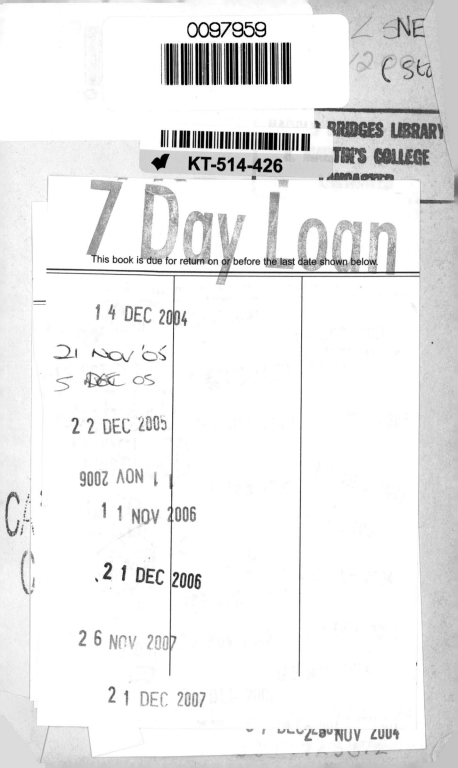

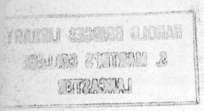
BOOKS BY KENNETH M. STAMPP

The Era of Reconstruction, 1865-1877

1965

The Peculiar Institution

1956

And the War Came

1950

Indiana Politics during the Civil War

1949

THE PECULIAR INSTITUTION

Slavery in the Ante-Bellum South

by Kenneth M· Stampp

Vintage Books
A Division of Random House, Inc.
New York

Vintage Books Edition, December 1989

Copyright © 1956 by Kenneth M. Stampp

Copyright renewed 1984 by Kenneth M. Stampp

All rights reserved under International and Pan-American
Copyright Conventions. Published in the United States by Vin-
tage Books, a division of Random House, Inc., New York, and
simultaneously in Canada by Random House of Canada Limited,
Toronto. Originally published, in hardcover, by Alfred A.
Knopf, Inc., New York in 1956 and in softcover by Vintage
Books, a division of Random House, Inc. in 1964.

ISBN: 0-679-72307-2
Library of Congress Catalog Card Number: 77-18363

Manufactured in the United States of America
10   9   8   7   6

For my father and mother

PREFACE

Prior to the Civil War southern slavery was America's most profound and vexatious social problem. More than any other problem, slavery nagged at the public conscience; offering no easy solution, it demanded statesmanship of uncommon vision, wisdom, and boldness. This institution deserves close study if only because its impact upon the whole country was so disastrous. But, in addition, such a study has a peculiar urgency, because American Negroes still await the full fruition of their emancipation—still strive to break what remains of the caste barriers first imposed upon them in slavery days. With the historian it is an article of faith that knowledge of the past is a key to understanding the present. In this instance I firmly believe that one must know what slavery meant to the Negro and how he reacted to it before one can comprehend his more recent tribulations.

Yet there is a strange paradox in the historian's involvement with both present and past, for his knowledge of the present is clearly a key to his understanding of the past. Today we are learning much from the natural and social sciences about the Negro's potentialities and about the basic irrelevance of race, and we are slowly discovering the roots and meaning of human behavior. All this is of immense value to the historian when, for example, he tries to grasp the significance of the Old South's "peculiar institution." I have assumed that the slaves were merely ordinary human beings, that innately Negroes *are*, after all, only white men with black skins, nothing more, nothing less.

I did not, of course, assume that there have been, or are today, no cultural differences between white and black Americans. Nor do I regard it as flattery to call Negroes white men with black skins. It would serve my purpose as well to call Caucasians black men with white skins I have simply found no convincing evidence that there are any significant differences between the innate emotional traits and intellectual capacities of Negroes and whites. This gives quite a new and different meaning to the bondage of black men; it gives their story a relevance to men of all races which it never seemed to have before.

What I have written about slavery is built, as all books about history are built, upon what others have already written. Those who have made major contributions to this subject are cited in my footnotes. Ulrich B. Phillips's *American Negro Slavery* (1918) is the pioneer work of scholarship in this field; and though he approached the subject with different assumptions and from a different perspective, I learned much from his methods, his sources, and his findings. Since 1918 many others have written more specialized books and articles about slavery, and the best of them have pointed toward revisions of some of Phillips's conclusions. Without these recent studies an attempt at a new synthesis would have been infinitely more difficult, if not impossible.

Among the more outrageous forms of human exploitation is the kind to which an author subjects his friends. To acknowledge their patience and pains afterward is a feeble gesture, but I can at least absolve them from responsibility for the stylistic gaucheries and interpretive errors that survive their labors. My entire manuscript was read and criticized by Carl Bridenbaugh, Richard N. Current, Frank Freidel, Richard Hofstadter, Henry F. May, and Paul S. Taylor. In addition, I have received valuable advice at different times from Reinhard Bendix, John Hope Franklin,

R. A. Gordon, Fred H. Harrington, William B. Hesseltine, John D. Hicks, and James F. King.

I am grateful to the staffs of the various libraries I visited for the numerous courtesies they extended to me. A John Simon Guggenheim Memorial Foundation Fellowship enabled me to devote a year to research; and the Institute of Social Sciences of the University of California provided funds for typists and travel.

For her assistance during the research, her criticism of the manuscript, and her aid in the proofreading, my wife, Katherine Mitchell Stampp, has my deepest appreciation.

KENNETH M. STAMPP

Berkeley, October, 1955

CONTENTS

The Peculiar Institution

CHAPTER ONE

The Setting

To understand the South is to feel the pathos in its history. This aura of pathos is more than a delusion of historians, more than the vague sensation one gets when looking down an avenue of somber, moss-draped live oaks leading to stately ruins or to nothing at all. For Southerners live in the shadow of a real tragedy; they know, better than most other Americans, that little ironies fill the history of mankind and that large disasters from time to time unexpectedly help to shape its course.

Their tragedy did not begin with the ordeal of Reconstruction, or with the agony of civil war, but with the growth of a "peculiar institution" (as they called it) in ante-bellum days. It began, in short, with chattel slavery whose spiritual stresses and unremitting social tensions became an inescapable part of life in the Old South.

What caused the growth of this institutional affliction which had so severe an impact upon the lives of so many Southerners? Some historians have traced the origin of southern slavery to a morbific quality in the southern climate. Though admitting great climatic variations within the South and the normal mildness of the winter season, they have emphasized the weather's fiercer moods—the torrential rains, the searing droughts, above all, the humid heat of subtropical summers. Since Southerners were unable to control the weather, they had to come to terms with it. So it was the climate that determined the nature of their institutions and the structure of their society. "Let us begin by discussing the weather," wrote one historian who saw here "the chief agency in making the South distinctive." [1] To such climatic determinists the social significance of "ninety degrees in the shade" was too real to be ignored.

If climate alone could not explain everything, then perhaps certain additional factors, such as soil, topography, and watercourses, contributed to a broader geographical determinism. Combine the hot summers and long growing seasons with the rich southern soils—the alluvial river bottoms, the sandy loams of the coastal plains, the silt loams of the Black Belt, and the red clays of the piedmont—and an agricultural economy was the logical result. Add the many navigable rivers which facilitated the movement of bulky staples from considerable distances inland to coastal ports, and all the requirements for a commercial form of agriculture were at hand. Commercial agriculture induced a trend toward large landholdings which in turn created a demand for labor. Thus some have argued that Southerners, in permitting slavery to grow, had merely submitted to compelling natural forces.

Human institutions, however, have not been formed by forces as rigidly deterministic as this. To be sure, men must inevitably make certain adjustments to fixed environmental conditions. But, within limits, these adjustments may take a variety of forms. At different times and in different places roughly similar environmental conditions have produced vastly different human responses. Some human adaptations have been far more successful than others. For this reason one must examine the forms of southern

---

[1] Ulrich B. Phillips, *Life and Labor in the Old South* (Boston, 1929), p. 1.

I: *The Setting*

institutions as closely as the facts of the southern environment.

It may be that unfree labor alone made possible the early rise of the plantation system, but this proves neither the necessity nor the inevitability of slavery. Actually, the southern plantation was older than slavery and survived its abolition. More important, there was nothing inevitable about the plantation. Without a continuing supply of bondsmen southern agriculture, in its early development at least, would probably have depended more upon small-farm units and given less emphasis to the production of staple crops. Under these circumstances the South might have developed more slowly, but it would not have remained a wilderness. There was no crop cultivated by slaves that could not have been cultivated by other forms of labor, no area fit for human habitation that would have been passed by for want of a slave force. The slave-plantation system answered no "specific need" that could not have been answered in some other way.[2]

Slavery, then, cannot be attributed to some deadly atmospheric miasma or some irresistible force in the South's economic evolution. The use of slaves in southern agriculture was a deliberate choice (among several alternatives) made by men who sought greater returns than they could obtain from their own labor alone, and who found other types of labor more expensive. "For what purpose does the master hold the servant?" asked an ante-bellum Southerner. "Is it not that by his labor he, the master, may accumulate wealth?"[3] The rise of slavery in the South was inevitable only in the sense that every event in history seems inevitable after it has occurred.

Southerners who chose to develop and to preserve slavery

---

[2] For such a defense of the system see Ulrich B. Phillips (ed.), *Plantation and Frontier: 1649–1863* (Cleveland, 1910), I, p. 71.

[3] *Farmer's Journal*, II (1853), p. 52.

could no more escape responsibility for their action than they could escape its consequences. But to judge them without compassion is to lack both the insight and the sensitivity needed to understand the nature of their tragedy. For the South began with good human material; its tragedy did not spring from the inherent depravity of its people. Southerners did not create the slave system all at once in 1619; rather, they built it little by little, step by step, choice by choice, over a period of many years; and all the while most of them were more or less blind to the ultimate consequences of the choices they were making. Somehow, at crucial times, their vision failed them; somehow it was their misfortune to have built a social structure wanting in flexibility. Ultimately Southerners became the victims of their own peculiar institution; they were unwilling to adjust it, or themselves, to the ideological and cultural realities of the nineteenth century.

Not that slavery failed as a practical labor system. In that narrow sense it was a success, and it was still flourishing as late as 1860. In terms of its broad social consequences for the South as a whole, however, slavery must be adjudged a failure. Few slaves ever really adapted successfully to their servitude, and few whites could defend the system without betraying the emotional stresses to which slavery subjected them. Eventually the omnipresent slave became the symbol of the South and the cornerstone of its culture. When that happened, disaster was close at hand—in fact, that in itself was a disaster.

2

An essential point about the South's peculiar institution was this: its slaves were Negroes (that is, they possessed one or more Negro ancestors) . The presence of Negroes in the South was indeed significant, but the significance of their presence must be neither exaggerated nor misunderstood. The folklore regarding the Negro and his role in southern history must not be mistaken for fact.

According to tradition, Negroes had to be brought to the South for labor that Europeans themselves could not perform. "The white man will never raise—*can* never raise a cotton or a sugar crop in the United States. In our swamps and under our suns the negro thrives, but the white man dies." Without the productive power of the African whom an "all-wise Creator" had perfectly adapted to the labor needs of the South, its lands would have remained "a howling wilderness." [4]

Such is the myth. The fact is that, ever since the founding of Jamestown, white men have performed much of the South's heavy agricultural labor. For a century and a half white farmers have tended their own cotton fields in every part of the Deep South. In the 1850's Frederick Law Olmsted saw many white women in Mississippi and Alabama "at work in the hottest sunshine . . . in the regular cultivation of cotton." [5] In 1855, even a South Carolinian vigorously disputed "the opinion frequently put forth, that white labor is unsuited to the agriculture of this State." All that such laborers required was to be properly acclimatized. "The white man—born, raised and habituated to exposure and labor in the field in our climate—will be found equal to the task in any part of this State free from the influence of the excessive malaria of stagnant waters." Then this Carolinian observed an important fact: in the swamplands Negroes did not thrive any better than white men. [6] But Negro slaves, unlike free whites, could be forced to toil

---

[4] *DeBow's Review*, XXI (1856), p. 467; XXIV (1858), p. 63; *Southern Cultivator*, XVI (1858), pp. 233–36.

[5] Frederick Law Olmsted, *A Journey in the Back Country* (New York, 1860), pp. 298, 349–50.

[6] *Columbian Carolinian*, quoted in Charleston *Courier*, September 6, 1855.

in the rice swamps regardless of the effect upon their health. That was the difference.

An equally durable myth is that Negroes, in contrast to peoples of other races, possess certain racial traits which uniquely fitted them for bondage, and which created in the South a lasting "race problem." As other defenses of slavery became increasingly untenable, nineteenth-century Southerners gave special emphasis to this racist argument. Doctors, scientists, and pseudo-scientists—phrenologists had a substantial following—found a physiological basis for alleged temperamental and intellectual differences. Dr. Samuel W. Cartwright, of Louisiana, argued that the visible difference in skin pigmentation also extended to "the membranes, the muscles, the tendons, and . . . [to] all the fluids and secretions. Even the negro's brain and nerves, the chyle and all the humors, are tinctured with a shade of the pervading darkness." Dr. Josiah C. Nott, of Mobile, was the leader of a small group who carried racism to the extreme position of denying that Negroes and whites belonged to the same species.[7]

Racist doctrines did not die with slavery. Around the time of the Spanish-American War the imperialist concept of the "white man's burden" and the writings of such scholars as John Fiske and John W. Burgess gave added strength to the belief in white superiority in general and Anglo-Saxon superiority in particular. As late as 1918, Professor Ulrich B. Phillips premised his study of slavery upon the assumption that Negroes "by racial quality" are "submissive," "light-hearted," "amiable," "ingratiating," and "imitative." The removal of the Negro from Africa to America had "had little more effect upon his temperament than upon his complexion." Hence the progress of the "gener-

---

[7] *DeBow's Review*, IX (1850), p. 231; X (1851), pp. 113–32; XI (1851), p. 65; James B. Sellers, *Slavery in Alabama* (University, Alabama, 1950), pp. 344–45.

ality" of slaves "was restricted by the fact of their being negroes." More than a decade later an agricultural economist expressed serious doubts whether it was really slavery that made many ante-bellum Negroes inefficient and irresponsible laborers. As late as 1953, a distinguished biochemist suggested that races of men, like breeds of dogs, may possess distinctive emotional characteristics, and that the Negro's "inborn temperament" may have made his enslavement feasible.[8]

These ideas continue to have wide currency despite the impossibility of generalizing, without extreme caution, even about the external physical traits of American Negroes. While most of their ancestors were "true Negroes" from the coastal areas of West Africa, some came from Central Africa, South Africa, East Africa, and Madagascar. These Bantus, Bushmen, and Hottentots, though dark-skinned, frizzly-haired peoples, deviate significantly from some of the physical characteristics that are regarded as typically Negroid. In skin coloration the yellowish-browns found among the Bantus distinguish them from the darker shaded "true Negroes." This kind of physical diversity is as common among members of the Negro race as it is among members of other races.[9]

In so far as the southern "race problem" grew out of such external differences as skin pigmentation, it has always been an artificial problem created by white men who by the nineteenth century had made an obsession of these racial superficialities. Few would argue seriously that the Negro's physical make-up accounted in any way for his al-

---

[8] Ulrich B. Phillips, *American Negro Slavery* (New York, 1918), pp. 291–92, 339, 341–42; Lewis C. Gray, *History of Agriculture in the Southern United States to 1860* (Washington, D.C., 1933), I, pp. 464–66; Roger J. Williams, *Free and Unequal: The Biological Basis of Individual Liberty* (Austin, Texas, 1953), pp. 121–28.

[9] Julian H. Lewis, *The Biology of the Negro* (Chicago, 1942), pp. 19–22.

leged special fitness for servitude. If this belief has a more substantial foundation in his innate emotional traits or intellectual inferiority, no one has yet turned up any convincing evidence to demonstrate it—though many have tried. Instead, modern biologists, psychologists, sociologists, and anthropologists offer an impressive accumulation of evidence that Negroes and whites have approximately the same intellectual potentialities. The seemingly unavoidable subjective element in testing devices may make it impossible ever to settle this point conclusively through exact measurements of intelligence. But as the tests have been refined in an effort to eliminate environmental factors, their results have become increasingly embarrassing to the racists.

One fact is established beyond any reasonable doubt. This is the fact that variations in the capacities and personalities of *individuals* within each race are as great as the variations in their physical traits. Therefore it is impossible to make valid generalizations about races as such. Negroes as a race were no more psychically fitted for slavery than were white men as a race.[1] Either slavery was a desirable status for some whites as well as for some Negroes, or it was not a desirable status for anyone. Finally, in view of the fact that certain groups of Caucasians at different times have also been forced to submit to various forms of bondage, it would appear to be a little preposterous to generalize about the peculiarities of Negroes in this respect.

But perhaps it is not enough merely to reject the first

[1] For a summary of the evidence and literature on this subject see Gunnar Myrdal, *An American Dilemma: The Negro Problem and Modern Democracy* (New York, 1944) , esp. Vol. I, Chap. VI, and the footnotes to this chapter, Vol. II, pp. 1212–18. Two recent additions to the literature are Otto Klineberg (ed.) , *Characteristics of the American Negro* (New York, 1944) ; Theodosius Dobzhansky, "The Genetic Nature of Differences Among Men," in Stow Persons (ed.) , *Evolutionary Thought in America* (New Haven, 1950) , pp. 85–155.

myth that an "all-wise Creator" had designed the Negro
for labor in the South, and the second myth that by intel-
lect and temperament he was the natural slave of the white
man. For there is a third myth which offers still another
reason why Negroes were kept in bondage for two centuries. The substance of this tradition is that Africans were
barbarians who therefore needed to be subjected to rigid
discipline and severe controls. Their enslavement was essential for their own good and for the preservation of white
civilization. The Negroes, declared the preamble to South
Carolina's code of 1712, were "of barbarous, wild, savage
natures, and . . . wholly unqualified to be governed by
the laws, customs, and practices of this province." They
had to be governed by such special laws "as may restrain
the disorders, rapines, and inhumanity to which they are
naturally prone and inclined, and [as] may also tend to the
safety and security of the people of this province and their
estates." [2]

Whether colonial South Carolinians regarded this as
more than an immediate and temporary problem they did
not make entirely clear. But it is quite evident that many
others since then have viewed it as a persistent problem
which has perplexed each generation of Southerners. According to their belief, the primitive Negroes who were
brought to America could only learn the ways of the civilized white man in the course of many generations of gradual cultural growth. One historian described the southern
plantation as "a school constantly training and controlling
pupils who were in a backward state of civilization. . . .
On the whole the plantations were the best schools yet invented for the mass training of that sort of inert and backward people which the bulk of the American negroes rep-

---

[2] John C. Hurd, *The Law of Freedom and Bondage in the United States* (Boston, 1858–62), I, p. 299.

resented." [3] This belief is implicit in some other historical treatises on southern slavery.

Unquestionably when adult Negroes were imported from Africa they had trouble learning to live in a strange environment and to understand unfamiliar social institutions. But the idea that Negroes needed to be civilized by a slow evolutionary process, during which they would gradually acquire and transmit to their descendants the white man's patterns of social behavior, contains two fallacies. One of them results from a misconception of the problem. Actually, the first generation of Negroes born in America in the seventeenth century was just as well prepared for freedom as the generation that was emancipated in the 1860's. The adaptation to the white man's culture involved a process of education, not one of biological evolution. The only way that Negroes ever learned how to live in America as responsible free men was by experience—by *starting* to live as free men. The plantation school never accomplished this: its aim was merely to train them to be slaves.

The second fallacy results from a total misapprehension of the Negro's African background. There may be objective standards by which one can designate as "primitive" the cultures of the Ashantis and Fantis of the Gold Coast, the Yorubas and Binis of Nigeria, the Mandingos and Hausas of the western Sudan, the people of Dahomey, and the various tribes of the Congo. But to describe these people as savages who led an animal-like existence is a serious distortion. Long before the seventeenth century they had evolved their own intricate cultures. It is always wise to be cautious about making subjective comparisons of cultures in terms of the superiority of one over the other. It is easy, and perhaps natural, for one people to regard the strange

---

[3] Phillips, *American Negro Slavery*, pp. 342–43. For a somewhat similar view see Gray, *History of Agriculture*, I, pp. 464–66.

customs of another people as inferior to their own familiar customs. And it is easy to forget that white men were scarcely in a position to judge Africans severely for sanctioning slavery, indulging in inter-tribal warfare, and cherishing superstitions.

The African ancestors of American Negroes had developed an economy based upon agriculture which in some places approached the complex organization of a plantation system. The cultivation of their crops required hard work which both men and women performed in accordance with a division of tasks fixed by custom. Skilled craftsmen—potters, basketmakers, wood carvers, weavers, and ironworkers—played important roles in African society. Professional traders negotiated exchanges of goods with the aid of monetary systems. Social and political institutions matched the complexity of the economy. To dismiss African religion as mere superstition or fetishism is to oversimplify a highly involved system of thought about the supernatural. In the aesthetic sphere Africans expressed themselves through music, the dance, and the graphic and plastic arts. A rich folklore was the surrogate for literature among these nonliterate peoples.[4] Indeed, it was because of the relative complexity of their cultures, their familiarity with a sedentary, agricultural way of life, that white men found it profitable to use native Africans as slaves. Nomadic peoples from relatively simpler cultures were enslaved with less success.

When Negroes and whites first mingled with each other in colonial America their cultural differences obstructed a process of quick and easy assimilation. But their striking similarities as human beings could have made this the problem of a generation or two and not of centuries. That Ne-

---

[4] Melville J. Herskovits, *The Myth of the Negro Past* (New York, 1941), pp. 54–85; John Hope Franklin, *From Slavery to Freedom* (New York, 1948), pp. 11–41.

groes and whites originally spoke different languages was less important than that each used speech as a means of communication. Their mutual understanding of the value of labor, of the social importance of the family, and of the need for political authority gave them a body of common experience however much it may have differed in detail. Both used music and art to express their love of beauty, their fears and anxieties, and their hopes and dreams. Their ethical codes were different, but they shared a desire to distinguish between moral and immoral, good and evil, right and wrong. Above all, they both had the resilience and adaptability of rational, educable creatures who depended upon their brains rather than their instincts for survival. These human qualities, in all of which Negroes and whites were so much alike, indicate that the third myth—the cultural justification of slavery—was made from the same flimsy material as the others.

The Negro, then, was deeply involved in the southern tragedy, but through no peculiar fault of his own. His presence in the South did not of itself create an unhealthy social condition. His involvement in the southern tragedy was not as a Negro but as the embodiment of the South's peculiar institution—as a type of labor and as a species of property. Not the Negro but slavery was the Old South's great affliction—the root of its tragedy.

3

Ante-bellum Southerners attached considerable significance to, and found considerable solace in, the fact that they had not invented human bondage. Apologists for slavery traced the history of servitude back to the dawn of civilization and showed that it had always existed in some form until their own day. They were not willingly isolated from the traditions of western culture.

I: *The Setting*

If all men are somehow naturally endowed with such "unalienable rights" as life, liberty, and the pursuit of happiness, this principle was discovered relatively late in human history. Many centuries earlier some men learned that they could gain practical advantages from an unequal distribution of rights and from transgressions upon the liberties of others. The application of this concept to prisoners of war was doubtless an improvement over the more primitive practice of putting them to death. The extermination of prisoners became less fashionable whenever a group of people abandoned nomadic pursuits for the more sedentary life of townsmen and agriculturists. Then it seemed desirable to spare the lives of at least some captives in order to exploit their labor.

Thus the ancient Egyptians reached out among their Semitic and Ethiopian neighbors for slave laborers. The Athenians, as Americans of the ante-bellum South were fond of recalling, attained unprecedented heights of intellectual and artistic achievement in a society built upon a foundation of servitude. The Romans made chattel slaves of captives taken in Gaul, Spain, Sardinia, North Africa, and western Asia. Some of these bondsmen worked on the country estates of Roman squires; others were consigned to frightful toil in the mines and on merchant ships; still others were converted into fawning domestics; and the most robust among them amused the multitude in the role of gladiators. Slavery was clearly one of the legacies of antiquity.

In the Middle Ages bondage was still flourishing in various forms. The lands of European nobles were cultivated by serfs whose status was above that of chattel slaves but who were nevertheless bound to the soil in a condition of hereditary servitude. The ultimate decline of villeinage in England did not mean that all Englishmen were at last free, for in the seventeenth century they were still familiar

15

with other types of bondage. Debtors, rogues, vagabonds, and paupers were legally deprived of their freedom and endured the indignity of the lash. Economic necessity reduced other poor men to the same condition when they indentured themselves for a term of years.

These forms of white servitude were introduced into the English colonies almost as soon as they were founded. Redemptioners paid their passage to America by binding themselves as servants for terms of from two to seven years. In the seventeenth century most of the servants were English; in the eighteenth century most of them were Germans, Swiss, Scots, Scotch-Irish, and Irish. Victims of kidnappers and convicts sentenced to transportation by English courts supplemented this flow of unfree labor. Probably more than half of the immigrants to the thirteen English colonies in North America came as bondsmen. After the horrors of the passage they often endured the cruelty of masters determined to extract from them the maximum of labor at a minimum of expense. Though they ultimately gained their freedom, they nevertheless made servitude an established labor system in all the colonies.[5]

Meanwhile, the religious zeal of Christians and Moslems had helped to revive and spread a form of servitude once justified primarily by the ancient laws of war. Members of each faith looked upon the other as infidels, and hence each felt doubly entitled to make slaves of the other when taken as captives. Moors captured in North Africa and in the Spanish peninsula were held in bondage in Italy, Spain, Portugal, and France. Christian prisoners suffered the same fate in the lands of Islam.

Christians and Moslems alike believed it just to hold

[5] Oscar and Mary F. Handlin, "Origins of the Southern Labor System," *William and Mary Quarterly*, 3rd Ser., VII (1950), pp. 200–204; Richard B. Morris, *Government and Labor in Early America* (New York, 1946), pp. 315 ff.

heathens in servitude, and both found victims among the Negroes of Africa. Their operations were facilitated by the fact that slavery already existed among the Negro tribes and that native dealers were often willing participants in this trade in human flesh. The Christian purchasers liked to think of themselves as the agents of civilization and of the true religion. The native traders were less philosophical about their business.[6]

During the fifteenth century Spaniards and Portuguese brought cargoes of Negro servants to Europe from their trading centers on the west coast of Africa south of the Sahara. In the early sixteenth century the Portuguese in Brazil and the Spanish in other parts of the New World found more heathens eligible for bondage. In the West Indies the Christianizing and civilizing influence of the *encomenderos* was costly to the Indians who first lost their freedom and then their lives through disease and heavy labor in mines and sugar cane fields. As the supply of Indians dwindled, Negroes were imported in increasing numbers. Before 1600, Negro labor was being utilized in nearly every part of the sprawling Spanish and Portuguese empires.

By the seventeenth century, the Dutch, French, and English had entered the profitable slave trade and had seized colonies of their own in the Caribbean. The Dutch in Curaçao, St. Eustatius, and Tobago, the French in Guadeloupe and Martinique, and the English in Jamaica and Barbados helped to develop Negro slavery and the plantation system in the New World. For many years the English esteemed their sugar islands more highly than any of their other possessions in America. In these islands planters, merchants, and Negro traders shared in the profits extracted from the labor of black bondsmen.[7]

[6] Hurd, *Law of Freedom and Bondage*, I, pp. 159–62; Franklin, *From Slavery to Freedom*, pp. 42–45; Phillips, *American Negro Slavery*, pp. 1–13.
[7] Hurd, *Law of Freedom and Bondage*, I, pp. 205–206; Franklin, *From*

When a "Dutch man of warre" brought the first cargo of twenty "negars" to Virginia in 1619, John Rolfe and his neighbors sanctioned a trade and tapped a source of labor that had been familiar to some Europeans for nearly two centuries. Virginia landholders received a small trickle of Negro servants during the next fifty years and worked them on tobacco plantations along with their infinitely more numerous white servants. As early as the 1630's, Maryland planters began to use black labor; in 1669, Carolina's Lords Proprietors promulgated John Locke's "Fundamental Constitutions" which gave every freeman "absolute power and authority over his negro slaves"; by 1750, Georgia colonists had persuaded the trustees to rescind their original policy of prohibiting slavery.[8]

The middle colonies also purchased a substantial number of Negroes. If only a few New Englanders became slave-holders, some merchants of Newport, Providence, Boston, and Salem were vigorous and eminently successful participants in the slave trade.[9] Later generations of Southerners did not forget that the ancestors of the abolitionists had helped to keep them well supplied with slaves.

Ante-bellum Southerners understood this world of the seventeenth and eighteenth centuries better than they understood their own. The quest for enlarged opportunities which brought their colonial forebears to America was a personal objective which did not necessarily mean that they believed in the equality of all men. If southern colonists did little to improve the lot of propertyless laborers, their neighbors were hardly in a position to criticize them for it. To the north and to the south of them Englishmen, Dutch-

Slavery to Freedom, pp. 46–49, 59–69, 111–24; Phillips, *American Negro Slavery*, pp. 13–19, 46–66.

8 Franklin, *From Slavery to Freedom*, pp. 70–84; Phillips, *American Negro Slavery*, pp. 74–75, 85–86, 93–95.

9 Franklin, *From Slavery to Freedom*, pp. 88–110; Phillips, *American Negro Slavery*, pp. 98–114.

men, Spaniards, and Portuguese held Indians, Negroes, and whites in bondage. This being the case, their use of unfree labor demanded of them a minimum of soul searching. Since their social institutions were not peculiar in any fundamental way, they lived comfortably in their world.

But ante-bellum Southerners lived less comfortably in the world of the nineteenth century. They found themselves increasingly isolated, increasingly on the defensive, increasingly compelled to improvise, as the code by which their fathers had justified the holding of slaves became less and less intelligible. The heathens they had imported from Africa had now become Christians. The theory that it was proper to enslave prisoners taken in "just wars" belonged to the dead past. The fact that many of the ancestors of southern Negroes had been slaves in their own lands now seemed strangely irrelevant. Above all, the ideals of the Enlightenment, especially the doctrine of natural rights and the belief in the inherent goodness and dignity of man, had found one of their most eloquent champions in the South's greatest statesman. An impressive number of Southerners never would agree that Jefferson's philosophy was wrong.

The facts were no less disturbing than the theories. Outside the South reformers everywhere made the destruction of legal servitude one of their major goals. By 1860, economic liberals, who linked social progress with the concept of free labor in a competitive society, had won a series of decisive victories. In the northern states slavery did not long survive the social upheaval which was part of the American Revolution. Not because slave labor was unprofitable, but because they were given no choice, northern slaveholders accepted a domestic application of the principles which had justified resistance to British authority. During the 1780's, these states put slavery "in the course of ultimate extinction," usually through a system of gradual emancipation which took a generation to complete.

The new spirit was contagious. In Haiti, when the French seemed inclined to restrict the benefits of their own revolution to the white race, the Negro slaves helped themselves to freedom by a rebellion which all but destroyed the old master class. In 1833, the British government made provision for the abolition of slavery in its possessions. Slavery entered a period of decline in the new Spanish-American republics, until the last of them abolished it during the 1850's.

But in spite of these cataclysmic events, most Southerners clung to slavery. It survived the ordeal of the Revolution and the assaults of the South's own revolutionary radicals. It survived the French Revolution, though Southerners shuddered at the price Toussaint L'Ouverture and his Negro followers exacted from Haitian masters. Slavery survived the liberalism of Jeffersonian Democracy and the egalitarianism of Jacksonian Democracy. It survived the persistent criticism and the emancipation schemes of native Southerners, especially in the Upper South, and a month of antislavery debate carried on during January, 1832, in the Virginia legislature. It survived a thirty-year crusade against it conducted by northern abolitionists. Southern slavery more than survived: the slaveholders enlarged their domain, tightened the slave's shackles, and defiantly told outsiders to mind their own affairs. The South of 1860, big and prosperous, still boldly defended its peculiar institution.

Its trouble, however, was manifest in the term itself. For by 1860 chattel slavery had become in literal truth a *peculiar* institution, and Southerners knew it. The fact that they had inherited slavery and not invented it was now quite beside the point, and many Southerners knew this too. The one supremely relevant fact was that Southerners were among slavery's last apologists—that theirs was a

"Lost Cause" even before they took up arms to defend it. Being culturally isolated, living in an unfriendly world, was a frightening experience which made many of them angry and aggressive. Outside of Africa itself, they now could look only to Brazil, Cuba, Porto Rico, and Dutch Guiana for societies which, like their own, contained masters and slaves. The rest of the world was inhabited by strangers.

4

In its early stages the South's peculiar institution grew slowly and uncertainly. The specific form it took in the eighteenth and nineteenth centuries was unknown to English law, and in some respects unlike the forms of servitude which had developed in other places. During most of the seventeenth century the Negro's status was so vague and amorphous that his ultimate position might conceivably have been defined in several different ways. In any case, the Negro's presence in the South antedated by many years the legal existence of chattel slavery. That some early colonial statutes used the term "slave" had no decisive significance, because the term had sometimes been applied loosely to white servants.

In the main, Maryland and Virginia masters first subjected their Negroes to the customary forms of servitude. Like white servants, some of them gained their freedom after serving a term of years, or after conversion to Christianity. If their bondage tended to be more severe, their terms of service longer or even of indefinite duration, this merely indicated that attractive inducements did not have to be held out to servants whose coming to America was not a matter of free choice.

Moreover, the Negro and white servants of the seventeenth century seemed to be remarkably unconcerned about their visible physical differences. They toiled together in the fields, fraternized during leisure hours, and, in and out of wedlock, collaborated in siring a numerous progeny. Though the first southern white settlers were quite familiar with rigid class lines, they were as unfamiliar with a caste system as they were with chattel slavery.

The statutes which made clear distinctions between white and Negro bondsmen evolved piecemeal. No specific date marked the legal establishment of chattel slavery in the South; but there were few obstacles in the way of its development. Neither the provisions of their charters nor the policy of the English government limited the power of colonial legislatures to control Negro labor as they saw fit. Negroes did not have the benefit of written indentures which defined their rights and limited their terms of service. Their unprotected condition encouraged the trend toward special treatment, and their physical and cultural differences provided handy excuses to justify it. More than anything else, however, the landholders' growing appreciation of the advantages of slavery over the older forms of servitude gave a powerful impetus to the growth of the new labor system. Southern masters developed much—though not all—of the system by custom before it was recognized in law.

Not until the 1660's did Maryland and Virginia make the first important legal distinctions between white and Negro servants. During this decade various statutes provided that Negroes were to be slaves for life, that the child was to inherit the condition of the mother, and that Christian baptism did not change the slave's status. Even then it took many more years and many additional statutes to define clearly the nature of slaves as property, to confer upon the masters the required disciplinary power, to enact the codes by which the slaves' movements were subjected to public control, and to give them a peculiar position in

courts of law. Other statutes prohibited interracial marriages, in order to prevent "that abominable mixture and
spurious issue." By the eighteenth century color had become not only the evidence of slavery but also a badge of
degradation. Thus the master class, for its own purposes,
wrote chattel slavery, the caste system, and color prejudice
into American custom and law.[1]

The general trend of colonial policy toward American
Indians was against their enslavement. It is not necessary
to search for innate psychic qualities in the Indians to explain why most of them were not reduced to the status of
the Negroes. In the West Indies it was not so much the humiliation of bondage as its rigors that caused Indian slaves
to perish so rapidly. In the English colonies, especially in
the Carolinas, at various times some Indian captives were
held as servants or slaves. Whenever Negroes and Indians
were thus brought in contact with each other they inter-
married, with the result that a considerable number of
southern slaves were of mixed Negro and Indian ancestry.[2]

But Indian servitude was never an adequate or satisfactory answer to the labor needs of southern landholders.
Cultural factors made it difficult for Indians to adapt to the
plantation regime. Unlike the Negroes, Indian slaves found
it relatively easy to escape along familiar forest trails to the
protection of their own people. The weakness of the early
white settlements ordinarily caused them to value the
friendship of neighboring Indians more than their potential labor. As early as 1656 the Virginia Assembly passed

---

[1] Handlin, "Origins of the Southern Labor System," *loc. cit.*, pp. 199–
222; Gray, *History of Agriculture*, I, pp. 351–71; James C. Ballagh, *A
History of Slavery in Virginia* (Baltimore, 1902), pp. 27 ff.; Hurd,
Law of Freedom and Bondage, I, pp. 225–54, 291–311; Wilbert E.
Moore, "Slave Law and the Social Structure," *Journal of Negro His-
tory*, XXVI (1941), pp. 171–84.

[2] Kenneth W. Porter, "Relations between Negroes and Indians within
the Present Limits of the United States," *Journal of Negro History*,
XVII (1932), pp, 287–367.

the first of a series of statutes prohibiting the enslavement of Indians. By the eighteenth century Virginia's courts distinguished between descent from Africans and from native American Indians and accepted proof of the latter as evidence of freedom.[3] Here and elsewhere in the South only a predominantly Negro ancestry created the presumption of slavery.

During the seventeenth century the South's Negro population increased very slowly. In 1649, thirty years after the arrival of the first Africans, Virginia counted only three hundred black laborers in its population. Until the end of this century southern landholders relied chiefly upon the labor of white servants. Then, when English and colonial merchants entered the slave trade on a large scale, and when the advantages of slavery were fully understood, Negroes began to arrive in substantial numbers. In the eighteenth century thousands of them were imported annually, some from the West Indies but most directly from Africa. By the eve of the American Revolution Virginia's population was nearly evenly divided between Negroes and whites; in South Carolina the Negroes outnumbered the whites by two to one.[4]

It was the common lot of poor emigrants from Europe to suffer great hardship in making the passage to America. Not only in the colonial period but also in the nineteenth century, the ordeal of leaving familiar places, breaking old ties, making the journey on overcrowded vessels, and adjusting to a strange environment was a dreadful experience. But none of the European immigrant groups felt the

---

[3] Almon W. Lauber, *Indian Slavery in Colonial Times within the Present Limits of the United States* (New York, 1913); Gray, *History of Agriculture*, I, pp. 360–61; Wesley F. Craven, *The Southern Colonies in the Seventeenth Century, 1607–1689* (Baton Rouge, 1949), pp. 366–68; Helen T. Catterall, *Judicial Cases Concerning American Slavery and the Negro* (Washington, D.C., 1926–37), I, pp. 112–13.

[4] Morris, *Government and Labor in Early America*, pp. 36–37; Phillips, *American Negro Slavery*, pp. 74–75, 87.

shock of these experiences quite as severely as did the Africans. The inhumanity of the traders, the terrors of the Middle Passage, and the "breaking in" process in America gave these involuntary immigrants a vivid impression of the white man and his culture which they did not soon forget. Estimates of the total number of Negroes torn from their African homes and carried to the New World range upward from five million. Of these, perhaps a half million were brought to the South legally before 1808, and thousands more illegally thereafter.[5]

Eighteenth-century Southerners, their humanitarianism fortified by practical considerations, made the first attempts to control or abolish the African slave trade. These measures were motivated by the desire of established planters to keep prices up and restrict competition, by the fear of too high a proportion of slaves in the total population, and by the danger of receiving rebellious slaves from the West Indies. But before the Revolution all restrictions on the trade were disallowed by the English government in the interest of the traders. Delaware finally prohibited importations of Africans in 1776, Virginia in 1778, Maryland in 1783, South Carolina in 1787, North Carolina in 1794, and Georgia in 1798. South Carolina reopened the trade in 1803 and imported 39,000 additional black laborers before it was closed by Federal action five years later.[6] After that the natural increase of the existing stock had to be the main reliance for an increased supply. By 1810 the southern slave population had grown to more than a million.

The closing of the African slave trade did not prove to

---

[5] For the African slave trade see Elizabeth Donnan (ed.), *Documents Illustrative of the History of the Slave Trade to America* (Washington, D.C., 1930–35) ; W. E. Burghardt DuBois, *The Suppression of the African Slave-Trade to the United States of America, 1638–1870* (New York, 1896) ; Franklin, *From Slavery to Freedom*, pp. 42–58; Phillips, *American Negro Slavery*, pp. 20–45.

[6] Phillips, *American Negro Slavery*, pp. 121, 132–49.

be the first step toward the abolition of slavery itself. For at the very time that the foreign supply was being cut off, another fateful development was taking place: slavery was spreading beyond the limits of the original southern states. The Federal Constitution had placed no obstacles in the way of its expansion, for it accepted slavery as a local institution to be protected or prohibited according to the wishes of individual states. The exclusion of slavery from the territory north of the Ohio River, written into the Ordinance of 1787, was not applied to the territory south of it. Accordingly, one by one, Kentucky, Tennessee, Mississippi, and Alabama entered the Union as slave states. Slavery already existed in the regions acquired from France and Spain by the Louisiana and Florida purchases. Four more slave states—Louisiana, Missouri, Arkansas, and Florida—were carved out of these lands. Before the annexation of Texas in 1845, Americans had firmly planted slavery in its soil. By then slavery's empire included fifteen states ranging southward and westward from the Delaware River to the Rio Grande.

Was this the end? Had slavery now reached the "natural limits" of its expansion? If it had, there were many Americans who still hoped—or feared—that it had not. New Mexico and Utah were opened to slavery by the Compromise of 1850, the territory north of the Missouri Compromise line by the Kansas-Nebraska Act. Manifest Destiny held the glittering promise of more land for slavery in Mexico, Central America, and Cuba. In the Dred Scott case the Supreme Court gave judicial sanction to the proslavery doctrine that the peculiar institution could not be excluded from any of the territories of the United States. In 1860 the expansion of slavery still remained a lively issue.

"Somehow this *must* end," said Northerners as they cast their votes for Abraham Lincoln.

"But it *cannot* end, for that would destroy us," replied

secessionists as they launched the Confederate States of America.

So came the harvest. Planted experimentally in the seventeenth century, cultivated systematically in the eighteenth, sheltered from the storms of the Revolution, then transplanted to new lands in the West, chattel slavery reached maturity in the ante-bellum period. The nature of its fruit was determined not by the climate, not by the soil, but by the kinds of seeds sown by men. But how could the first Southerners have known that they had sown a crop of weeds? How long should it have taken their descendants to realize that this rank crop was choking every other growing thing? Only this can be said: All along a few southern skeptics had been predicting that at harvest time it would be this way.

5

By the 1830's southern agriculture had regained much of the vitality it had possessed in colonial days. Virginians were beginning to recover from an agricultural depression which had plagued them for half a century. They were improving their methods, reclaiming their worn-out lands, and finding new crops to free them from the tyranny of tobacco. Carolinians and Georgians were busy feeding cotton to the mills of Manchester and Lowell. Many emigrants from these older states were finding opportunities to grow one of the great southern staples on the virgin lands of the Southwest. If a Virginian or Carolinian did not get the "Alabama fever" himself, he at least knew that in these new regions there were ready markets for as many Negroes as he could spare. Everywhere—in Virginia as well as in Georgia or Mississippi or Louisiana—slaves were a more or less vital part of the economy, an important source of labor, and a valuable type of property. Southerners measured their rank in society by counting their slaves.

By the 1830's the fateful decision had been made. Slavery, now an integral part of the southern way of life, was to be preserved, not as a transitory evil, an unfortunate legacy of the past, but as a permanent institution—a *positive good*. To think of abolition was an idle dream. Now even native Southerners criticized the peculiar institution at their peril.

Finally, by the 1830's slavery had assumed the rigidity of an entrenched institution. It no longer had the plasticity—the capacity to modify its shape—that it had in the colonial period. Slavery had crystallized; its form was fixed. In 1860 the peculiar institution was almost precisely what it had been thirty years before. If anything, the chains of bondage were strengthened, not weakened, in this ante-bellum period. In the hardened pattern of southern law and custom the twin functions of the slaves were now clearly defined: they were to labor diligently and breed prolifically for the comfort of their white masters.

The rigid and static nature of ante-bellum slavery, 1830–1860, makes it possible to examine it institutionally with only slight regard for chronology. The important variations in detail that were apparent in the three decades before 1860 were not evidences of progressive changes in the nature of southern bondage. Rather, they were evidences of regional variations within the South itself and of natural variations among individual masters and slaves. For, of course, the inflexibility of the status of slaves did not mean that they all did the same kind of work or lived under exactly the same conditions, or that they or their masters were all alike.

Nor did it mean that slavery was of equal importance in the lives of all southern whites or in the economies of all the South's many regions. Far from it. Two of the persistent characteristics of the South's peculiar institution were the unequal size of individual slaveholdings and the uneven geographic distribution of the slave population. It is essential to understand these characteristics if the nature of slavery in the ante-bellum South is to be fully comprehended. The pattern of slave ownership and distribution was part of the larger pattern of southern society.

At the end of each decade the Federal census takers assembled facts and figures which refuted the plantation legend of the Old South. The data showed that the South was not simply—or even chiefly—a land of planters, slaves, and degraded "poor whites." Together these three groups constituted less than half of the total southern population. Most of the remaining Southerners (and the largest single group) were independent yeoman farmers of varying degrees of affluence. If there were such a thing as a "typical" ante-bellum Southerner, he belonged to the class of land-owning small farmers who tilled their own fields, usually without any help except from their wives and children. He might have devoted a few acres to one of the staples for a "cash crop," but he devoted most of his land and time to food crops for the subsistence of his own family.[7] Other smaller groups of Southerners included businessmen, professional men, skilled artisans, overseers, tenant farmers, and unskilled urban and farm laborers.

The South of 1860 was still overwhelmingly rural. Five southern states—North Carolina, Florida, Mississippi, Arkansas, and Texas—did not have a single city with a population of 10,000. New Orleans was the only big American city that was truly southern. The peculiar institution, then, was part of an agrarian civilization.

If the direct ownership of slave property had been the only way in which Southerners had become personally involved in the slave system, relatively few of them would have had an interest in preserving it. In 1860, there were

---

[7] The yeoman farmers receive full and sympathetic treatment in Frank L. Owsley, *Plain Folk of the Old South* (Baton Rouge, 1949).

in the South 385,000 owners of slaves distributed among 1,516,000 free families.[8] Nearly three-fourths of all free Southerners had no connection with slavery through either family ties or direct ownership. The "typical" Southerner was not only a small farmer but also a nonslaveholder.

The proportions of slaveholding and nonslaveholding families varied considerably in different parts of the South. In South Carolina and Mississippi, approximately half of the families owned slaves; in Georgia, two-fifths; in Alabama, Louisiana, and Florida, one-third; in Virginia, North Carolina, Kentucky, Tennessee, and Texas, one-fourth; in Arkansas, one-fifth; in Maryland and Missouri, one-eighth; and in Delaware, one-thirtieth. These same striking variations occurred regionally within each state.[9]

If membership in the planter class required the ownership of at least twenty slaves, the "typical" slaveholder of 1860 certainly did not belong to it. For 88% of the owners held less than that number, 72% held less than ten, and almost 50% held less than five. Not only was the "typical" slaveholder not a planter, but the "typical" planter worked only a moderate-sized gang of from twenty to fifty slaves. The planter aristocracy was limited to some ten thousand families who lived off the labor of gangs of more than fifty slaves. The extremely wealthy families who owned more

[8] The slave states (including the District of Columbia) had a total population of 12,302,000, of which 8,098,000 were whites, 3,954,000 were slaves, and 250,000 were free colored.

Unless otherwise indicated, these and subsequent statistics were compiled from the printed decennial returns of the United States Bureau of the Census, and from two other Bureau publications: *A Century of Population Growth from the First Census of the United States to the Twelfth, 1790–1900* (Washington, D.C., 1909) ; *Negro Population in the United States, 1790–1915* (Washington, D.C., 1918) .

[9] See, for example, Chase C. Mooney, "Some Institutional and Statistical Aspects of Slavery in Tennessee," *Tennessee Historical Quarterly*, I (1942) , pp. 211–12; Harry L. Coles, Jr., "Some Notes on Slaveownership and Landownership in Louisiana," *Journal of Southern History*, IX (1943) , pp. 382–85.

than a hundred slaves numbered less than three thousand, a tiny fraction of the southern population.

However, it does not follow that most of the slaves therefore lived on small agricultural units, for by 1860 slaves were heavily concentrated in the hands of a few owners. Only one-fourth of them belonged to masters who owned less than ten. Considerably more than half of them lived on plantation units of more than twenty slaves, and one-fourth lived on units of more than fifty. That the majority of slaves belonged to members of the planter class, and not to those who operated small farms with a single slave family, is a fact of crucial importance concerning the nature of bondage in the ante-bellum South.

Large slaveholdings were proportionally more numerous in the Deep South than in the Upper South.[1] Thus in Louisiana about one-sixth of the slaves lived on units of less than ten, while in Kentucky almost half lived on such units. In all of the southern states the bulk of the big slaveholdings were clustered together in restricted areas. These were always the areas best suited for the production of staple crops; for example, the alluvial river bottoms where the soil was rich and markets were easily accessible. Concentrations of the southern plantation aristocracy could be found in the sugar parishes of Louisiana, in the Yazoo Basin and around Natchez in Mississippi, in the Black Belt of Alabama, and in the rice swamps and sea islands of South Carolina and Georgia. In marked contrast, every southern state had counties containing not a single large plantation.

The South's nearly four million slaves were as unevenly distributed geographically as were the big slaveholders. Few of them—probably not many more than ten per cent—lived in cities and towns. Though Virginia had more

---

[1] There were 12.7 slaves per slaveholder in the Deep South and 7.7 slaves per slaveholder in the Upper South.

bondsmen than any other state, most of the slaves—2,312,000—lived in the seven states of the Deep South. The proportions of slaves in total state populations ranged from 57% in South Carolina to 1.5% in Delaware.[2]

The heavy concentrations of slaves were naturally in the same regions in which there were heavy concentrations of big slaveholders. In many counties in the Deep South the slaves exceeded the free population by more than two to one. In Issaquena and Washington counties in Mississippi they outnumbered the whites by more than ten to one. Even in the Upper South most of the bondsmen lived in a limited number of staple-producing regions. Some counties in western Virginia had just a few score slaves, while some in southeastern Virginia counted more slaves than whites. In Kentucky, though the whites outnumbered the slaves by four to one, the two groups were nearly equal in the Bluegrass counties of Fayette, Bourbon, and Woodford.

This complex pattern of slave distribution and ownership had an important bearing upon the lives of all Southerners and upon their relationship to the peculiar institution. Most of the slaves lived in a rural environment, on plantation-sized units, where they cultivated the great staple crops, on the richest lands of the South. Most of them lived in the cotton states, and only a few hundred thousand of them in border states such as Delaware, Maryland, Kentucky, and Missouri.

For a small percentage of southern whites the pattern provided the economic rewards and social prestige of the plantation. For the great majority of slaveholders it provided the more modest advantages of moderate-sized agricultural units. For the nearly three-fourths of the southern

---

[2] The proportions in other states were 55% in Mississippi, 47% in Louisiana, 45% in Alabama and Florida, 44% in Georgia, 33% in North Carolina, 31% in Virginia, 30% in Texas, 26% in Arkansas, 25% in Tennessee, 20% in Kentucky, 13% in Maryland, and 10% in Missouri.

I: *The Setting*

whites who owned no slaves it provided less tangible things: a means of controlling the social and economic competition of Negroes, concrete evidence of membership in a superior caste, a chance perhaps to rise into the planter class. Whatever the reason, most of the nonslave-holders seemed to feel that their interest required them to defend the peculiar institution.

So the slaves labored on the plantations and the white yeomen on their farms, but seldom with that mutual sympathy which is befitting to fellow tillers of the soil.

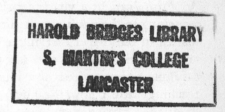
33

CHAPTER TWO

From Day Clean to First Dark

One summer afternoon in 1854, a traveler in Mississippi caught a vivid picture of a gang of field-hands
returning to their toil after a thundershower. "First came,
led by an old driver carrying a whip, forty of the largest
and strongest women I ever saw together; they were all in
a simple uniform dress of a bluish check stuff, the skirts
reaching little below the knee; their legs and feet were
bare; they carried themselves loftily, each having a hoe
over the shoulder, and walking with a free, powerful swing,
like chasseurs on the march." Then came the plow-hands
with their mules, "the cavalry, thirty strong, mostly men,
but a few of them women. . . . A lean and vigilant white
overseer, on a brisk pony, brought up the rear." [1] In this
procession were the chief components of the plantation's
production machinery—the regimented laborers whom
slavery was expected to provide.

Slavery was above all a labor system. Wherever in the
South the master lived, however many slaves he owned, it
was his bondsmen's productive capacity that he generally
valued most. And to the problem of organizing and exploiting their labor with maximum efficiency he devoted
much of his attention.

On small agricultural units—and the great majority of

[1] Olmsted, *Back Country*, pp. 14–15.

them were small—the organization was simple: the masters usually gave close personal supervision to the unspecialized labor of a few slaves. Most of these masters could not afford merely to act as managers; and many of them were obliged to enter the fields with their bondsmen and drive a plow or wield a hoe. Farmers who worked alongside their slaves could be found throughout the South. The son of a small slaveholder in the South Carolina Low Country remembered that his mother ran a spinning wheel, wove cloth, did her own cooking, and milked the cows, while his father plowed, drove the wagon, and made shoes.[2] In the Upper South, as a contemporary student of southern society observed, it was not unusual to see "the sturdy yeoman and his sons working in company of their negroes." One could hear "the axe of master and man falling with alternate strokes" and watch "the negroes and their masters ploughing side by side."[3]

Masters who had at their command as few as a half dozen field-hands, however, were tempted to improve their social status by withdrawing from the fields and devoting most of their time to managerial functions. Lacking skilled craftsmen in their small slave forces, they still found it necessary to perform certain specialized tasks such as carpentering and repairing tools; and in an emergency (a crop rarely went from spring planting to fall harvesting without a crisis of some kind) they temporarily forgot their pride. If some of the land needed to be replanted, if a crop was "in the grass"—i.e., overgrown with weeds—after a long spell of wet weather, or if illness created a shortage of plow-hands, a master often had to choose between losing his crop and pitching in with his slaves.[4] Cotton farmers who did

2 David Gavin Ms. Diary, entry for May 31, 1856.
3 Daniel R. Hundley, *Social Relations in Our Southern States* (New York, 1860), pp. 195–97.
4 John W. Brown Ms. Diary, entry for June 9, 1853; Henry Marston Ms. Diary, entries for May 3, 13, 1825; April 11, May 1, 1826.

not do ordinary field work helped with the picking in the fall, for that was a time when the labor force was seldom adequate.

But most slaves never saw their masters toiling in the fields, because most did not live on farms of the size where such intimate relationships and unspecialized economic functions existed. The great majority of bondsmen belonged to those whose holdings were large enough to enable them to escape routine farm labor. Even the slaves in the more modest holdings did not always work with their masters on small farms. Some of them worked in the cities. Others belonged to overseers and hence labored on the plantations. Still others belonged to the children or grandchildren of large planters and were used on the family estates. Hence the normal relationship between field-hands and their masters was not that of fellow workers but of labor and management.

Occasionally a small slaveholder, either temporarily or for a long period of time, left farm operations entirely in the hands of his slaves. Thus the head of an academy in Hillsboro, North Carolina, owned a farm nearby which his two bondsmen managed and worked for him. Another master in Harford County, Maryland, put his wheat farm under the control of three male slaves and gave them virtually no supervision.[5] But these informal managerial arrangements were exceptional; slaves rarely enjoyed such relative autonomy.

The substantial farmers and small planters who owned from ten to thirty slaves had at their disposal enough field-hands to make the problems of organization and supervision more complex. Members of this class usually handled these problems themselves without the aid of an overseer—

[5] W. J. Bingham to Ebenezer Pettigrew, January 10, 1842, Pettigrew Family Papers; James W. Williams Ms. Farm Books, in Neilson Record Books.

unless they operated more than one farm or combined farming with some other business or profession. In such cases the owner often required his overseer to work in the field as well as to manage the slaves. James M. Torbert, of Macon County, Alabama, who ran a shop in town, hired a young man "to work as a hand and oversee" his dozen bondsmen. A visitor to the Great Valley of Virginia noticed that where overseers were employed they almost always "participate[d] in the labors of the field." [6]

But everywhere in the South the normal pattern for a master in this class was to live on his own land and devote his full time to the supervision of his slaves and the general management of his agricultural enterprise. If he had assistance it came from his own sons or from a slave foreman, or driver. If the foreman knew his business the master did not have to be in constant attendance in the fields and even found it possible to be absent from home for short periods of time. Some of the foremen were able farmers; one observer suggested that many masters would have learned a great deal by consulting them.[7]

On these units of ten to thirty slaves there was customarily a limited amount of labor specialization. In addition to the field-hands and slave foreman, a slave or two might have been trained in any number of different manual skills useful in agriculture. Almost always at least one of them performed domestic work. But these slaves were not necessarily full-time specialists: they often had to divide their time between carpentry or cooking and field labor. For example, a small Virginia planter owned a slave woman whom he expected "to be a good deal occupied about the house in cooking etc. But she works in the field about half

[6] James M. Torbert Ms. Plantation Diary, entry at end of the year 1852; Edward S. Abdy, *Journal of a Residence and Tour in the United States* (London, 1835), II, p. 291.

[7] Columbia *South Carolinian*, quoted in *Southern Cultivator*, II (1844), p. 108.

of every day." [8] When the crops required it, every able-bodied hand was called upon for help. In the cotton districts at picking time the domestics, skilled workers, and small children were mobilized along with the regular field-hands.

The planters who owned more than thirty slaves were the ones who achieved maximum efficiency, the most complex economic organization, and the highest degree of specialization within their labor forces. Slightly less than half of the slaves belonged to the approximately twenty-five thousand masters operating plantations of these dimensions. Planters in this group who did not use overseers were as rare as the smaller slaveholders who did. In 1860 the number of Southerners who were employed as overseers about equalled the number of plantations with more than thirty slaves.[9]

The planter who hired a full-time overseer limited his direction of routine crop cultivation to periodic inspections of the fields and concentrated upon problems of marketing, finance, and general plantation administration. Being free from the need to give constant attention to his labor force, he enjoyed greater leisure and was able to absent himself from the plantation more or less at his discretion. He employed his overseer on a year-to-year basis, usually by a written contract which could be terminated at the will of either party. The planter paid his overseer an annual salary ranging all the way from $100 to $1200, in addition to furnishing a house, an allowance of corn and pork, and a slave servant.

A prudent planter defined the overseer's duties in a detailed set of written instructions. Each planter had his own

[8] Edmund Ruffin, Jr., Ms. Farm Journal, entry for March 6, 1843.

[9] For a detailed analysis of these ratios in Mississippi, see Charles S. Sydnor, *Slavery in Mississippi* (New York, 1933), pp. 67–69.

peculiar notions about the proper way to manage an estate, but his instructions tended to follow a somewhat standardized pattern. A Mississippian generalized about the overseer's responsibilities in a way that almost any planter would have endorsed: "The Overseer will never be expected to work in the field, but he must always be with the hands when not otherwise engaged in the Employers business and must do every thing that is required of him, provided it is directly or indirectly connected with the planting or other pecuniary interest of the Employer."[1] Specific instructions related to the care and control of the slaves, the amount and kinds of labor to be performed, the care of plantation tools and livestock, and the behavior and activities of the overseer himself. The owner often required his overseer to keep a daily record of general plantation activities and to make regular oral or written reports. In short, he expected the overseer to be an efficient general manager and a careful guardian of his employer's property.

The overseer's performance rarely satisfied the planter. To find an overseer with the skill to operate a large estate, the self-discipline and understanding of human psychology needed to control a body of slaves, and the physical energy to perform the countless duties assigned to him, was the dream of every planter but the realization of few. Since the social prestige and monetary rewards were seldom commensurate with the responsibilities, the profession did not attract many of the South's most talented men. The countless essays on the shortcomings of overseers in southern periodicals and the rapid turnover on most plantations gave evidence that this was one of the planter's major problems. Only in exceptional cases did he retain the same overseer for more than a year or two. The record of a Louisiana sugar planter who employed fourteen different overseers

---

[1] "Plantation Rules" in Andrew Flinn Ms. Plantation Book.

in a period of seventeen years was in no respect unusual. "They are as a class a worthless set of vagabonds," complained a Mississippian who recalled his own unhappy experiences.[2]

Now and then a planter, despairing of finding a satisfactory overseer, tried to do without one. For many years Ebenezer Pettigrew and two of his sons ran their three Tyrrell County, North Carolina, plantations with the assistance of trusted slave foremen only. An Alabama cotton planter pursued a more familiar course when he tried the same experiment for two years and then abandoned it.[3] Others periodically resolved to dispense with an overseer but never found it convenient to do so. Most planters simply did not wish to give up so much of their freedom; they looked upon the overseer, with all his faults, as an indispensable cog in the plantation machinery. Hence, although the conscientious master kept a close check on him, the usual arrangement was to delegate direct responsibility for routine operations to a white overseer.

In working the slave force the overseer generally made use of one or more slave drivers. If there were several of them one was designated head driver and acted almost as a sub-overseer. Sometimes the drivers were required to work and thus to set the pace for the rest of the slaves; sometimes they were exempted from labor and urged the gangs on by word or whip. A South Carolina rice planter defined their duties in his plantation rules: "Drivers are, under the Overseer, to maintain discipline and order on the place. They are to be responsible for the quiet of the negro-houses, for the proper performance of tasks, for bringing

[2] Plantation Ledger in Thomas W. Butler Papers; Everard Green Baker Ms. Diary, entry for July 1, 1858.

[3] William S. Pettigrew to James C. Johnston, December 31, 1845; December 7, 1848; October 3, 1850, Pettigrew Family Papers; Weymouth T. Jordan, *Hugh Davis and His Alabama Plantation* (University, Alabama, 1948), pp. 62–63.

out the people early in the morning, and generally for the immediate inspection of such things as the Overseer only generally superintends." [4] Planters thus called upon trusted slaves to become part of the plantation's command hierarchy. A Georgia planter described the efficient managerial system that existed on his estate:

> Every evening the drivers . . . make a report to the overseer in my presence of the employment of their respective hands. The drivers report . . . the quantity and kind of work they have done, and the field in which it is done. . . . These reports . . . are copied into the "Journal of Plantation Work," which forms a minute and daily record of the occupation and quantity of work done by the different gangs. After the reports are received, the work for the following day is arranged, and the head driver is directed what is to be done, and the manner in which it is to be executed. He distributes the orders to the sub-drivers and others:—the sub-drivers to the hands composing the gangs.
>
> As the quantity of land in each field is accurately known, a constant check is had on the fidelity of the reports as to the quantity of work done. It only remains, by a daily inspection, to see that all operations have been well performed.[5]

On a plantation containing more than thirty slaves there was always considerable labor specialization, the amount depending upon its size. The minimum was a clear distinction between household servants and field-hands, the latter in turn being divided into plow and hoe gangs. On the larger plantations some slaves devoted their full time to such occupations as ditching, tending livestock, driving wagons, and cultivating vegetable gardens. Here, too, there were substantial numbers of skilled slave artisans, and a

---

[4] *De Bow's Review*, XXI (1857), pp. 38–44.
[5] *Southern Agriculturist*, VI (1833), pp. 571–73.

high degree of specialization among household servants. In addition, each of the southern staples demanded its own kinds of specialists. These agricultural enterprises, with their business directors, production managers, labor foremen, and skilled and unskilled workers, approached the organizational complexity of modern factories. Though agriculture was not yet mechanized, the large plantations were to a considerable extent "factories in the fields."

Planters differed about how many slaves could be directed efficiently by one overseer on a single agricultural unit. Some divided their plantations when they owned less than a hundred slaves; others worked many more than that on undivided estates. But usually a large landowner whose slave force had grown to more than a hundred observed a decline in efficiency, because of the long distances the hands had to walk from their quarters to the fields, and because of the inability of an overseer to give close supervision to so many laborers. Such a large planter might split his estate into two or more separate enterprises. James H. Hammond, of South Carolina, noted in his diary that his overseer had proved himself to be "wholly incompetent" to manage his slave force. "Begin to believe no overseer capable of handling 125 hands and that they *must* be divided," he concluded.[6]

A division of this kind increased the complexity of the planter's economic operations. Though he sometimes elected to manage one plantation himself or depended on one overseer to run several, he normally employed an overseer for each plantation. On a very large establishment a general manager, or steward, helped the owner run his estate. The holdings of Colonel J. A. S. Acklen, of West Feliciana Parish, Louisiana, illustrate the magnitude of some of these enterprises. Acklen owned seven hundred slaves and

---

[6] James H. Hammond Ms. Diary, entry for July 8, 1846.

twenty thousand acres of land organized into six plantations. A visitor to his estate reported that he employed six overseers, a general agent, a bookkeeper, two physicians, a head carpenter, a tinner, a ditcher, and a preacher. "Every thing moves on systematically, and with the discipline of a regular trained army." [7]

Plantation magnates such as Acklen, most of whom were located in the sugar, rice, and cotton regions of the Lower South, were central figures in the ante-bellum plantation legend. A fact that was somehow lost in this legend was that these entrepreneurs operated their estates and made their fortunes in a competitive society in which success was the reward of careful financing, shrewd management, and a constant search for the most efficient methods of utilizing slave labor. The traits ascribed to the legendary genteel planter might even have been a handicap in the struggle for success.

Though the number of absentee owners among southern planters was relatively small, they were found most frequently among the owners of large estates. Those who divided their holdings into several plantations often maintained their residences on one of them—the "home plantation"—and made only periodic visits to the others. A few owned plantations long distances from their homes. They made annual visits to them and the rest of the time kept in touch through correspondence with their overseers. A small number of Virginians and Carolinians preferred to live in the states of their birth while depending upon incomes from sugar or cotton plantations in the Southwest. Some Alabamians and Mississippians in turn operated plantations in Texas and Arkansas.

Other slaveholders resided upon their estates only part of the year. Planters who were also lawyers, politicians, or

---

[7] *Southern Cultivator*, X (1852), p. 227.

merchants were necessarily absent much of the time and maintained residences in the towns. In summer, those who could afford it escaped to mountain or seashore. Few South Carolina and Georgia rice planters remained on their lands during the "sickly season." They fled from this malaria-infested region in May and did not return until after the first frost in the fall. The overseers of these temporary or permanent absentees were the only white men who made a direct impact upon the daily lives of the slaves.

The agricultural organizations of southern slaveholders, then, ranged from the simple systems of small farmers who toiled in the fields with their slaves, to the intricate systems of opulent planters whose lands stretched beyond the horizon and whose slaves were too numerous to be more than names in their plantation records. But, in either case, the primary function of slavery was to provide labor which, when utilized efficiently, could bring rich harvests from the land.

2

The day's toil began just before sunrise. A visitor on a Mississippi plantation was regularly awakened by a bell which was rung to call the slaves up. "I soon hear the tramp of the laborers passing along the avenue. . . . All is soon again still as midnight. . . . I believe that I am the only one in the house that the bell disturbs; yet I do not begrudge the few minutes' loss of sleep it causes me, it sounds so pleasantly in the half dreamy morning" [8] On James H. Hammond's South Carolina plantation a horn was blown an hour before daylight. "All work-hands are [then] required to rise and prepare their cooking, etc. for the day. The second horn is blown just at good day-light, when it is the duty of the driver to visit every house and see that all

---

[8] Joseph H. Ingraham (ed.), *The Sunny South; or, The Southerner at Home* (Philadelphia, 1860), pp. 51–52.

have left for the field." [9] At dusk the slaves put away their tools and returned to their quarters.

The working day was shorter in winter than in summer, but chiefly because there was less daylight, not because there was much less to do. Seldom at any time of the year was the master at a loss to find essential work to keep his hands busy. Those who planned the routine carefully saved indoor tasks for rainy days. An Alabama planter told his father in Connecticut that cotton picking continued until January, "and after that [we] gathered our corn which ripened last August. We then went to work with the waggons ha[u]ling rails and repairing and rebuilding fences, say two weeks, we then knocked down cotton stalks and pulled up corn stalks and commenced plowing. There is no lying by, no leisure, no long sleeping season such as you have in New England." [1] The terse plantation records of the year-round routine of slaves whose principal work was growing cotton usually ran something like this:

January–February: Finished picking, ginning, and pressing cotton and hauling it in wagons to the point of shipment; killed hogs and cut and salted the meat; cut and hauled wood; cut and mauled fence rails; repaired buildings and tools; spread manure; cleaned and repaired ditches; cleared new ground by rolling and burning logs and grubbing stumps; knocked down corn and cotton stalks and burned trash; plowed and "bedded up" corn and cotton fields; planted vegetables.

March–April: Opened "drills," or light furrows, in the corn and cotton beds; sowed corn and cotton seeds in the drills and covered them by hand or with a harrow; replanted where necessary; cultivated the vegetable garden; plowed and hoed in the corn fields.

---

[9] Plantation Manual in James H. Hammond Papers.
[1] Henry Watson, Jr., to his father, February 24, 1843 (copy), Henry Watson, Jr., Papers.

May–August: "Barred" cotton by scraping dirt away from it with plows; "chopped" cotton with hoes to kill weeds and grass and to thin it to a "stand"; "molded" cotton by "throwing dirt" to it with plows; cultivated corn and cotton until it was large enough to be "laid by"; made repairs; cleared new ground; "pulled fodder," i.e., stripped the blades from corn stalks; cleaned the gin house.

September–December: Picked, ginned, pressed, and shipped cotton; gathered peas; hauled corn and fodder; dug potatoes; shucked corn; cleaned and repaired ditches; repaired fences; cut and hauled wood; cleared new ground.[2]

Thus the operations of one growing cycle overlapped those of the next. There were, of course, variations from planter to planter and differences in the time of planting crops in the upper and lower parts of the cotton belt. Slaves who grew long-staple, or sea-island, cotton in the coastal areas of South Carolina and Georgia had to exercise greater care in picking, ginning, and packing this finer and more expensive variety. But these were differences only in detail. The routine work of cotton growers was essentially the same everywhere, and their basic tools were always the hoe and the plow.

Slaves who cultivated sugar, rice, tobacco, or hemp were involved in a similar year-round routine. They used the same basic tools and much of the time performed the same kinds of supplementary tasks. But each of the staples required special techniques in planting, cultivating, harvesting, and preparing for market.

Some slaves in Texas, Florida, Georgia, and other scattered places in the Deep South produced a little sugar, but those who worked on plantations lining the rivers and bayous of southern Louisiana produced ninety-five per cent of

---

[2] This is a generalized description obtained from the records of many slaveholders who grew cotton in widely scattered parts of the cotton belt.

this crop. Most of them were attached to large estates whose owners had heavy investments in land, labor, and machinery. On sugar plantations in the late fall and winter the slaves prepared the land with plows and harrows; before the end of February they planted the seed cane in deep furrows. The shoots grew from eyes at the joints of the seed cane, or ratooned from the stubble of the previous crop. Then came months of cultivation with hoes and plows until the crop was laid by in July. Meanwhile, other slaves cut huge quantities of wood and hauled it to the sugar house, and coopers made sugar hogsheads and molasses barrels. Much heavy labor also went into ditching to provide drainage for these lands which sloped gently from the rivers toward the swamps.

The first cane cut in October was "matalayed" (laid on the ground and covered with a little dirt) to be used as the next year's seed cane. During the frantic weeks from then until December most of the slaves worked at cutting the cane and stripping the leaves from the stalks, loading it into carts, and hauling it to the sugar house. At the mill other slaves fed the cane through the rollers, tended the open kettles or vacuum pans, kept the fires burning, hauled wood, and packed the unrefined sugar into hogsheads. When the last juice was boiled, usually around Christmas, it was almost time to begin planting the next crop.[3]

Soon after the Revolution South Carolina planters abandoned the cultivation of one of their staples—indigo.[4] But to the end of the ante-bellum period rice continued to be the favorite crop of the great planters along the rivers of the South Carolina and Georgia Low Country. Slaves had turned the tidal swamps into fertile rice fields by construct-

---

[3] J. Carlyle Sitterson, *Sugar Country: The Cane Sugar Industry in the South, 1753–1950* (Lexington, Kentucky, 1953), pp. 112–56.

[4] Michael Gramling, a small planter in the Orangeburg District, who was still producing indigo as late as 1845 was a rare exception. Michael Gramling Ms. Record Book.

ing an intricate system of banks, "trunks" (sluices), and ditches which made possible periodic flooding and draining with the rising and falling tides. Throughout the year slaves on rice plantations devoted much of their time to cleaning the ditches, repairing the banks and trunks, and keeping the tide-flow irrigation system in efficient operation.

In winter the slaves raked the rice fields and burned the stubble. After the ground was broken and "trenched" into drills, the seeds were planted in March and early April. During the first flooding (the "sprout flow") other crops on higher ground were cultivated. When the rice fields were drained and dried they were hoed to loosen the ground and to kill grass and weeds. The next flooding (the "stretch flow") was followed by a long period of "dry growth" during which hoeing went on constantly. Then came the final flooding (the "harvest flow") which lasted until September when the rice was ready to be cut. The slaves cut the rice with sickles, tied it into sheaves, and stacked it to dry. After it had dried they carried the rice to the plantation mill to be threshed, "pounded" to remove the husks from the kernels, winnowed, screened, and packed in barrels.[5] The other crops grown on lands above the swamps were gathered in time to begin preparations for the next year's planting.

The Tobacco Kingdom stretched into the border states of Maryland, Kentucky, and Missouri, but in the antebellum period its heart was still the "Virginia District." This district embraced the piedmont south of Fredericksburg, including the northern tier of counties in North Carolina. Here the plantations were smaller than in the

[5] Duncan Clinch Heyward, *Seed from Madagascar* (Chapel Hill, 1937), pp. 27–44; J. H. Easterby (ed.), *The South Carolina Rice Plantation as Revealed in the Papers of Robert F. W. Allston* (Chicago, 1945), pp. 31–32; Phillips, *Life and Labor in the Old South*, pp. 115–18.

Lower South, because each hand could cultivate fewer acres and because the crop had to be handled with great care. The unique aspects of tobacco culture included the preparing of beds in which the tiny seeds were sown during the winter, the transplanting of the shoots in May, and the worming, topping, and suckering of the plants during the summer months. In the late summer the tobacco stalks were split, cut, and left in the fields to wilt. Then they were carried to the tobacco houses to be hung and cured during the fall and winter. The following year, when work had already begun on the next crop, the leaves were stripped from the stalks, sorted, tied into bundles, and "prized" into hogsheads.[6]

The Bluegrass counties of Kentucky and the Missouri River Valley were the chief hemp producing regions of the Old South. Slaves were almost always the working force on hemp farms, because free labor avoided the strenuous, disagreeable labor required to prepare a crop for market. After the ground was prepared, the seeds were sown broadcast in April and May and covered lightly with a harrow or shovel plow. Unlike the other staples, hemp required no cultivation during the growing season, and slaves were free to tend other crops. In late summer the hemp was cut, laid on the ground to dry, and then tied in sheaves and stacked. In November or December it was again spread out in the fields for "dew rotting" to loosen the fiber. A month or so later the hemp was stacked once more, and the lint was laboriously separated from the wood with a hand "brake." The fiber was taken to the hemp house where it was hackled or sold immediately to manufacturers.[7]

In 1850, the Superintendent of the Census estimated that

---

[6] Joseph Clarke Robert, *The Tobacco Kingdom* (Durham, 1938), pp. 32-50.

[7] James F. Hopkins, *A History of the Hemp Industry in Kentucky* (Lexington, Kentucky, 1951), pp. 24-30, 39-64; Harrison A. Trexler, *Slavery in Missouri, 1804-1865* (Baltimore, 1914), pp. 23-25.

2,500,000 slaves of all ages were directly employed in agriculture. Of these, he guessed that 60,000 were engaged in the production of hemp, 125,000 in the production of rice, 150,000 in the production of sugar, 350,000 in the production of tobacco, and 1,815,000 in the production of cotton. Somewhat casually he observed that these slaves also produced "large quantities of breadstuffs." [8] This was scarcely adequate recognition of the amount of time they devoted to such crops, even on many of the plantations which gave chief attention to one of the five staples.

To be sure, some planters in the Lower South were so preoccupied with staple production that they grew almost nothing else—not even enough corn and pork to feed their slaves. This pattern was common in the Louisiana sugar district. One planter explained that when sugar sold for fifty dollars a hogshead, "it is cheaper to buy pork[,] for it is utterly impossible to raise hogs here without green pastures and plenty of corn[,] and all lands here fit for pasturage will make a hogshead [of] sugar pr acre—The great curse of this country is that we are all planters and no farmers." [9] An Alabama cotton planter was alarmed when pork failed to arrive from Tennessee: "All of our towns and most of our large Planters are dependent on Drovers for their meat." Even some of the cotton and tobacco planters in North Carolina bought food supplies for their slaves.[1] Such planters were convinced that it was most profitable to concentrate on the production of a single cash crop.

Most planters, however, did not share this point of view. Almost all of the hemp and tobacco growers of the Upper

8 *Compendium of the Seventh Census* (Washington, 1854), p. 94.
9 Kenneth M. Clark to Lewis Thompson, June 20, 1853, Lewis Thompson Papers.
1 Columbus Morrison Ms. Diary, entry for November 27, 1845; Rosser H. Taylor, *Slaveholding in North Carolina: An Economic View* (Chapel Hill, 1926), pp. 36–37.

South planted many acres of food crops to supply their own needs—and frequently additional acres to produce surpluses for sale. A major feature of the agricultural revival in ante-bellum Virginia was an improved system of crop rotation with increased emphasis upon corn, wheat, and clover.[2] Many of the tobacco planters gave enough attention to these and other crops to approximate a system of diversified farming. Their field-hands often devoted less than half of their time to tobacco.

Few planters in the Deep South approached such levels of diversification, but most of them produced sizeable food crops for their families and slaves. In southern agricultural periodicals they constantly admonished each other to strive for self-sufficiency. They instructed their overseers to produce adequate supplies of corn, sweet potatoes, peas, and beans, and to give proper attention to the poultry, hogs, and cattle. A Mississippi planter warned his overseer "that a failure to make a bountiful supply of corn and meat for the use of the plantation, will be considered as notice that his services will not be required for the succeeding year." [3] The average planter, however, was tempted to forgive a great deal if his overseer managed to make enough cotton. Interest in other crops tended to vary with fluctuations in cotton prices. Even so, most of the field-hands on cotton plantations were at least familiar with the routine of corn cultivation.

Though southern planters showed that slaves could grow other crops besides the five great staples, there was a widespread belief that it was impractical to devote plantations to them exclusively. But here and there in the Lower South a planter disproved this assumption. In Richmond County,

---

[2] Avery O. Craven, *Soil Exhaustion as a Factor in the Agricultural History of Virginia and Maryland* (Urbana, Illinois, 1926), pp. 122–61; Robert, *Tobacco Kingdom*, pp. 18–19.

[3] *De Bow's Review*, X (1851), pp. 625–27.

Georgia, an owner of more than a hundred slaves successfully used his labor force to raise grain and meat for sale in Augusta.[4]

In the Upper South many large slaveholders grew neither tobacco nor hemp but engaged in diversified farming. In Talbot County, Maryland, Colonel Edward Lloyd worked his two hundred and seventy-five slaves on profitable farms which produced wheat, corn, hams, wool, and hides.[5] On Shirley Plantation on the James River, Hill Carter, like many of his Virginia neighbors, made wheat his major cash crop. An incomplete list of the products of a plantation in King and Queen County included wheat, corn, oats, rye, vegetables, Irish potatoes, sweet potatoes, wool, hogs, apples, and strawberries.[6]

In North Carolina, corn was the chief crop on a number of Roanoke River plantations. In Tyrrell County, Ebenezer Pettigrew annually shipped thousands of bushels of wheat and corn to Norfolk and Charleston.[7] Clearly, the slave-plantation system had greater flexibility and was less dependent upon the production of a few staples than some have thought.

There is a different tradition about the agricultural operations of farmers who owned less than ten slaves. Here a high degree of diversification is assumed—presumably the smaller farms were better adapted to this type of farming than to the cultivation of the staples. Thousands of slaveholders in this group did engage in what was almost subsistence farming with cash incomes well below five hundred

---

[4] Ralph B. Flanders, *Plantation Slavery in Georgia* (Chapel Hill, 1933), p. 158.

[5] Records of sales in Lloyd Family Papers. See also Frederick Law Olmsted, *A Journey in the Seaboard Slave States* (New York, 1856), p. 10.

[6] Shirley Plantation Ms. Farm Journal; John Walker Ms. Diary.

[7] Pettigrew Family Papers; Bennett H. Wall, "Ebenezer Pettigrew, An Economic Study of an Ante-Bellum Planter" (unpublished doctoral dissertation, University of North Carolina, 1946), *passim; Farmer's Journal,* I (1852), p. 147.

dollars a year. Others, especially in the Upper South, marketed large surpluses of pork, corn, and wheat. The amount of commercialization in the operations of non-staple producing small slaveholders depended upon the quality of their lands, their proximity to markets and transportation, and their managerial skill.

But a large proportion of these slaveholding farmers depended upon one of the five southern staples for a cash crop. In Kentucky and Missouri many of them produced a few tons of hemp; there and in Virginia and North Carolina they often gave tobacco their chief attention. A few small slaveholders in the Deep South even planted rice and sugar—sometimes surprisingly large amounts—in spite of the handicaps they faced in trying to compete with the planters. In St. Mary Parish, Louisiana, for example, an owner of seven slaves in 1859 produced forty hogsheads of sugar. These small operators depended upon their neighbors' sugar making facilities or ran their own crude horse-driven mills.[8]

In cotton production those with modest slaveholdings faced no overwhelming competitive disadvantage. Some of the smaller cotton growers were as preoccupied with this staple as were their neighbors on the large plantations. Some even depended upon outside supplies of food. Many of them reported astonishing cotton-production records to the census takers, the number of bales per hand easily matching the records of the planters.[9]

Nevertheless, the majority of small slaveholders did engage in a more diversified type of agriculture than most of the large planters. Slavery could be, and was, adapted to diversified agriculture and to the labor needs of small

---

8 Sitterson, *Sugar Country*, pp. 50–51.
9 This information about small slaveholders was derived from a study of their production records in representative counties throughout the South as reported in the manuscript census returns for 1860.

farms. It did not necessarily depend upon large plantations or staple crops for its survival.

3

For the owner of a few slaves, labor management was a problem of direct personal relationships between individuals. For the owner of many, the problem was more difficult and required greater ingenuity. Both classes of masters desired a steady and efficient performance of the work assigned each day. They could not expect much cooperation from their slaves, who had little reason to care how much was produced. Masters measured the success of their methods by the extent to which their interest in a maximum of work of good quality prevailed over the slaves' predilection for a minimum of work of indifferent quality. Often neither side won a clear victory.

Slaveowners developed numerous variations of two basic methods of managing their laborers: the "gang system" and the "task system." Under the first of these systems, which was the one most commonly used, the field-hands were divided into gangs commanded by drivers who were to work them at a brisk pace. Competent masters gave some thought to the capacities of individual slaves and to the amount of labor that a gang could reasonably be expected to perform in one day. But the purpose of the gang system was to force every hand to continue his labor until all were discharged from the field in the evening.

Under the task system, each hand was given a specific daily work assignment. He could then set his own pace and quit when his task was completed. The driver's job was to inspect the work and to see that it was performed satisfactorily before the slave left the field. "The advantages of this system," according to a Georgia rice planter, "are encouragement to the laborers, by equalizing the work of each

54

agreeable to strength, and the avoidance of watchful superintendence and incessant driving. As . . . the task of each [slave] is separate, imperfect work can readily be traced to the neglectful worker." [1]

The task system was best adapted to the rice plantation, with its fields divided into small segments by the network of drainage ditches. Outside the Low Country of South Carolina and Georgia planters occasionally used this system or at least experimented with it, but many of them found it to be unsatisfactory. For one thing, they could get no more work out of their stronger slaves than out of their weaker ones, since the tasks were usually standardized. The planters also found that the eagerness of slaves to finish their tasks as early as possible led to careless work. After using the task system for twenty years, an Alabama planter abandoned it because of evils "too numerous to mention." A South Carolina cotton planter, who also gave it up, noted with satisfaction that under the gang system his slaves did "much more" and were "not so apt to strain themselves." [2]

Actually, most planters used a combination of the two systems. Cotton planters often worked plow-hands in gangs but gave hoe-hands specific tasks of a certain number of cotton rows to hoe each day. Each hand was expected to pick as much cotton as he could, but he might be given a minimum quota that had to be met. Sugar, rice, and tobacco planters applied the task system to their coopers, and hemp growers used it with hands engaged in breaking or hackling hemp. Masters generally tasked their hands for digging ditches, cutting wood, or mauling rails.

Thus most slaves probably had some experience with both systems. From their point of view each system doubtless had its advantages and drawbacks. A strong hand might

---

[1] *Southern Agriculturist*, VI (1833), p. 576.

[2] Sellers, *Slavery in Alabama*, p. 67; Hammond Diary, entry for May 16, 1838.

have preferred to be tasked if he was given an opportunity to finish early. But many slaves must have been appalled at the ease with which they could be held responsible for the quality of their work. The gang system had the disadvantages of severe regimentation and of hard driving which was especially onerous for the weaker hands. But there was less chance that a slave would be detected and held individually responsible for indifferent work. In the long run, however, the rigors of either system were determined by the demands of masters and overseers.

The number of acres a slaveholder expected each of his field-hands to cultivate depended in part upon how hard he wished to work them. It also depended upon the nature of the soil, the quality of the tools, and the general efficiency of the agricultural enterprise. Finally, it depended upon the crop. Cotton growers on flat prairies and river bottoms planted as many as ten acres per hand but rarely more than that. Those on hilly or rolling lands planted from three to eight acres per hand. Since a slave could ordinarily cultivate more cotton than he could pick, acreage was limited by the size of the available picking force. By the 1850's each hand was expected to work from nine to ten acres of sugar but seldom more than five acres of rice or three of tobacco, plus six or more of corn and other food crops.[3] The yield per acre and per hand varied with the fertility of the soil, the care in cultivation, the damage of insects, and the whims of the weather.

When calculating his yield per field-hand a slaveholder was not calculating his yield per slave, for he almost always owned fewer field-hands than slaves. Some of his slaves performed other types of work, and the very young and the

[3] These are generalized figures from a survey of many plantation records. See also *De Bow's Review*, II (1846), pp. 134, 138; X (1851), p. 625; Sydnor, *Slavery in Mississippi*, pp. 13–14; Gray, *History of Agriculture*, II, pp. 707–708; Sitterson, *Sugar Country*, pp. 127–28; Robert, *Tobacco Kingdom*, p. 18.

very old could not be used in the fields. The master's diseased, convalescing, and partially disabled slaves, his "breeding women" and "sucklers," his children just beginning to work in the fields, and his slaves of advanced years were incapable of laboring as long and as hard as full-time hands.

Most masters had systems of rating such slaves as fractional hands. Children often began as "quarter hands" and advanced to "half hands," "three-quarter hands," and then "full hands." As mature slaves grew older they started down this scale. "Breeding women" and "sucklers" were rated as "half hands." Some planters organized these slaves into separate gangs, for example, into a "sucklers gang." Children sometimes received their training in a "trash gang," or "children's squad," which pulled weeds, cleaned the yard, hoed, wormed tobacco, or picked cotton. Seldom were many more than half of a master's slaves listed in his records as field-hands, and always some of the hands were classified as fractional. Olmsted described a typical situation on a Mississippi cotton plantation: "There were 135 slaves, big and little, of which 67 went to the field regularly—equal, the overseer thought, to 60 able-bodied hands." [4]

The master, not the parents, decided at what age slave children should be put to work in the fields. Until they were five or six years old children were "useless articles on a plantation." Then many received "their first lessons in the elementary part of their education" through serving as "water-toters" or going into the fields alongside their mothers.[5] Between the ages of ten and twelve the children be-

---

[4] Olmsted, *Back Country*, p. 47; *id., Seaboard*, p. 433; *Southern Agriculturist*, VI (1833), pp. 571–73; Sydnor, *Slavery in Mississippi*, pp. 18–20; Sellers, *Slavery in Alabama*, p. 66.

[5] [Joseph H. Ingraham], *The South-West. By a Yankee* (New York, 1835), II, p. 126; Charles S. Davis, *The Cotton Kingdom in Alabama* (Montgomery, 1939), p. 58.

came fractional hands, with a regular routine of field labor. By the time they were eighteen they had reached the age when they could be classified as "prime field-hands."

Mature slaves who did not work in the fields (unless they were totally disabled or extremely old) performed other kinds of valuable and productive labor. Old women cooked for the rest of the slaves, cared for small children, fed the poultry, mended and washed clothes, and nursed the sick. Old men gardened, minded stock, and cleaned the stable and the yard.

Old or partially disabled slaves might also be put to spinning and weaving in the loom houses of the more efficient planters. The printed instructions in a popular plantation record book advised overseers to adopt this policy: "Few instances of good management will better please an employer, than that of having all the winter clothing spun and woven on the place. By having a room devoted to that purpose . . . where those who may be complaining a little, or convalescent after sickness, may be employed in some light work, and where all of the women may be sent in wet weather, more than enough of both cotton and woolen yarn can be spun for the supply of the place." [6] One planter reported that he had his spinning jenny "going at a round rate[.] Old Charles [is] Spinning and Esther reeling the thread. . . . Charles will in this way be one of my most productive laborers and so will several of the women[.]" [7] Thus a master's productive slaves were by no means limited to those listed as field-hands.

The bondsmen who were valued most highly were those who had acquired special skills which usually exempted them from field work entirely. This select group of slave

[6] Thomas Affleck, *The Cotton Plantation Record and Account Book* (Louisville and New Orleans, 1847–) .

[7] Gustavus A. Henry to his wife, December 3, 1846, Gustavus A. Henry Papers; Herbert A. Kellar (ed.) , *Solon Robinson, Pioneer and Agriculturist* (Indianapolis, 1936) , II, p. 203.

craftsmen included engineers, coopers, carpenters, blacksmiths, brickmakers, stone masons, mechanics, shoemakers,
weavers, millers, and landscapers. The excellence of the
work performed by some of them caused slaveowners to
make invidious comparisons between them and the free
artisans they sometimes employed. An Englishman recalled
an interview with the overseer on a Louisiana sugar plantation: "It would have been amusing, had not the subject
been so grave, to hear the overseer's praises of the intelligence and skill of these workmen, and his boast that they
did all the work of skilled laborers on the estate, and then
to listen to him, in a few minutes, expatiating on the utter
helplessness and ignorance of the black race, their inca-
pacity to do any good, or even to take care of themselves." [8]

Domestic servants were prized almost as much as craftsmen. The number and variety of domestics in a household
depended upon the size of the establishment and the wealth
of the master. They served as hostlers, coachmen, laun-
dresses, seamstresses, cooks, footmen, butlers, housemaids,
chambermaids, children's nurses, and personal servants.
On a large plantation specialization was complete: "The
cook never enters the house, and the nurse is never seen in
the kitchen; the wash-woman is never put to ironing, nor
the woman who has charge of the ironing-room ever put to
washing. Each one rules supreme in her wash-house, her
ironing-room, her kitchen, her nursery, her house-keeper's
room; and thus . . . a complete system of domesticdom is
established to the amazing comfort and luxury of all who
enjoy its advantages." [9]

But the field-hands remained fundamental in the slave
economy. Though their work was classified as unskilled
labor, this of course was a relative term. Some visitors described the "rude" or "slovenly" manner in which slaves

---

[8] William H. Russell, *My Diary North and South* (Boston, 1863), p. 273.
[9] Ingraham (ed.), *Sunny South*, pp. 179–81.

cultivated the crops, how "awkwardly, slowly, and undecidedly" they moved through the fields.[1] But other observers were impressed with the success of many masters in training field-hands to be efficient workers, impressed also by the skill these workers showed in certain crucial operations in the production of staple crops. Inexperienced hands had their troubles in sugar houses and rice fields, in breaking and hackling hemp, and in topping, suckering, sorting, and prizing tobacco. Even the neophyte cotton picker soon wondered whether this was unskilled labor, as one former slave testified: "While others used both hands, snatching the cotton and depositing it in the mouth of the sack, with a precision and dexterity that was incomprehensible to me, I had to seize the boll with one hand, and deliberately draw out the white, gushing blossom with the other." On his first day he managed to gather "not half the quantity required of the poorest picker."[2]

Field workers kept up a ceaseless struggle to make the lands fruitful, against the contrary efforts of the insects and the elements. The battle seemed at times to be of absorbing interest to some of the slaves, conscripts though they were. In a strange and uneasy kind of alliance, they and their masters combatted the foes that could have destroyed them both.

4

In 1860, probably a half million bondsmen lived in southern cities and towns, or were engaged in work not directly or indirectly connected with agriculture. Some farmers and planters found it profitable, either temporarily or permanently, to employ part of their hands in non-agricultural occupations. Along the rivers slaves cut wood to pro-

---

[1] Henry Watson, Jr., to Theodore Watson, March 3, 1831, Watson Papers; Olmsted, *Seaboard*, pp. 18–19.

[2] Solomon Northup, *Twelve Years a Slave* (Buffalo, 1853), pp. 178–79.

vide fuel for steamboats and for sale in neighboring towns. In swamplands filled with juniper, oak, and cypress trees they produced shingles, barrel and hogshead staves, pickets, posts, and rails. In North Carolina's Dismal Swamp slave gangs labored as lumberjacks.[3] In the eastern Carolina pine belt several thousand slaves worked in the turpentine industry. An owner of one hundred and fifty slaves in Brunswick County, North Carolina, raised just enough food to supply his force; he made his profits from the annual sale of thousands of barrels of turpentine. Many smaller operators also combined turpentine production with subsistence farming.[4]

Elsewhere in the South bondsmen worked in sawmills, gristmills, quarries, and fisheries. They mined gold in North Carolina, coal and salt in Virginia, iron in Kentucky and Tennessee, and lead in Missouri. On river boats they were used as deck hands and firemen. Slave stokers on a Mississippi River steamer bound for New Orleans, who sang as they fed wood to the boiler fires, intrigued a European traveler: "It was a fantastic and grand sight to see these energetic black athletes lit up by the wildly flashing flames . . . while they, amid their equally fantastic song, keeping time most exquisitely, hurled one piece of firewood after another into the yawning fiery gulf."[5]

Other slaves were employed in the construction and maintenance of internal improvements. They worked on the public roads several days each year in states which required owners to put them to such use. For many years

---

[3] Gustavus A. Henry to his wife, December 12, 1848, Henry Papers; John Nevitt Ms. Plantation Journal; William S. Pettigrew to James C. Johnston, January 24, 1856, Pettigrew Family Papers; Olmsted, *Seaboard*, pp. 153–55.

[4] Olmsted, *Seaboard*, pp. 339–42; Guion G. Johnson, *Ante-Bellum North Carolina* (Chapel Hill, 1937), pp. 487–88.

[5] Fredrika Bremer, *The Homes of the New World* (New York, 1853), II, p. 174.

slaves owned by the state of Louisiana built roads and cleared obstructions from the bayous. Slaves also worked for private internal improvements companies, such as the builders of the Brunswick and Altamaha Canal in Georgia and the Cape Fear and Deep River Navigation Company in North Carolina. In Mississippi a hundred were owned by a firm of bridge contractors, the Weldon brothers.[6]

Railroad companies employed bondsmen in both construction and maintenance work. As early as 1836 the Richmond, Fredericksburg, and Potomac Railroad Company advertised for "a large number" of slave laborers. In the same year the Alabama, Florida, and Georgia Railroad Company announced a need for five hundred "able-bodied negro men . . . to be employed in felling, cutting, and hewing timber, and in forming the excavations and embankments upon the route of said Rail Road." During the 1850's southern newspapers carried the constant pleas of railroad builders for slaves. Almost every railroad in the ante-bellum South was built at least in part by bondsmen; in Georgia they constructed more than a thousand miles of roadbed. In 1858, a Louisiana newspaper concluded: "Negro labor is fast taking the place of white labor in the construction of southern railroads."[7]

Bondsmen in southern cities and towns, in spite of the protests of free laborers, worked in virtually every skilled and unskilled occupation. They nearly monopolized the domestic services, for most free whites shunned them to avoid being degraded to the level of slaves. Many of the Southerners who owned just one or two slaves were urban

[6] Joe Gray Taylor, "Negro Slavery in Louisiana" (unpublished doctoral dissertation, Louisiana State University, 1951), pp. 43-44, 115-17; Raleigh *North Carolina Standard*, June 6, 1855; August 13, 1859; Horace S. Fulkerson, *Random Recollections of Early Days in Mississippi* (Vicksburg, 1885), pp. 130-31.

[7] Richmond *Enquirer*, August 2, 1836; Sellers, *Slavery in Alabama*, pp. 200-201; Flanders, *Plantation Slavery in Georgia*, pp. 197-98; Taylor, "Negro Slavery in Louisiana," pp. 112-13.

dwellers who used them as cooks, housekeepers, and gardeners. The wealthier townspeople often had staffs of domestic servants as large as those of rural planters. Other domestics found employment in hotels and at watering places.

Town slaves worked in cotton presses, tanneries, shipyards, bakehouses, and laundries, as dock laborers and stevedores, and as clerks in stores. Masters who owned skilled artisans such as barbers, blacksmiths, cabinet makers, and shoemakers often provided them with shops to make their services available to all who might wish to employ them. Many white mechanics used slave assistants. In short, as a visitor to Natchez observed, town slaves included "mechanics, draymen, hostlers, labourers, hucksters, and washwomen, and the heterogeneous multitude of every other occupation, who fill the streets of a busy city—for slaves are trained to every kind of manual labour. The blacksmith, cabinet-maker, carpenter, builder, wheelwright,—all have one or more slaves labouring at their trades. The negro is a third arm to every working man, who can possibly save money enough to purchase one. He is emphatically the 'right-hand man' of every man." [8] The quality of the work of slave artisans had won favorable comment as early as the eighteenth century. Among them were "many ingenious Mechanicks," wrote a colonial Georgian, "and as far as they have had opportunity of being instructed, have discovered as good abilities, as are usually found among people of our Colony." [9]

Some Southerners were enthusiastic crusaders for the development of factories which would employ slaves. They were convinced that bondsmen could be trained in all the

---

[8] [Ingraham], *South-West*, II, p. 249.

[9] Quoted in Flanders, *Plantation Slavery in Georgia*, p. 47. See also Leonard P. Stavisky, "Negro Craftsmanship in Early America," *American Historical Review*, IV (1949), 315–25.

necessary skills and would provide a cheaper and more manageable form of labor than free whites. "When the channels of agriculture are choked," predicted an industrial promoter, "the manufacturing of our own productions will open new channels of profitable employment for our slaves." Others thought that slavery was one of the South's "natural advantages" in its effort to build industries to free it from "the incessant and vexatious attacks of the North." [1] They believed that industrialization and slavery could proceed hand in hand.

Southern factory owners gave evidence that this was more than idle speculation. Every slave state had industrial establishments which made some use of slave labor. In Kentucky, the "ropewalks" which manufactured cordage and the hemp factories which produced cotton bagging and "Kentucky jeans" employed slaves extensively. [2] Almost all of the thirteen thousand workers in the tobacco factories of the Virginia District were bondsmen. The majority of them were employed in the three leading tobacco manufacturing cities—Richmond, Petersburg, and Lynchburg. These slave workers were not only a vital part of this industry but also a curiously paradoxical element in the society of the tobacco towns. [3]

From its earliest beginnings the southern iron industry depended upon skilled and unskilled slaves. Negro iron workers were employed in Bath County, Kentucky, and along the Cumberland River in Tennessee. In the Cumberland country the majority of laborers at the iron furnaces were slaves. Montgomery Bell, owner of the Cumberland Iron Works, engaged his own three hundred slaves and

---

[1] *De Bow's Review*, VIII (1850), p. 76; IX (1850), pp. 432–33.

[2] Hopkins, *Hemp Industry*, pp. 135–37; J. Winston Coleman, Jr., *Slavery Times in Kentucky* (Chapel Hill, 1940), pp. 81–82.

[3] Robert, *Tobacco Kingdom*, pp. 197–203; Alexander MacKay, *The Western World; or Travels in the United States in 1846–47* (London, 1849), II, p. 74.

many others in every task connected with the operation of forge and furnace.[4] In the Great Valley of Virginia, where the southern industry was centered during the early nineteenth century, slaves constituted the chief labor supply.

Until the 1840's, the famed Tredegar Iron Company in Richmond used free labor almost exclusively. But in 1842, Joseph R. Anderson, then commercial agent of the company, proposed to employ slaves as a means of cutting labor costs. The board of directors approved of his plan, and within two years Anderson was satisfied with "the practicability of the scheme." In 1847, the increasing use of slaves caused the remaining free laborers to go out on strike, until they were threatened with prosecution for forming an illegal combination. After this protest failed, Anderson vowed that he would show his workers that they could not dictate his labor policies: he refused to re-employ any of the strikers. Thereafter, as Anderson noted, Tredegar used "almost exclusively slave labor except as the Boss men. This enables me, of course, to compete with other manufacturers."[5]

But it was upon the idea of bringing textile mills to the cotton fields that southern advocates of industrialization with slave labor pinned most of their hopes. In cotton factories women and children were needed most, and hence it was often argued that they would provide profitable employment for the least productive workers in agriculture. Though the majority of southern textile workers were free whites, and though some believed that this work ought to be reserved for them, a small number of slaves were nevertheless employed in southern mills.

Occasionally mill owners managed to work slaves and

[4] Coleman, *Slavery Times in Kentucky*, p. 64; Robert E. Corlew, "Some Aspects of Slavery in Dickson County," *Tennessee Historical Quarterly*, X (1951), pp. 226–29.

[5] Kathleen Bruce, *Virginia Iron Manufacture in the Slave Era* (New York, 1931), pp. 231–38.

free whites together with a minimum of friction. A visitor found equal numbers of the two groups employed in a cotton factory near Athens, Georgia: "There is no difficulty among them on account of colour, the white girls working in the same room and at the same loom with the black girls; and boys of each colour, as well as men and women, working together without apparent repugnance or objection." [6] But even if some white workers would tolerate this, slave-owners ordinarily looked upon it as a dangerous practice.

The southern press gave full reports of cotton mills which used slave labor and ecstatic accounts of their success. A Pensacola newspaper cited the local Arcadia Cotton Factory, which employed only slaves, to prove that "with the native skill and ingenuity of mere labor—the labor of the hands—the negro is just as richly endowed as the white." The Saluda mill, near Columbia, South Carolina, operated on the "slave-labor, or anti free-soil system." The white managers testified to the "equal efficiency, and great superiority in many respects" of slaves over free workers. [7] During the 1830's and 1840's, a half dozen other cotton mills in South Carolina's Middle and Low Country employed bondsmen. Most other southern states could point to one or more mills which used this type of labor. To many observers the enterprises of Daniel Pratt at Prattsville, near Montgomery, Alabama, provided models for other Southerners to copy. Pratt worked slaves not only in his cotton mill but also in his cotton gin factory, iron foundry, sash and door factory, machine shop, and carriage and wagon shop. [8]

6 James S. Buckingham, *The Slave States of America* (London, [1842]), II, p. 112.
7 Pensacola *Gazette*, April 8, 1848; *De Bow's Review*, IX (1850), pp. 432-33.
8 E. M. Lander, Jr., "Slave Labor in South Carolina Cotton Mills," *Journal of Negro History*, XXXVIII (1953), pp. 161-73; Charles H. Wesley, *Negro Labor in the United States, 1850-1925* (New York,

Actually, the ante-bellum South had relatively few cotton mills, and most of them were small enterprises manufacturing only the coarser grades of cloth. In 1860, the fifteen slave states together had only 198 mills each employing an average of 71 workers, whereas Massachusetts alone had 217 mills each employing an average of 177 workers. Many of the southern factories resembled the one owned by a small manufacturer in East Tennessee which contained only three hundred spindles operated by fourteen slave hands.[9]

Still, in these textile mills and in what little other industry existed in the Old South there was abundant evidence that slaves could be trained to be competent factory workers. The evidence was sufficient to raise serious doubts that slavery was tied to agriculture, as some defenders and some critics of the institution believed.

5

Each year, around the first of January, at southern crossroad stores, on the steps of county courthouses, and in every village and city, large crowds of participants and spectators gathered for "hiring day." At this time masters with bondsmen to spare and employers in search of labor bargained for the rental of slave property. Thus thousands of nonslaveholders managed temporarily to obtain the services of slaves and to enjoy the prestige of tenuous membership in the master class. Thus, too, many bondsmen found it their lot to labor for persons other than their owners. Hired slaves were most numerous in the Upper South; dur-

---

1927), pp. 15–20; *American Cotton Planter and Soil of the South*, I (1857), pp. 156–57.
[9] William B. Lenoir to William Lenoir, May 18, 1833, Lenoir Family Papers.

ing the 1850's perhaps as many as fifteen thousand were hired out annually in Virginia alone. But slave-hiring was a common practice everywhere.[1]

In December and January southern newspapers were filled with the advertisements of those offering or seeking slaves to hire. Some of the transactions were negotiated privately, some by auctioneers who bid slaves off at public outcry, and some by "general agents" who handled this business for a commission. In Richmond, P. M. Tabb & Son, among many others, advertised that they attended "to the hiring out of negroes and collecting the hires" and promised to give "particular attention . . . through the year to negroes placed under their charge."[2]

Though slaves were occasionally hired for short terms, it was customary to hire them from January until the following Christmas. Written contracts specified the period of the hire, the kind of work in which the slaves were to be engaged, and the hirer's obligation to keep them well clothed. Usually an owner could spare only a few, but occasionally a single master offered as many as fifty and, rarely, as many as a hundred. Though most slaves were hired in the vicinity of their masters' residences, many were sent long distances from home. Hamilton Brown, of Wilkes County, North Carolina, hired out slaves in Virginia, Tennessee, and Georgia; and Jeremiah Morton, of Orange County, Virginia, hired out fifty-two of his Negroes through an agent in Mobile.[3]

A variety of circumstances contributed to this practice. If for some reason the owner was unable to use his slaves profitably, if he was in debt, or if he had a surplus of la-

---

[1] Frederic Bancroft, *Slave-Trading in the Old South* (Baltimore, 1931), pp. 404–405.

[2] Richmond *Enquirer*, January 1, 1850; Bancroft, *Slave-Trading*, p. 149.

[3] Hamilton Brown Papers; Memorandum dated December 15, 1860, in Morton-Halsey Papers.

borers, he might prefer hiring to selling them. Executors hired out slave property while estates were being settled. Sometimes lands and slaves together were rented to tenants. Heirs who inherited bondsmen for whom they had no employment put them up for hire. Many spinsters, widows, and orphans lived off the income of hired slaves who were handled for them by administrators. Masters often directed in their wills that slaves be hired out for the benefit of their heirs, or that cash be invested in slave property for this purpose. A widow in Missouri hired out most of her slaves, because she found it to be "a better business" than working them on her farm.[4] Occasionally a slaveowner endowed a church or a benevolent institution with slaves whose hire was to aid in its support.

In addition, urban masters often hired out the husbands or children of their female domestics. Both they and planters who had more domestics than they could use or afford disposed of them in this manner. It was also very common for urban and rural owners of skilled slaves to hire them to others at least part of the time. Planters hired their carpenters and blacksmiths to neighbors when they had no work for them and thus substantially augmented their incomes. A master sometimes hired a slave to a white artisan with the understanding that the slave was to be taught his skill. For example, a contract between a North Carolina master and a white blacksmith provided that the hirer was to work a slave "at the Forge during the whole time and learn him or cause him to be learned the arts and mysteries of the Black Smith's trade."[5]

A few Southerners bought slaves as business ventures with the intention of realizing profits solely through hiring

[4] S. E. Lenoir to her sisters, November 18, 1851, Lenoir Family Papers; Bancroft, *Slave-Trading*, pp. 145–47.
[5] Contract between William Frew and R. S. Young, dated December 30, 1853, in Burton-Young Papers.

them to others. Between 1846 and 1852, Bickerton Lyle Winston, of Hanover County, Virginia, purchased at least fifteen slaves for this purpose. Winston kept careful records of these investments, noting the purchase prices, the annual income from and expenses of each slave, and the net profit. The slaves Randal and Garland were his first speculations. Randal's record ended abruptly in 1853 with the terse notation: "Deduct medical and funeral expenses: $20." Four years later Winston recorded the fact that "Garland came to his end . . . by an explosion in the Black Heath Pits." [6] Some overseers pursued a similar course by investing in slaves whom they hired to their employers. A resident in Mississippi knew families "who possess not an acre of land, but own many slaves, [and] hire them out to different individuals; the wages constituting their only income, which is often very large." [7]

Farmers and planters frequently hired field-hands to neighbors for short periods of time. Cotton growers who finished their picking early contracted to help others pick their cotton for a fee. When a planter's crop was "in the grass" he tried to borrow hands from neighbors with the understanding that the labor would be repaid in the future. Small slaveholders sometimes made less formal agreements to help each other. A Virginia farmer lent his neighbor two mules and received in return "the labor of one man for the same time." [8] Many masters were generous in lending the labor of their slaves to friends.

The demand for hired slaves came from numerous groups. The shortage of free agricultural labor caused planters to look to this practice as a means of meeting their seasonal needs for additional workers. During the grinding season sugar growers hired hands from Creole farmers or

6 Bickerton Lyle Winston Ms. Slave Account Book.
7 [Ingraham], *South-West*, II, pp. 251–52.
8 Edmund Ruffin, Jr., Farm Journal, entry for September 7, 1843.

from cotton planters after their crops were picked.[9] Small farmers who could not afford to buy slaves were well represented in the "hiring-day" crowds. Some landowners employed free Negroes, Indians, or poor whites, but they generally preferred to hire slaves when they were available.

The great majority of hired slaves, however, were employed by those who sought a supply of nonagricultural labor. Many urban families hired rather than owned their domestic servants. Advertisements such as these appeared in every southern newspaper: "Wanted immediately, a boy, from 14 to 19 years of age, to do house work. One that can be well recommended from his owner." "Wanted a Black or Colored Servant, to attend on a Gentleman and take care of a Horse." [1] Hotels and watering places hired most of their domestics; laundries, warehouses, shipyards, steamships, cotton presses, turpentine producers, mine operators, lumberers, and drayage companies all made considerable use of hired slaves. Free artisans seldom could afford to own bondsmen and therefore hired them instead. Even a free Negro cooper in Richmond for many years hired a slave assistant.[2]

In most cases southern railroad companies did not own the slaves they employed; rather, they recruited them by promising their owners generous compensation. Railroad builders obtained most of their hands in the neighborhood of their construction work, but they often bid for them in distant places. In 1836, the Alabama, Florida, and Georgia Railroad Company advertised for a hundred slaves in Maryland, Virginia, and North Carolina. The Florida Railroad Company, in 1857, announced that for the past two years it had been employing slaves from Virginia and the

---

9 Sitterson, *Sugar Country*, pp. 61–62; Taylor, "Negro Slavery in Louisiana," p. 94.

1 Charleston *Courier*, August 16, 1852.

2 Copies of letters to "James Sims a Colored man," in Walker Diary.

Carolinas and offered to give masters evidence "of the health, climate, and other points of interest connected with the country and work." [3]

An advertisement in a Kentucky newspaper for "twenty-five Negro Boys, from thirteen to fifteen years old, to work in a woolen factory" pointed to another source of the demand for hired slaves. Gristmills, sawmills, cotton factories, hemp factories, iron foundries, and tobacco factories used them extensively, especially the smaller enterprises with limited capital. In 1860, about half of the slave laborers in Virginia tobacco factories were hired.[4]

A small group of slaves obtained from their masters the privilege of "hiring their own time." These bondsmen enjoyed considerable freedom of movement and were permitted to find work for themselves. They were required to pay their masters a stipulated sum of money each year, but whatever they could earn above that amount was theirs to do with as they wished. Almost all of the slaves who hired their own time were skilled artisans; most of them were concentrated in the cities of the Upper South. Though this practice was illegal nearly everywhere and often denounced as dangerous, there were always a few slaves who somehow managed to work in this manner under the most nominal control of their owners.

By permitting a trusted slave artisan to hire his own time the master escaped the burden of feeding and clothing him and of finding employment for him. Then, as long as his slave kept out of trouble, the master's sole concern was getting his payments (which were almost the equivalent of a quitrent) at regular intervals. Frederick Douglass described the terms by which he hired his own time to work

[3] Richmond *Enquirer*, August 8, 1836; Wilmington (N.C.) *Journal*, December 28, 1857.
[4] Lexington *Kentucky Statesman*, December 26, 1854; Robert, *Tobacco Kingdom*, p. 198.

as a calker in the Baltimore shipyards: "I was to be allowed all my time; to make all bargains for work; to find my own employment, and to collect my own wages; and, in return for this liberty, I was required, or obliged, to pay . . . three dollars at the end of each week, and to board and clothe myself, and buy my own calking tools. A failure in any of these particulars would put an end to my privilege. This was a hard bargain." [5]

But whatever the terms, most slave artisans eagerly accepted this arrangement when it was offered to them. A Negro blacksmith in Virginia pleaded with his master for the privilege of hiring his own time: "I would . . . be much obliged to you if you would authorize me to open a shop in this county and carry it on. . . . I am satisfied that I can do well and that my profits will amount to a great deal more than any one would be willing to pay for my hire." [6]

This slave had his wish granted, but few others shared his good fortune. It was the lot of the ordinary bondsman to work under the close supervision of his master or of some employer who hired his services. For him bondage was not nominal. It was what it was intended to be: a systematic method of controlling and exploiting labor.

6

Mammy Harriet had nostalgic memories of slavery days: "Oh, no, we was nebber hurried. Marster nebber once said, 'Get up an' go to work,' an' no oberseer ebber said it, neither. Ef some on 'em did not git up when de odders went out to work, marster nebber said a word. Oh, no, we was

---

[5] Frederick Douglass, *My Bondage and My Freedom* (New York, 1855), p. 328.
[6] Charles White to Hamilton Brown, December 20, 1832, Hamilton Brown Papers.

nebber hurried." [7] Mammy Harriet had been a domestic at "Burleigh," the Hinds County, Mississippi, estate of Thomas S. Dabney. She related her story of slave life there to one of Dabney's daughters who wrote a loving volume about her father and his cotton plantation.

Another slave found life less leisurely on a plantation on the Red River in Louisiana: "The hands are required to be in the cotton field as soon as it is light in the morning, and, with the exception of ten or fifteen minutes, which is given them at noon to swallow their allowance of cold bacon, they are not permitted to be a moment idle until it is too dark to see, and when the moon is full, they often times labor till the middle of the night." Work did not end when the slaves left the fields. "Each one must attend to his respective chores. One feeds the mules, another the swine—another cuts the wood, and so forth; besides the packing [of cotton] is all done by candle light. Finally, at a late hour, they reach the quarters, sleepy and overcome with the long day's toil." [8] These were the bitter memories of Solomon Northup, a free Negro who had been kidnapped and held in bondage for twelve years. Northup described his experiences to a Northerner who helped him prepare his autobiography for publication.

Mammy Harriet's and Solomon Northup's disparate accounts of the work regimen imposed upon slaves suggest the difficulty of determining the truth from witnesses, Negro and white, whose candor was rarely uncompromised by internal emotions or external pressures. Did Dabney's allegedly unhurried field-hands (who somehow produced much cotton and one of whom once tried to kill the overseer) feel the same nostalgia for slavery days? How much

---

[7] Susan Dabney Smedes, *Memorials of a Southern Planter* (Baltimore, 1887) , p. 57.
[8] Northup, *Twelve Years a Slave*, pp. 166–68.

was Northup's book influenced by his amanuensis and by the preconceptions of his potential northern readers?

And yet there is nothing in the narratives of either of these ex-slaves that renders them entirely implausible. The question of their complete accuracy is perhaps less important than the fact that both conditions actually did exist in the South. Distortion results from exaggerating the frequency of either condition or from dwelling upon one and ignoring the other.

No sweeping generalization about the amount of labor extracted from bondsmen could possibly be valid, even when they are classified by regions, or by occupations, or by the size of the holdings upon which they lived. For the personal factor transcended everything else. How hard the slaves were worked depended upon the demands of individual masters and their ability to enforce them. These demands were always more or less tempered by the inclination of most slaves to minimize their unpaid toil. Here was a clash of interests in which the master usually, but not always, enjoyed the advantage of superior weapons.

Not only must glib generalizations be avoided but a standard must be fixed by which the slave's burden of labor can be judged. Surely a slave was overworked when his toil impaired his health or endangered his life. Short of this extreme there are several useful standards upon which judgments can be based. If, for example, the quantity of labor were compared with the compensation the inevitable conclusion would be that most slaves were overworked. Also by present-day labor standards the demands generally made upon them were excessive. These, of course, were not the standards of the nineteenth century.

Another standard of comparison—though not an altogether satisfactory one—is the amount of work performed by contemporary free laborers in similar occupations. Independent farmers and artisans set their own pace and planned their work to fit their own convenience and interests, but they nevertheless often worked from dawn to dusk. Northern factory workers commonly labored twelve hours a day. This was arduous toil even for free laborers who enjoyed the advantages of greater incentives and compensation. Yet contemporaries did not think that slaves were overworked when their masters respected the normal standards of their day. Some slaveowners did respect them, and some did not.

Unquestionably there were slaves who escaped doing what was then regarded as a "good day's work," and there were masters who never demanded it of them. The aphorism that it took two slaves to help one to do nothing was not without its illustrations. After lands and slaves had remained in the hands of a single family for several generations, planters sometimes developed a patriarchal attitude toward their "people" and took pride in treating them indulgently. Such masters had lost the competitive spirit and the urge to increase their worldly possessions which had characterized their ancestors. To live gracefully on their declining estates, to smile tolerantly at the listless labor of their field-hands, and to be surrounded by a horde of pampered domestics were all parts of their code.

In Virginia, the easygoing manner of the patricians was proverbial. But Virginia had no monopoly of them; they were scattered throughout the South. Olmsted visited a South Carolina rice plantation where the tasks were light enough to enable reasonably industrious hands to leave the fields early in the afternoon. Slaves on several sea-island cotton plantations much of the time did not labor more than five or six hours a day.[9]

The production records of some of the small slavehold-

---

[9] Olmsted, *Seaboard*, pp. 434–36; Guion G. Johnson, *A Social History of the Sea Islands* (Chapel Hill, 1930), pp. 124–25; E. Merton Coulter, *Thomas Spalding of Sapelo* (Baton Rouge, 1940), p. 85.

ing farmers indicated that neither they nor their slaves exerted themselves unduly. These masters, especially when they lived in isolated areas, seemed content to produce little more than a bare subsistence. In addition, part of the town slaves who hired their own time took advantage of the opportunity to enjoy a maximum of leisure. The domestics of some wealthy urban families willingly helped to maintain the tradition that masters with social standing did not examine too closely into the quantity or efficiency of their work.

From these models proslavery writers drew their sentimental pictures of slave life. The specific cases they cited were often valid ones; their profound error was in generalizing from them. For this leisurely life was the experience of only a small fraction of the bondsmen. Whether they lived in the Upper South or Deep South, in rural or urban communities, on plantations or farms, the labor of the vast majority of slaves ranged from what was normally expected of free labor in that period to levels that were clearly excessive.

It would not be too much to say that masters usually demanded from their slaves a long day of hard work and managed by some means or other to get it. The evidence does not sustain the belief that free laborers generally worked longer hours and at a brisker pace than the unfree. During the months when crops were being cultivated or harvested the slaves commonly were in the fields fifteen or sixteen hours a day, including time allowed for meals and rest.[1] By ante-bellum standards this may not have been excessive, but it was not a light work routine by the standards of that or any other day.

In instructions to overseers, planters almost always cautioned against overwork, yet insisted that the hands be

---

[1] Gray, *History of Agriculture*, I, pp. 556–57.

made to labor vigorously as many hours as there was daylight. Overseers who could not accomplish this were discharged. An Arkansas master described a work day that was in no sense unusual on the plantations of the Deep South: "We get up before day every morning and eat breakfast before day and have everybody at work before day dawns. I am never caught in bed after day light nor is any body else on the place, and we continue in the cotton fields when we can have fair weather till it is so dark we cant see to work, and this history of one day is the history of every day." [2]

Planters who contributed articles on the management of slaves to southern periodicals took this routine for granted. "It is expected," one of them wrote, "that servants should rise early enough to be at work by the time it is light. . . . While at work, they should be brisk. . . . I have no objection to their whistling or singing some lively tune, but no *drawling* tunes are allowed in the field, for their motions are almost certain to keep time with the music." [3] These planters had the businessman's interest in maximum production without injury to their capital.

The work schedule was not strikingly different on the plantations of the Upper South. Here too it was a common practice to regulate the hours of labor in accordance with the amount of daylight. A former slave on a Missouri tobacco and hemp plantation recalled that the field-hands began their work at half past four in the morning. Such rules were far more common on Virginia plantations than were the customs of languid patricians. An ex-slave in Hanover County, Virginia, remembered seeing slave women hurrying to their work in the early morning "with their shoes and stockings in their hands, and a petticoat wrapped over

---

[2] Gustavus A. Henry to his wife, November 27, 1860, Henry Papers.
[3] *Southern Cultivator*, VIII (1850), p. 163.

their shoulders, to dress in the field the best way they could." [4] The bulk of the Virginia planters were business-men too.

Planters who were concerned about the physical condition of their slaves permitted them to rest at noon after eating their dinners in the fields. "In the Winter," advised one expert on slave management, "a hand may be pressed all day, but not so in Summer. . . . In May, from one and a half to two hours; in June, two and a half; in July and August, three hours rest [should be given] at noon." [5] Except for certain essential chores, Sunday work was uncommon but not unheard of if the crops required it. On Saturdays slaves were often permitted to quit the fields at noon. They were also given holidays, most commonly at Christmas and after the crops were laid by.

But a holiday was not always a time for rest and relaxation. Many planters encouraged their bondsmen to cultivate small crops during their "leisure" to provide some of their own food. Thus a North Carolina planter instructed his overseer: "As soon as you have laid by the crop give the people 2 days but . . . they must work their own crops." Another planter gave his slaves a "holiday to plant their potatoes," and another "holiday to get in their potatoes." James H. Hammond once wrote in disgust: "Holiday for the negroes who fenced in their gardens. Lazy devils they did nothing after 12 o'clock." In addition, slave women had to devote part of their time when they were not in the fields to washing clothes, cooking, and cleaning their cabins. An Alabama planter wrote: "I always give them half of each Saturday, and often the whole day, at which

---

[4] William W. Brown, *Narrative of William W. Brown, a Fugitive Slave* (Boston, 1847), p. 14; Olmsted, *Seaboard*, p. 109; *De Bow's Review*, XIV (1853), pp. 176–78; Benjamin Drew, *The Refugee: or the Narratives of Fugitive Slaves in Canada* (Boston, 1856), p. 162.

[5] *Southern Cultivator*, VIII (1850), p. 163.

time . . . the women do their household work; therefore they are never idle." [6]

Planters avoided night work as much as they felt they could, but slaves rarely escaped it entirely. Night work was almost universal on sugar plantations during the grinding season, and on cotton plantations when the crop was being picked, ginned, and packed. A Mississippi planter did not hesitate to keep his hands hauling fodder until ten o'clock at night when the hours of daylight were not sufficient for his work schedule.[7]

Occasionally a planter hired free laborers for such heavy work as ditching in order to protect his slave property. But, contrary to the legend, this was not a common practice. Most planters used their own field-hands for ditching and for clearing new ground. Moreover, they often assigned slave women to this type of labor as well as to plowing. On one plantation Olmsted saw twenty women operating heavy plows with double teams: "They were superintended by a male negro driver, who carried a whip, which he frequently cracked at them, permitting no dawdling or delay at the turning." [8]

Among the smaller planters and slaveholding farmers there was generally no appreciable relaxation of this normal labor routine. Their production records, their diaries and farm journals, and the testimony of their slaves all suggest the same dawn-to-dusk regimen that prevailed on the large plantations.[9] This was also the experience of most slaves engaged in nonagricultural occupations. Every-

[6] Henry K. Burgwyn to Arthur Souter, August 6, 1843, Henry King Burgwyn Papers; John C. Jenkins Diary, entries for November 15, 1845; April 22, 1854; Hammond Diary, entry for May 12, 1832; *De Bow's Review*, XIII (1852), pp. 193–94.

[7] Jenkins Diary, entry for August 7, 1843.

[8] Olmsted, *Back Country*, p. 81; Sydnor, *Slavery in Mississippi*, p. 12.

[9] See, for example, Marston Papers; Torbert Plantation Diary; *De Bow's Review*, XI (1851), pp. 369–72; Drew, *Refugee*; Douglass, *My Bondage*, p. 215; Trexler, *Slavery in Missouri*, pp. 97–98.

where, then, masters normally expected from their slaves, in accordance with the standards of their time, a full stint of labor from "day clean" to "first dark."

Some, however, demanded more than this. Continuously, or at least for long intervals, they drove their slaves at a pace that was bound, sooner or later, to injure their health. Such hard driving seldom occurred on the smaller plantations and farms or in urban centers; it was decidedly a phenomenon of the large plantations. Though the majority of planters did not sanction it, more of them tolerated excessively heavy labor routines than is generally realized. The records of the plantation regime clearly indicate that slaves were more frequently overworked by calloused tyrants than overindulged by mellowed patriarchs.

That a large number of southern bondsmen were worked severely during the colonial period is beyond dispute. The South Carolina code of 1740 charged that "many owners . . . do confine them so closely to hard labor, that they have not sufficient time for natural rest." [1] In the nineteenth century conditions seemed to have improved, especially in the older regions of the South. Unquestionably the ante-bellum planter who coveted a high rank in society responded to subtle pressures that others did not feel. The closing of the African slave trade and the steady rise of slave prices were additional restraining influences. "The time has been," wrote a planter in 1849, "that the farmer could kill up and wear out one Negro to buy another; but it is not so now. Negroes are too high in proportion to the price of cotton, and it behooves those who own them to make them last as long as possible." [2]

But neither public opinion nor high prices prevented some of the bondsmen from suffering physical breakdowns

---

[1] Hurd, *Law of Freedom and Bondage*, I, p. 307; Flanders, *Plantation Slavery in Georgia*, p. 42.
[2] *Southern Cultivator*, VII (1849), p. 69.

and early deaths because of overwork. The abolitionists never proved their claim that many sugar and cotton growers deliberately worked their slaves to death every seven years with the intention of replacing them from profits. Yet some of the great planters came close to accomplishing that result without designing it. In the "race for wealth" in which, according to one Louisiana planter, all were enlisted, few proprietors managed their estates according to the code of the patricians.[3] They were sometimes remarkably shortsighted in the use of their investments.

Irresponsible overseers, who had no permanent interest in slave property, were frequently blamed for the overworking of slaves. Since this was a common complaint, it is important to remember that nearly half of the slaves lived on plantations of the size that ordinarily employed overseers. But planters could not escape responsibility for these conditions simply because their written instructions usually prohibited excessive driving. For they often demanded crop yields that could be achieved by no other method.

Most overseers believed (with good reason) that their success was measured by how much they produced, and that merely having the slave force in good condition at the end of the year would not guarantee re-employment. A Mississippi overseer with sixteen years of experience confirmed this belief in defending his profession: "When I came to Mississippi, I found that the overseer who could have the most cotton bales ready for market by Christmas, was considered best qualified for the business—consequently, every overseer gave his whole attention to cotton bales, to the exclusion of everything else."[4]

More than a few planters agreed that this was true. A committee of an Alabama agricultural society reported: "It

---

[3] Kenneth M. Clark to Lewis Thompson, December 29, 1859, Thompson Papers.
[4] *American Cotton Planter and Soil of the South*, II (1858), pp. 112-13.

is too commonly the case that masters look only to the yearly products of their farms, and praise or condemn their overseers by this standard alone, without ever once troubling themselves to inquire into the manner in which things are managed on their plantations, and whether he may have lost more in the diminished value of his slaves by over-work than he has gained by his large crop." This being the case, it was understandably of no consequence to the overseer that the old hands were "worked down" and the young ones "overstrained," that the "breeding women" miscarried, and that the "sucklers" lost their children. "So that he has the requisite number of cotton bags, all is overlooked; he is re-employed at an advanced salary, and his reputation increased." [5]

Some planters, unintentionally perhaps, gave overseers a special incentive for overworking slaves by making their compensation depend in part upon the amount they produced. Though this practice was repeatedly denounced in the ante-bellum period, many masters continued to follow it nevertheless. Cotton growers offered overseers bonuses of from one to five dollars for each bale above a specified minimum, or a higher salary if they produced a fixed quota. A Louisiana planter hired an overseer on a straight commission basis of $2.75 per bale of cotton and four cents per bushel of corn. A South Carolina rice planter gave his overseer ten per cent of the net proceeds. And a Virginian offered his overseer "the seventh part of the good grain, tobacco, cotton, and flax" that was harvested on his estate. "Soon as I hear [of] such a bargain," wrote a southern critic, "I fancy that the overseer, determined to save his salary, adopts the song of 'drive, drive, drive.'" [6]

---

5 *American Farmer*, II (1846), p. 78; *Southern Cultivator*, II (1844), pp. 97, 107.
6 *North Carolina Farmer*, I (1845), pp. 122–23. Agreements of this kind with overseers are in the records of numerous planters.

Masters who hired their slaves to others also helped to create conditions favoring ruthless exploitation. The over-working of hired slaves by employers with only a tempo-rary interest in their welfare was as notorious as the harsh practices of overseers. Slaves hired to mine owners or rail-road contractors were fortunate if they were not driven to the point where their health was impaired. The same dan-ger confronted slaves hired to sugar planters during the grinding season or to cotton planters at picking time. Few Southerners familiar with these conditions would have chal-lenged the assertion made before a South Carolina court that hired slaves were "commonly treated more harshly . . . than those in possession of their owner[s]." [7]

But the master was as responsible for the conduct of those who hired his slaves as he was for the conduct of the overseers he employed. Overworked slaves were not always the innocent victims of forces beyond his control; there were remedies which he sometimes failed to apply. A stanch defender of slavery described a set of avaricious planters whom he labeled "Cotton Snobs," or "Southern Yankees." In their frantic quest for wealth, he wrote indig-nantly, the crack of the whip was heard early and late, until their bondsmen were "bowed to the ground with over-task-ing and over-toil." [8] A southern physician who practiced on many cotton plantations complained, in 1847, that some masters still regarded "their sole interest to consist in large crops, leaving out of view altogether the value of negro property and its possible deterioration." During the eco-nomic depression of the 1840's, a planter accused certain cotton growers of trying to save themselves by increasing their cotton acreage and by driving their slaves harder, with the result that slaves broke down from overwork. An

---

[7] Catterall, *Judicial Cases*, II, p. 374.
[8] Hundley, *Social Relations*, pp. 132, 187–88.

Alabama newspaper attributed conditions such as these to "avarice, the desire of growing rich." [9]

On the sugar plantations, during the months of the harvest, slaves were driven to the point of complete exhaustion. They were, in the normal routine, worked from sixteen to eighteen hours a day, seven days a week.[1] Cotton planters who boasted about making ten bales per hand were unconsciously testifying that their slaves were overworked. An overseer on an Arkansas plantation set his goal at twelve bales to the hand and indicated that this was what his employer desired. On a North Carolina plantation a temporary overseer assured the owner that he was a "hole hog man rain or shine" and boasted that the slaves had not been working like men but "like horses." "I'd ruther be dead than be a nigger on one of these big plantations," a white Mississippian told Olmsted.[2]

Sooner or later excessive labor was bound to take its toll. In the heat of mid-summer, slaves who could not bear hard driving without sufficient rest at noon simply collapsed in the fields. In Mississippi a planter reported "numerous cases" of sunstroke in his neighborhood during a spell of extreme heat. His own slaves "gave out." On a Florida plantation a number of hands "fainted in the field" one hot August day. Even in Virginia hot weather and heavy labor caused "the death of many negroes in the harvest field." [3]

---

9 *De Bow's Review*, I (1846), pp. 434–36; III (1847), p. 419; Selma *Free Press*, quoted in Tuscaloosa *Independent Monitor*, July 14, 1846.

1 This is apparent from the records of sugar planters. See also Sitterson, *Sugar Country*, pp. 133–36; Olmsted, *Seaboard*, pp. 650, 667–68.

2 P. Weeks to James Sheppard, September 20, 1854, James Sheppard Papers; Doctrine Davenport to Ebenezer Pettigrew, April 24, 1836, Pettigrew Family Papers; Olmsted, *Back Country*, pp. 55–57, 202.

3 Jenkins Diary, entries for August 9, 1844; July 7, 1846; June 30, 1854; Ulrich B. Phillips and James D. Glunt (eds.), *Florida Plantation Records from the Papers of George Noble Jones* (St. Louis, 1927), p. 90; John B. Garrett Ms. Farm Journal, entry for July 19, 1830.

CHAPTER THREE

A Troublesome Property

Slaves apparently thought of the South's peculiar institution chiefly as a system of labor extortion. Of course they felt its impact in other ways—in their social status, their legal status, and their private lives—but they felt it most acutely in their lack of control over their own time and labor. If discontented with bondage, they could be expected to direct their protests principally against the master's claim to their work. Whether the majority were satisfied with their lot, whether they willingly obeyed the master's commands, has long been a controversial question.

It may be a little presumptuous of one who has never been a slave to pretend to know how slaves felt; yet defenders of slavery did not hesitate to assert that most of them were quite content with servitude. Bondsmen generally were cheerful and acquiescent—so the argument went —because they were treated with kindness and relieved of all responsibilities; having known no other condition, they unthinkingly accepted bondage as their natural status. "They find themselves first existing in this state," observed a Northerner who had resided in Mississippi, "and pass through life without questioning the justice of their allotment, which, if they think at all, they suppose a natural one." [1] Presumably they acquiesced, too, because of innate racial traits, because of the "genius of African temperament," the Negro being "instinctively . . . contented" and "quick to respond to the stimulus of joy, quick to forget his grief." Except in rare instances when he was cruelly treated, his "peaceful frame of mind was not greatly disturbed by the mere condition of slavery." [2]

Though sometimes asserted with such assurance, it was never proved that the great majority of bondsmen had no concept of freedom and were therefore contented. It was always based upon inference. Most masters believed they understood their slaves, and most slaves apparently made no attempt to discourage this belief. Instead, they said the things they thought their masters wanted to hear, and they conformed with the rituals that signified their subservience. Rare, no doubt, was the master who never heard any of his humble, smiling bondsmen affirm their loyalty and contentment. When visitors in the South asked a slave whether he wished to be free, he usually replied: "No, massa, me no want to be free, have good massa, take care of me when I sick, never 'buse nigger; no, me no want to be free." [3]

This was dubious evidence, as some slaveholders knew and others learned. (They would have acknowledged the validity of an affirmation later to be made by a post-bellum South Carolinian: "the white man does not know the Negro so well as he thinks he does." [4]) A Virginia master believed that slaves had their faculties "sharpened by constant exercise" and that their perceptions were "extremely fine and acute." An overseer decided that a man who "put his con-

---

1 [Ingraham], *South-West*, II, p. 201.
2 Francis P. Gaines, *The Southern Plantation: A Study in the Development and the Accuracy of a Tradition* (New York, 1924), p. 244.
3 Ethan A. Andrews, *Slavery and the Domestic Slave Trade in the United States* (Boston, 1836), pp. 97–99.
4 Mason Crum, *Gullah: Negro Life in the Carolina Sea Islands* (Durham, 1940), p. 80.

fidence in a Negro . . . was simply a Damned Fool." A Georgia planter concluded: "So deceitful is the Negro that as far as my own experience extends I could never in a single instance decipher his character. . . . We planters could never get at the truth." [5] When advertising for runaways, masters repeatedly confirmed these opinions by describing them as being "very artful," as acting and conversing in a way "calculated to deceive almost any one," and (most frequently) as possessing a "pretty glib and plausible tongue." Yet proslavery writers swallowed whole the assurances of contentment which these glib-tongued "scoundrels" gave them.

Since there are few reliable records of what went on in the minds of slaves, one can only infer their thoughts and feelings from their behavior, that of their masters, and the logic of their situation. That they had no understanding of freedom, and therefore accepted bondage as their natural condition, is hard to believe. They had only to observe their masters and the other free men about them to obtain a very distinct idea of the meaning and advantages of freedom. All knew that some Negroes had been emancipated: they knew that freedom was a *possible* condition for any of them. They "continually have before their eyes, persons of the same color, many of whom they have known in slavery . . . freed from the control of masters, working where they please, going whither they please, and expending their money how they please." So declared a group of Charleston whites who petitioned the legislature to expel all free persons of color from South Carolina. [6]

Untutored slaves seldom speculated about freedom as an abstraction. They naturally focused their interest upon

[5] Abdy, *Journal*, II, pp. 216–17; Manigault Ms. Plantation Records, summary of plantation events, May, 1863–May, 1864; entry for March 22, 1867.
[6] Phillips (ed.), *Plantation and Frontier*, II, pp. 108–11.

88

such immediate and practical benefits as escaping severe discipline and getting increased compensation for less labor. An ex-slave explained simply what freedom meant to her: "I am now my own mistress, and need not work when I am sick. I can do my own thinkings, without having any to think for me,—to tell me when to come, what to do, and to sell me when they get ready." [7] Though she may never have heard of the doctrine of natural rights, her concept of freedom surely embraced more than its incidental aspects.

If slaves had some understanding of the pragmatic benefits of freedom, no doubt most of them desired to enjoy these benefits. Some, perhaps the majority, had no more than a vague, unarticulated yearning for escape from burdens and restraints. They submitted, but submission did not necessarily mean enjoyment or even contentment. And some slaves felt more than a vague longing, felt a sharp pang and saw a clear objective. They struggled toward it against imposing obstacles, expressing their discontent through positive action.

Were these, the actively discontented, to be found only among slaves exposed to great physical cruelty? Apparently not. Slaves of gentle masters might seek freedom as eagerly as those of cruel ones. Frederick Douglass, the most famous refugee from slavery, testified: "Beat and cuff your slave, keep him hungry and spiritless, and he will follow the chain of his master like a dog; but feed and clothe him well,—work him moderately—surround him with physical comfort,—and dreams of freedom intrude. Give him a *bad* master, and he aspires to a *good* master; give him a good master, and he wishes to become his *own* master." [8] Here was a problem confronting conscientious slaveholders. One confessed that slaveownership subjected "the man of care and feeling to more dilemmas than perhaps any other voca-

---

[7] Drew, *The Refugee*, p. 177.
[8] Douglass, *My Bondage*, pp. 263–64.

tion he could follow. . . . To moralize and induce the slave to assimilate with the master and his interest, has been and is the great desideratum aimed at; but I am sorry to say I have long since desponded in the completion of this task." [9] Another slaveholder who vaguely affirmed that his bondsmen were "as contented as their nature will permit" was in reality agreeing with what a white man once bluntly stated before the Louisiana Supreme Court: The desire for freedom "exists in the bosom of *every* slave—whether the recent captive, or him to whom bondage has become a habit." [1]

Slaves showed great eagerness to get some—if they could not get all—of the advantages of freedom. They liked to hire their own time, or to work in tobacco factories, or for the Tredegar Iron Company, because they were then under less restraint than in the fields, and they had greater opportunities to earn money for themselves. They seized the chance to make their condition approximate that of freemen.

But they were not satisfied with a mere loosening of the bonds. Former slaves affirmed that one had to "know the *heart* of the poor slave—learn his secret thoughts—thoughts he dare not utter in the hearing of the white man," to understand this. "A man who has been in slavery knows, and no one else can know, the yearnings to be free, and the fear of making the attempt." While he was still in bondage Douglass wondered how white people knew that God had made black people to be slaves. "Did they go up in the sky and learn it? or, did He come down and tell them so?" [2] A slave on a Louisiana sugar plantation assured Olmsted that slaves did desire freedom, that they talked about

[9] *Southern Agriculturist*, III (1830), p. 238.
[1] Ebenezer Pettigrew to Mrs. Mary Shepard, September 22, 1847, Pettigrew Family Papers; Catterall (ed.), *Judicial Cases*, III, p. 568.
[2] Northup, *Twelve Years a Slave*, pp. 206–207; Drew, *The Refugee*, pp. 43, 115; Douglass, *My Bondage*, pp. 89–91.

it among themselves, and that they speculated about what they would do if they were emancipated. When a traveler in Georgia told a slave he understood his people did not wish to be free, "His only answer was a short, contemptuous laugh." [3]

If slaves yielded to authority most of the time, they did so because they usually saw no other practical choice. Yet few went through life without expressing discontent somehow, some time. Even the most passive slaves, usually before they reached middle age, flared up in protest now and then. The majority, as they grew older, lost hope and spirit. Some, however, never quite gave in, never stopped fighting back in one way or another. The "bad character" of this "insolent," "surly," and "unruly" sort made them a liability to those who owned them, for a slave's value was measured by his disposition as much as by his strength and skills. Such rebels seldom won legal freedom, yet they never quite admitted they were slaves.

Slave resistance, whether bold and persistent or mild and sporadic, created for all slaveholders a serious problem of discipline. As authors or as readers they saw the problem discussed in numberless essays with such titles as "The Management of Negroes," essays which filled the pages of southern agricultural periodicals. Many masters had reason to agree with the owner of a hundred slaves who complained that he possessed "just 100 troubles," or with the North Carolina planter who said that slaves were "a troublesome property." [4]

The record of slave resistance forms a chapter in the story of the endless struggle to give dignity to human life. Though the history of southern bondage reveals that men

[3] Olmsted, *Seaboard*, pp. 679–80; James Stirling, *Letters from the Slave States* (London, 1857) , p. 201.

[4] Gustavus A. Henry to his wife, November 25, 1849, Henry Papers; William S. Pettigrew to James C. Johnston, January 6, 1847 (copy), Pettigrew Family Papers.

can be enslaved under certain conditions, it also demonstrates that their love of freedom is hard to crush. The subtle expressions of this spirit, no less than the daring thrusts for liberty, comprise one of the richest gifts the slaves have left to posterity. In making themselves "troublesome property," they provide reassuring evidence that slaves seldom wear their shackles lightly.

The record of the minority who waged ceaseless and open warfare against their bondage makes an inspiring chapter, also, in the history of Americans of African descent. True, these rebels were exceptional men, but the historian of any group properly devotes much attention to those members who did extraordinary things, men in whose lives the problems of their age found focus, men who voiced the feelings and aspirations of the more timid and less articulate masses. As the American Revolution produced folk heroes, so also did southern slavery—heroes who, in both cases, gave much for the cause of human freedom.

2

Now and then a slave happened to get a chance for freedom but rejected it. A body servant devoted to his master might accompany him into the free states and then willingly return to the land of slavery. Or a slave might decline to be emancipated in accordance with a provision in his master's will. A free Negro might even seek a master and petition to be enslaved. Proslavery men seized upon instances such as these to support the argument that Negroes were better off and happier as slaves than as freemen.

Why, actually, did an occasional Negro refuse to be freed or even ask to be enslaved? One of the reasons is suggested by the petition a slave once sent to the Virginia legislature. This slave, Washington, by his master's will, had the choice of accepting freedom or selecting a new master from among the relatives of his late owner. Washington chose freedom, but he asked the legislature to exempt him from the law which then required freed Negroes to leave the state. He declared in his petition that he had no money to pay the cost of moving, that he was advanced in years, and that he had a family living in Virginia.[5]

Given the general hostility toward free Negroes in both the North and South and the severe handicaps which they faced, the choice between "freedom" and slavery did not always seem to be an altogether clear one. A South Carolina doctor therefore disagreed with one of his professional colleagues who claimed that Negroes had a "natural" preference for slavery. "To offer to the race the nominal freedom which a free colored person possesses in our land, is a test by no means satisfactory," the physician said. "About as reasonable would it be to put a muzzle on a pig's nose, and then invite him into the potatoe patch. Of course, he would *prefer* to remain in his pen, and drink the swill you might be pleased to give him."[6]

But proslavery writers exaggerated both the number and the significance of instances in which slaves rejected an offer of freedom. They usually welcomed the chance even though aware of the hard role and inferior status of "free persons of color." This was one of the ways in which they demonstrated their prevalent longing to be free. The action of twenty-two Virginia Negroes who thought that their deceased master had emancipated them by his will indicated that they had a vigorous interest in the prospect. These freedmen—as they thought they were—invaded the office of the clerk of the Hustings Court in Richmond and demanded legal proof of their status. They were arrested for their pains and brought before the mayor who informed

---

[5] Petition, dated December 8, 1836, in Virginia Ms. Legislative Petitions.

[6] *Charleston Medical Journal and Review*, VII (1852), p. 97.

them "that they were all slaves, having no claim whatever
to freedom; and that if they were again caught going at
large . . . he would punish each and all with 30 stripes." [7]

With rare exceptions slaves eagerly accepted offers of
emancipation regardless of the conditions imposed upon
them. In some cases they were required to leave not merely
the state but the country. One Virginia master offered freedom to his fourteen slaves if they would agree to move to
Liberia at the expense of the American Colonization Society. Though they were thus forced to part with friends
and relatives and to settle in a strange land, only one of
them rejected the terms. All of the one hundred and
twenty-three slaves of Isaac Ross, of Mississippi, elected the
option of being transported to Africa to obtain the freedom provided in his will.[8]

Southern court records contain innumerable suits in behalf of Negroes who claimed that they were being held in
bondage illegally. They based their cases upon claims that
they had been kidnapped, or that a female ancestor had
been free, or that they had been emancipated by a will or
by some other legal document. These suits were filled with
human drama which, from the slave's point of view, sometimes ended tragically and sometimes joyously. In one case
before the Virginia Court of Appeals, "Daniel and twenty-
three others filed their bill . . . stating that they were the
only slaves of a certain Miss Mary Robinson" whose will
provided "that the whole of them . . . as far as the law
enables me to do it, be emancipated." However, Mary Robinson had previously deeded these slaves to a nephew, and
the court therefore ordered "that the appellees be delivered
to . . . [him] as his proper slaves." [9]

---

[7] Richmond *Enquirer*, July 19, 1853.
[8] Catterall (ed.), *Judicial Cases*, I, p. 171: III, pp. 290–92.
[9] *Ibid.*, I, pp. 114–15.

In another case before the same court a group of Negroes won a suit against certain persons who had attempted to deprive them of the freedom granted in their master's will. They then sued for compensation for the period of their illegal detention. This the court refused to grant, because emancipation was "a benefit rather in name than in fact." In bondage they were cared for "in infancy, old age, and infirmity," they were exempted from the "anxieties of a precarious existence," and they enjoyed the "humane indulgence" of their master. Hence no "practical injustice" was done them "by striking an even balance of profit and loss" while they were illegally held in servitude.[1] The freedmen in this case apparently did not agree.

The emancipating clauses in the wills of slaveholders were often the products of philanthropy or of a troubled conscience, but some of them were the products (at least in part) of pressures applied by the slaves themselves. Bondsmen occasionally persuaded their masters to make this philanthropic gesture, or promised to give faithful service as part of an agreement leading to eventual emancipation. It is quite likely that many slaves who could get no such commitment nevertheless hoped ultimately to receive this reward for their loyalty and devotion. This seemed to be the objective of a slave carpenter named Jim who belonged to Ebenezer Pettigrew, of North Carolina. Jim had been known for his "humility" and "good manners" during the many years that he gave Pettigrew "faithful service." But immediately after his master's death Jim's conduct changed when he found that he was not going to be emancipated. His new master discovered a "deformity" in his character resulting from his "proud and wicked spirit." Jim was "haunted . . . with a desire for freedom" and

---

[1] *Ibid.*, I, pp. 214–15.

indulged in "harsh strictures" against his owner for not granting it to him.[2] Eventually Jim was shipped to New Orleans.

A few slaves (usually skilled ones in the towns of the Upper South) won the opportunity to purchase their own freedom. Occasionally, they earned the necessary funds by working nights and Sundays. More often, they hired their own time. Either way, they gradually accumulated enough money to pay their masters an amount equal to their value and thus obtained deeds of emancipation. Benevolent masters helped ambitious bondsmen by permitting them to make the payments in installments over a period of years or by accepting a sum lower than the market price. Now and then a slave convinced his master of the wisdom of this policy by making himself an economic liability. A Virginia slave was a chronic malingerer until he was given a chance to purchase his freedom. He then took a job in a tobacco factory and soon earned his emancipation by diligent toil.[3]

The long struggle of a bondsman, in effect, to buy himself was invariably a moving story. Sometimes it led to bitter disappointment when a master repudiated the bargain or died before the transaction was completed. Sometimes it led to success, as in the case of Charles White, a slave blacksmith in Bath County, Virginia. White, an "exceedingly capable and efficient laborer" who would "do well anywhere," began his campaign for freedom in 1832 when he petitioned his master for permission to hire his own time. His owner agreed, and White began to save whatever he could earn above his expenses and what he paid for his hire. By 1841, the goal seemed to be in sight, for there was talk of "freedom papers" for White, who sent his master "many

[2] William S. Pettigrew to John Williams, November 4, 1852; *id.* to J. Johnston Pettigrew, March 17, 1853; undated memorandum in handwriting of William S. Pettigrew, Pettigrew Family Papers.

[3] Olmsted, *Seaboard*, pp. 103–104.

thanks of gratitude . . . with tears in his eyes." But four years later he was still eighty dollars short, because he found it difficult as a slave to collect fees that were due him. Finally, in 1847, after fifteen years, Charles White paid the balance of his owner's claim against him and obtained his "freedom papers." [4] Few have earned their freedom more honestly than this Virginia blacksmith.

Some self-bought freedmen attempted to buy the freedom of other members of their families. A husband might labor to purchase his wife and children, or a wife might earn her freedom first, then purchase her husband. No case is more touching than that of a slave woman in Augusta, Georgia, who remained in bondage herself but used her earnings from extra work to pay for the emancipation of her five children.[5] A free person of color occasionally gave financial assistance to slaves who were not members of his own family.

Only a small number of bondsmen ever had the chance to show their desire for freedom by embracing an opportunity to gain legal emancipation. The handful who were permitted to buy themselves, or who were freed by their masters' wills, left little doubt about how much they valued liberty. But most slaves had to register their protests against bondage and express their yearning for freedom in less orderly ways.

3

The masses of slaves, for whom freedom could have been little more than an idle dream, found countless ways to exasperate their masters—and thus saw to it that bondage as a labor system had its limitations as well as its advantages. Many slaves were doubtless pulled by conflicting im-

---

[4] A series of letters concerning Charles White from 1832 to 1847 are in the Hamilton Brown Papers.
[5] Bremer, *Homes of the New World*, I, p. 363.

pulses: a desire for the personal satisfaction gained from doing a piece of work well, as against a desire to resist or outwit the master by doing it badly or not at all. Which impulse dominated a given slave at a given time depended upon many things, but the latter one was bound to control him at least part of the time. Whether the master was humane or cruel, whether he owned a small farm or a large plantation, did not seem to be crucial considerations, for almost all slaveholders had trouble in managing this kind of labor.

Not that every malingering or intractable bondsman was pursuing a course calculated to lead toward freedom for his people, or at least for himself. He was not always even making a conscious protest against bondage. Some of his "misdeeds" were merely unconscious reflections of the character that slavery had given him—evidence, as one planter explained, that slavery tended to render him "callous to the ideas of honor and even honesty" (as the master class understood those terms). "Come day, go day, God send Sunday," eloquently expressed the indifference of the "heedless, thoughtless," slave.[6]

But the element of conscious resistance was often present too; whether or not it was the predominant one the master usually had no way of knowing. In any case, he was likely to be distressed by his inability to persuade his slaves to "assimilate" their interest with his. "We all know," complained one slaveholder, that the slave's feeling of obligation to his master "is of so flimsy a character that none of us rely upon it." [7]

Slaveholders disagreed as to whether "smart" Negroes or "stupid" ones caused them the greater trouble. A Missis-

---

[6] Johnson, *Ante-Bellum North Carolina*, p. 496; W. P. Harrison, *The Gospel Among the Slaves* (Nashville, 1893), p. 103.

[7] James W. Bell to William S. Pettigrew, May 3, 1853, Pettigrew Family Papers.

sippian told Olmsted that the "smart" ones were "rascally" and constantly "getting into scrapes," and a Louisianian confessed that his slave Lucy was "the greatest rascal" and the "smartest negro of her age" he had ever known.[8] On the other hand, many masters were annoyed by the seeming stupidity of some of their slaves, by their unwillingness to "think for themselves." A Negro recently imported from Africa was said to be especially prone to this kind of stubborn obtuseness: "let a hundred men shew him how to hoe, or drive a wheelbarrow, he'll still take the one by the Bottom and the other by the Wheel." [9]

According to a former slave, the bondsmen had good reason for encouraging their master to underrate their intelligence. Ignorance was "a high virtue in a human chattel," he suggested, and since it was the master's purpose to keep his bondsmen in this state, they were shrewd enough to make him think he succeeded.[1] A Virginia planter concluded from his own long experience that many slaveholders were victimized by the "sagacity" of Negroes whom they mistakenly thought they understood so well. He was convinced that the slaves, "under the cloak of great stupidity," made "dupes" of their masters: "The most general defect in the character of the negro, is hypocrisy; and this hypocrisy frequently makes him pretend to more ignorance than he possesses; and if his master treats him as a fool, he will be sure to act the fool's part. This is a very convenient trait, as it frequently serves as an apology for awkwardness and neglect of duty." [2]

Slaveowners generally took it as a matter of course that

---

8 Olmsted, *Back Country*, pp. 154–55; Edwin A. Davis (ed.), *Plantation Life in the Florida Parishes of Louisiana, 1836–1846. As Reflected in the Diary of Bennet H. Barrow* (New York, 1943), p. 164.

9 E. B. R. to James B. Bailey, March 24, 1856, James B. Bailey Papers; Gray, *History of Agriculture*, I, p. 519.

1 Douglass, *My Bondage*, p. 81.

2 *Farmers' Register*, V (1837), p. 32.

a laborer would shirk when he could and perform no more work than he had to. They knew that, in most cases, the only way to keep him "in the straight path of duty" was to watch him "with an eye that never slumbers." [3] They frequently used such terms as "slow," "lazy," "wants pushing," "an eye servant," and "a trifling negro" when they made private appraisals of their slaves. "Hands won't work unless I am in sight," a small Virginia planter once wrote angrily in his diary. "I left the Field at 12 [with] all going on well, but very little done after [that]." [4] Olmsted, watching an overseer riding among the slaves on a South Carolina plantation, observed that he was "constantly directing and encouraging them, but . . . as often as he visited one end of the line of operations, the hands at the other end would discontinue their labor, until he turned to ride towards them again." Other visitors in the South also noticed "the furtive cessation from toil that invariably took place, as the overseer's eye was turned from them." [5]

Slaves sought to limit the quantity of their services in many different ways. At cotton picking time they carried cotton from the gin house to the field in the morning to be weighed with the day's picking at night. They concealed dirt or rocks in their cotton baskets to escape punishment for loafing. They fixed their own work quotas, and masters had to adopt stern measures to persuade them that they had been unduly presumptuous. Where the task system was used, they stubbornly resisted any attempt to increase the size of the daily tasks fixed by custom. [6] Athletic and mus-

---

[3] William S. Pettigrew to [James C. Johnston], October 3, 1850, Pettigrew Family Papers.

[4] William C. Adams Ms. Diary, entries for July 18, 20, 1857.

[5] Olmsted, *Seaboard*, pp. 387–88; Abdy, *Journal*, II, p. 214; William Chambers, *Things as They Are in America* (London, 1854), pp. 269–70.

[6] [Ingraham], *South-West*, II, p. 286; Hammond Diary, entries for October 23, 24, 1834; Olmsted, *Seaboard*, pp. 434–36.

cular slaves, as Frederick Douglass recalled, were inclined
to be proud of their capacity for labor, and the master often
sought to promote rivalry among them; but they knew that
this "was not likely to pay," for "if, by extraordinary exertion, a large quantity of work was done in one day, the
fact, becoming known to the master, might lead him to require the same amount every day." Some refused to become
skilled craftsmen, for, as one of them explained, he would
gain nothing by learning a craft.[7] Few seemed to feel any
personal shame when dubbed "eye servants."

Slaves retaliated as best they could against those who
treated them severely, and sometimes their reprisals were
at least partly successful. Experience taught many slaveholders "that every attempt to force a slave beyond the
limit that he fixes himself as a sufficient amount of labor to
render his master, instead of extorting more work, only
tends to make him unprofitable, unmanageable, a vexation
and a curse. If you protract his regular hours of labor, his
movements become proportionally slower." The use of
force might cause him to work still more slowly until he
fell "into a state of impassivity" in which he became "in-
sensible and indifferent to punishment, or even to life." [8]
After a slave was punished in the Richmond tobacco factories, the other hands "gave neither song nor careless
shout for days, while the bosses fretted at slackened production." [9]

Besides slowing down, many slaves bedeviled the master
by doing careless work and by damaging property. They
did much of this out of sheer irresponsibility, but they did
at least part of it deliberately, as more than one master

---

[7] Douglass, *My Bondage*, pp. 261–62; Catterall (ed.), *Judicial Cases*,
II, pp. 73–74, 210–11.

[8] *De Bow's Review*, VII (1849), p. 220; XVII (1854), p. 422; XXV
(1858), p. 51.

[9] Joseph C. Robert, *The Story of Tobacco in America* (New York,
1949), p. 89.

suspected. A Louisiana doctor, Samuel W. Cartwright, attributed their work habits to a disease, peculiar to Negroes, which he called *Dysaethesia Æthiopica* and which overseers "erroneously" called "rascality." An African who suffered from this exotic affliction was "apt to do much mischief" which appeared "as if intentional." He destroyed or wasted everything he touched, abused the livestock, and injured the crops. When he was driven to his labor he performed his tasks "in a headlong, careless manner, treading down with his feet or cutting with his hoe the plants" he was supposed to cultivate, breaking his tools, and "spoiling everything." This, wrote the doctor soberly, was entirely due to "the stupidity of mind and insensibility of the nerves induced by the disease." [1]

But slaveowners ignored this clinical analysis and persisted in diagnosing the disease as nothing but "rascality." To overcome it, they had to supervise the work closely. They searched for methods to prevent slaves from abusing horses and mules, plowing and hoeing "badly," damaging tools, killing young plants, and picking "trashy cotton." James H. Hammond noted in his diary: "I find [hoe-hands] chopping up cotton dreadfully and begin to think that my stand has every year been ruined in this way." A Louisiana sugar planter advised his son to turn to cotton production, because it was "trouble enough to have to manage negroes in the simplest way, without having to overlook them in the manufacture of sugar and management of Machinery." [2] "Rascality" was also a major problem for those who employed slaves in factories.

Olmsted found slaveholders fretting about this problem everywhere in the South. In Texas an angry mistress complained that her domestics constantly tracked mud through

---

[1] *De Bow's Review,* XI (1851), pp. 333–34.
[2] Hammond Diary, entry for June 7, 1839; Lewis Thompson to Thomas Thompson, December 31, 1858, Lewis Thompson Papers.

the house: "What do they care? They'd just as lief clean the mud after themselves as [do] anything else—*their time isn't any value to themselves.*" A Virginia planter said that he grew only the coarser and cheaper tobaccos, because the finer varieties "required more pains-taking and discretion than it was possible to make a large gang of negroes use." Another Virginian complained that slaves were "excessively careless and wasteful, and, in various ways . . . subject us to very annoying losses." Some masters used only crude, clumsy tools, because they were afraid to give their hands better ones.[3] One slaveholder felt aggrieved when he saw that the small patches which his Negroes cultivated for themselves were better cared for and more productive than his own fields.[4]

Masters were also troubled by the slave who idled in the quarters because of an alleged illness or disability. They often suspected that they were being victimized, for feigning illness was a favorite method of avoiding labor. Olmsted found one or more bondsmen "complaining" on almost every plantation he visited, and the proprietor frequently expressed "his suspicion that the invalid was really as well able to work as anyone else." Some masters and overseers believed that they could tell when a slave was deceiving them, but others were afraid to risk permanent injury to their human property. According to one overseer, trying to detect those who were "shamming illness" was "the most disagreeable duty he had to perform. Negroes were famous for it."[5]

Slave women had great success with this stratagem. The overseer on Pierce Butler's Georgia plantation reported that they were constantly "*shamming* themselves into the

3 Olmsted, *A Journey Through Texas* (New York, 1857), p. 120; *id., Seaboard,* pp. 44–45, 91, 480–82.

4 *American Farmer,* 4th Ser., I (1846), p. 295.

5 Olmsted, *Seaboard,* pp. 186–90; *id., Back Country,* pp. 77–79.

family-way in order to obtain a diminution of their labor."
One female enjoyed a "protracted pseudo-pregnancy" during which she "continued to reap increased rations as the
reward of her expectation, till she finally had to disappoint
and receive a flogging." [6] A Virginian asserted that a slave
woman was a less profitable worker after reaching the
"breeding age," because she so often pretended to be suffering from what were delicately called "female complaints." "You have to take her word for it . . . and you
dare not set her to work; and so she will lay up till she feels
like taking the air again, and plays the lady at your expense." [7]

Almost every slaveholder discovered at one time or another that a bondsman had outwitted him by "playing
possum" or by some ingenious subterfuge. One Negro
spread powdered mustard on his tongue to give it a foul
appearance before he was examined by a doctor. Another
convinced his owner that he was totally disabled by rheumatism, until one day he was discovered vigorously rowing
a boat. A master found two of his slaves "grunting" (a common term), one affecting a partial paralysis and the other
declaring that he could not walk; but he soon learned that
they "used their limbs very well when they chose to do so."
For many years a slave on a Mississippi plantation escaped
work by persuading his master that he was nearly blind.
After the Civil War, however, he produced "no less than
eighteen good crops for himself" and became one of "the
best farmers in the country." [8]

In these and other ways a seemingly docile gang of
slaves drove an inefficient manager well nigh to distrac-

[6] Frances Anne Kemble, *Journal of a Residence on a Georgian Plantation in 1838–1839* (New York, 1863), pp. 135–36, 235.

[7] Olmsted, *Seaboard*, pp. 188–90.

[8] Buckingham, *Slave States*, I, pp. 135, 402; Clement Claiborne Clay to
Clement Comer Clay, April 19, 1846, Clement C. Clay Papers; Smedes,
Memorials, p. 80.

tion. They probed for his weaknesses, matched their wits against his, and constantly contrived to disrupt the work routine. An efficient manager took cognizance of the fact that many of his bondsmen were "shrewd and cunning," ever ready to "disregard all reasonable restraints," and eager "to practice upon the old maxim, of 'give an inch and take an ell.' "[9] This was the reason why the owner of a small cotton plantation rejoiced when at last he could afford to employ an overseer: "I feel greatly relieved at the idea of getting a lazy trifling set of negroes off my hands. . . . They have wearied out all the patience I had with them."[1]

Whenever a new master assumed control of a gang of slaves, there was a period of tension; the outcome of this crucial period might determine the success or failure of his enterprise. The bondsmen seemed to think that if the work burden were to be reduced, or the discipline relaxed, it would have to be accomplished at a time such as this. If during this crisis the master had the advantage of superior authority, the slaves at least had the advantage of superior numbers. They could share the results of their experiments as they put him to the test; and, therefore, they probably knew him sooner than he knew them. (Doubtless slaves *always* knew their master better than he knew them.) Shortly after James H. Hammond took over Silver Bluff Plantation on the Savannah River, he wrote in his diary: "All confusion here yet. Just getting things in order and negroes trying me at every step."[2]

In these contests the bondsmen were sometimes able to celebrate a victory over their unhappy master, frustrated in his efforts to make profitable use of their labor. Once they found an incompetent owner, they pressed their ad-

---

[9] *Southern Cultivator*, VII (1849), p. 140; XII (1854), p. 206.
[1] John W. Brown Diary, entry for January 24, 1854.
[2] Hammond Diary, entry for December 13, 1831.

vantage to the point where normal discipline was completely destroyed. Cases can be found of slaves who established a dominating influence over their master, or who, "for want of a better control, would not make crops adequate to the[ir] support." The slaves of a small South Carolina planter were so "unmanageable" and so "unproductive as to render it necessary for him to borrow money." [3] This kind of situation was almost certain to culminate in a sale of the slaves to a new owner. And this in turn marked the beginning of another contest of wills.

A similar period of crisis developed each time a new overseer took command of a plantation labor force. The chances were that discipline had been lax and affairs generally in an unfavorable state during the last weeks of the previous overseer's regime. The first problem, therefore, was to restore order and to re-establish discipline, while the slaves tried every trick they knew to spread and perpetuate chaos.

Though the early weeks of an overseer's administration were the most critical ones, his problems were never permanently solved. His interests and those of the workers under his control clashed at almost every point, and so a feud between them continuously smoldered and occasionally, perhaps, flared up. Let an overseer slacken his control momentarily, let him permit some plantation rule to be violated with impunity, let him tolerate some slipshod work, and the slaves lost no time in putting him to a thorough test. In an essay entitled "Overseers and Their Enjoyments" a Louisiana overseer described graphically what it was like to be "bedeviled with 40 niggers." He concluded bitterly: "Oh, what a fine time of it a manager of a large Louisiana plantation does have." [4]

Plantation records amply illustrate the ways that slaves

---

[3] See, for example, Catterall (ed.), *Judicial Cases*, II, pp. 129, 421, 438.
[4] *Southern Cultivator*, XVIII (1860), p. 151.

capitalized upon the weaknesses of an overseer. In Arkansas, an overseer "made himself so familiar with the hands, that they do [with] him as they please." Another, on a Georgia plantation, "elated by a strong and very false religious feeling," placed himself "on a par with the Negroes, by even joining with them at their prayer meetings, breaking down long established discipline, which in every Case is so *difficult* to preserve." [5] Still another, employed on the North Carolina plantation of Ebenezer Pettigrew, found the slaves more than he could handle when the owner was away. They even "had a great feast" to which they invited the slaves on a neighboring plantation. By the end of a year, as he confessed, they had bothered him "near a bout to death." [6]

When a severe overseer assumed control of one of the Florida plantations of George Noble Jones, the slaves resorted to nearly every conceivable method of active and passive resistance. Eventually they attempted a deliberate slowdown at cotton picking time. "I regret to say," the overseer reported to Jones, "that I never have had as hard work to git cotton picked and that don in good order befor. It seames that those people was determine to not pick cotton." [7]

If an overseer emerged the victor in such a struggle, as he usually did, the slaves might try one last stratagem. They might attempt to cause trouble between the overseer and his employer. An Arkansas planter warned slaveholders that Negroes were "unprincipled creatures" who would "frequently evince a great deal of shrewdness in fixing up a 'tale' on an overseer they do not like." It was his policy, therefore, to whip any slave who made complaints against the overseer. "The impropriety and absurdity of listening

---

5 Willie [Empie] to James Sheppard, October 27, 1859, Sheppard Papers; Manigault Plantation Records.

6 Doctrine Davenport to Ebenezer Pettigrew, February 21, May 16, December 31, 1836, Pettigrew Papers.

7 Phillips and Glunt (eds.), *Florida Plantation Records*, pp. 107–18.

to what negroes have to say about their overseer, is perfectly evident to any who will reflect a minute on the subject." [8]

But frequent complaints nevertheless might weaken a master's confidence in his overseer and lead to his dismissal. Anyhow, an overseer was likely to be more circumspect in his treatment of a slave who had the courage to approach the master. Some planters permitted their slaves to bring in their grievances and prohibited overseers from punishing them for it. Overseers always deplored this practice as a sure way to undermine their authority. "Your Negroes behave badly behind my back and then Run to you and you appear to beleave what they say," one complained to his employer as he tendered his resignation. On another plantation a slave managed to produce a long controversy between owner and overseer until his responsibility was finally discovered. [9] Occasionally the slaves had the pleasure of watching a hated overseer depart in a futile rage. An Alabama planter was troubled with a recently discharged overseer who threatened "to shoot and whip sundries of the Negroes" for "telling tales on him." He behaved "like a madman." [1]

For the most part the slaves who thus provoked masters and overseers were the meek, smiling ones whom many thought were contented though irresponsible. They were not reckless rebels who risked their lives for freedom; if the thought of rebellion crossed their minds, the odds against success seemed too overwhelming to attempt it. But the inevitability of their bondage made it none the more attractive. And so, when they could, they protested by

---

[8] *Southern Cultivator*, XVIII (1860), p. 131.

[9] Phillips and Glunt (eds.), *Florida Plantation Records*, p. 150; John Berkeley Grimball Ms. Diary, entries for October 12, 17, 20, November 2, 3, 1832.

[1] James Pickens to Samuel Pickens, June 15, 1827 (typescript), Israel Pickens and Family Papers.

shirking their duties, injuring the crops, feigning illness, and disrupting the routine. These acts were, in part, an unspectacular kind of "day to day resistance to slavery." [2]

4

According to Dr. Cartwright, there was a second disease peculiar to Negroes which he called *Drapetomania:* "the disease causing negroes to run away." Cartwright believed that it was a "disease of the mind" and that with "proper medical advice" it could be cured. The first symptom was a "sulky and dissatisfied" attitude. To forestall the full onset of the disease, the cause of discontent must be determined and removed. If there were no ascertainable cause, then "whipping the devil out of them" was the proper "preventive measure against absconding." [3]

Though Cartwright's dissertations on Negro diseases are mere curiosities of medical history, the problem he dealt with was a real and urgent one to nearly every slaveholder. Olmsted met few planters, large or small, who were not more or less troubled by runaways. A Mississippian realized that his record was most unusual when he wrote in his diary: "Harry ran away; *the first* negro that ever ran from me." Another slaveholder betrayed his concern when he avowed that he would "rather a negro would do anything Else than runaway." [4]

The number of runaways was not large enough to threaten the survival of the peculiar institution, because slaveholders took precautions to prevent the problem from growing to such proportions. But their measures were never entirely successful, as the advertisements for fugitives in

---

2 Raymond A. and Alice H. Bauer, "Day to Day Resistance to Slavery," *Journal of Negro History*, XXVII (1942) , pp. 388–419.

3 *De Bow's Review*, XI (1851) , pp. 331–33.

4 Olmsted, *Back Country*, p. 476; Newstead Plantation Diary, entry for June 7, 1860; Davis (ed.) , *Diary of Bennet H. Barrow*, p. 165.

southern newspapers made abundantly clear. Actually, the problem was much greater than these newspapers suggested, because many owners did not advertise for their absconding property. (When an owner did advertise, he usually waited until his slave had been missing for several weeks.) In any case, fugitive slaves were numbered in the thousands every year. It was an important form of protest against bondage.

Who were the runaways? They were generally young slaves, most of them under thirty, but occasionally masters searched for fugitives who were more than sixty years old. The majority of them were males, though female runaways were by no means uncommon. It is not true that most of them were mulattoes or of predominantly white ancestry. While this group was well represented among the fugitives, they were outnumbered by slaves who were described as "black" or of seemingly "pure" African ancestry. Domestics and skilled artisans—the ones who supposedly had the most intimate ties with the master class—ran away as well as common field-hands.

Some bondsmen tried running away only once, or on very rare occasions. Others tried it repeatedly and somehow managed to escape in spite of their owners' best efforts to stop them. Such slaves were frequently identified as "habitual" or "notorious" runaways. While a few of them were, according to their masters, "unruly scoundrels" or "incorrigible scamps," most of them seemed to be "humble," inoffensive," or "cheerful" slaves. Thus an advertisement for a Maryland fugitive stated: he "always appears to be in a good humor, laughs a good deal, and runs on with a good deal of foolishness." A Louisiana master gave the following description of three slaves who escaped from him: the first was "very industrious" and always answered "with a smile" when spoken to; the second, a "well-disposed and industrious boy," was "very timid" and spoke to white men "very humbly, with his hand to his hat"; and the third addressed whites "humbly and respectfully with a smile." [5] Slaves such as these apparently concealed their feelings and behaved as they were expected to—until one day they suddenly made off.

Runaways usually went singly or in small groups of two or three. But some escaped in groups of a dozen or more, and in a few instances in groups of more than fifty. They ran off during the warm summer months more often than during the winter when sleeping out of doors was less feasible and when frost-bitten feet might put an end to flight.

Many fugitives bore the marks of cruelty on their bodies, but humane treatment did not necessarily prevent attempts to escape. More than a few masters shared the bewilderment of a Marylander who advertised for his slave Jacob: "He has no particular marks, and his appearance proves the fact of the kind treatment he has always received." Slaveholders told Olmsted that slaves who were treated well, fed properly, and worked moderately ran away even when they knew that it would cause them hardship and, eventually, severe punishment. "This is often mentioned to illustrate the ingratitude and especial depravity of the African race." [6]

In advertising for a runaway, owners frequently insisted that he had absconded for no cause, or for none that they could understand. A Virginia slave ran off without the excuse "either of whipping, or threat, or angry word"; the slaves Moses and Peter left an Alabama plantation "without provocation." A small Virginia planter recorded in his diary that he had punished a slave woman for running away, because there was "no cause" for it but "badness." [7]

---

5 Baltimore *Sun*, September 25, 1856; New Orleans *Picayune*, March 17, 1846.

6 Baltimore *Sun*, August 1, 1840; Olmsted, *Seaboard*, pp. 190–91.

7 Richmond *Enquirer*, August 1, 1837; Mobile *Commercial Register*, November 20, 1837; John Walker Diary, entry for December 16, 1848.

"Poor ignorant devils, for what do they run away?" asked a puzzled master. "They are well clothed, work easy and have all kinds of plantation produce." [8] Some masters, it appears, were betrayed by their own pessimistic assumptions about human nature, especially about the nature of Negroes!

When slaves protested against bondage (or some specific aspect of it) by flight, however, they normally had a clear personal grievance or an obvious objective. One of their most common grievances was being arbitrarily separated from families and friends. Hired slaves often became fugitives as they attempted to get back to their homes. Many of the runaways had recently been carried from an eastern state to the Southwest; torn by loneliness they tried frantically to find their ways back to Virginia or to one of the Carolinas. Sometimes a timid slave had never before attempted escape until he was uprooted by sale to a trader or to another master.

The advertisements for runaways were filled with personal tragedies such as the following: "I think it quite probable that this fellow has succeeded in getting to his wife, who was carried away last Spring out of my neighborhood." Lawrence, aged fourteen, was trying to make his way from Florida to Atlanta where "his mother is supposed to be." Mary "is no doubt lurking about in the vicinity of Goose Creek, where she has children." Will, aged fifty, "has recently been owned in Savannah, where he has a wife and children." [9] Items such as these appeared regularly in the southern press.

Occasionally running away enabled a slave to defeat an attempt to move him against his will. A North Carolina slave fled to the woods when his master tried to take him to

[8] Sellers, *Slavery in Alabama*, pp. 13–14.
[9] Huntsville *Southern Advocate*, December 11, 1829; Tallahassee *Floridian and Journal*, May 20, 1854; Charleston *Courier*, April 10, 1847; March 10, 1856.

Tennessee, and a Georgia slave escaped to his old home after being taken to Alabama. In both cases the owners decided to sell them to owners in the neighborhoods where they wished to remain, rather than be troubled with potential "habitual runaways." [1]

Flight was also a means by which slaves resisted attempts to work them too severely. The heavier labor burdens as well as the more favorable climatic conditions accounted for the higher incidence of runaways in summer. Cotton growers found the number increasing at picking time, sugar growers during the grinding season. Planters who used the task system faced the danger of "a general stampede to the 'swamp'" when they attempted to increase the standardized tasks. The overseer on a Florida plantation, dissatisfied with the rate at which the hands were picking cotton, tried "pushing them up a Little," whereupon some of them retaliated by absconding. Sometimes these escapes resembled strikes, and master or overseer had to negotiate terms upon which the slaves would agree to return. A small slaveholder in Louisiana once wrote in his diary: "I arose this morning as usual to proceed to the day's work, but there were none to do it, with the exception of Sib and Jess." The rest had run off in protest against his work regimen. [2]

Slaves ran away to avoid punishment for misdeeds or to get revenge for punishments already received. Most masters knew that it was folly to threaten slaves with "correction," for this usually caused them to disappear. An overseer reported the escape of a slave to his employer: "I went to

---

1 Balie Peyton to Samuel Smith Downey, January 6, March 7, 1831, Samuel Smith Downey Papers; John C. Pickens to Samuel Pickens, June 28, 1827, Pickens Papers.

2 Olmsted, *Seaboard*, pp. 100–101, 434–36; Phillips and Glunt (eds.), *Florida Plantation Records*, p. 95; Phillips, *American Negro Slavery*, p. 303; John Spencer Bassett, *The Southern Plantation Overseer As Revealed in His Letters* (Northampton, Mass., 1925), p. 18; Marston Diary, entry for May 19, 1828.

give him a Floging for not coming to work in due time and he told me that he would not take it and run off." [3] Olmsted learned that slaves "often ran away after they had been whipped, or something else had happened to make them angry." Those who advertised for fugitives confirmed this fact; they frequently stated that a bondsman "was well paddled before he left," or that "on examination he will be found to have been severely whipped." Slaveholders discovered that some of their human chattels would not tolerate being "dealt harshly with—otherwise they will run off—and if once the habit of absconding is fixed, it is difficult to conquer it." [4]

In other cases escape was simply the result of a longing for at least temporary relief from the restraints and discipline of slavery. "John's running off," explained an overseer, "was for no other cause, than that he did not feel disposed to be governed, by the same rules and regulations that the other negroes . . . are governed by." [5] This seemed to be the most common motive, and in spite of severe punishment some ran away time after time. The most talented fugitives reduced the technique to a science. For example, Remus and his wife Patty escaped from James Battle's Alabama plantation; were caught and jailed in Montgomery; escaped again; were caught and jailed in Columbus, Georgia; escaped again; and were then still at large. Battle urged the next jailer to "secure Remus well." [6]

Slaves like Remus set "evil" examples for others. A small slaveholder in South Carolina was distressed by his "runaway fellow" Team: "this is the 2ᵈ or 3ᵈ time he has rana-

[3] Phillips and Glunt (eds.) , *Florida Plantation Records*, p. 57.
[4] Olmsted, *Back Country*, p. 79; Memphis *Daily Appeal*, July 23, 1859; New Orleans *Picayune*, October 5, 1847; Stephen Duncan to Thomas Butler, September 20, 1851, Butler Family Papers.
[5] Elisha Cain to Alexander Telfair, October 10, 1829, Telfair Plantation Records.
[6] Milledgeville *Southern Recorder*, February 16, 1836.

way, and lost together nearly a years work, I cannot afford to keep him at this rate, he will spoil the rest of my people by his bad example." Moreover, the skilled, "habitual" runaway often persuaded friends or relatives to decamp with him. A Mississippian advertised for his slave Jim, "a dangerous old scoundrel to be running at large, as he has the tact of exercising great influence with other negroes to induce them to run away." [7] No punishment could break the spirit of such a slave, and he remained an "incorrigible scamp" as long as he lived.

In most cases the runaways were at large for only a short time—a few days or, at most, a few weeks—before they were caught or decided to return voluntarily. But some of them, though remaining in the South, eluded their pursuers with amazing success. It took a South Carolinian a year to catch a slave woman who was over fifty years old. A Florida master advertised for a slave who had been a fugitive for three years. In 1832, a Virginia master was still searching for two slaves who had escaped fifteen years earlier. And a jailer in Jones County, North Carolina, gave notice that he had captured a bondsman who had been a runaway for twenty-five years. [8]

The success of runaway expeditions depended upon the willingness of other slaves to give the fugitives aid. Some of them were helped by literate bondsmen who provided them with passes. One slave carpenter made a business of writing passes for his friends; when he was finally detected he ran away himself. [9] Slaveholders knew that their bondsmen fed and concealed runaways, but they were unable to stop

---

7 Gavin Diary, entry for July 4, 1857; Vicksburg *Weekly Sentinel*, August 9, 1849.

8 Wilmington (N.C.) *Journal*, September 5, 1851; July 5, 1855; Tallahassee *Floridian*, March 13, 1847; Richmond *Enquirer*, September 4, 1832.

9 Rachel O'Connor to Mary C. Weeks, April 9, 1833, David Weeks and Family Collection.

them. In Louisiana a fugitive was found to have been "lurking" about his master's premises for nearly a year while sympathetic bondsmen "harbored" him.[1]

A few slaves betrayed runaways, but usually it was futile for a master to expect their help in catching his property. Even domestics often refused to be informers. One house servant was whipped for not reporting that she had heard a runaway "talking in the yard." James H. Hammond demoted two domestics to field labor for aiding runaways and cut off the meat allowance of all his slaves until they would help him bring them in. A Mississippi planter wrote angrily that his slave woman Nancy, who had been treated "with the greatest indulgence," was "taken in the very act" of carrying food to some runaways. "There is no gratitude among them," he concluded, "and there is nothing more true, than that they will not bear indulgence."[2]

Bands of fugitives sometimes fled into the fastness of a forest or swamp where they established camps and lived in rude huts. Occasionally they tried to grow their own food, but more often they obtained it by raiding nearby farms. One such camp in South Carolina was in a "clearing in a very dense thicket" from which the runaways "killed the hogs and sheep and robbed the fields of the neighbors." A party hunting fugitives in the same state found another camp which was "well provided with meal, cooking utensils, blankets, etc," and near which "corn, squashes, and peas were growing." Slaves rarely betrayed the locations of these camps. A Louisiana planter, searching for runaways, "very foolish[ly]" tried to force a captured slave woman to

---

1 Davis (ed.), *Diary of Bennet H. Barrow*, pp. 226–27; Northup, *Twelve Years a Slave*, pp. 236–49.

2 Mrs. Andrew McCollam Ms. Diary, entry for April 20, 1847; Hammond Diary, entries for July 1, 18, 19, 1832; Stephen Duncan to Thomas Butler, July 1, 1823, Butler Family Papers.

lead him to their camp and thus "fooled the day off to no purpose." [3]

Some bold fugitives, because of the lightness of their complexions or because they possessed forged "free papers," made no attempt to conceal themselves. An Alabama master sounded a warning that appeared frequently in fugitive-slave advertisements: Daniel would "no doubt change his name and have a free pass, or pass to hire his time as he has done before." [4] This Negro was, in effect, trying to work and live as a free man while remaining in the South. A fugitive blacksmith repeatedly wrote passes for himself authorizing him to travel about and work at his trade; another managed to find employment in the turpentine industry for nearly two years. [5] Still others, pretending to be "free persons of color," were eventually caught working in the fisheries, on the wharves, or on river boats. They could scarcely have given stronger evidence of their longing for freedom and of their ability to take care of themselves.

But slaves who ran away with the hope of gaining permanent freedom usually attempted to get out of the South. This fearful enterprise involved a dangerous journey along the back ways in the dead of night. Most of the time it ended in the tragedy of failure, which meant certain punishment and possibly no second opportunity. When it ended in success, the fugitive at best faced an uncertain future among strangers. But a passionate desire for a new and better life in freedom caused many bondsmen to take all these risks. How often they succeeded there is no way of

---

[3] Catterall (ed.), *Judicial Cases*, II, p. 434; Howell M. Henry, *The Police Control of the Slaves in South Carolina* (Emory, Va., 1914), p. 121; Davis (ed.), *Diary of Bennet H. Barrow*, pp. 341–43.

[4] Pensacola *Gazette*, November 3, 1838.

[5] Milledgeville *Southern Recorder*, July 18, 1843; Raleigh *North Carolina Standard*, November 7, 1855.

knowing accurately. The claim of a southern judge in 1855 that the South had by then lost "upwards of 60,000 slaves" to the North was a reasonable estimate.[6] In any case, the number was large enough to keep southern masters on guard and to remind Northerners that defenders of slavery did not speak for the slaves.

Most of the fugitives who tried to reach the free states naturally came from the Upper South where the distance was relatively short and the chance of success accordingly greater. In 1847, a Louisville newspaper reported that nearly fifty Kentucky slaves had recently escaped across the Ohio River; slave property, the paper commented, was becoming "entirely insecure" in the river counties.[7] Maryland lacked even a river barrier, and probably more bondsmen fled to the North through this state than through any other. In Cecil County, slaves were reported in 1848 to be "running away in droves." In Charles County, a "strange and singular spirit" once came over the bondsmen, with the result that more than eighty fled in a single group. (Their recapture made it evident again that it was foolhardy to attempt escape in groups of this size.) On various occasions Maryland slaveholders assembled to consider measures "to put a stop to the elopement" of Negroes.[8] They never succeeded.

Fear of being sold to the Deep South, as well as fear of having their families broken, often caused bondsmen in the Upper South to flee to the North. Many ran away when the estates of deceased masters were being settled. Sometimes the mere threat of a sale was sufficient provocation. A Virginia Negro who escaped to Canada recalled: "Master used

---

[6] Catterall (ed.), *Judicial Cases*, III, pp. 45–46; Franklin, *From Slavery to Freedom*, p. 255–56.
[7] Louisville *Democrat*, September 6, 1847; Coleman, *Slavery Times in Kentucky*, p. 219.
[8] Baltimore *Sun*, July 10, 14, 22, 1845; April 22, 1848.

to say, that if we didn't suit him, he would put us in his pocket quick—meaning he would sell us."[9]

A few runaways from the Deep South also attempted to reach the free states in spite of their slender chances of success. An Alabama master advertised for his slave Gilbert, "a carpenter by trade and an excellent workman," who would probably "endeavor to get to Ohio, as he ran away . . . once before, and his aim was to get to that state." Archy and his wife Maria escaped from their master in Wilkes County, Georgia: "They will make for a free State, as the boy Archy has heretofore made several attempts to do." Prince, a South Carolina fugitive, was doubtless aiming for a free state, "having runaway . . . [before] and got as far as Salisbury, N.C., before he was apprehended."[1] These slaves often tried to reach a seaport and get aboard a vessel bound for the North. Generally they were caught before the vessel left port.

Abraham, who lived in Mobile and was for many years his master's "confidential servant," was one of the few slaves from the Deep South who actually got all the way to a free state. "By dint of his ingenuity and adroitness at forgery, and a good share of cunning," Abraham made his way unhindered until he reached Baltimore. Here he was arrested and taken before a magistrate, "but his fictitious papers were so well executed . . . [that] he was at once suffered to go free." He then went on to New York where he found employment as a hotel porter. Eventually, however, his master found him and under the provisions of the fugitive-slave law carried him back to bondage.[2] Not many runaways from the Deep South experienced Abraham's bitter disappointment, because not many came so close to having freedom within their grasp.

---

9 Drew, *The Refugee*, passim.
1 Mobile *Commercial Register*, March 17, 1834; Nashville *Republican Banner*, July 3, 1843; Columbia *South Carolinian*, July 20, 1847.
2 Baltimore *Sun*, August 15, 1842.

While the North Star was the fugitives' traditional guide, some saw liberty beckoning from other directions. They fled to the British during the American Revolution and the War of 1812, and to the Spanish before the purchases of Louisiana and Florida. At a later date Florida slaves escaped to the Seminole Indians, aided them in their war against the whites, and accompanied them when they moved to the West.[3] At Key West, in 1858, a dozen slaves stole a small boat and successfully navigated it to freedom in the Bahamas.[4] Arkansas runaways often tried to make their way to the Indian country. For Texas slaves, Mexico was the land of freedom, and most of those who sought it headed for the Rio Grande. In Mexico the fugitives generally were welcomed and protected, and in some cases sympathetic peons guided them in their flight.[5]

How often runaways received assistance from free persons residing in the South is hard to determine, but it seems likely that they seldom trusted anyone but fellow slaves. A few white Southerners who opposed slavery gave sanctuary to fugitives or directed them along their routes. Slaveholders sometimes suspected that runaways were being harbored by some "evil disposed person" or "unprincipled white." Now and then free Negroes also gave aid to the less fortunate members of their race. One of them, Richard Buckner, was convicted of assisting slaves to escape from Kentucky and sentenced to two years in prison. Free Negroes who were employed on river boats or on vessels engaged in the coastal trade occasionally concealed slaves who

---

[3] Kenneth W. Porter, "Florida Slaves and Free Negroes in the Seminole War, 1835–1842," *Journal of Negro History*, XXVIII (1943), pp. 390–421.

[4] Tallahassee *Floridian and Journal*, February 20, 1858.

[5] Austin *Texas State Gazette*, September 23, 1854; April 7, June 2, 1855; San Antonio *Ledger*, September 21, 1854; Olmsted, *Texas*, pp. 323–27; Paul S. Taylor, *An American-Mexican Frontier* (Chapel Hill, 1934), pp. 33–39.

were trying to reach the free states.[6]

Many Southerners were convinced that the slave states were honeycombed with northern abolitionist agents seeking to create discontent among the slaves and to urge them to abscond. While this was an exaggeration, a few Northerners did undertake this hazardous enterprise. In 1849, a Missouri newspaper complained that almost every day slaves were induced "by the persuasions of Abolitionists, to abandon comfortable homes." Supporters of the antislavery movement operated in Kentucky (sometimes disguised as peddlers) and guided hundreds to freedom across the Ohio River. On one occasion three Northerners made an unsuccessful effort to help seventy-eight slaves escape from the District of Columbia by boat down the Potomac River. In 1844, Jonathan Walker, a New Englander, was severely punished for attempting to ferry seven fugitives from Pensacola to the Bahamas. Ten years later, James Redpath, the Massachusetts abolitionist, traveled through the slave states trying to persuade slaves to run away.[7] But the bondsmen generally needed assistance more than persuasion.

Not the least of those who gave assistance to fugitives were former slaves who had themselves escaped and then returned to help others. One of them was Ben, "a stout hearty negro," who absconded from Kentucky but "was not satisfied with letting 'well enough alone.'" Instead he engaged in "running off the 'property' of his late master at every opportunity." When at length Ben was caught, he "fought with the desperation of a man who had once tasted

---

[6] Louisville *Democrat*, October 26, 1858; Richmond *Enquirer*, August 3, 1847; Trexler, *Slavery in Missouri*, p. 178.

[7] St. Louis *Missouri Republican*, November 5, 1849; Lexington *Kentucky Statesman*, June 20, 1854; Baltimore *Sun*, April 18, 19, 21, 1848; Edwin L. Williams, Jr., "Negro Slavery in Florida," *Florida Historical Quarterly*, XXVIII (1950), p. 185; James Redpath, *The Roving Editor: or, Talks with Slaves in the Southern States* (New York, 1859), *passim*.

the sweets of liberty"; but he was overpowered and re-enslaved. Harriet Tubman, after twenty-five years in bondage, escaped from her master who lived on the Eastern Shore of Maryland. During the 1850's she returned nineteen times to deliver parties of fugitives.[8] There were others whose careers were less spectacular.

Harriet Tubman was one of the many ex-slaves who served as "conductors" on the famed Underground Railroad. Along its various routes in the Northeast and Northwest they, together with northern free Negroes and sympathetic whites, sheltered the frightened fugitives and sped them on their way.[9] These runaway slaves did much to disturb the consciences of the northern people and to arouse sympathy for those they left behind.

But southern masters were less disturbed about the ultimate consequences than they were about their immediate losses. Moreover, every successful runaway was bound to encourage other slaves to try their luck in the same enterprise. When a Tennessee master learned that several of his bondsmen had escaped to Canada, he vowed that he would recover them if it cost all that they were worth. "I intend going to Canada next spring and if there is no other choice I will kidnap them, or have them at the risk of my life."[1] This was idle talk; his slaves were lost forever.

Only a few of the runaways left records of their feelings at the time they made their break for liberty. One of them, Anthony Chase, the property of a Baltimore widow, composed a priceless document. In 1827, after failing to get permission to purchase his freedom, Chase escaped from

[8] Louisville *Democrat*, October 27, 1857; Sarah H. Bradford, *Scenes in the Life of Harriet Tubman* (Auburn, N.Y., 1869), *passim*.
[9] William Still, *The Underground Railroad* (Philadelphia, 1879), *passim;* Wilbur H. Siebert, *The Underground Railroad from Slavery to Freedom* (New York, 1898), *passim*.
[1] John P. Chester to Hamilton Brown, September 13, 1837, Hamilton Brown Papers.

the man to whom he was hired. It was to him, rather than to his owner, that Chase penned his personal Declaration of Independence:

> I know that you will be astonished and surprised when you becom acquainted with the unexspected course that I am now about to take, a step that I never had the most distant idea of takeing, but what can a man do who has his hands bound and his feet fettered [?] He will certainly try to get them loosened in any way that he may think the most adviseable. I hope sir that you will not think that I had any fault to find of you or your family[.] No sir I have none and I could of hired with you all the days of my life if my conditions could of been in any way bettered which I intreated with my mistress to do but it was all in vain[.] She would not consent to anything that would melorate my condition in any shape or measure[.] So I shall go to sea in the first vesel that may offer an opportunity and as soon as I can acumulate a sum of money suficient I will remit it to my mistress to prove to her and to [the] world that I dont mean to be dishonest but wish to pay her every cent that I think my servaces is worth. . . . I dont supose that I shall ever be forgiven for this act but I hope to find forgiveness in that world that is to com.

After wishing his former employer "helth and happyness," Anthony Chase, with an unconscious touch of irony, signed himself "your most obedient serv[an]t." [2] And thus another slaveholder was left to meditate upon the folly of placing confidence in the loyalty of slaves.

The bondsmen who protested against bondage by running away or by some form of malingering were a perplexing lot. Since, by all outward appearances, they usually seemed cheerful and submissive, masters could never be

---

2 Anthony Chase to Jeremiah Hoffman, August 8, 1827, Otho Holland Williams Papers.

sure whether their misdeeds were purposeful or capricious.
Their smiling faces were most disarming.

There were some bondsmen, however, who did not smile.

5

"His look is impudent and insolent, and he holds himself
straight and walks well." So a Louisiana master described
James, a runaway slave.[3] There were always bondsmen like
James. In 1669, a Virginia statute referred to "the obsti-
nacy of many of them"; in 1802, a South Carolina judge declared that they were "in general a headstrong, stubborn
race of people"; and in 1859, a committee of a South Carolina agricultural society complained of the "insolence of
disposition to which, as a race, they are remarkably liable."
An overseer on a Louisiana plantation wrote nervously
about the many "outrageous acts" recently committed by
slaves in his locality and insisted that he scarcely had time
to eat and sleep: "The truth is no man can begin to attend
to Such a business with any Set of negroes, without the
Strictest vigilance on his part."[4] It was the minority of
slaves whom his discipline could not humble (the "insolent," "surly," and "unruly" ones) that worried this overseer—and slaveholders generally. These were the slaves
whose discontent drove them to drastic measures.

Legally the offenses of the rebels ranged from petty misdemeanors to capital crimes, and they were punished accordingly. The master class looked upon any offense as
more reprehensible (and therefore subject to more severe
penalties) when committed by a slave than when committed by a free white. But how can one determine the proper

[3] New Orleans *Picayune*, November 4, 1851.
[4] Hurd, *Law of Freedom and Bondage*, I, p. 232; Catterall (ed.), *Judicial Cases*, II, pp. 281–82; *De Bow's Review*, XXVI (1859), p. 107;
Moore Rawls to Lewis Thompson, May 9, 1858, Lewis Thompson
Papers.

ethical standards for identifying undesirable or even criminal behavior among slaves? How distinguish a "good"
from a "bad" slave? Was the "good" slave the one who was
courteous and loyal to his master, and who did his work
faithfully and cheerfully? Was the "bad" slave the one who
would not submit to his master, and who defiantly fought
back? What were the limits, if any, to which a man deprived of his freedom could properly go in resisting bondage? How accountable was a slave to a legal code which
gave him more penalties than protection and was itself a
bulwark of slavery? This much at least can be said: many
slaves rejected the answers which their masters gave to
questions such as these. The slaves did not thereby repudi-
ate law and morality: rather, they formulated legal and
moral codes of their own.

The white man's laws against theft, for example, were
not supported by the slave's code. In demonstrating the
"absence of moral principle" among bondsmen, one master
observed: "To steal and not to be detected is a merit among
them." Let a master turn his back, wrote another, and
some "cunning fellow" would appropriate part of his
goods. No slave would betray another, for an informer was
held "in greater detestation than the most notorious
thief." [5]

If slaveholders are to be believed, petty theft was an almost universal "vice"; slaves would take anything that was
not under lock and key. Field-hands killed hogs and robbed
the corn crib. House servants helped themselves to wines,
whiskey, jewelry, trinkets, and whatever else was lying
about. Fugitives sometimes gained from their master unwilling help in financing the journey to freedom, the advertisements often indicating that they absconded with
money, clothing, and a horse or mule. Thefts were not nec-

---

[5] Harrison, *Gospel Among the Slaves*, p. 103; *Farmers' Register*, V
(1837), p. 302.

essarily confined to the master's goods: any white man might be considered fair game.

Some bondsmen engaged in theft on more than a casual and petty basis. They made a business of it and thus sought to obtain comforts and luxuries which were usually denied them. A South Carolina master learned that his house servants had been regularly looting his wine cellar and that one of them was involved in an elaborate "system of roguery." A planter in North Carolina found that three of his slaves had "for some months been carrying on a robbery" of meat and lard, the leader being "a young carpenter, remarkable for smartness . . . and no less worthy for his lamentable deficiency in common honesty." [6]

If the stolen goods were not consumed directly, they were traded to whites or to free Negroes. This illegal trade caused masters endless trouble, for slaves were always willing to exchange plantation products for tobacco, liquor, or small sums of money. Southern courts were kept busy handling the resulting prosecutions. One slaveholder discovered that his bondsmen had long been engaged in an extensive trade in corn. "Strict vigilance," he concluded, was necessary "to prevent them from theft; particularly when dishonesty is inherent, as is probably the case with some of them." [7] Dishonesty, as the master understood the term, indeed seemed to be a common if not an inherent trait of southern slaves.

The slaves, however, had a somewhat different definition of dishonesty in their own code, to which they were reasonably faithful. For appropriating their master's goods they might be punished and denounced by him, but they were not likely to be disgraced among their associates in the

---

[6] Hammond Diary, entry for October 16, 1835; William S. Pettigrew to [James C. Johnston], October 3, 1850, Pettigrew Family Papers.

[7] William S. Pettigrew to J. Johnston Pettigrew, March 9, 1849, Pettigrew Family Papers; Catterall (ed.), *Judicial Cases, passim.*

slave quarters, who made a distinction between "stealing" and "taking." Appropriating things from the master meant simply taking part of his property for the benefit of another part or, as Frederick Douglass phrased it, "taking his meat out of one tub, and putting it in another." Thus a female domestic who had been scolded for the theft of some trinkets was reported to have replied: "Law, mam, don't say I's wicked; ole Aunt Ann says it allers right for us poor colored people to 'popiate whatever of de wite folk's blessings de Lord puts in our way." Stealing, on the other hand, meant appropriating something that belonged to another slave, and this was an offense which slaves did not condone.[8]

The prevalence of theft was a clear sign that slaves were discontented, at least with the standard of living imposed upon them. They stole food to increase or enrich their diets or to trade for other coveted commodities. Quite obviously they learned from their masters the pleasures that could be derived from the possession of worldly goods; and when the opportunity presented itself, they "took" what was denied them as slaves.

Next to theft, arson was the most common slave "crime," one which slaveholders dreaded almost constantly. Fire was a favorite means for aggrieved slaves to even the score with their master. Reports emanated periodically from some region or other that there was an "epidemic" of gin-house burnings, or that some bondsman had taken his revenge by burning the slave quarters or other farm buildings. More than one planter thus saw the better part of a year's harvest go up in flames.[9] Southern newspapers and court records

[8] Douglass, *My Bondage*, pp. 189–91; Austin Steward, *Twenty-Two Years a Slave* (Canandaigua, N.Y., 1856), p. 29; Olmsted, *Seaboard*, pp. 116–17; Sellers, *Slavery in Alabama*, p. 257.
[9] Davis (ed.), *Diary of Bennet H. Barrow*, p. 131 n.; Rachel O'Conner to David Weeks, June 16, 1833, Weeks Collection; S. Porcher Gaillard Ms. Plantation Journal, entry for May 9, 1856.

are filled with illustrations of this offense, and with evidence of the severe penalties inflicted upon those found guilty of committing it.

Another "crime" was what might be called self-sabotage, a slave deliberately unfitting himself to labor for his master. An Arkansas slave, "at any time to save an hour's work," could "throw his left shoulder out of place." A Kentucky slave made himself unserviceable by downing medicines from his master's dispensary (thus showing a better understanding of the value of these nostrums than his owner). A slave woman was treated as an invalid because of "swellings in her arms"—until it was discovered that she produced this condition by thrusting her arms periodically into a beehive. Yellow Jacob, according to his master's plantation journal, "had a kick from a mule and when nearly well would bruise it and by that means kept from work." [1] Another Negro, after being punished by his owner, retaliated by cutting off his right hand; still another cut off the fingers of one hand to avoid being sold to the Deep South. [2]

A few desperate slaves carried this form of resistance to the extreme of self-destruction. Those freshly imported from Africa and those sold away from friends and relatives were especially prone to suicide. [3] London, a slave on a Georgia rice plantation, ran to the river and drowned himself after being threatened with a whipping. His overseer gave orders to leave the corpse untouched "to let the [other] negroes see [that] when a negro takes his own life they will be treated in this manner." A Texas planter be-

[1] Helena (Ark.) *Southern Shield*, July 23, 1853; Buckingham, *Slave States*, I, p. 402; Gaillard Plantation Journal, entry for May 9, 1856.

[2] Harriet Martineau, *Society in America* (New York, 1837), II, p. 113; Drew, *The Refugee*, p. 178.

[3] Phillips (ed.), *Plantation and Frontier*, II, p. 31; Catterall (ed.), *Judicial Cases*, II, pp. 425–26; III, pp. 216–17; Drew, *The Refugee*, p. 178.

wailed the loss of a slave woman who hanged herself after two unsuccessful breaks for freedom: "I had been offered $900.00 for her not two months ago, but damn her . . . I would not have had it happened for twice her value. *The fates pursue me.*" [4]

Some runaways seemed determined to make their recapture as costly as possible and even resisted at the risk of their own lives. One advertisement, typical of many, warned that an escaped slave was a "resolute fellow" who would probably not be taken without a "show of competent force." When, after a day-long chase, three South Carolina fugitives were cornered, they "fought desperately," inflicted numerous wounds upon their pursuers with a barrage of rocks, and "refused to surrender until a force of about forty-five or fifty men arrived." [5] In southern court records there are numerous cases of runaway slaves who killed whites or were themselves killed in their frantic efforts to gain freedom.

In one dramatic case, a Louisiana fugitive was detected working as a free Negro on a Mississippi River flatboat. His pursuers, trailing him with a pack of "Negro dogs," finally found him "standing at bay upon the outer edge of a large raft of drift wood, armed with a club and pistol." He threatened to kill anyone who got near him. "Finding him obstinately determined not to surrender, one of his pursuers shot him. He fell at the third fire, and so determined was he not to be captured, that when an effort was made to rescue him from drowning he made battle with his club, and sunk waving his weapon in angry defiance." [6]

An effort to break up an organized gang of runaways was a dangerous business, because they were often unwilling to

[4] Phillips (ed.), *Plantation and Frontier*, II, p. 94; John R. Lyons to William W. Renwick, April 4, 1854, William W. Renwick Papers.

[5] Petition of William Boyd to South Carolina legislature, November 29, 1858, in South Carolina Slavery Manuscripts Collection.

[6] *Feliciana Whig*, quoted in Olmsted, *Back Country*, p. 474.

surrender without a fight. The fugitives in one well-armed band in Alabama were building a fort at the time they were discovered. Their camp was destroyed after a "smart skirmish" during which three of them were killed.[7] Such encounters did not always end in defeat for the slaves; some runaway bands successfully resisted all attempts at capture and remained at large for years.

Ante-bellum records are replete with acts of violence committed by individual slaves upon masters, overseers, and other whites. A Texan complained, in 1853, that cases of slaves murdering white men were becoming "painfully frequent." "Within the last year or two many murders have taken place, by negroes upon their owners," reported a Louisiana newspaper. And a Florida editor once wrote: "It is our painful duty to record another instance of the destruction of the life of a white man by a slave." [8]

Many masters owned one or more bondsmen whom they feared as potential murderers. A Georgia planter remembered Jack, his plantation carpenter, "the most notoriously bad character and worst Negro of the place." Jack "was the only Negro ever in our possession who I considered capable of Murdering me, or burning my dwelling at night, or capable of committing any act." [9]

Slaves like Jack could be watched closely; but others appeared to be submissive until suddenly they turned on their masters. Even trusted house servants might give violent expression to long pent up feelings. One "first rate" female domestic, while being punished, abruptly attacked her mistress, "threw her down, and beat her unmercifully on the head and face." A "favorite body servant" of a "humane master who rarely or never punished his slaves" one day

[7] Phillips (ed.), *Plantation and Frontier*, II, pp. 90–91; Bassett, *Plantation Overseer*, pp. 78–79.

[8] Austin *Texas State Gazette*, September 3, 1853; Alexandria (La.) *Red River Republican*, April 24, 1852; Pensacola *Gazette*, May 4, 1839.

[9] Manigault Plantation Records, entry for March 22, 1867.

became insolent. Unwilling to be disciplined, this slave waylaid his owner, "knocked him down with a whiteoak club, and beat his head to a pumice." [1] Here was another reason why it seemed foolish for a master to put his "confidence in a Negro."

At times these acts of violence appeared to be for "no cause"—that is, they resulted from a slave's "bad disposition" rather than from a particular grievance. But more often they resulted from a clash of personalities, or from some specific incident. For example, a slave who had been promised freedom in his master's will, poisoned his master to hasten the day of liberation. A South Carolina bondsman was killed during a fight with an overseer who had whipped his son. In North Carolina a slave intervened while the overseer was whipping his wife, and in the ensuing battle the overseer met his death. [2]

The most common provocation to violence was the attempt of a master or overseer either to work or to punish slaves severely. An Alabama bondsman confessed killing the overseer because "he was a hard down man on him, and said he was going to be harder." Six Louisiana slaves together killed an overseer and explained in their confession that they found it impossible to satisfy him. Three North Carolina slaves killed their master when they decided that "the old man was too hard on them, and they must get rid of him." [3] During one of these crises an overseer called upon his hands to help him punish an "unmanageable" slave: "not one of them paid the least attention to me but kept on at their work." These encounters did not

---

1 Rachel O'Conner to A. T. Conrad, May 26, 1836, Weeks Collection; Austin *Texas State Gazette*, September 23, 1854.

2 Martineau, *Society in America*, II, pp. 110–11; Catterall (ed.), *Judicial Cases*, II, pp. 206–207, 434–35.

3 Catterall (ed.), *Judicial Cases*, III, pp. 238–41; Reuben Carnal to Lewis Thompson, June 17, 1855, Lewis Thompson Papers; Hardy Hardison to William S. Pettigrew, February 11, 1858, Pettigrew Family Papers.

always lead to death, but few plantations escaped without at least one that might easily have ended in tragedy. "Things move on here in the old Style except that now and then a refractory negro has to be taken care of," was the off-hand comment of a planter.[4]

Sometimes a slave who showed sufficient determination to resist punishment managed to get the best of his owner or overseer. A proud bondsman might vow that, regardless of the consequences, he would permit no one to whip him.[5] An overseer thought twice before precipitating a major crisis with a strong-willed slave; he might even overlook minor infractions of discipline.

But an impasse such as this was decidedly unusual; if it had not been, slavery itself would have stood in jeopardy. Ordinarily these clashes between master and slave were fought out to a final settlement, and thus a thread of violence was woven into the pattern of southern bondage. Violence, indeed, was the method of resistance adopted by the boldest and most discontented slaves. Its usual reward, however, was not liberty but death!

6

No ante-bellum Southerner could ever forget Nat Turner. The career of this man made an impact upon the people of his section as great as that of John C. Calhoun or Jefferson Davis. Yet Turner was only a slave in Southampton County, Virginia—and during most of his life a rather unimpressive one at that. He was a pious man, a Baptist exhorter by avocation, apparently as humble and docile as a slave was expected to be. There is no evidence that he was underfed, overworked, or treated with special cruelty. If

---

[4] Taylor, "Negro Slavery in Louisiana," pp. 258–59; Charles L. Pettigrew to William S. Pettigrew, October 9, 1837, Pettigrew Family Papers.

[5] Douglass, *My Bondage*, pp. 95, 242–46; Brown, *Narrative*, pp. 17–18.

III: *A Troublesome Property*

Nat Turner could not be trusted, what slave could? That was what made his sudden deed so frightening.

Somehow Turner came to believe that he had been divinely chosen to deliver his people from bondage, and he persuaded several other slaves to assist him. In due time he saw the sign for which he had waited, and early in the morning of August 22, 1831, he and his followers rose in rebellion. They began by killing the family to whom Turner belonged. As they marched through the Southampton countryside they gained additional recruits, making a total of about seventy. (Others seemed ready to join if the rebels came their way. The slave Jacob, for example, proclaimed "that if they came by he would join them and assist in killing all the white people.") Within two days they killed nearly sixty whites. They could have killed more. They left undisturbed at least one poor white family, "because they thought no better of themselves than they did of the negroes." To justify the killings, members of Turner's band declared that they had had enough of punishment, or that they now intended to be as rich as their masters. One rebel demonstrated his new status by walking off in his late owner's shoes and socks.

The Nat Turner rebellion lasted only forty-eight hours. Swiftly mobilizing in overwhelming strength, the whites easily dispersed the rebels. Then followed a massacre during which not only the insurrectionists but scores of innocent bondsmen were slaughtered. Others, charged with "felonously consulting, advising and conspiring . . . to rebel . . . and making insurrection and taking the lives of divers free white persons of this Commonwealth," were tried before a court of oyer and terminer during the months of September and October. Some were executed, others transported. Most of those transported had not actively participated in the rebellion; they had merely expressed sympathy for the rebels.

Nat Turner himself was not captured until October 30, more than two months after the uprising. He was brought to trial on November 5, convicted the same day, and hanged six days later.[6] Thus ended an event which produced in the South something resembling a mass trauma, from which the whites had not recovered three decades later. The danger that other Nat Turners might emerge, that an even more serious insurrection might some day occur, became an enduring concern as long as the peculiar institution survived. Proslavery writers boldly asserted that Southerners did not fear their slaves, that a rebellion of the laboring class was more likely to transpire in the North than in the South; but the fear of rebellion, sometimes vague, sometimes acute, was with them always.

Though it was the most disastrous (for both slaves and masters), Nat Turner's was not the first insurrection. Several earlier conspiracies, which narrowly missed being carried into execution might easily have precipitated rebellions much more extensive than that of Turner.[7] These uprisings and conspiracies began as early as the seventeenth century and kept Southerners apprehensive throughout the colonial period. The preamble to a South Carolina statute of 1740 defining the duties of slave patrols stated that many "horrible and barbarous massacres" had been committed or plotted by the slaves who were "generally prone to such

---

[6] Details of the Turner insurrection can be found in contemporary Richmond newspapers, and in the manuscript records of the trials in Southampton County Minute Book, 1830–1835. See also William S. Drewry, *The Southampton Insurrection* (Washington, D.C., 1900); Thomas R. Gray, *The Confessions of Nat Turner* (Baltimore, 1831).

[7] Herbert Aptheker, *American Negro Slave Revolts* (New York, 1943) presents evidence of many conspiracies and a few rebellions, each involving ten or more slaves, from the colonial period to the end of the Civil War. See also Joseph C. Carroll, *Slave Insurrections in the United States, 1800–1865* (Boston, 1938); Harvey Wish, "American Slave Insurrections before 1861," *Journal of Negro History*, XXII (1937), pp. 299–320.

cruel practices." [8] On the eve of the American Revolution a Charlestonian wrote about a "disturbance" among the bondsmen who had "mimicked their betters in crying *Liberty*." In 1785, a West Florida slaveholder was dismayed to learn that several of his slaves were involved in an insurrection plot: "Of what avail is kindness and good usage when rewarded by such ingratitude . . . [?]" [9] Such incidents set the pattern for the nineteenth century.

The new century opened with the Gabriel Conspiracy (August, 1800) in Henrico County, Virginia, in which at least a thousand slaves were implicated. The warnings of two bondsmen and a severe storm enabled the whites to forestall a projected march upon Richmond. A decade later some five hundred slaves in St. John the Baptist Parish, Louisiana, armed with cane knives and other crude weapons, advanced toward New Orleans. But the planters and a strong detachment of troops put them to flight. In 1822, Denmark Vesey, a free Negro in Charleston, planned a vast conspiracy which came to nothing after it was given away by a slave. These and other plots were invariably followed by severe reprisals, including the indiscriminate killing of slaves as well as mass executions after regular trials. The heads of sixteen Louisiana rebels were stuck upon poles along the Mississippi River as a grim warning to other slaves. After the Vesey conspiracy, Charlestonians expressed disillusionment with the idea that by generous treatment the slaves "would become more satisfied with their condition and more attached to the whites." [1]

---

[8] Hurd, *Law of Freedom and Bondage*, I, p. 308.

[9] Henry Laurens to J. Gervais, January 29, 1766, Henry Laurens Ms. Letter Book, 1762–1766, Historical Society of Pennsylvania, Philadelphia (copy in possession of Professor Carl Bridenbaugh) ; Sellers, *Slavery in Alabama*, pp. 13–14.

[1] Aptheker, *American Negro Slave Revolts*, pp. 209–92; Taylor, "Negro Slavery in Louisiana," pp. 268–74; Phillips, *Plantation and Frontier*, II, pp. 103–104.

The shock of Nat Turner caused Southerners to take preventive measures, but these never eliminated their apprehension or the actual danger. Hardly a year passed without some kind of alarming disturbance somewhere in the South. When no real conspiracy existed, wild rumors often agitated the whites and at times came close to creating an insurrection panic. The rumors might be entirely unfounded, or they might grow out of some local incident which was magnified by exaggeration. Even the historian cannot always distinguish between the rumors and the facts. Most of the stories seem to have had a foundation in at least a minor disturbance, limited perhaps to a single plantation where the slaves suddenly became insubordinate, or to a whole neighborhood where they showed signs of becoming restive. Whether caused by rumor or fact, the specter of rebellion often troubled the sleep of the master class.

The Turner rebellion itself produced an insurrection panic that swept the entire South. A Richmond editor wondered whether the southern press was trying to give the slaves "false conceptions of their numbers and capacity, by exhibiting the terror and confusion of the whites, and to induce them to think that practicable, which they see is so much feared by their superiors." [2] In eastern North Carolina the panic caused the arrest of scores of slaves and the execution of more than a dozen. A South Carolinian reported that there was "considerable alarm" in his state too and that some slaves were hanged to prevent a rumored uprising. [3] The excitement spread into the Southwest where it was feared that the bondsmen would become "troublesome." A Mississippian, confessing "great apprehension,"

---

[2] Richmond *Whig*, quoted in Alexandria (Va.) *Phenix Gazette*, September 6, 1831.

[3] Johnson, *Ante-Bellum North Carolina*, pp. 519–20; Rosannah P. Rogers to David S. Rogers, October 29, 1831, Renwick Papers.

noted that "within 4 hours march of Natchez" there were "2200 able bodied male slaves." He warned: "It behooves [us] to be vigilent—but silent." [4]

Similar insurrection panics developed from time to time thereafter. In 1835, one of these frightful disturbances centered in Mississippi and Louisiana; before it subsided, numerous bondsmen had been legally or extra-legally executed. This panic even spread into Roane County in East Tennessee, though that county contained a very small slave population. There was "a great deal of talk and some dread of the negroes rising at Christmas or new year," reported a local slaveholder. "I can not say that I have had much fear of their rising here, but have thought it right to be careful and watchful. It is a disagreeable state of living to be ever suspicious of those with whom we live." [5] This point was illustrated by a not uncommon incident in a small village on the Eastern Shore of Virginia. One night in 1849, the firing of guns "alarmed the people very much. They at once thought that the Slaves had risen to murder the white people. Many immediately left their houses and fled to the woods. . . . But it was afterwards ascertained that it was a false alarm." [6] This was indeed a "disagreeable state of living"!

The most acute and widespread insurrection panics, after the Turner rebellion, occurred in 1856 and 1860, each of them resulting in part from the rise of the Republican party and the exciting political campaigns. On both occasions alarming stories of huge conspiracies spread through every slave state, stories frequently mentioning "unscrupulous" white men (presumably abolitionist emissaries like

---

[4] Nevitt Plantation Journal, entry for October 28, 1831; Stephen Duncan to Thomas Butler, October 4, 1831, Butler Family Papers.

[5] William B. Lenoir to Thomas Lenoir, December 27, 1835, Lenoir Family Papers.

[6] J. Milton Emerson Ms. Journal, entry for September 29, 1849.

John Brown) who were "tampering" with the Negroes and encouraging them to rebel. "All at once, in Kentucky, Tennessee, Missouri, Arkansas, Louisiana and Texas, it is discovered that the slaves are meditating schemes of insurrection," proclaimed a Richmond newspaper in a hysterical editorial. "From almost every point in the Southwest, rumors of insurrectionary movements among the negroes come upon us with more or less distinct and authentic detail." In Virginia, as a slaveholder noted, "reports of negro plots" had "induced proper measures of vigilance." [7] A South Carolinian observed privately that there was "a good deal of anxiety," but little was being said about it, "as every one felt it should not be the subject of general talk." In Texas, one of the principal centers of these insurrection panics, vigilance committees were hastily formed to deal with the expected emergency. [8] On these occasions, as on others, there was some substance to the rumors, however much they were exaggerated. In 1856 slave unrest did increase noticeably in certain areas, including Texas where there was at least one well authenticated conspiracy. [9]

Sometimes rebellions took odd forms. The Seminole War in Florida was in part a slave revolt, for many fugitive Negroes fought alongside the Indian warriors. In 1841, a group of slaves being carried from Virginia to New Orleans on the brig *Creole* rose in rebellion, seized the ship, and sailed it to the Bermudas. In 1848, about seventy-five slaves from Fayette County, Kentucky, led by a white man, made a break for the Ohio River. They waged a brisk battle with

---

[7] Richmond *Enquirer*, December 16, 1856; Edmund Ruffin Ms. Diary, entry for December 25, 1856.

[8] Easterby (ed.), *South Carolina Rice Plantation*, p. 136; Austin *Texas State Gazette*, November 15, 22, 29, 1856; Harvey Wish, "The Slave Insurrection Panic of 1856," *Journal of Southern History*, V (1939), pp. 206–22.

[9] Aptheker, *American Negro Slave Revolts*, pp. 325–58; Wendell G. Addington, "Slave Insurrections in Texas," *Journal of Negro History*, XXXV (1950), pp. 408–35.

their pursuers before they were forced to surrender. More than forty of them were tried for "most wickedly, seditiously, and rebelliously" making a "public insurrection." Three of the slaves were executed, and their white leader was sentenced to twenty years in prison.[1]

One of the last ante-bellum slave conspiracies occurred in October, 1860, in the neighborhood of Plymouth, in eastern North Carolina. It began when a score of slaves met in a swamp to plan an insurrection. Their plan was to persuade several hundred bondsmen to join them in a march on Plymouth; they would kill all the whites they met on the road, burn the town, take money and weapons, and escape by ship through Albemarle Sound. The plot was betrayed by a slave, and once again panic spread throughout the neighborhood. "When I reached Plymouth," wrote a local planter, "the town was in the greatest of commotion, and, as even calm persons thought, with some reason." The country people were "so much excited and alarmed as to vow themselves as ready to slaughter the negroes indiscriminately." This planter believed that during an insurrection panic "the negroes are in much more danger from the non slave holding whites than the whites are from the negroes." [2] He was probably right, though the slaveholders were hardly less inclined, on that account, to be ruthless whenever rumors of rebellion swept through the land.

That there was no slave conspiracy comparable to Denmark Vesey's and no rebellion comparable to Nat Turner's, during the three decades before the Civil War, has been explained in many ways. The explanations, however, do not sufficiently emphasize the impact which the Turner rebellion had on the slaves themselves. The speed with which it

---

1 Porter, "Florida Slaves and Free Negroes in the Seminole War, 1835–1842," *loc. cit.*, pp. 420–21; Catterall (ed.), *Judicial Cases*, III, pp. 565–67; Coleman, *Slavery Times in Kentucky*, pp. 88–92.
2 William S. Pettigrew to James C. Johnston, October 25, 1860, Pettigrew Family Papers.

was crushed and the massacre that followed were facts soon known, doubtless, to every slave in Virginia and, before long, to almost every slave in the South. Among the Negroes everywhere, news generally spread so far and so fast as to amaze the whites. The Turner story was not likely to encourage slaves to make new attempts to win their freedom by fighting for it. They now realized that they would face a united white community, well armed and quite willing to annihilate as much of the black population as might seem necessary.

In truth, no slave uprising ever had a chance of ultimate success, even though it might have cost the master class heavy casualties. The great majority of the disarmed and outnumbered slaves, knowing the futility of rebellion, refused to join in any of the numerous plots. Most slaves had to express their desire for freedom in less dramatic ways. They rarely went beyond disorganized individual action—which, to be sure, caused their masters no little annoyance. The bondsmen themselves lacked the power to destroy the web of bondage. They would have to have the aid of free men inside or outside the South.

The survival of slavery, then, cannot be explained as due to the contentment of slaves or their failure to comprehend the advantages of freedom. They longed for liberty and resisted bondage as much as any people could have done in their circumstances, but their longing and their resistance were not enough even to render the institution unprofitable to most masters. The masters had power and, as will be seen, they developed an elaborate technique of slave control. Their very preoccupation with this technique was, in itself, a striking refutation of the myth that slavery survived because of the cheerful acquiescence of the slaves.

CHAPTER FOUR

To Make Them Stand in Fear

I t is a pity," a North Carolina planter wrote sadly, "that agreeable to the nature of things Slavery and Tyranny must go together and that there is no such thing as having an obedient and useful Slave, without the painful exercise of undue and tyrannical authority." The legislatures and courts of the ante-bellum South recognized this fact and regulated the relationship of master and slave accordingly. "The power of the master must be absolute, to render the submission of the slave perfect," a southern judge once affirmed.[1] Short of deliberately killing or maliciously maiming them, the owner did have almost absolute power over his chattels.

If a bondsman ran away, if he stole the goods, injured the property, or disobeyed the commands of the master, he was guilty of a private and not a public offense; and the state left the prevention and punishment of such offenses to the owner.[2] In governing his bondsmen, therefore, the master made the law, tried offenders, and administered penalties. Whether he exercised his despotic authority benevolently or malevolently depended upon his nature.

Masters were not all alike. Some governed their slaves

1 Charles Pettigrew to Ebenezer Pettigrew, May 19, 1802, Pettigrew Family Papers; Catterall (ed.), *Judicial Cases*, II, p. 57.
2 Catterall (ed.), *Judicial Cases*, I, p. 382; V, p. 249.

with great skill and induced them to submit with a minimum of force. Others, lacking the personal qualities needed to accomplish this, governed inefficiently. For example, an Alabama woman with an undisciplined temper found it nearly impossible to control her domestics. Two of them, Alex and Hampton, obeyed her commands only when they found it agreeable to do so; the rest of the time they treated her orders with "the utmost contempt." Hampton "has often laughed in my face and told me that I was the only mistress he ever failed to please, on my saying he should try another soon, he said he could not be worsted, and was willing to go." During a dinner with a friend this mistress was astonished to see how smoothly his household ran. His servants were perfectly trained: "you hear no noise, see·no confusion, . . . and their master has no need to point them to their duty. By what secret does he manage all this? The contrast with me is mortifying, truly." [3]

Slaves were not all alike either. They reacted to a particular master or overseer in different ways, some acquiescing in his authority and others rebelling against it. Some, because of their temperaments, found it impossible to get along with even a humane master. Ephraim, the property of a kind and pious small Virginia slaveholder, was in trouble so frequently that his master labeled him a "bad negro." After running away Ephraim was sold to a New Orleans slave trader; according to his owner, it was "his wish . . . to be sold." [4] Sometimes a restless slave became passive when transferred to another owner.

A master valued each slave not only on the basis of his physical condition and proficiency as a worker but also in terms of mutual compatibility. For this reason southern courts repeatedly ruled that it was impossible to give any

---

[3] Sarah A. Gayle Ms. Journal, entries for March 24, September 15, November 10, 1833.
[4] Walker Diary, entry for October 5, 1846.

slave an objective valuation. "One man will give or take fifty or one hundred dollars more or less in the purchase of one [bondsman] than another man will," declared a judge. Two prospective purchasers might come to opposite conclusions about the character of a slave: "A habit that would render him useless to one man, would scarcely be considered a blot upon his character in the hands of another." Indeed, the value of slaves depended "upon a thousand things"; it was in the "wretched market of the mere slave trader" that they were rated only "by pound avoirdupois."[5]

The successful master was often a keen student of human psychology. Those who discussed the problem of managing slaves advised owners to study carefully the character of each chattel. "As . . . some negroes are greater offenders than others, so does it require different management for differently disposed negroes. You should *not* 'treat them all alike.' " Too many masters did not understand this. Some bondsmen, warned a Virginian, required "spurring up, some coaxing, some flattery, and others nothing but good words." Many a valuable slave had been "broken down by injudicious management."[6]

It was within this framework of human relationships that the peculiar institution had to operate. To achieve the "perfect" submission of his slaves, to utilize their labor profitably, each master devised a set of rules by which he governed. These were the laws of his private domain—and the techniques which enabled him to minimize the bondsmen's resistance to servitude. The techniques of control were many and varied, some subtle, some ingenious, some brutal. Slaveholders generally relied upon more than one.

---

[5] Catterall (ed.), *Judicial Cases*, II, pp. 97, 318, 530.
[6] *Southern Cultivator*, XVIII (1860), p. 287; *Farmers' Register*, I (1834), pp. 564–65; IV (1836), p. 115.

2

A wise master did not take seriously the belief that Negroes were natural-born slaves. He knew better. He knew that Negroes freshly imported from Africa had to be broken in to bondage; that each succeeding generation had to be carefully trained. This was no easy task, for the bondsman rarely submitted willingly. Moreover, he rarely submitted completely. In most cases there was no end to the need for control—at least not until old age reduced the slave to a condition of helplessness.

Masters revealed the qualities they sought to develop in slaves when they singled out certain ones for special commendation. A small Mississippi planter mourned the death of his "faithful and dearly beloved servant" Jack: "Since I have owned him he has been true to me in all respects. He was an obedient trusty servant. . . . I never knew him to steal nor lie and he ever set a moral and industrious example to those around him. . . . I shall ever cherish his memory." A Louisiana sugar planter lost a "very valuable Boy" through an accident: "His life was a very great one. I have always found him willing and obedient and never knew him to fail to do anything he was put to do." [7] These were "ideal" slaves, the models slaveholders had in mind as they trained and governed their workers.

How might this ideal be approached? The first step, advised those who wrote discourses on the management of slaves, was to establish and maintain strict discipline. An Arkansas master suggested the adoption of the "Army Regulations as to the discipline in Forts." "They must obey at all times, and under all circumstances, cheerfully and with alacrity," affirmed a Virginia slaveholder. "It greatly

---

[7] Baker Diary, entry for July 1, 1854; Alexander Franklin Pugh Ms. Plantation Diary, entry for June 21, 1860.

impairs the happiness of a negro, to be allowed to cultivate an insubordinate temper. Unconditional submission is the only footing upon which slavery should be placed. It is precisely similar to the attitude of a minor to his parent, or a soldier to his general." A South Carolinian limned a perfect relationship between a slave and his master: "that the slave should know that his master is to govern absolutely, and he is to obey implicitly. That he is never for a moment to exercise either his will or judgment in opposition to a positive order." [8]

The second step was to implant in the bondsmen themselves a consciousness of personal inferiority. They had "to know and keep their places," to "feel the difference between master and slave," to understand that bondage was their natural status. They had to feel that African ancestry tainted them, that their color was a badge of degradation. In the country they were to show respect for even their master's nonslaveholding neighbors; in the towns they were to give way on the streets to the most wretched white man. The line between the races must never be crossed, for familiarity caused slaves to forget their lowly station and to become "impudent." [9]

Frederick Douglass explained that a slave might commit the offense of impudence in various ways: "in the tone of an answer; in answering at all; in not answering; in the expression of countenance; in the motion of the head; in the gait, manner and bearing of the slave." Any of these acts, in some subtle way, might indicate the absence of proper subordination. "In a well regulated community," wrote a Texan, "a negro takes off his hat in addressing a white

---

[8] *Southern Cultivator,* IV (1846), pp. 43–44; XVIII (1860), pp. 304–305; *Farmers' Register,* V (1837), p. 32.

[9] *Southern Planter,* XII (1852), pp. 376–79; *Southern Cultivator,* VIII (1850), p. 163; *Farmers' Register,* I (1834), pp. 564–65.

man. . . . Where this is not enforced, we may always look for impudent and rebellious negroes." [1]

The third step in the training of slaves was to awe them with a sense of their master's enormous power. The only principle upon which slavery could be maintained, reported a group of Charlestonians, was the "principle of fear." In his defense of slavery James H. Hammond admitted that this, unfortunately, was true but put the responsibility upon the abolitionists. Antislavery agitation had forced masters to strengthen their authority: "We have to rely more and more on the power of fear. . . . We are determined to continue masters, and to do so we have to draw the reign tighter and tighter day by day to be assured that we hold them in complete check." A North Carolina mistress, after subduing a troublesome domestic, realized that it was essential "to make them stand in fear"! [2]

In this the slaveholders had considerable success. Frederick Douglass believed that most slaves stood "in awe" of white men; few could free themselves altogether from the notion that their masters were "invested with a sort of sacredness." Olmsted saw a small white girl stop a slave on the road and boldly order him to return to his plantation. The slave fearfully obeyed her command. A visitor in Mississippi claimed that a master, armed only with a whip or cane, could throw himself among a score of bondsmen and cause them to "flee with terror." He accomplished this by the "peculiar tone of authority" with which he spoke. "Fear, awe, and obedience . . . are interwoven into the very nature of the slave." [3]

---

[1] Douglass, *My Bondage*, p. 92; Austin *Texas State Gazette*, October 10, 1857.
[2] Phillips (ed.), *Plantation and Frontier*, II, pp. 108–11; *De Bow's Review*, VII (1849), p. 498; Mary W. Bryan to Ebenezer Pettigrew, October 20, 1835, Pettigrew Family Papers.
[3] Douglass, *My Bondage*, pp. 250–51; Olmsted, *Back Country*, pp. 444–45; [Ingraham], *South-West*, II, pp. 260–61.

The fourth step was to persuade the bondsmen to take an interest in the master's enterprise and to accept his standards of good conduct. A South Carolina planter explained: "The master should make it his business to show his slaves, that the advancement of his individual interest, is at the same time an advancement of theirs. Once they feel this, it will require but little compulsion to make them act as it becomes them." [4] Though slaveholders induced only a few chattels to respond to this appeal, these few were useful examples for others.

The final step was to impress Negroes with their helplessness, to create in them "a habit of perfect dependence" upon their masters. [5] Many believed it dangerous to train slaves to be skilled artisans in the towns, because they tended to become self-reliant. Some thought it equally dangerous to hire them to factory owners. In the Richmond tobacco factories they were alarmingly independent and "insolent." A Virginian was dismayed to find that his bondsmen, while working at an iron furnace, "got a habit of roaming about and *taking care of themselves*." Permitting them to hire their own time produced even worse results. "No higher evidence can be furnished of its baneful effects," wrote a Charlestonian, "than the unwillingness it produces in the slave, to return to the regular life and domestic control of the master." [6]

A spirit of independence was less likely to develop among slaves kept on the land, where most of them became accustomed to having their master provide their basic needs, and where they might be taught that they were unfit to look out for themselves. Slaves then directed their energies to the attainment of mere "temporary ease and enjoy-

4 *Farmers' Register*, IV (1837), p. 574.
5 *Southern Cultivator*, IV (1846), p. 44.
6 *Southern Planter*, XII (1852), pp. 376–79; Olmsted, *Seaboard*, pp. 58–59; Charleston *Courier*, September 12, 1850.

ment." "Their masters," Olmsted believed, "calculated on it in them—do not wish to cure it—and by constant practice encourage it." [7]

Here, then, was the way to produce the perfect slave: accustom him to rigid discipline, demand from him unconditional submission, impress upon him his innate inferiority, develop in him a paralyzing fear of white men, train him to adopt the master's code of good behavior, and instill in him a sense of complete dependence. This, at least, was the goal.

But the goal was seldom reached. Every master knew that the average slave was only an imperfect copy of the model. He knew that some bondsmen yielded only to superior power—and yielded reluctantly. This complicated his problem of control.

3

"Never be induced by a course of good behavior on the part of the negroes, to relax the strictness of your discipline. . . . The only way to keep a negro honest is not to trust him. This seems a harsh assertion; but it is unfortunately, too true." So wrote a Southerner who was giving advice to overseers. To a former slave it sometimes appeared that masters, "with skilled and practiced eyes," probed into the chattel's mind and heart to detect his changing moods. A slave, Olmsted observed, "is trusted as little as possible to use his own discretion, and it is taken for granted that he will never do anything desired of him that he dares avoid." [8]

Because most Negroes were imperfect slaves, because they needed to be watched constantly, each master devised

---

[7] Olmsted, *Seaboard*, pp. 128–29.
[8] Printed instructions in Affleck, *Cotton Plantation Record and Account Book*; Douglass, *My Bondage*, pp. 276–77; Olmsted, *Seaboard*, pp. 478–79.

a set of rules for the efficient day-by-day operation of his enterprise. Slaveholders were not always in accord about the value of specific rules, but there were large areas of agreement nevertheless. They recorded the rules they considered most important in their private journals, in their instructions to overseers, and in essays published in agricultural periodicals. Here are the ones they generally accepted:

1. An overseer was not to be absent from the estate without his employer's consent. He was to stay constantly in the fields while the hands were at work, to search the cabins periodically for weapons or stolen goods, and to guard the keys to the corn crib, smoke house, and stable. If there were no overseer, the master (even on small establishments) assumed responsibility for these police measures.

2. A slave was not to be out of his cabin after "hornblow," usually at eight o'clock in winter and nine o'clock in summer. The master or overseer was to tour the cabins at night to see that none were missing. Some masters established a system of regular night watches.

3. A slave was not to leave the estate without a pass which gave his destination and the time he was to return. Some owners issued passes generously when slaves were not at work; others issued them sparingly. Many agreed that bondsmen should not visit neighboring estates, or associate with "mean white men" who might be disposed to make them dissatisfied. By keeping them at home "they do not know what is going on beyond the limits of the plantation, and feel satisfied that they could not . . . accomplish anything that would change their condition." Strangers, white and black, were to be "run off" the plantations.[9]

4. Free Negroes or whites were not to work with slaves. One planter, for example, discharged a white mechanic for

---

[9] *Southern Cultivator*, XVIII (1860), p. 305; St. John R. Liddell Ms. Diary, entry for October 18, 1841.

"talking with the negroes." Another believed that the
value of a slave was "always impaired by contact with
white labor," because the whites worked less, received
"more consideration," and enjoyed "higher privileges." [1]
Whites who associated with slaves became objects of suspicion. According to a Texan, "no white men will ever be
found on familiar terms with negroes, who are not either
of an abandoned or worthless character or are abolitionists." [2]

5. Slaves were not to marry free Negroes, though some
were permitted to marry slaves living on other estates.
Often they were required to select their spouses only among
the master's own chattels. Men who married away from
home were frequently absent and thus exposed "to temptations from meeting and associating with negroes . . . with
various habits and views." Women with husbands abroad
brought to the home estate slaves accustomed to different
treatment and thus created a rendezvous for a "medley of
characters." It was better for a master to buy husbands or
wives for his bondsmen when necessary. Otherwise, "if
they cannot be suited at home," it should be a settled principle that "they must live single." [3]

6. A slave was not to sell anything without a permit, have
whiskey in his cabin, quarrel or fight, or use abusive language.

These rules were to be enforced consistently, and no violations were to pass unnoticed. Master and overseer must
make it clear that they were in perfect agreement, for
slaves soon discovered "any little jarring" between them
and were "sure to take advantage of it." Moreover, each
neighborhood of slaveholders needed to be harmonious;

[1] *Southern Planter*, XIII (1853), p. 23.
[2] Austin *Texas State Gazette*, June 16, 1855; J. Benwell, *An Englishman's Travels in America* (London, n.d.), pp. 165–66.
[3] *Southern Cultivator*, IV (1846), p. 44; VIII (1850), p. 164.

when all enforced similar rules and maintained effective discipline, the government of slaves was easier. "A good disciplinarian in the midst of bad managers . . . cannot do much." [4]

Some also believed it undesirable to have groups of lower-class whites living shiftlessly on the fringes of plantations where they could corrupt the slaves. Planters sometimes bought the lands of their poor neighbors to get them out of the way.[5] Thus the plantation often became a kind of isolated, autonomous enclave.

The slaveholder needed the willing cooperation of some of his bondsmen to make his government work efficiently. Knowing that the majority could not be trusted, he tried to recruit a few who would be loyal to him and take his side against the others. Usually he found his allies among the domestics, skilled artisans, and foremen, all of whom he encouraged to feel superior to, and remain apart from, the field-hands. He gave them better clothes, more food, and special privileges as long as they remained true to his interests. He withdrew these favors and demoted them to field labor when they failed him.

"The head driver . . . is to be treated with more respect than any other negro," wrote James H. Hammond in his plantation manual. A South Carolina overseer always required his driver to dress better than the other slaves. "This caused him to maintain a pride of character before them that was highly beneficial. . . . The more the driver is kept aloof from the negroes, the better." [6]

In this manner some planters gained the assistance of chattels who identified themselves wholly with the master class. Jefferson Davis found such a bondsman in James

---

[4] *Farmers' Register*, I (1834), pp. 564–65.

[5] Olmsted, *Seaboard*, pp. 673–74.

[6] James H. Hammond Ms. Plantation Manual, Hammond Papers, Library of Congress; *Farmers' Register*, IV (1836), p. 115.

Pemberton, who was first his body-servant and then his able plantation manager. Fanny Kemble reported that the head driver on Pierce Butler's Georgia plantation was reserved in his relations with other slaves, and completely faithful in handling his master's business.[7]

William S. Pettigrew, a Tyrrell County, North Carolina, planter, rejoiced that he owned two excellent slave foremen who were "subservient, without a murmur," to his will. "What a blessing it is to have two such men . . . whose chief desire I think is to relieve me of as much burden as possible; . . . also to add to their own character as men of honesty, industry, faithfulness and success." In the summer Pettigrew was able to leave his estate in their charge (under the nominal direction of a white man) while he vacationed at the Virginia springs. In his letters Pettigrew warned the foremen that any disorder during his absence would disgrace them. "I am anxious for your credit as well as my own ...hat all things should go on well, and it would be distressing and mortifying to me to hear the contrary on my return." One of the foremen replied (through an amanuensis) : "I have don[e] all . . . in my power towa[r]ds your benefit. . . . our respects to master wanting to see you very bad." [8]

Some domestics also became "white folk's servants"— i.e., devoted to the master and his family and alienated from the other slaves. "They are just the same as white men," said a former slave in disgust. "Some of them will betray another to curry favor with the master." In this way, observed a visitor in Virginia, the master destroyed "the

---

[7] Walter L. Fleming, "Jefferson Davis, The Negroes and the Negro Problem," *Sewanee Review*, XVI (1908) , pp. 408–409; Kemble, *Journal*, pp. 43–45.

[8] William S. Pettigrew to James C. Johnston, December 31, 1845; May 11, 1856, Pettigrew Family Papers. Correspondence between Pettigrew and his foremen during the summers of 1856–58 is in this collection.

sympathy that unites . . . the victims of the same oppression. . . . He has but to arm the human passions against each other." [9]

The recruitment of a slave elite was related in part to the runaway problem, for some of these favored slaves helped to catch the fugitives. But there were other groups whose assistance was even more valuable. Legally all white men were authorized to seize runaways; some of them, tempted by the rewards masters were willing to pay, made a profession of it. Poor white men habitually kept their eyes open for strange Negroes without passes, for the apprehension of a fugitive was a financial windfall. Few southern white laborers showed much sympathy for the runaway slave. For example, white workingmen on the Baltimore and Susquehanna Railroad caught several Maryland bondsmen who had escaped to within five miles of the Pennsylvania border. The workingmen returned them to their owners and collected the rewards.[1]

Nor was a runaway necessarily beyond his master's grasp if he managed to reach a free state. The Federal fugitive-slave law still enabled his master to claim him if he could be found. In the North, too, the runaway had to be wary of professional slave catchers—of men such as F. H. Pettis, a lawyer in New York City. Pettis advertised in the southern newspapers that he had much experience "in causing fugitive slaves to be secured . . . in defiance of the Abolitionists." Masters who desired his services were to forward him power of attorney, a description of the runaway, "and also a fee of $20." "When the slave shall have been secured and handed over to the master, $100 additional charge will be made." [2]

[9] Drew, *The Refugee*, p. 211; Abdy, *Journal*, II, pp. 215–16.
[1] Baltimore *Sun*, July 1, 1850.
[2] Charleston *Courier*, June 9, 1840.

Not only the slave's fear of capture but his limited knowledge of geography made the prospect of successful escape seem discouragingly dim. Frederick Douglass gave a graphic description of the fears he and several other slaves shared when they planned to escape. They were afraid that their owner would discover the plot, that he would discern their thoughts from their behavior. Often they wondered whether bondage might not be easier than the "doubts, fears and uncertainties" which now perplexed them. "The case, sometimes, to our excited visions, stood thus: At every gate through which we had to pass, we saw a watchman; at every ferry, a guard; on every bridge, a sentinel; and in every wood, a patrol or slave-hunter. . . . No man can tell the intense agony which is felt by the slave, when wavering on the point of making his escape." [3]

Slaves in the Upper South knew that the probable penalty for an unsuccessful attempt at escape was to be sold to the Deep South. They knew that slaveholders in the border states seldom gambled with bondsmen who showed any inclination to seek freedom through flight. In fact, runaways were often sold to speculators at a reduced price even before they were recaptured. As they were driven southward, freedom slipped from their grasp forever.

The mere threat of sale was an effective method of discouraging potential runaways. Many slaves believed that bondage in some distant state would be infinitely worse than the bondage they knew, because their masters painted terrifying pictures of what was in store for those who were sold. Virginia slaves heard of the horrors of the Georgia rice swamps, while Georgia slaves trembled at the thought of being shipped to the Louisiana sugar district. A trouble-maker belonging to a Georgia planter was warned that "if he don't change for the better I'll sell him to a slave trader who will send him to New Orleans, where I have already

---

[3] Douglass, *My Bondage*, pp. 273-98.

sent several of the gang for their misconduct, or their running away for no cause." [4]

According to the South Carolina Court of Appeals: "The owners of slaves frequently send them off from amongst their kindred and associates as a punishment, and it is frequently resorted to, as the means of separating a vicious negro from amongst others exposed to be influenced and corrupted by his example." [5] When no method of discipline worked, this was the master's last resort. An Alabama planter sold two chattels and invested the proceeds "in like property," for he was determined "not to keep a mean negro." A North Carolina planter disposed of a "malignant enemy" in the heart of his establishment who was "poisoning the minds of all around him" and "disturbing the quiet" of the estate.[6] Those who had a surplus of slaves for sale naturally marketed the ones they found most difficult to control.

If the new master had no greater success than the old, he might put the ungovernable bondsman up for sale again. In this manner slaveholders passed a considerable number of the incorrigibles from hand to hand. Six different owners, for example, found an "old scoundrel," who had been sent from South Carolina to Mississippi, more than they could handle; in 1848, his most recent master advertised that he was a runaway.[7] Because slaveholders had to manage less-than-perfect slaves, they found that their government never worked perfectly.

---

4 Phillips, *American Negro Slavery*, pp. 304–305; *id., Plantation and Frontier*, II, pp. 31–32.
5 Catterall (ed.), *Judicial Cases*, II, p. 352.
6 James H. Taylor to Franklin H. Elmore, March 24, 1836, Franklin H. Elmore Papers; William S. Pettigrew to John Williams, November 4, 1852; *id.* to [James C. Johnston], January 27, 1853, Pettigrew Family Papers.
7 Vicksburg *Weekly Sentinel*, August 9, 1848.

4

"I greatly desire that the Gospel be preached to the Negroes when the services of a suitable person can be procured," wrote a Mississippian to his overseer. Religious instruction "not only benefits the slave in his moral relations, but enhances his value as an honest, faithful servant and laborer," affirmed an Alabama judge.[8] Pious masters regarded their bondsmen as human beings with immortal souls and therefore felt an obligation to look after their spiritual life. Many of them also considered Christian indoctrination an effective method of keeping slaves docile and contented.

When the first Africans were imported in the seventeenth century, some purchasers opposed converting them to Christianity lest baptism give them a claim to freedom. After the colonial legislatures provided that conversion would not have this effect, the opposition diminished. Thereafter most masters encouraged Christian proselytizing among their bondsmen, and conversion proceeded rapidly.

A minority, however, continued to be indifferent. Even in the nineteenth century a southern clergyman complained that some, "forgetful of God and eternity," treated their slaves "too much as creatures of profit." In "extensive districts" thousands of bondsmen never heard the voices of those who brought "the glad tidings of salvation to perishing men." Another clergyman was "astonished to find planters of high moral pretensions" who kept their slaves "shut out almost entirely from the privileges of the Gospel." [9]

---

[8] Phillips (ed.) , *Plantation and Frontier*, I, pp. 112–15; Catterall (ed.) , *Judicial Cases*, III, p. 238.

[9] Charles Colcock Jones, *Suggestions on the Religious Instruction of the Negroes in the Southern States* (Philadelphia, 1847) , pp. 7–9, 31; *Southern Cultivator*, IX (1851) , pp. 84–85.

A few were openly hostile. "Be assured," wrote a North Carolinian, "that religion among the mass of negroes who profess, is nothing more than a humbug." He did not believe "in the efficacy of preaching to negroes and would never contribute a cent for that purpose." A Louisianian considered attempts to convert slaves the "greatest piece of foolishness"; the only way to improve them, he thought, was through "proper discipline." Olmsted met other slaveholders who shared these views. A Mississippian told him that religious exercises excited the slaves so much that it was difficult to control them. "They would be singing and dancing every night in their cabins, till dawn of day, and utterly unfit themselves for work." [1]

Since Nat Turner had been a slave preacher, the Southampton insurrection temporarily increased sentiment of this kind. Its lasting effect was to convince the master class that the religious life of the slaves needed rigid supervision. In December, 1831, James H. Hammond resolved "to break up negro preaching and negro Churches." Many years later another South Carolinian was still warning slaveholders, "Do not, I beseech you, send off your negroes to worship . . . by themselves. I have known great mischief to have grown out of such meetings." [2]

The early attitude of certain Protestant sects toward slavery also accounted for some of the surviving suspicion. In the eighteenth century and early nineteenth century, southern Baptists and Methodists exhibited considerable anti-slavery sentiment. Many slaveholders were therefore reluctant to have the preachers and missionaries of these

---

[1] Ebenezer Pettigrew to James C. Johnston, July 16, 1838, Pettigrew Family Papers; Davis (ed.), *Diary of Bennet H. Barrow*, pp. 323–24; Olmsted, *Back Country*, pp. 92–93, 107–108.

[2] Hammond Diary, entries for December 15, 16, 1831; *De Bow's Review*, XXIV (1858), p. 64; Luther P. Jackson, "Religious Development of the Negro in Virginia from 1760 to 1860," *Journal of Negro History*, XVI (1931), p. 206.

denominations work among their slaves. But when the southern wings of these churches changed their positions, when southern clergymen became ardent defenders of slavery, the master class could look upon organized religion as an ally. Church leaders now argued "that the gospel, instead of becoming a means of creating trouble and strife, was really the best instrument to preserve peace and good conduct among the negroes." This was a persuasive argument. "In point of fact," recalled one churchman, "it was this conviction that ultimately opened the way for the gospel on the large plantations." [3]

Through religious instruction the bondsmen learned that slavery had divine sanction, that insolence was as much an offense against God as against the temporal master. They received the Biblical command that servants should obey their masters, and they heard of the punishments awaiting the disobedient slave in the hereafter. They heard, too, that eternal salvation would be their reward for faithful service, and that on the day of judgment "God would deal impartially with the poor and the rich, the black man and the white." Their Christian preceptors, Fanny Kemble noted, "jump[ed] the present life" and went on "to furnish them with all the requisite conveniences for the next." [4]

Numerous slaveholders agreed that this indoctrination had a felicitous effect. A committee of a South Carolina agricultural society reported that religion contributed much to "the government and discipline of the slave population." A traveler in Mississippi met a planter who was himself "a most decided infidel" but who nevertheless saw "the advantage of giving religious instruction to slaves." Many claimed that imparting Christian doctrine to impressionable slave children was especially beneficial. It taught

---

[3] Harrison, *Gospel Among the Slaves*, pp. 149–51.
[4] Sir Charles Lyell, *A Second Visit to North America* (London, 1849), II, pp. 2–3; Kemble, *Journal*, p. 57.

them "respect and obedience to their superiors," made them "more pleasant and profitable servants," and aided "the discipline of a plantation in a wonderful manner." [5]

Others noticed a decline in theft when bondsmen "got religion." A Methodist missionary related a slave's confession that the Gospel "had saved more rice for massa than all the locks and keys on the plantation." Moreover, religious services on Sundays kept idle slaves at home and out of mischief. Indeed, one planter even used a Methodist exhorter as an overseer, with gratifying success; another, hearing of it, tried to get one too. [6]

In 1845, a group of distinguished South Carolina slaveholders published a pamphlet illustrating "the practical working and wholesome effects of religious instruction, when properly and judiciously imparted to our negro peasantry." Each plantation, they believed, ought to become a "religious or parochial family," for religion could play a major role in the perpetuation of slavery. "Precepts that inculcated good-will, forbearance and forgiveness; that enjoin meekness and patience under evils; that demand truth and faithfulness under all circumstances; a teaching that sets before men a righteous judgment, and happiness or misery in the life to come, according to our course of faith and practice in the life that now is, must . . . change the general character of persons thus taught." [7]

The master class understood, of course, that only a carefully censored version of Christianity could have this desired effect. Inappropriate Biblical passages had to be deleted; sermons that might be proper for freemen were not

[5] *De Bow's Review*, VII (1849), p. 221; XXVI (1859), p. 107; *Southern Agriculturist*, IV (1831), pp. 351–52; Jones, *Suggestions on the Religious Instruction of the Negroes*, pp. 34–35.
[6] Harrison, *Gospel Among the Slaves*, pp. 205, 210–11; *Farmers' Register*, IV (1837), p. 574; Henry, *Police Control*, p. 139.
[7] Quoted in Charleston *Courier*, August 28, 1845.

necessarily proper for slaves. Church leaders addressed themselves to this problem and prepared special catechisms and sermons for bondsmen, and special instructions for those concerned with their religious indoctrination. In 1847, for example, Charles Colcock Jones, of Georgia, wrote a book entitled *Suggestions on the Religious Instruction of the Negroes in the Southern States*, which was published by the Presbyterian Board of Publications. From his own experience Jones advised missionaries to ignore the "civil condition" of the slaves and to listen to no complaints against masters or overseers. In preaching to the bondsmen missionaries should condemn "every vice and evil custom," advocate the "discharge of every duty," and support the "peace and order of society." They should teach the slaves to give "respect and obedience [to] all those whom God in his providence has placed in authority over them." Religion, in short, should underwrite the status quo.

Owners had various methods of providing religious training. Most of them believed it "pernicious and evil" for slaves to preach at their own services or prayer meetings.[8] Nevertheless, some permitted it. The master or overseer usually attended such meetings, as required by law—and the preacher, naturally, was a trusted slave. In a number of southern towns the bondsmen attended their own churches. Richmond had four African Baptist Churches before 1860, each controlled by a governing board of whites and served by a white pastor. In Savannah, Andrew Marshall, a free Negro, was the minister of the First African Baptist Church. Until his death in 1856, Marshall was "greatly respected" by the whites and the "idol" of his slave congregation.[9]

---

[8] *De Bow's Review*, XXVI (1859), p. 107.
[9] Jackson, "Religious Development . . . ," *loc. cit.*, pp. 221–22; Savannah *Republican*, December 15, 1856.

In the regions of small slaveholdings whites and blacks commonly belonged to the same churches; on the large plantations only the domestics accompanied their masters to worship. When there were mixed congregations the slaves sat in the galleries, or were grouped together at the rear. Sometimes they attended special services on Sunday afternoon. Whatever the arrangements, whites admitted Negro members to their churches everywhere in the antebellum South.

The white-controlled churches made an important contribution to the governing of their slave communicants. They disciplined or "excluded from fellowship" bondsmen guilty of such offenses as "disorder," thievery, "selling spirits on the Lord's day at meeting," "unchristian conduct," and "immorality." For instance, the slave Peter, a member of a Presbyterian church in Iredell County, North Carolina, confessed that he had forged a pass. Because forgery and falsehood were such "flagrant crimes," he was suspended from membership and "exhorted to repentence and [a] better life." A year later, Peter applied for the restoration of his church privileges, "professing a deep penitence for his sins, and a strong determination to lead hereafter a life of greater watchfulness and more prayer." Peter was forgiven.[1]

Large slaveholders occasionally built churches on their estates and hired clergymen to preach to their bondsmen each Sunday. The proprietor of a Mississippi plantation maintained a "beautiful little Gothic church" where a resident pastor administered to the spiritual needs of both master and slaves. Other planters, depending upon missionaries who visited their estates periodically, made no provision for regular religious services. Their slaves apparently had mixed feelings about the occasional visitations of the

---

white preachers. One divine noted sadly that some of them made it "a settled point to sleep during sermons." [2]

The best system, many agreed, was one in which the master himself assumed responsibility for the religious life of his slaves. Gathering his "people" around him on the Sabbath, he preached to them from one of the handbooks or read to them from the Scriptures. The advantage of this system, according to a South Carolina planter, was that it created "a feeling of interest between the master and the slave." It produced "that happy state of protection on the one part, and obedience on the other." [3]

Whatever form the bondsmen's religious training took, it appeared that piety increased their value. A former slave remembered hearing a Missouri auctioneer expounding the virtues of a female domestic who was up for sale. She was a good cook and an obedient servant. Moreover, "She has got religion!" Why should this have mattered? Because "the religious teaching consists in teaching the slave that he must never strike a white man; that God made him for a slave; and that, when whipped, he must not find fault,—for the Bible says, 'He that knoweth his master's will and doeth it not, shall be beaten with many stripes!' And slaveholders find such religion very profitable to them." [4]

5

One of the inherent tragedies of slavery was that a humane master's impulse to be kind to his slaves was severely circumscribed by the inescapable problem of control. He

[2] *De Bow's Review*, VII (1849), p. 221; *Southern Cultivator*, IX (1851), p. 85.
[3] Northup, *Twelve Years a Slave*, pp. 97–98; Charleston *Courier*, April 15, 1851.
[4] Brown, *Narrative*, pp. 83–84.

could indulge only the most obsequious of them, and only within the bounds of essential discipline. He knew, too, that some of his bondsmen would show precious little gratitude for his benevolence.

Moreover, a conscientious slaveholder might be disturbed by the thought that his humanitarianism could be interpreted as merely a form of enlightened self-interest. For some did suggest that a policy of kindness was a practical method of binding a certain type of slave to his owner. Though many paternalistic masters had no conscious ulterior motive for their liberality, others were clearly seeking a way to induce their workers to be more productive.

"Now, I contend that the surest and best method of managing negroes, is to love them," wrote a Georgia patriarch. "We know . . . that if we love our horse, we will treat him well, and if we treat him well he will become gentle, docile and obedient; . . . and if this treatment has this effect upon all the animal creation . . . why will it not have the same effect upon slaves?" Many of them, he added, responded to praise more readily than to punishment. A few kind words, a little flattery, would sometimes go a long way. Negroes, like children, instinctively loved a kind master who ministered generously to their wants.[5]

An Alabama planter assured slaveholders that the Negro had "self-respect" and was capable of "moral elevation." Much could be gained by "exciting his pride," by cultivating in him a desire to have a reputation for honesty and fidelity. By winning his bondsman's love the master solved the problem of control. Such a slave "is more *contented* and *profitable* . . . [and] will bring more money when offered for sale; will make as many bales of cotton with less trouble to the owner; will steal fewer chickens and drink

---

[5] *Southern Cultivator*, XVIII (1860), p. 326; *De Bow's Review*, XI (1851), p. 67; XXI (1856), p. 279; *Farmers' Register*, I (1834), pp. 564–65.

less whiskey without watching than the one whose spirit is crushed and whose self-respect is trampled upon." [6]

Some masters—often the ones with modest holdings—pursued a policy of kindness as far as possible. Olmsted frequently heard slaves singing or whistling as they worked on southern farms. A Mississippi farmer explained his method thus: "If I ever notice one of 'em getting a little slack, I just talk to him; tell him we must get out of the grass, . . . and then, maybe, I slip a dollar into his hand, and when he gits into the field he'll go ahead, and the rest seeing him, won't let themselves be distanced by him." [7]

The dollar may have been as important as the kind words. Some slaveholders apparently thought so; even though they had the power to coerce their workers to toil without compensation, they saw the wisdom of providing incentives for faithful service. "Hope, that great prompter to cheerful action," had to be cultivated in the slaves, one master contended. "In order to beget in mine this essential principle, the hope of reward is constantly held out as an inducement." [8]

The rewards and incentives took numerous forms. Giving slaves a small plot of ground in which to cultivate their own crops during spare hours was one of the most popular. If this was not simply a means of forcing them to grow part of their essential food, as it sometimes was, it was an effective incentive. Bondsmen were thus able to add to the minimum diet provided them and to exchange the surplus for luxuries such as tobacco, sugar, coffee, and bits of finery.

Each slave might cultivate his plot independently, or all of them might cultivate a larger plot collectively and divide the harvest. Either way, their usual crops were vegetables and corn—seldom cotton or tobacco lest they be

---

[6] *Southern Cultivator*, XVIII (1860), p. 176–77.
[7] Olmsted, *Back Country*, pp. 155–56, 220.
[8] *American Cotton Planter and Soil of the South*, I (1857), pp. 374–75.

tempted to augment their yield by theft from the master. In addition, they were frequently permitted to raise chickens, occasionally swine, and in a few instances a cow. They also made baskets, cut puncheons, caught fish, or gathered Spanish moss. They sold all of these commodities along with the surplus from their "patches." In this manner many slaves earned a few dollars a year.

Some masters permitted them to sell their goods in town, while others bought for their own use whatever their bondsmen produced. A large Mississippi planter once paid his slaves two hundred dollars for their hay crop; and a South Carolinian obtained his pork in this way.[9] These masters acted as bankers for their bondsmen and kept careful accounts in their plantation records. They debited the slaves for items purchased for them during the year and made a cash settlement at the end of the year.

Olmsted described the agreement a South Carolina planter made with his hands: "He has a rule to purchase everything they desire to sell. . . . Eggs constitute a circulating medium on the plantation. The negroes do not commonly take money for the articles he has of them, but the value of them is put to their credit, and regular accounts kept with them. He has a store, usually well supplied with articles that they most want. . . . His slaves are sometimes his creditors to large amounts; at the present time he says he owes them about five hundred dollars." [1]

Many believed that this form of incentive was beneficial, even indispensable. Since the money settlements did not come until after the crops were harvested, deductions could be made for misbehavior. "This I have found to be a powerful lever in my hands to enforce obedience and fidelity," reported a Virginian. "No Negro with a well stocked poul-

---

9 Jenkins Diary, entry for January 1, 1852; Easterby (ed.), *South Carolina Rice Plantation*, p. 350.
1 Olmsted, *Seaboard*, pp. 442–43.

try house, a small crop advancing, a canoe partly finished, or a few tubs unsold, all of which he calculate[d] soon to enjoy," would run away, insisted a Georgia overseer.[2]

A minority, however, thought it unwise to permit slaves to raise and sell produce. They complained that bondsmen cultivated their own crops at night and on Sunday instead of getting needed rest, fell into the habit of trading, and were tempted to mix some of their master's goods with their own. Critics also argued that when slaves *earned* money they became "vain and arrogant" and felt "more independent." It was better to make them work full time for their masters who might *give* money rewards to those who served faithfully. Accordingly, a Mississippi planter, instead of permitting them to have a "truck patch," presented five dollars to each head of a family and each unmarried adult on Christmas.[3]

Distributing gifts at the end of the year was a common practice. At Christmas time one rice planter gave each adult a bonus of twelve quarts of rough rice, one quart of molasses, two pipes, and three "hands" of tobacco. A Mississippian purchased nearly ten dollars' worth of molasses, coffee, tobacco, calico, and "Sunday tricks" for each of his bondsmen. Most slaveholders gave them articles of clothing, usually handkerchiefs for the women and hats for the men.[4] The value and quantity of the presents often depended upon their conduct during the past year.

Another form of incentive was to compensate slaves for work performed beyond what was normally expected of

2 *American Farmer*, VII (1852), p. 397; *Southern Agriculturist*, I (1828), p. 525.
3 *De Bow's Review*, X (1851), p. 624; XVII (1854), p. 424; XIX (1855), p. 362; *American Cotton Planter and Soil of the South*, II (1858), pp. 20–21.
4 John B. Milliken Ms. Plantation Journal, entry for December 26, 1853; James A. Gillespie Ms. Diary, entry for December 24, 1854; Olmsted, *Back Country*, pp. 50–51.

them, for example, for night and Sunday work. A small Louisiana cotton farmer noted in his diary one Sunday: "To day I gave the hands leave to go into the cotton field to pick on wages." Besides "keeping them out of mischief," this gave them a chance "to earn something for themselves." [5] Those who owned or hired skilled artisans frequently paid them for their labor above a specified minimum; factory owners paid their hands for overtime. In the tobacco factories many bondsmen earned several dollars a month, and in Richmond's Tredegar Iron Works a few earned as much as ten dollars a month.

Cotton growers were resourceful in devising inducements for diligent toil at picking time. Some divided their pickers into competing teams; others promoted competition between individuals. Thomas Dabney, of Mississippi, gave a prize of a dollar to the best picker each week and smaller amounts to all who had worked well. An Alabama planter incited two gangs of pickers to race for a prize of two and a half pounds of tobacco. [6]

A few masters stimulated their laborers by making profit sharing agreements with them. A sugar planter gave his slaves a dollar for each hogshead of sugar they produced. An Alabamian at various times permitted his slaves to share in the profits of the cotton, peanut, and pea crops. Another Alabamian developed a system of share-cropping. He gave his slaves two-thirds of the cotton and corn crops and kept the other third himself. He instructed them to appropriate the proceeds from their share in the following manner: "You are then to pay your overseer his part and pay me [for] what I furnish, clothe yourselves, pay your own taxes and doctor's fee with all expenses of the farm. . . . You have the use of the stock and plantation tools. You are to return them as good as they are and the

[5] Marston Diary, entry for October 20, 1822.
[6] Smedes, *Memorials*, pp. 68–70; Jordan, *Hugh Davis*, p. 105.

167

plantation to be kept in good repair, and what clear money you make shall be divided equally amongst you in a fair proportion agreeable to the services rendered by each hand." [7] These, however, were rare procedures.

The promise of periodic relief from the labor routine was still another form of incentive. Those who used the task system dangled the privilege of leaving the fields early before bondsmen who worked with speed and care. Almost all masters gave them Sunday for rest and relaxation. Many thought it wise to give half of Saturday, and occasionally the whole day, at least to those who had been working well. One slaveholder let his bondsmen know that, to be excused from the fields at noon on Saturday, they had to behave themselves all week. "It is a very great stimulus to labor, and I really believe more work will be done by hands treated in this way than by those who know that to them, work as they may, they never stop." [8]

During these respites some slaveholders, especially the smaller ones, gave their workers passes to visit a nearby town or to visit friends or relatives in the neighborhood. They occasionally permitted the bondsmen to have a dance on Saturday night. "I have a good fiddler, and keep him well supplied with catgut, and I make it his duty to play for the negroes every Saturday night until 12 o'clock," wrote a Mississippi planter. A North Carolina court once rebuked a slave patrol for trying to stop one of these boisterous affairs. "We may let them make the most of their idle hours," said the court, "and may well make allowances for the noisy outpourings of glad hearts, which providence bestows as a blessing on corporeal vigor united to a vacant mind." [9]

---

[7] Olmsted, *Seaboard*, p. 660; Jordan, *Hugh Davis*, pp. 104–105; Sellers, *Slavery in Alabama*, p. 59.

[8] *Southern Cultivator*, IX (1851), p. 85.

[9] *De Bow's Review*, X (1851), p. 625; Catterall (ed.), *Judicial Cases*, II, pp. 139–41.

IV: *To Make Them Stand in Fear*

Nearly every master observed a number of special holidays, the most common being Good Friday, Independence Day, "laying-by time," and Christmas. These were occasions not only for the granting of passes but also for feasting. After the crops were laid by, a Mississippian "Called off the hands . . . to take holiday for the balance of the week. . . . Gave the negroes a dinner; and they did eat, and were filled. They demolished a beef, two shoats and two lam[b]s. . . . Sent down for Courtney's colored band to play for my negroes to dance tonight, which pleases them greatly." [1] Similar banquets and celebrations occurred at corn shuckings and at weddings.

Christmas was the festival that bondsmen looked forward to most, for they enjoyed a general relaxation of discipline along with the gifts and feasts and the holiday from labor. Even the severest masters gave their slaves Christmas Day to celebrate; most gave them one or two additional days; and some gave them a whole week of vacation between Christmas and New Year's Day. "At Christmas a holyday of three or four days is given," James H. Hammond wrote in his plantation manual. "On that day . . . a barbecue is given, beef or mutton and pork, coffee and bread being bountifully provided." [2]

Some went to considerable expense and took great pains to make the Christmas holiday pleasant. "I have endeavored . . . to make my Negroes joyous and happy,—and am glad to see them enjoying themselves with such a contented hearty good will," exulted a small Mississippi slaveholder. Another Mississippian "Spent the day waiting on the negroes, and making them as comfortable as possible." A Tennesseean noted with satisfaction that his "people" were "as happy as Lords." Though most masters made it a policy to keep liquor away from their bondsmen, save for

---

[1] Newstead Plantation Diary, entries for August 20, 21, 1858.
[2] Plantation Manual in Hammond Papers.

medicinal purposes, they often made an exception of Christmas. At the end of the holiday one slaveholder observed that his chattels were "all drunk or asleep." [3]

Now and then a Southerner deplored the widespread practice of permitting slaves to have so much freedom at Christmas, especially the practice of giving them passes to wander about. No man of common sense, wrote one nervous critic, believed that this "idle, lounging, roving, drunken, and otherwise mischievous [Christmas] week fits the Negro in the least degree for the discharge of his duties." [4]

This was a narrow view of the matter. A former slave thought that the occasional festivities and holidays were an essential part of the master's system of control. They kept the minds of the bondsmen "occupied with prospective pleasures within the limits of slavery. . . . These holidays are conductors or safety valves to carry off the explosive elements inseparable from the human mind, when reduced to the condition of slavery." [5]

In general, the master class agreed. An Alabamian urged others to adopt his policy of giving the slaves occasional dances, dinners, holidays, and other harmless indulgences. It contributed to their happiness and caused them to become attached to their master, he claimed. "Some will say that this plan will not do to make money, but I know of no man who realizes more to the hand than I." [6]

---

[3] Baker Diary, entry for December 25, 1852; Newstead Plantation Diary, entry for December 25, 1858; John Houston Bills Ms. Diary, entry for December 30, 1843; Nevitt Plantation Journal, entry for December 30, 1827.

[4] Tallahassee *Floridian and Journal*, April 11, 1857.

[5] Douglass, *My Bondage*, pp. 253–54.

[6] *De Bow's Review*, XIII (1852), pp. 193–94.

6

A realistic Arkansas slaveholder once addressed himself to the great problem of his class, "the management of Negroes," and bluntly concluded: "Now, I speak what I know, when I say it is like 'casting pearls before swine' to try to *persuade* a negro to work. He must be *made* to work, and should always be given to understand that if he fails to perform his duty he will be punished for it." Having tested the *"persuasion* doctrine" when he began planting, he warned all beginners that if they tried it they would surely fail.[7]

Most masters preferred the "persuasion doctrine" nevertheless. They would have been gratified if their slaves had willingly shown proper subordination and wholeheartedly responded to the incentives offered for efficient labor. They found, however, that some did not respond at all, and that others responded only intermittently. As a result, slaveholders were obliged to supplement the lure of rewards for good behavior with the threat of punishment for bad. One Virginian always assumed that slaves would "not labor at all except to avoid punishment," and would "never do more than just enough to save themselves from being punished." Fortunately, said a Georgian, punishment did not make the Negro revengeful as it did members of other races. Rather, it tended "to win his attachment and promote his happiness and well being."[8]

Without the power to punish, which the state conferred upon the master, bondage could not have existed. By comparison, all other techniques of control were of secondary importance. Jefferson Davis and a few others gave their bondsmen a hand in the chastisement of culprits. On Da-

---

[7] *Southern Cultivator,* XVIII (1860), pp. 130–31, 239–40.
[8] Olmsted, *Seaboard,* pp. 104–105; *Southern Cultivator,* XII (1854), p. 206.

vis's Mississippi estate trusted slaves tried, convicted, and punished the violators of plantation law.[9] But this was an eccentric arrangement. Normally the master alone judged the seriousness of an offense and fixed the kind and amount of punishment to be administered.

Slaveholders devised a great variety of penalties. They demoted unfaithful domestics, foremen, and drivers to field labor. They denied passes to incorrigibles, or excluded them from participating in Saturday night dances. An Arkansas planter gave his bondsmen a dinner every Sunday and required those on the "punishment list" to wait on the others without getting any of the food themselves. Masters forced malingerers to work on Sundays and holidays and at night after the others had finished. They penalized them by confiscating the crops in their "truck patches," or by reducing the sums due them. They put them on short rations for a period of time, usually depriving them of their meat allowances. And they sold them away from their families and friends.

Some of the penalties were ingenious. A Maryland tobacco grower forced a hand to eat the worms he failed to pick off the tobacco leaves. A Mississippian gave a runaway a wretched time by requiring him to sit at the table and eat his evening meal with the white family. A Louisiana planter humiliated disobedient male field-hands by giving them "women's work" such as washing clothes, by dressing them in women's clothing, and by exhibiting them on a scaffold wearing a red flannel cap.[1]

A few slaveholders built private jails on their premises. They knew that close confinement during a working day was a punishment of dubious value, but they believed that

---

[9] Fleming, "Jefferson Davis, the Negroes and the Negro Problem," *loc. cit.*, pp. 410–11.

[1] John Thompson, *The Life of John Thompson, A Fugitive Slave* (Worcester, Mass., 1856), p. 18; Sydnor, *Slavery in Mississippi*, p. 89; Davis (ed.), *Diary of Bennet H. Barrow*, pp. 112, 154, 175.

it was effective during leisure hours. "Negroes are gregarious," explained a small planter, "they dread solitariness, and to be deprived from the little weekly dances and chit-chat. They will work to death rather than be shut up." Accordingly, a Louisianian locked runaways in his jail from Saturday night until Monday morning. When he caught a cotton picker with a ten pound rock in his basket, he jailed him every night and holiday for five months.[2]

Others made use of public jails, paying the jailer a fee for the service. One South Carolinian put a runaway in solitary confinement in the Charleston workhouse; another had a slave "shut in a darkcell" in the same institution. A Georgia planter advised his overseer to take a disobedient slave "down to the Savannah jail, and give him prison discipline and by all means solitary confinement for 3 weeks, when he will be glad to get home again." [3]

The stocks were still a familiar piece of equipment on the plantations of the ante-bellum South. Thomas Affleck's widely used plantation record book recommended incarceration in the stocks as an appropriate form of punishment: "So secured, in a lonely, quiet place, where no communication can be held with anyone, nothing but bread and water allowed, and the confinement extending from Saturday, when they drop work, until Sabbath evening, will prove . . . effectual." Heeding this advice, a Louisiana planter put his runaways in the stocks for a week. "Drunkenness," wrote a Georgia planter, "would be punished by lying in the stocks all night and drinking a pint of warm water." [4]

---

2 *De Bow's Review*, XI (1851), p. 371; Davis (ed.), *Diary of Bennet H. Barrow*, pp. 165, 269.

3 Gaillard Plantation Journal, entry for May 22, 1849; Gavin Diary, entry for March 26, 1856; Phillips (ed.), *Plantation and Frontier*, II, pp. 31–32.

4 McCollam Diary, entry for February 5, 1845; *Southern Agriculturist*, IV (1831), p. 352.

"Chains and irons," James H. Hammond correctly explained, were used chiefly to control and discipline runaways. "You will admit," he argued logically enough, "that if we pretend to own slaves, they must not be permitted to abscond whenever they see fit; and that if nothing else will prevent it these means must be resorted to." [5] Three entries in Hammond's diary, in 1844, indicated that he practiced what he preached. July 17: "Alonzo runaway with his irons on." July 30: "Alonzo came in with his irons off." July 31: ". . . re-ironed Alonzo."

Hammond was but one of many masters who gave critics of the peculiar institution a poignant symbol—the fettered slave. A Mississippian had his runaway Maria "Ironed with a shackle on each leg connected with a chain." When he caught Albert he "had an iron collar put on his neck"; on Woodson, a habitual runaway, he "put the ball and chain." A Kentuckian recalled seeing slaves in his state wearing iron collars, some of them with bells attached. The fetters, however, did not always accomplish their purpose, for numerous advertisements stated that fugitives wore these encumbrances when they escaped. For example, Peter, a Louisiana runaway, "Had on each foot when leaving, an iron ring, with a small chain attached to it." [6]

But the whip was the most common instrument of punishment—indeed, it was the emblem of the master's authority. Nearly every slaveholder used it, and few grown slaves escaped it entirely. Defenders of the institution conceded that corporal punishment was essential in certain situations; some were convinced that it was better than any other remedy. If slavery were right, argued an Arkansas planter, means had to be found to keep slaves in subjuga-

---

[5] *De Bow's Review*, VII (1849), p. 500.
[6] Nevitt Plantation Journal, entries for November 9, 1827; March 28, 1831; July 18, 1832; Coleman, *Slavery Times in Kentucky*, pp. 248–49; New Orleans *Picayune*, December 26, 1847.

tion, "and my opinion is, the lash—not used murderously, as would-be philanthropists assert, is the most effectual." A Virginian agreed: "A great deal of whipping is not necessary; *some* is." [7]

The majority seemed to think that the certainty, and not the severity, of physical "correction" was what made it effective. While no offense could go unpunished, the number of lashes should be in proportion to the nature of the offense and the character of the offender. The master should control his temper. "Never inflict punishment when in a passion," advised a Louisiana slaveholder, "but wait until perfectly cool, and until it can be done rather in sorrow than in anger." Many urged, therefore, that time be permitted to elapse between the misdeed and the flogging. A Georgian required his driver to do the whipping so that his bondsmen would not think that it was "for the pleasure of punishing, rather than for the purpose of enforcing obedience." [8]

Planters who employed overseers often fixed the number of stripes they could inflict for each specific offense, or a maximum number whatever the offense. On Pierce Butler's Georgia plantation each driver could administer twelve lashes, the head driver thirty-six, and the overseer fifty. A South Carolinian instructed his overseer to ask permission before going beyond fifteen. "The highest punishment must not exceed 100 lashes in one day and to that extent only in extreme cases," wrote James H. Hammond. "In general 15 to 20 lashes will be a sufficient flogging." [9]

The significance of these numbers depended in part upon the kind of whip that was used. The "rawhide," or

---

7 *Southern Cultivator*, XVIII (1860), p. 239-40; *Southern Planter*, XII (1852), p. 107.

8 *De Bow's Review*, XXII (1857), pp. 376–79; *Southern Agriculturist*, IV (1831), p. 350.

9 Kemble, *Journal*, pp. 42–43; Phillips (ed.), *Plantation and Frontier*, I, pp. 116–22; Plantation Manual in Hammond Papers.

"cowskin," was a savage instrument requiring only a few strokes to provide a chastisement that a slave would not soon forget. A former bondsman remembered that it was made of about three feet of untanned ox hide, an inch thick at the butt end, and tapering to a point which made it "quite elastic and springy." [1]

Many slaveholders would not use the rawhide because it lacerated the skin. One recommended, instead, a leather strap, eighteen inches long and two and a half inches wide, fastened to a wooden handle. In Mississippi, according to a visitor, the whip in general use consisted of a "stout flexible stalk" covered with a tapering leather plait, about three and a half feet in length, which formed the lash. "To the end of the lash is attached a soft, dry, buckskin cracker, about three eighths of an inch wide and ten or twelve inches long, which is the only part allowed to strike, in whipping on the bare skin. . . . When it is used by an experienced hand it makes a very loud report, and stings, or 'burns' the skin smartly, but does not bruise it." [2]

How frequently a master resorted to the whip depended upon his temperament and his methods of management. On some establishments long periods of time elapsed with relatively few whippings—until, as a rice planter explained, it seemed "as if the devil had got into" the hands, and for a time there was "a good deal of it." Or, occasionally, a normally amiable slave got out of hand and had to be flogged. "Had to whip my Man Willis for insolence to the overseer," wrote a Tennesseean. "This I done with much regret as he was never whipped before." [3]

On other establishments the whip was in constant use. The size of the estate may have had some relationship to

---

[1] Douglass, *My Bondage*, p. 103.
[2] *Southern Cultivator*, VII (1849), p. 135; [Ingraham], *South-West*, II, pp. 287–88.
[3] Olmsted, *Seaboard*, pp. 438–39; Bills Diary, entry for March 30, 1860.

the amount of whipping, but the disposition of the proprietor was decidedly more crucial. Small farmers, as well as large planters, often relied upon corporal punishment as their chief method of enforcing discipline. Southern women were sometimes equally prone to use the lash upon errant domestics.

Some overseers, upon assuming control, thought it wise to whip every hand on the plantation to let them know who was in command. Some masters used the lash as a form of incentive by flogging the last slave out of his cabin in the morning.[4] Many used it to "break in" a young slave and to "break the spirit" of an insubordinate older one. "If the negro is humble and appears duly sensible of the impropriety of his conduct, a very moderate chastisement will answer better than a severe one," advised a planter. "If, however, he is stubborn . . . a slight punishment will only make bad worse." Slaves had to be flogged, explained an Alabamian, until they manifested "submission and penitence."[5]

In short, the infliction of stripes curbed many a bondsman who could not be influenced by any other technique. Whipping had a dispiriting effect upon most of them. "Had to administer a little rod to Bob this morning," reported a Virginian. "Have seen for more than 3 months I should have to humble him some, hope it may benefit him."[6]

7

"To manage *negroes* without the exercise of too much passion, is next to an impossibility. . . . I would therefore put you on your guard, lest their provocations should

---

[4] *Southern Cultivator*, II (1844), pp. 169–70; Davis, *Cotton Kingdom in Alabama*, pp. 54–55.
[5] *Southern Cultivator*, VIII (1850), p. 164; William P. Gould Ms. Plantation Rules.
[6] Adams Diary, entry for July 2, 1860.

on some occasions transport you beyond the limits of decency and christian morality." The Reverend Charles Pettigrew, of North Carolina, gave this advice to his sons when he willed them his estate. John H. Cocke, of Virginia, cautioned the overseer on his Bremo Plantation: "Most persons are liable to be thrown into a passion by the improper conduct of those they have to govern." After traveling through the South, Olmsted wondered "whether humanity and the accumulation of wealth, the prosperity of the master and the happiness and improvement of the subject, are not in some degree incompatible." [7] Physical cruelty, as these observations suggest, was always a possible consequence of the master's power to punish. Place an intemperate master over an ill-disposed slave, and the possibility became a reality.

Not that a substantial number of slaveholders deliberately adopted a policy of brutality. The great majority, in fact, preferred to use as little violence as possible. Many small slaveholders, urban and rural, who had close personal contacts with their bondsmen and knew them as human beings, found it highly disagreeable to treat them unkindly. Large planters, in their instructions to overseers, frequently prohibited barbarous punishments. Thomas Affleck's plantation record book advised overseers that the "indiscriminate, constant and excessive use of the whip" was "altogether unnecessary and inexcusable." A Louisiana proprietor was very explicit on this point. In whipping a slave the overseer was never to be "cruel or severe," though he could repeat the whipping at intervals "until the most entire submission" was achieved. "I object to having the skin cut, or my negroes marked in any way by the lash. . . . I will most certainly discharge any overseer

---

[7] Johnson, *Ante-Bellum North Carolina*, p. 496; John H. Cocke Ms. Plantation Rules, in N. F. Cabell Collection of Agricultural Papers; Olmsted, *Seaboard*, pp. 367–68.

for striking any of my negroes with a club or the butt of his whip." [8]

A master who gave some thought to his standing in the community certainly wished to avoid a reputation for inordinate cruelty. To be counted a true Southern Gentleman one had to be humane to his bondsmen, to exercise self-control in dealing with them, to know how to give commands without raising his voice. Plenty of masters possessed these qualities. A European visitor marveled at the patience, the "mild forbearance," some of them exhibited. It seemed that every slaveholder's temper was subjected to a discipline which either ruined or perfected it. And more than a few met the test with remarkable success. [9]

Many openly censured those who were guilty of inhumanity. A Georgian told a Northerner that the government of slaves was necessarily despotic, but that Southerners despised ruthless masters. A South Carolinian wrote in a published letter, "The overseer whose constant and only resort is to the lash . . . is a brute, and deserves the penitentiary." And a North Carolinian denounced a neighbor as a "*moral miasma*" because of the way he treated his slaves. [1]

Those who were destitute of humane instincts might still be restrained by the slave's economic worth. To injure by harsh punishment a prime field-hand valued at a thousand dollars or more was a costly indulgence. It may be, therefore, that rising slave prices encouraged a decline in the incidence of brutality.

But these restraints were not always enough. Some masters, made irascible by the endless irritations which were

---

[8] *De Bow's Review*, XXII (1857), pp. 376–79.

[9] Martineau, *Society in America*, II, pp. 109–10.

[1] Lester B. Shippee (ed.), *Bishop Whipple's Southern Diary 1843–1844* (Minneapolis, 1937), pp. 31–32; *Southern Cultivator*, II (1844), p. 107; William S. Pettigrew to James C. Johnston, September 24, 1846, Pettigrew Family Papers.

...le part of owning slaves, were unmerciful in ex-
...heir almost unlimited powers. Some were indif-
...bout their reputations among neighbors, or hoped
...ceal the conditions that existed on their isolated estates. Some were as prodigal in the use of human chattels
as they were in the use of other property. Neither law, nor
social pressure, nor economic self-interest made Southern
Gentlemen out of all slaveholders. As long as the peculiar
institution survived, the master class contained a group of
unfeeling men.

Few who knew southern slavery intimately denied that
there existed within it an element of savagery. No apologist
disputed the evidence published by Theodore Dwight
Weld, the abolitionist, for he gathered it from southern
newspapers and public records.[2] It is unnecessary, however,
to turn to the abolitionists—or to former slaves—for proof.
Daniel R. Hundley, a Southerner who admired and defended his section's institutions, agreed that the South was
"no second paradise." He knew that slaves were "badly
treated" on some estates, and that masters were sometimes
unconcerned about it. Moreover, "he must be a very bold
man who will deny that the overseers on many southern
plantations, are cruel and unmercifully severe."[3]

A committee of an Alabama agricultural society reported
that there were "instances" in which self-interest and morality had "not been sufficient to restrain masters from cruelty to slaves." A former Mississippi slaveholder knew "of
his own knowledge, that cruelties and grievous wrongs were
perpetrated upon slaves by their owners." Another Mississippian hoped that southern public opinion would condemn the "many things" that were "cancerous" in slavery.
As an example he cited a "certain class of overseers" who

---

[2] Theodore Dwight Weld, *American Slavery As It Is: Testimony of a
Thousand Witnesses* (New York, 1839).
[3] Hundley, *Social Relations*, pp. 63–64, 187–88, 203–205.

were consistently bestial toward bondsmen. "It is this un-relenting, brutalizing, *drive, drive,* watch and whip, that furnishes *facts* to abolition writers that cannot be disputed, and that are infamous." [4]

Southerners themselves having established the fact of cruelty, it only remains to estimate its extent and to exam-ine is nature. Proslavery writers asserted that cases of cru-elty were the rare exceptions to the general rule of human-ity by which slaves were governed. Travelers in the South gave conflicting testimony. Abolitionists and ex-slaves in-sisted that cruelty was far more common than defenders of the institution would admit.

The exact truth will never be known, because surviving records are fragmentary and sometimes hint only vaguely at conditions. There is no way to discover what went on in the "voiceless solitudes" where no records were kept, or on hundreds of plantations where visitors were unwelcome and the proprietors were in residence only part of the year. (In 1860, several large planters in Rapides Parish, Louisiana, would not even permit the census takers to tres-pass upon their estates.) Even so, the public and private records that do survive suggest that, although the average slaveholder was not the inhuman brute described by the abolitionists, acts of cruelty were not as exceptional as pro-slavery writers claimed.

As a South Carolina judge sadly confessed, there were "men and women on earth who deserved no other name than *fiends,*" for they seemed to delight in brutality.[5] No southern state required masters to be tested for their com-petence to rule slaves. Instead, they permitted slaves to fall willy-nilly into the hands of whoever inherited them or had the cash or credit to buy them. As a result, bondsmen were

---

4 *American Farmer*, II (1846), pp. 77–78; Fulkerson, *Random Recollec-tions*, pp. 128–30; *Southern Culivator*, XVIII (1860), p. 258.
5 Charleston *Courier*, May 14, 1847.

owned by persons of unsound minds, such as the South Carolinian who had his chattels "throw dirt upon [his] roof . . . to drive off witches." They were owned by a woman "unable to read or write, . . . scarcely able to count ten," legally incompetent to contract marriage.[6] They were owned by drunkards, such as Lilburne Lewis, of Livingston County, Kentucky, who once chopped a slave to bits with an ax; and by sadists, such as Madame Lalaurie, of New Orleans, who tortured her slaves for her own amusement. It would be pointless to catalogue the atrocities committed by psychopaths.

Cruelty, unfortunately, was not limited to the mentally unbalanced. Men and women, otherwise "normal," were sometimes corrupted by the extraordinary power that slavery conferred upon them. Some made bondsmen the victims of their petulance. (The repentant wife of a Louisiana planter once wrote in her diary: "I feel badly got very angry and whipped Lavinia. O! for government over my temper." [7]) Others who were reasonably humane to most of their slaves made the ones who annoyed them beyond endurance the targets of their animosity. Still others who were merely irresponsible, rather than inherently brutal, made slaves the objects of their whims. In other words, masters were seldom consistent; they were apt to be indulgent or harsh depending upon their changing moods, or their feelings toward individual slaves. In truth, said one Southerner, "men of the right stamp to manage negroes are like Angels visits few and far between." [8]

Kindness was not a universal trait among small slaveholders, especially among those who were ambitious to climb the economic ladder. Both a shoemaker and a carpenter, each of whom owned a single slave, were guilty of

---

[6] Catterall (ed.), *Judicial Cases*, II, pp. 336, 427.

[7] Quoted in Taylor, "Negro Slavery in Louisiana," p. 254.

[8] Moore Rawls to Lewis Thompson (n.d.), Lewis Thompson Papers.

atrocities.[9] Southern farmers with modest holdings were also, on occasion, capable of extreme cruelty toward slaves.

But brutality was more common on the large plantations. Overseers, almost all of whom were native-born Southerners, seldom felt any personal affection for the bondsmen they governed. Their inclination in most cases was to punish severely; if their employers prohibited severity, they ignored such instructions as often as not. Planters complained that it was difficult to find an overseer who would "condescend to take orders from his employer, and manage according to the system of another man." The typical overseer seemed to have little confidence in the use of incentives as a method of governing slaves; he had a decided preference for physical force.[1]

Illustrations of this problem sometimes found their way into the records of southern courts. Overseers sued masters for their wages when discharged for cruelty; masters sued overseers for injuring slave property; occasionally the state intervened to prosecute an overseer for killing or maiming a bondsman.[2] Most of these cases never reached the courts, as the planter dealt with the problem himself. An Alabamian discovered that he had found no solution even when he employed a relative to oversee. "I want you to distinctly understand me," he scolded, "withhold your rushing whipping and lashing—for I will not stand it any longer." A Louisiana planter, returning to his estate after a year's absence, related in his journal the "most terrible account of the severity [and] cruelty" of his overseer. At least twelve slaves had died from "negligence and ill treatment." Discharging this overseer and employing another,

---

9 New Orleans *Picayune*, March 16, 1858; Northup, *Twelve Years a Slave*, pp. 105-16.

1 *Southern Cultivator*, II (1844), p. 107; Bassett, *Plantation Overseer*, pp. 3-5.

2 Catterall (ed.), *Judicial Cases, passim.*

he was dismayed to find that the new one also "punished severely without discretion."[3]

A planter was often in a quandary when his overseer was both brutal and efficient. "I do not know whether I will keep Harris another year or not," a Mississippian told his wife. "He is a first rate manager except he is too cruel. I have had my feelings greatly shocked at some of his conduct." But he re-employed Harris after exacting from him a promise to be less harsh. Harris, he explained, made big crops, and he did not wish "to break it all up by getting a new manager."

A few years later this same planter, having transferred his operations to Arkansas, viewed the problem of slave management in a different light. While Harris was away on a month's leave of absence, the proprietor ran the estate himself. He found governing slaves to be a "pretty rough business" and waited impatiently for his overseer to return.[4]

Ordinarily the owner of a large plantation was realistic enough to know that controlling a gang of field-hands was at best a wretched business, and that a certain amount of savagery was inevitable. There seemed to be no other way to keep certain bondsmen under control. "Experience and observation have taught me that some negroes require a vast deal more punishment than others to be brought to a performance of their duties," wrote an Arkansas planter. And a Louisiana sugar planter assured his distressed wife that he would not sanction the admitted cruelty of his overseer unless there was "a *great* necessity for it." Indeed,

[3] James P. Tarry to Samuel O. Wood, November 27, 1853; July 1, 1854, Samuel O. Wood Papers; Haller Nutt Ms. Journal of Araby Plantation, entries for November 1, 1843, *et seq.*
[4] Gustavus A. Henry to his wife, December 12, 17, 1848; December 7, 1857, Henry Papers.

he found the management of slaves "exceedingly disagree-able . . . under any and all circumstances." [5]

Although cruelty was endemic in all slaveholding com-munities, it was always most common in newly settled re-gions. Along the rough southern frontier thousands of am-bitious men were trying swiftly to make their fortunes. They operated in a frantically competitive society which provided few rewards for the virtues of gentility and almost put a premium upon ruthlessness. In the eastern tobacco and rice districts brutality was unquestionably less preva-lent in the nineteenth century than it had been during the colonial period. But in the Southwest only limited areas had developed a mellowed gentry as late as 1860. In the Alabama-Mississippi Black Belt, in the cotton and sugar parishes of Louisiana, along the Arkansas River, and in eastern Texas the master class included the "parvenus," the "cotton snobs," and the "Southern Yankees." If these plant-ers failed to observe the code of the patrician, they appar-ently thought none the less of each other for it.

The hired slave stood the greatest chance of subjection to cruel punishments as well as to overwork. His employer, a Kentucky judge confessed, had no incentive to treat him kindly "except the mere feelings of humanity, which we have too much reason to believe in many instances . . . are too weak to stimulate the active virtue." [6] This was no exaggeration.

Southerners who were concerned about the welfare of slaves found it difficult to draw a sharp line between acts of cruelty and such measures of physical force as were an in-extricable part of slavery. Since the line was necessarily ar-bitrary, slaveholders themselves disagreed about where it

---

[5] *Southern Cultivator*, XVIII (1860), p. 287; Sitterson, *Sugar Country*, p. 105.
[6] Catterall (ed.), *Judicial Cases*, I, p. 284.

should be drawn. Was it barbarous to "correct" a slave by putting him in the stocks, or by forcing him to wear chains or an iron collar? How severely might a slave be flogged before the punishment became brutal? These were matters of personal taste.

But no master denied the propriety of giving a moderate whipping to a disobedient bondsman. During the seventeenth and eighteenth centuries the lash was used to punish free men as well as slaves. By mid-nineteenth century, however, it was seldom used upon any but slaves, because public opinion now considered it to be cruel. Why it was less cruel to whip a bondsman was a problem that troubled many sensitive masters. That they often had no choice as long as they owned slaves made their problem no easier to resolve.

Bennet H. Barrow, a Louisiana planter, kept an unusually full record of punishments—a record which illustrates the difficulty of distinguishing between cruelty and reasonable "correction." A substantial and respected man in his community, Barrow inherited lands and slaves from his father; he was in no sense a crude parvenu. Yet he flogged his chattels freely, sometimes severely. On various occasions he had a "general whipping frollick," whipped "every hand in the field . . . comencing with the driver," or gave "a number of them a good flogging." He broke his sword cane on the head of one offending slave, "beat" another "very much" and "cut him with a club in 3 places verry bad." Barrow was one of the few large planters who refused to employ overseers, because of their bad reputation.[7]

If it was cruel to flog slaves so frequently and severely that their backs were permanently scarred, southern newspapers provided evidence of an abundance of this variety of inhumanity. The following illustrations are from ante-

---

[7] Davis (ed.), *Diary of Bennet H. Barrow*, *passim*.

bellum fugitive-slave advertisements and from sheriffs' committal notices: Charles, "an old sinner" who escaped from a Louisiana plantation, had "many stripes of the lash"; a Mississippi slave had "large raised scars or whelks in the small of his back and on his abdomen nearly as large as a person's finger"; Nancy, a Georgia slave, was "considerably marked by the whip"; Esther, an Alabama slave, was "marked about the shoulders from whipping"; a Missouri fugitive had "many scars on his back"; Gid, according to his North Carolina master, had a "remarkably bad temper" and had in consequence "marks of the lash upon his back"; Tom, who was held by the jailer of Augusta County, Virginia, had "the appearance of frequent and severe flogging"; Anaca, who escaped from her Kentucky master, had "a large scar immediately on her chest from the cut of a whip."

After northern abolitionists began scanning the southern press for atrocities, specific references to slaves who were "marked by the whip" declined. The number of slaves identified more vaguely as having "scars" or "burns" increased.

Beyond this were cases of pure brutality—cases of flogging that resulted in the crippling, maiming, or killing of slaves. An early nineteenth-century Charleston grand jury presented "as a serious evil the many instances of Negro Homicide" and condemned those who indulged their passions "in the barbarous treatment of slaves." [8] "Salting"— washing the cuts received from the whip with brine—was a harsh punishment inflicted upon the most obstinate bondsmen. Though all but a few deplored such brutality, slaveholders found themselves in a dilemma when nothing else could subdue a rebel.

If a master was too squeamish to undertake the rugged task of humbling a refractory bondsman, he might send

[8] Henry, *Police Control*, pp. 67–68.

him to a more calloused neighbor or to a professional "slave breaker." John Nevitt, a Mississippi planter not averse to the application of heroic remedies, received from another master a young chattel "for the purpose of punishing him for bad conduct." Frederick Douglass remembered a ruthless man in Maryland who had a reputation for being "a first rate hand at breaking young negroes"; some slaveholders found it beneficial to send their beginning hands to him for training.[9]

The branding of slaves was a widespread custom in colonial days; it was less common in the nineteenth century. But as late as 1838, a North Carolinian advertised that Betty, a fugitive, was recently "burnt . . . with a hot iron on the left side of her face; I tried to make the letter M." In 1848, a Kentuckian identified his runaway Jane by a brand mark "on the breast something like L blotched."[1] Mutilation as a form of punishment also declined without disappearing entirely. A Louisiana jailer, in 1831, gave notice that he had a runaway in his custody: "He has been lately gelded, and is not yet well." Another Louisianian recorded his disgust for a neighbor who had "castrated 3 men of his."[2]

Some masters who were otherwise as humane as the peculiar institution would permit tolerated almost anything that might "cure" habitual runaways. Andrew Jackson once offered fifty dollars reward for the capture of a fugitive, "and ten dollars extra for every hundred lashes any person will give him to the amount of three hundred." A Georgian punished his runaways by pulling out one of their toenails with a pair of pincers. Others hunted them

---

[9] Nevitt Plantation Journal, entry for June 5, 1828; Douglass, *My Bondage*, p. 203; Sydnor, *Slavery in Mississippi*, pp. 69–70.

[1] Johnson, *Ante-Bellum North Carolina*, pp. 493–94; Coleman, *Slavery Times in Kentucky*, pp. 248–49.

[2] Taylor, "Slavery in Louisiana," p. 236; Davis (ed.), *Diary of Bennet H. Barrow*, pp. 173–74.

with shotguns. A North Carolinian advertised for an escaped slave who had "some marks of shot about his hips, thighs, neck and face." Bennet H. Barrow caught Jerry "in the Bayou behind the Quarter, [and] shot him in the thigh"; when Jerry absconded again, Barrow vowed he would this time "shoot to kill." A Mississippian, apparently wishing to give his slaves a stern warning, promised to compensate whoever captured his fugitive "dead or alive." [3]

The tracking of runaways with dogs was no figment of abolitionist imaginations; it was a common practice in all slave states, defended and justified in the courts. Groups of slaveholders sometimes rode through the swamps with their dogs and made the search for fugitives a sport comparable to fox hunting. Others preferred to hire professional slave catchers who provided their own "Negro dogs." A Mississippi master described the talents of a slave catcher he employed: "He follows a negro with his dogs 36 hours after he has passed and never fails to overtake him. It is his profession and he makes some $600 per annum by it." [4] Southern newspapers carried the advertisements of professionals who solicited the patronage of slaveholders, and of those who trained "Negro dogs" for sale.

The dogs could give a fugitive a severe mauling if the owner was willing to permit it. After a Mississippi master caught an escaped slave he allowed his dogs to "bite him very severely." A Louisiana planter "treed" a runaway and then "made the dogs pull him out of the tree, Bit him very badly, think he will stay home a while." On another occasion his dogs tore a slave naked; he then "took him Home

---

[3] Phillips (ed.), *Plantation and Frontier*, II, pp. 85–88; Olmsted, *Texas*, pp. 104–105; Davis (ed.), *Diary of Bennet H. Barrow*, pp. 239, 242; Jackson *Mississippian*, July 11, 1834.

[4] Gustavus A. Henry to his wife, November 23, 1849, Henry Papers; Coleman, *Slavery Times in Kentucky*, pp. 61–62; Olmsted, *Back Country*, pp. 214–15.

Before the other negro[es] . . . and made the dogs give him another over hauling." [5]

The angry mobs who dealt extra-legal justice to slaves accused of serious crimes committed barbarities seldom matched by the most brutal masters. "They call it Lintch's Law," wrote a frightened Louisiana plantation mistress during a local insurrection panic. "If they continue hanging, as they have done for some time past, we should be careful of the children, otherwise the World might be left without people." [6] Fear turned groups of decent white men into ferocious mobs—fear and the knowledge that the law was not strong enough to touch them.

After the Nat Turner rebellion a Richmond newspaper declared that the reprisals of the whites were "hardly inferior in barbarity to the atrocities of the insurgents." During the insurrection panic of 1856, a Texas editor affirmed that at such a time "the popular vengeance may be meted out to the criminal with as much necessity as we would strike down an enemy in self-defence, or shoot a mad dog in our path." A Mississippian was ready for the "fagot and the flame" and to "let every tree in the country bend with negro meat." Four years later a Georgia editor urged the oldest and best citizens in each community to examine persons suspected of encouraging slave rebellions; if they were adjudged guilty, "swing the vagabonds from the nearest tree, and say nothing about it." [7]

Mobs all too frequently dealt with slaves accused of murder or rape. They conducted their own trials or broke into jails or court rooms to seize prisoners for summary execu-

[5] William Read to Samuel S. Downey, August 8, 1848, Downey Papers; Davis (ed.), *Diary of Bennet H. Barrow*, pp. 369–70, 376.
[6] Rachel O'Conner to Frances S. Weeks, September 7, 1835, Weeks Collection.
[7] Richmond *Whig*, quoted in Alexandria (Va.) *Phenix Gazette*, September 1, 1831; Austin *Texas State Gazette*, November 15, 1856; Jackson *Mississippian*, December 19, 1856; *Augusta Daily Chronicle and Sentinel*, September 9, 1860.

tion. Their more fortunate victims were hanged; the others were burned to death, sometimes in the presence of hundreds of bondsmen who were forced to attend the ceremony. Thus, wrote a Mississippian after one such incident, "justice was satisfied; the law of retaliation was inflicted . . . while the example made of this wretch had, no doubt, a salutary effect upon the two thousand slaves who witnessed his execution." An Alabama editor justified the burning of a slave at the stake by "the law of self-protection, which abrogates all other law. . . . There was no passionate conduct here. The whole subject was disposed of with the coolest deliberation and with regard only to the interest of the public." [8]

The abolition of slavery, of course, did not bring to a close the record of brutality in the South any more than it did elsewhere. But it did make less tenable the argument that brutality was sometimes in the public interest. And it did rescue many a master from the dilemma he faced when his desire to be humane was compromised by the demands of proper discipline.

Surely there is room for compassion for a profoundly disturbed North Carolinian who owned several plantations in Mississippi. "My great desire is to have my blacks taken proper care of," he wrote. "I would be content with much less . . . cotton if less cruelty was exercised. I fear I am near an abolition[i]st. But I should consider myself an unjust and unfeeling man if I did not have a proper regard for those who are making me so much money[.]" [9]

---

[8] Vicksburg *Weekly Sentinel*, June 13, 1855; Huntsville *Democrat*, quoted in Sellers, *Slavery in Alabama*, pp. 262–63.
[9] William Boylan to [George W. Mordecai], December 20, 1850, Cameron Family Papers.

CHAPTER FIVE

Chattels Personal

In Alabama's legal code of 1852 two clauses, standing in significant juxtaposition, recognized the dual character of the slave.[1]

The first clause confirmed his status as property—the right of the owner to his "time, labor and services" and to his obedient compliance with all lawful commands. Slavery thus being established by law, masters relied upon the state to use its power against white men who "tampered" with their bondsmen, and against bondsmen they could not subdue. Courts, police, and militia were indispensable parts of the machinery of control.

The second clause acknowledged the slave's status as a person. The law required that masters be humane to their slaves, furnish them adequate food and clothing, and provide care for them during sickness and in old age. In short, the state endowed masters with obligations as well as rights and assumed some responsibility for the welfare of the bondsmen.

But legislators and magistrates were caught in a dilemma whenever they found that the slave's status as property was

---

[1] Extracts from the slave codes presented in this chapter were taken from the legal codes or revised statutes of the southern states. See also Hurd, *Law of Freedom and Bondage*, and the various studies of slavery in individual states.

incompatible with his status as a person. Individual masters struggled with this dilemma in different ways, some conceding much to the dictates of humanity, others demanding the utmost return from their investment. Olmsted explained the problem succinctly: "It is difficult to handle simply as property, a creature possessing human passions and human feelings, . . . while, on the other hand, the absolute necessity of dealing with property as a thing, greatly embarrasses a man in any attempt to treat it as a person." [2]

After adopting Draconian codes in the early eighteenth century, the various legislatures in some respects gradually humanized them, while the courts tempered their application, but there was no way to resolve the contradiction implicit in the very term "human property." Both legislators and judges frequently appeared erratic in dealing with bondsmen as both *things* and *persons*. Alabama's code defined the property status of the slave before acknowledging his human status, and throughout the ante-bellum South the cold language of statutes and judicial decisions made it evident that, legally, the slave was less a person than a thing.

2

The fact that southern slavery was, in the main, Negro slavery gave an advantage to those who wished to preserve it. If he ran away, the Negro slave with his distinctive skin color could not so easily escape detection as could a white indentured servant. Moreover, all Negroes were brought to America in bondage, and legislatures soon adopted the principle of *partus sequitur ventrem*—the child inherits the condition of the mother. Therefore, the English common-law presumption in favor of freedom did not apply to

---

[2] Olmsted, *Back Country*, p. 64.

Negroes; in all the slave states (except Delaware) the presumption was that people with black skins were slaves unless they could prove that they were free. Any strange Negro found in a southern community without "freedom papers" was arrested as a fugitive.

But southern slavery was not *exclusively* Negro slavery. The status of a child of mixed Negro and white ancestry depended upon the status of the mother. The offspring of a Negro slave father and a free white mother was free. The offspring of a free white father and a Negro, mulatto, quadroon, or octoroon slave mother was a slave. In fact, the Texas Supreme Court once ruled that the child of a slave mother was a slave no matter how remote the Negro ancestry.[3] Hence some slaves were whites by any rational definition as well as by all outward appearances, even though some distant female ancestor may have been a Negro. One Virginia fugitive had a "complexion so nearly white, that . . . a stranger would suppose there was no African blood in him."[4]

Not all southern slaves were Negroes, and not all southern masters were whites. In 1830, more than thirty-six hundred free Negroes or persons of mixed ancestry owned slaves. The great majority of these colored slaveowners had merely purchased husbands, wives, or children and were unable to emancipate them under existing state laws. A few were substantial planters, such as the Negro in King George County, Virginia, who owned seventy-one slaves; another in St. Landry Parish, Louisiana, who owned seventy-five; and two others in Colleton District, South Carolina, who owned eighty-four apiece. Though southern whites overwhelmingly disapproved, only in Delaware and Arkansas did the courts refuse to sanction the ownership of slaves by "free persons of color." The Arkansas Supreme Court held

[3] Catterall (ed.), *Judicial Cases*, V, p. 295.
[4] Richmond *Enquirer*, February 7, 1837.

that slavery had its foundation "in an *inferiority of race*," and the bondage of one Negro to another lacked "this solid foundation to rest upon." [5]

Since Negroes were presumed to be slaves and whites were presumed to be free, the southern states found it essential in cases of mixed ancestry to decide who were to be treated as Negroes and who as whites. No state adopted the principle that "a single drop of Negro blood" made a person legally a member of the "inferior race." Each state prescribed the proportion of Negro ancestry which excluded a person from the privileges enjoyed by white men.

In Virginia, according to the code of 1849, "Every person who has one-fourth part or more of negro blood shall be deemed a mulatto, and the word 'negro' . . . shall be construed to mean mulatto as well as negro." In Alabama a "mulatto" was "a person of mixed blood, descended, on the part of the mother or father, from negro ancestors, to the third generation inclusive, though one ancestor of each generation may have been a white person." In other southern states also the term *mulatto* was defined loosely, so as to include as a rule persons with one Negro grandparent (quadroon) or great grandparent (octoroon); such persons were treated in law as Negroes. Only in South Carolina did the statutes refer to "negroes, mulattoes and persons of color" without defining these terms. The Court of Appeals, however, refused to infer from this that all persons "of *any* mixture of negro blood" were legally Negroes. Rather, it ruled that there must be a "visible mixture" and that much depended upon a person's "reputation" among his neighbors.[6]

Any person with Negro ancestors too remote to cause

---

[5] Carter G. Woodson, *Free Negro Owners of Slaves in the United States in 1830* (Washington, D.C., 1924) ; Catterall (ed.) , *Judicial Cases*, IV, p. 215; V, p. 257.

[6] Catterall (ed.) , *Judicial Cases*, II, pp. 358–59.

him to be classified as a mulatto was by law a white man. While such a person could be held as a slave, the burden of proof was placed upon the putative master. In Kentucky, affirmed the Court of Appeals, "it has been well settled, that . . . having less than a fourth of African blood, is *prima facie* evidence of freedom." A Virginia jury having found that a woman suing for her freedom was white, it was incumbent upon her master to prove that she "was descended in the maternal line from a slave. Having not proved it, she and her children must be considered free." [7]

Some slaveholders preferred to use "bright mulattoes" as domestics; a few paid premium prices for light-skinned females to be used as concubines or prostitutes. But most masters saw the inconvenience of owning slaves who were nearly white: the presumption of freedom in their favor, and the greater ease with which they could escape. One former bondsman, a "white man with blue eyes," recalled his master's repeated attempts to sell him, always unsuccessful. A Kentucky slave, "owing to his being almost white, and to the consequent facilities of escape," was adjudged to be worth only "half as much as other slaves of the ordinary color and capacities." [8] Here was convincing evidence of the importance of racial visibility in keeping the Negro in bondage.

3

In the customary phraseology of the ante-bellum codes, South Carolina's slaves were "deemed, held, taken, reputed and adjudged in law to be chattels personal, in the hands of their owners and possessors and their executors, administrators and assigns, to all intents, constructions and pur-

---

[7] Catterall (ed.), *Judicial Cases*, I, pp. 121, 330.

[8] Drew, *The Refugee*, pp. 123–32; Catterall (ed.), *Judicial Cases*, I, p. 278.

poses whatsoever." Slaves had the attributes of personal property everywhere, except in Louisiana (and Kentucky before 1852) where they had the attributes of real estate. Neither the laws nor the courts, however, were altogether consistent. In states where slaves were generally considered as personalty, they were treated as realty for purposes of inheritance. In Louisiana, where they were supposedly like real property, they retained many of the characteristics of "chattels personal."

Though the slave was property "of a distinctive and peculiar character," though recognized as a person, he was legally at the disposal of his master, whose property right was very nearly absolute. "The master," proclaimed the Louisiana code, "may sell him, dispose of his person, his industry, and his labor: he can do nothing, possess nothing, nor acquire anything but what must belong to his master." Even in Kentucky, slaves had "no rights secured to them by the constitution, except of trial by jury in cases of felony." [9]

Legally a bondsman was unable to acquire title to property by purchase, gift, or devise; he could not be a party to a contract. No promise of freedom, oral or written, was binding upon his master. According to the Arkansas Supreme Court, "If the master contract . . . that the slave shall be emancipated upon his paying to his master a sum of money, or rendering him some stipulated amount of labor, although the slave may pay the money, . . . or perform the labor, yet he cannot compel his master to execute the contract, because both the money and the labor of the slave belong to the master and could constitute no legal consideration for the contract." [1]

Nor could a chattel be a party to a suit, except indirectly when a free person represented him in a suit for freedom. In court he was not a competent witness, except in a case

[9] Catterall (ed.), *Judicial Cases*, I, p. 311.
[1] *Ibid.*, V, pp. 250–51.

involving another slave. He had no civil rights, no political rights, no claim to his time, no freedom of movement.

Since slaves, as chattels, could not make contracts, marriages between them were not legally binding. "The relation between slaves is essentially different from that of man and wife joined in lawful wedlock," ruled the North Carolina Supreme Court, for "with slaves it may be dissolved at the pleasure of either party, or by the sale of one or both, depending upon the caprice or necessity of the owners." Their condition was compatible only with a form of concubinage, "voluntary on the part of the slaves, and permissive on that of the master." In law there was no such thing as fornication or adultery between slaves; nor was there bastardy, for, as a Kentucky judge noted, the father of a slave was "unknown" to the law.[2] No state legislature ever seriously entertained the thought of encroaching upon the master's rights by legalizing slave marriages.

On the contrary, the states guaranteed the rights of property in human chattels in every way feasible. Most southern constitutions prohibited the legislatures from emancipating slaves without both the consent of the owners and the payment of a full equivalent in money. Every state provided severe penalties for the theft of a slave—a common crime in the ante-bellum South. In Virginia the penalty was two to ten years in the penitentiary, in Tennessee it was five to fifteen years, and in many states it was death.

When a bondsman was executed for a capital crime the state usually compensated the owner, the normal compensation being something less than the full value assessed by a jury. In Arkansas, which gave no compensation, a slaveholder complained bitterly of the "injustice" done him when one of his slaves was hanged for rape. "I had, or ought to have, some claims upon the State for the destruc-

2 Catterall (ed.), *Judicial Cases*, I, p. 287; II, pp. 76–77, 221.

tion of my property," he thought. "That would be good policy and good law." [3] Since the execution of a slave resembled the public seizure or condemnation of private property, most of the states recognized the justice of the owner's claim. Sometimes they levied a special tax on slaves and established a separate public fund for this purpose.

There were virtually no restrictions upon the owner's right to deed his bondsmen to others. Normally the courts nullified such transfers only if the seller fraudulently warranted a slave to be "free from defects" or "vices" such as the "habit of running away." In devising his chattels a testator had the power to divide them among his heirs in any way he saw fit—including the power to dissolve families for the purpose of making an equitable distribution. If a master died intestate, the division was made in accordance with the state's laws of inheritance.

Sometimes the division provided by a will, or the claims of heirs of a master who died intestate, could not be realized without a sale of slaves. In such cases the southern courts seldom tried to prevent the breaking up of slave families. The executor of an estate was expected to dispose of human chattels, like other property, in the way that was most profitable to the heirs. It may be "harsh" to separate members of families, said the North Carolina Supreme Court, yet "it must be done, if the executor discovers that the interest of the estate requires it; for he is not to indulge his charities at the expense of others." [4]

Advertisements of administrators' sales appeared constantly in southern newspapers. Among several dozen in a single issue of a Georgia newspaper were these: "A negro boy, George, about 25 years old," to be sold "for division

---

[3] Francis Terry Leak Ms. Diary, entries for September 22, October 23, November 5, 1856.

[4] Catterall (ed.), *Judicial Cases*, II, pp. 58–59.

among the heirs"; two Negro girls, Ann and Lucy, "the former 13, the latter 9 years old," to be sold "for the benefit of the legatees"; fifteen Negroes, "most of them likely and very valuable," to be sold to the highest bidder to settle an estate. Some administrators had to find purchasers for scores of slaves. One lot of a hundred, sold "for the benefit of the heirs," included "a large number of healthy fine children, boys and girls, young men and young women, a house carpenter, a plantation blacksmith and a miller; almost every description of servants can be had out of the above negroes."

Since slaves were frequently sold on credit or used as security for loans, they were subject to seizure and sale for the benefit of creditors. A clause in the Virginia code added the proviso that human chattels were not to be seized "without the debtor's consent" when there were "other goods and chattels of such debtor for the purpose." Slaves who were seized were to be sold "at the court house of the county or corporation, between the hours of ten in the morning and four in the afternoon . . . on the first day of the court." In "execution sales," except for mothers and small children, family ties were ignored whenever it was beneficial to the debtor. As a witness testified before the Georgia Supreme Court, "It is not usual to put up negroes in families at Sheriff's sales." [5]

For several weeks prior to a public auction the sheriff advertised the event in a local newspaper. "Will be sold before the Court-house door in the town of Covington," ran a typical sheriff's notice in Newton County, Georgia, "within the usual hours of sale, on the first Tuesday in February next, the following property, to-wit: Three Negroes—John, a boy about 18 years old; Ann, a girl about 4 years old; Riley, a boy about three years old; all levied on

---

[5] Catterall (ed.), *Judicial Cases*, III, p. 68.

as the property of Burwell Moss, to satisfy a mortgage . . . in favor of Alfred M. Ramsey." [6]

Executors and administrators also sold slaves when it was necessary to satisfy the creditors of the deceased. Their notices of sales "for the purpose of paying debts" against estates appeared in the newspapers alongside the sheriff's notices. Sometimes their advertisements listed bondsmen together with horses, mules, cows, farm implements, and other forms of personal property.

4

The unsentimental prose of legal codes and court records, of sheriff's notices and administrator's accounts, gave some indication of the dehumanizing effects of reducing people to "chattels personal." Masters who claimed their rights under the laws of property, and who developed the habit of thinking of their chattels in impersonal terms, provided further evidence. The laws, after all, were not abstractions; they were written by practical men who expected them to be applied to real situations. Accordingly, slaves *were* bartered, deeded, devised, pledged, seized, and auctioned. They were awarded as prizes in lotteries and raffles; they were wagered at gaming tables and horse races. They were, in short, property in fact as well as in law.

Men discussed the price of slaves with as much interest as the price of cotton or tobacco. Commenting upon the extraordinarily good prices in 1853, a South Carolina editor reported, "Boys weighing about fifty lbs. can be sold for about five hundred dollars." "It really seems that there is to be no stop to the rise," added a North Carolina editor. "This species of property is at least 30 per cent higher now, (in the dull season of the year), than it was last Janu-

---

[6] Milledgeville *Southern Recorder*, January 7, 1851.

ary. . . . What negroes will bring next January, it is impossible for mortal man to say." [7]

Olmsted noticed how frequently the death of a slave, when mentioned in a southern newspaper, was treated as the loss of a valuable piece of property. A Mississippi editor reported a tragedy on the Mississippi River involving the drowning of six "likely" male slaves "owned by a couple of young men who had bought and paid for them by the sweat of their brows." A young North Carolina planter, who seemed "doomed to misfortune," lost through an accident a slave he had inherited from his grandmother and was thus "minus the whole legacy." One morning James H. Hammond discovered that his slave Anny had "brought forth a dead child." "She has not earned her salt for 4 months past," he grumbled. "Bad luck—my usual luck in this way." [8]

In new regions—for example, in Alabama and Mississippi during the 1830's—the buying and selling of slaves and plantations was the favorite operation of speculators. Everywhere people invested cash in bondsmen as people in an industrial society would invest in stocks and bonds. Affluent parents liked to give slaves to their children as presents. "With us," said a Virginia judge, "nothing is so usual as to advance children by gifts of slaves. They stand with us instead of money." A Kentuckian, "in easy circumstances," was "in the habit of . . . presenting a slave to each of his grandchildren." "I buy . . . Negro boy Jessee," wrote a Tennessee planter, "and send him as a gift to my daughter Eva and the heirs of her body." [9]

[7] Wilmington (N.C.), *Journal*, July 12, 1853, quoting and commenting upon an editorial in the Anderson (S.C.) *Gazette.*
[8] Olmsted, *Back Country*, p. 63; Sydnor, *Slavery in Mississippi*, p. 250; Ebenezer Pettigrew to James C. Johnston, February 22, 1842, Pettigrew Family Papers; Hammond Diary, entry for February 26, 1838.
[9] Catterall (ed.), *Judicial Cases*, I, pp. 149–50, 311; II, p. 112; Bills Diary, entry for January 7, 1860.

V: *Chattels Personal*

Slaveholders kept the courts busy with litigation involving titles and charges of fraudulent sales. "The plaintiff declares that the defendent . . . deceitfully represented the . . . slave to be sound except one hip, and a good house servant," ran a typical complaint. A lawyer, searching for legal precedents which might justify a claim of "unsoundness" in a slave recently sold, cited past judicial opinions "as regards horseflesh." Two South Carolinians presented to the state Court of Appeals the question of whether the seller or buyer must suffer the loss of a slave who had committed suicide during the course of the transaction.[1] Families were sometimes rent asunder as relatives fought for years, in court and out, over claims to bondsmen.

Litigation between slaveholders and their creditors also brought much business to the southern courts. Many masters who would have refused to sell bondsmen to traders nevertheless mortgaged them and thus often made sales inevitable when their estates were settled, if not before. A Tennesseean with "heavy debts over him" escaped the sheriff by fleeing to Texas with his slaves. This was a familiar story in the Old South, so familiar that the phrase "gone to Texas" was applied to any debtor who fled from his creditors. A slaveholder would abandon his lands and escape in the night with his movable chattels. The courts heard case after case like that of a Georgian who "clandestinely removed his property, consisting of negroes, to . . . Alabama, . . . to avoid the payment of his debts," and of a Mississippian, who "ran off . . . into Texas, certain negro slaves, with a view of defrauding his creditors." [2]

The reduction of bondsmen to mere pawns in disputes over titles and in actions by creditors was a sordid business.

---

1 Catterall (ed.), *Judicial Cases*, II, pp. 425–26, 561; Easterby, (ed.), *South Carolina Rice Plantation*, p. 69.

2 Allen Brown to Hamilton Brown, March 4, 1833, Hamilton Brown Papers; Catterall (ed.), *Judicial Cases*, II, p. 440; III, p. 24.

But the suits for trespass masters brought against those who had injured their chattels were no less depressing. For example, when a Kentucky bondsman "died in consequence of injuries inflicted on him by Thos. Kennedy and others," the owner sued and recovered a judgment for one hundred and ninety-five dollars and costs. A Tennessee slave was hired to a man who permitted him to die of neglect. An indignant judge affirmed that "the hirer of a slave should be taught . . . that more is required of him than to exact from the slave the greatest amount of service, with the least degree of attention to his comfort, health, or even life"— and gave a judgment of five hundred dollars for the master, the sole penalty. An Alabama slave was scarred by severe whippings inflicted by his hirer. The owner brought suit on the ground that the slave's "market value . . . was permanently injured." [3]

In all these ways the slave as property clearly had priority over the slave as a person. Contrary to tradition, this was equally the case when masters executed their last wills and testaments. To be sure, some exhibited tender solicitude for their "people" and made special provisions for them, but they were decidedly exceptional. In addition to those who died intestate and thus left the fate of their slaves to be settled by the courts, most testators—Virginians as well as Mississippians, large as well as small—merely explained how they wished their chattels to be divided among the heirs.

John Ensor, of Baltimore County, Maryland, who died in 1831, bequeathed to a daughter "three negroes . . . also one gray mare and one cow." He gave a second daughter "one negro boy called Lee, one horse called Tom, and one cow." Ensor's will made no further reference to his slaves. [4]

---

[3] Catterall (ed.), *Judicial Cases*, I, p. 390; II, pp. 103, 541-42; III, p. 224.

[4] These and subsequent quotations are from ms. county will books listed in the bibliography.

In 1851, Elizabeth Ann Boswell, of Prince Georges County Maryland, willed to her three children eight slaves to be "divided among them in equal portions, share and share alike"—and thus made the sale of all or part of these slaves inevitable for the division she required. Time after time devisors uprooted small slave communities, as did Sherwood Barksdale, of Cumberland County, North Carolina, in 1841, when he divided his twenty-five slaves among nine heirs.

Testators often specifically authorized or ordered the sale of slaves. In 1849, Martha DuBose, of Fairfield District, South Carolina, provided for a division of slaves among her devisees "either by sale or otherwise." Stephen Taylor, of Edgecombe County, North Carolina, in 1848, bequeathed to his wife five slaves during her life, after which they were "to be sold and the money arising therefrom to be equally divided" among several heirs. In 1842, James Atkinson, also of Edgecombe County, instructed his executor to sell nine slaves immediately after his death; upon his wife's death his two remaining slaves were to be "sold at public sale to the highest bidder and the monies arising from said sale equally divided among my lawful heirs."

The offspring of slave women were frequently devised before they were born—occasionally before they were conceived. In Fairfield District, South Carolina, in 1830, Mary Kincaid gave a slave woman named Sillar to a grandchild, and Sillar's two children to other grandchildren. If Sillar should have a third child, it was to go to still another grandchild. If not, "I will that her two children now living be sold at twelve years of age and the proceeds equally divided among my said grand children." In Mecklenburg County, North Carolina, George Houston, in 1839, willed to one daughter a slave named Charity, and to another daughter "the first child that . . . Charity shal have."

Thomas Harvey, of Prince Georges County, Maryland, a

kind and thoughtful grandfather, in 1851, inserted the following item in his will: "I give and bequeath to my Grandchild . . . a little negro girl by the name of Sally who is the daughter of my woman Harriet. . . . It is my desire that . . . the little negro Sally remain and live with my aforesaid Grand-child to wait on her and attend to her comforts until she arrives at the age of eighteen; when she is to have full possession of the said negro Sally and her children should she have any at that time."

5

Every slave state had a slave code. Besides establishing the property rights of those who owned human chattels, these codes supported masters in maintaining discipline and provided safeguards for the white community against slave rebellions. In addition, they held slaves, as thinking beings, morally responsible and punishable for misdemeanors and felonies.

Fundamentally the slave codes were much alike. Those of the Deep South were somewhat more severe than those of the Upper South, but most of the variations were in minor details. The similarities were due, in part, to the fact that new states patterned their codes after those of the old. South Carolina's code of 1712 was almost a copy of the Barbadian code; Georgia's code of 1770 duplicated South Carolina's code of 1740; and later the Gulf states borrowed heavily from both. In the Upper South, Tennessee virtually adopted North Carolina's code, while Kentucky and Missouri lifted many passages from Virginia's. But the similarities were also due to the fact that slavery, wherever it existed, made necessary certain kinds of regulatory laws. The South Carolina code would probably have been essentially the same if the Barbadian code had never been written.

After a generation of liberalization following the American Revolution, the codes underwent a reverse trend toward increasing restrictions. This trend was clearly evident by the 1820's, when rising slave prices and expansion into the Southwest caused more and more Southerners to accept slavery as a permanent institution. The Nat Turner rebellion and northern abolitionist attacks merely accelerated a trend which had already begun.

In practice the slave codes went through alternating periods of rigid and lax enforcement. Sometimes slaveholders demanded even more rigorous codes, and sometimes they were remiss in enforcing parts of existing ones. When the danger of attack from without or of rebellion from within seemed most acute, they looked anxiously to the state governments for additional protection. After the Turner uprising, Governor John Floyd advised the Virginia legislature: "As the means of guarding against the possible repetition of these sanquinary scenes, I cannot fail to recommend to your early attention, the revision of all the laws, intended to preserve in due subordination the slave population of our State." [5] The legislature responded with several harsh additions to the code, but enforcement during the next three decades continued to be spasmodic.

At the heart of every code was the requirement that slaves submit to their masters and respect all white men. The Louisiana code of 1806 proclaimed this most lucidly: "The condition of the slave being merely a passive one, his subordination to his master and to all who represent him is not susceptible of modification or restriction . . . he owes to his master, and to all his family, a respect without bounds, and an absolute obedience, and he is consequently to execute all the orders which he receives from him, his said master, or from them." A slave was neither to raise his hand against a white man nor to use insulting or abusive language. Any number of acts, said a North Carolina judge,

---

[5] Richmond *Enquirer*, December 8, 1831.

may constitute "insolence"—it may be merely "a look, the pointing of a finger, a refusal or neglect to step out of the way when a white person is seen to approach. But each of such acts violates the rules of propriety, and if tolerated, would destroy that subordination, upon which our social system rests." [6]

The codes rigidly controlled the slave's movements and his communication with others. A slave was not to be "at large" without a pass which he must show to any white man who asked to see it; if he forged a pass or free papers he was guilty of a felony. Except in a few localities, he was prohibited from hiring his own time, finding his own employment, or living by himself. A slave was not to preach, except to his master's own slaves on his master's premises in the presence of whites. A gathering of more than a few slaves (usually five) away from home, unattended by a white, was an "unlawful assembly" regardless of its purpose or orderly decorum.

No person, not even the master, was to teach a slave to read or write, employ him in setting type in a printing office, or give him books or pamphlets. A religious publication asked rhetorically: "Is there any great moral reason why we should incur the tremendous risk of having our wives slaughtered in consequence of our slaves being taught to read incendiary publications?" They did not need to read the Bible to find salvation: "Millions of those now in heaven never owned a bible." [7]

Farms and plantations employing slaves were to be under the supervision of resident white men, and not left to the sole direction of slave foremen. Slaves were not to beat drums, blow horns, or possess guns; periodically their cabins were to be searched for weapons. They were not to ad-

---

[6] Catterall (ed.), *Judicial Cases*, II, p. 168.
[7] *Southern Presbyterian*, quoted in *De Bow's Review*, XVIII (1855), p. 52; *Farmers' Register*, IV (1836), p. 181.

minister drugs to whites or practice medicine. "A slave under pretence of practicing medicine," warned a Tennessee judge, "might convey intelligence from one plantation to another, of a contemplated insurrectionary movement; and thus enable the slaves to act in concert." [8]

A slave was not to possess liquor, or purchase it without a written order from his owner. He was not to trade without a permit, or gamble with whites or with other slaves. He was not to raise cotton, swine, horses, mules, or cattle. Allowing a slave to own animals, explained the North Carolina Supreme Court, tended "to make other slaves dissatisfied . . . and thereby excite . . . a spirit of insubordination." [9]

Southern cities and towns supplemented the state codes with additional regulations. Most of them prohibited slaves from being on the streets after curfew or living in dwellings separate from their masters. Richmond required Negroes and mulattoes to step aside when whites passed by, and barred them from riding in carriages except in the capacity of menials. Charleston slaves could not swear, smoke, walk with a cane, assemble at military parades, or make joyful demonstrations. In Washington, North Carolina, the town Commissioners prohibited "all disorderly shouting and dancing, and all disorderly . . . assemblies . . . of slaves and free Negroes in the streets, market and other public places." In Natchez, all "strange slaves" had to leave the city by four o'clock on Sunday afternoon. [1]

Violations of the state and local codes were misdemeanors or felonies subject to punishment by justices, sheriffs, police, and constabulary. Whipping was the most common form of public punishment for less than capital offenses.

8 Catterall (ed.), *Judicial Cases*, II, pp. 520–21.
9 *Ibid.*, II, pp. 240–41.
1 *Ibid.*, II, p. 182; Henry, *Police Control*, p. 48; [Ingraham], *South-West*, II, pp. 72–73; Phillips, *American Negro Slavery*, pp. 497–98.

Except in Louisiana, imprisonment was rare. By mid-nineteenth century branding and mutilation had declined, though they had not been abolished everywhere. South Carolina did not prohibit branding until 1833, and occasionally thereafter slave felons still had their ears cropped. Mississippi and Alabama continued to enforce the penalty of "burning in the hand" for felonies not capitally punished.[2]

But most slave offenders were simply tied up in the jail or at a whipping post and flogged. Some states in the Upper South limited to thirty-nine the number of stripes that could be administered at any one time, though more could be given in a series of whippings over a period of days or weeks. In the Deep South floggings could legally be more severe. Alabama permitted up to one hundred stripes on the bare back of a slave who forged a pass or engaged in "riots, routs, unlawful assemblies, trespasses, and seditious speeches."

State criminal codes dealt more severely with slaves and free Negroes than with whites. In the first place, they made certain acts felonies when committed by Negroes but not when committed by whites; and in the second place, they assigned heavier penalties to Negroes than whites convicted of the same offense. Every southern state defined a substantial number of felonies carrying capital punishment for slaves and lesser punishments for whites. In addition to murder of any degree, slaves received the death penalty for attempted murder, manslaughter, rape and attempted rape upon a white woman, rebellion and attempted rebellion, poisoning, robbery, and arson. A battery upon a white person might also carry a sentence of death under certain circumstances. In Louisiana, a slave who struck his master, a member of the master's family, or the overseer, "so as to

---

[2] Henry, *Police Control*, p. 52; Sydnor, *Slavery in Mississippi*, p. 83.

cause a contusion, or effusion or shedding of blood," was to suffer death—as was a slave on a third conviction for striking a white.

The codes were quite unmerciful toward whites who interfered with slave discipline. Heavy fines were levied upon persons who unlawfully traded with slaves, sold them liquor without the master's permission, gave them passes, gambled with them, or taught them to read or write. North Carolina made death the penalty for concealing a slave "with the intent and for the purpose of enabling such slave to escape." Aiding or encouraging a bondsman to rebel was the most heinous crime of all. "If a free person," said the Alabama code, "advise or conspire with a slave to . . . make insurrection, . . . he shall be punished with death, whether such rebellion or insurrection be made or not."

Every slave state made it a felony to say or write anything that might lead, directly or indirectly, to discontent or rebellion. In 1837, the Missouri legislature passed an act "to prohibit the publication, circulation, and promulgation of the abolition doctrines." The Virginia code of 1849 provided a fine and imprisonment for any person who maintained "that owners have not right of property in their slaves." Louisiana made it a capital offense to use "language in any public discourse, from the bar, the bench, the stage, the pulpit, or in any place whatsoever" that might produce "insubordination among the slaves." Most southern states used their police power to prohibit the circulation of "incendiary" material through the United States mail; on numerous occasions local postmasters, public officials, or mobs seized and destroyed antislavery publications.

Southerners justified these seizures on the ground that some slaves were literate in spite of the laws against teaching them to read. A petition to the South Carolina legislature claimed that "the ability to read exists on probably every plantation in the State; and it is utterly impossible for even the *masters* to prevent this—as is apparent from the cases in which servants learn to write by stealth." But whether or not slaves could read, the "corrupting influence" of antislavery propaganda was bound to reach them unless it was suppressed. There seemed to be no choice but to construct an "intellectual blockade" against ideas hostile to slavery if property were to be protected and the peace of society secured. Hence the laws controlled the voices and pens of white men as well as black.[3]

In brief, Southerners were not to do or say anything which might destroy what the Louisiana code called "that line of distinction . . . established between the several classes" of the community. If a white man fraternized with another man's slave, he became an object of suspicion; sometimes he found himself in trouble with the law. "On Sunday evening last," ran an item in a Richmond newspaper, "while Officer Reed, of the Police, was passing down Broad Street, he met a white man, walking arm-in-arm with a black man. Officer Reed stopped them and demanded to know the why and the wherefore of such a cheek by jowl business. . . . They were both arrested and taken to the cage." Happily for the white man, he could produce witnesses who testified that he was a person "of general good character, who happened to be 'on a spree' at the time he was found in company with the negro." He was therefore discharged "with an admonition."[4]

Southern slave codes protected the owners of bondsmen who attempted to abscond by requiring officers to assist in their recapture and by giving all white men power to arrest them. Every state required the owner of a fugitive to com-

---

[3] Undated petition from Chester District, South Carolina Slavery Manuscripts Collection; Clement Eaton, *Freedom of Thought in the Old South* (Durham, 1940), *passim*.

[4] Richmond *Enquirer*, August 30, 1853.

pensate the captor for his trouble. Because of the magnitude of the problem, Kentucky obligated masters to pay a reward of one hundred dollars for runaways taken "in a State where slavery is not tolerated by law." In an effort to induce the return of fugitives escaping to Mexico, Texas promised a reward of one-third the value of a slave who fled "beyond the limits of the slave territories of the United States." [5]

A slave was legally a runaway if found without a pass beyond a certain prescribed distance from home—eight miles in Mississippi, twenty in Missouri. If his master could not be located or lived far away, the fugitive was delivered to a justice of the peace who committed him to jail. The slave of an unknown master was advertised for a period ranging from three months to one year, and if he was not claimed by the end of this time he was sold to the highest bidder. The proceeds of the sale, minus the reward, jail fees, and other costs, were recoverable by the master should he appear at some future date.

North Carolina authorized the outlawing of a "vicious" runaway. For example, two justices of New Hanover County gave notice that the slave London was "lurking about" and "committing acts of felony and other misdeeds." London was therefore outlawed; unless he surrendered immediately, "any person may KILL and DESTROY the said slave by such means as he or they may think fit, without accusation or impeachment of any crime or offense for so doing." At the same time, London's master offered a reward of fifty dollars for his confinement in jail, or one hundred dollars for his head. Louisiana permitted a person to shoot a runaway who would not stop when ordered to do so. The state Supreme Court cautioned pursuers that they ought to try to avoid giving a fugitive a "mortal

---

[5] Austin *Texas State Gazette*, February 19, 1859.

wound," but if he were killed "the homicide is a consequence of the permission to fire upon him." [6]

Occasionally a band of runaways was too formidable to
be dispersed by volunteers, and the governor called upon
the militia to capture or destroy it. Ordinarily, however,
this and other organized police activity was delegated to the
slave patrols. A system of patrols, often more or less loosely
connected with the militia, existed in every slave state. Virginia empowered each county or corporation court to "ap-
point, for a term not exceeding three months, one or more
patrols" to visit "all negro quarters and other places suspected of having therein unlawful assemblies," and to arrest "such slaves as may stroll from one plantation to another without permission." Alabama compelled every
slaveowner under sixty and every nonslaveholder under
forty-five to perform patrol duty. The justices of each pre-
cinct divided the eligible males into detachments which
had to patrol at least one night a week during their terms
of service. Everywhere the patrols played a major role in
the system of control.

The patrols were naturally more active and efficient in
regions with many slaves than in regions with few. In some
places patrol activity was sporadic, at least between insurrection panics. "We should always act as if we had an enemy
in the very bosom of the State," warned a group of Charlestonians after the Vesey conspiracy.[7] But when their fears
subsided, many Southerners looked upon patrol service as
an irksome duty and escaped it when possible. Even the
slaveholders often preferred to pay the fines levied for non-
performance of this duty, or to hire substitutes as they were
sometimes permitted to do. The complaint of an editor in
Austin, Texas, that the state patrol law was not effective,

[6] Wilmington (N.C.) *Journal*, August 24, 1849; Catterall (ed.), *Judicial Cases*, III, p. 666.
[7] Phillips (ed.), *Plantation and Frontier*, II, pp. 113–14.

"in consequence of the indisposition of parties to perform their duties," was frequently heard—until the whites were again alarmed by rumors of rebellion.[8]

But complaints about patrols abusing their powers were as common as complaints about their failing to function. The nonslaveholding whites, to whom most patrol service was relegated, frequently disliked the masters almost as intensely as the Negroes, and as patrollers they were in a position to vent their feelings toward both. Slaveholders repeatedly went to the courts with charges that patrollers had invaded their premises and whipped their slaves excessively or illegally. The slaves in turn both hated and feared the "paterollers" and retaliated against them when they could. Yet masters looked upon the patrol as an essential police system, and none ever seriously suggested abolishing it.

The final clauses in the southern legal codes relating directly to the control of slaves were those governing free Negroes. The laws reflected the general opinion that these people were an anomaly, a living denial "that nature's God intended the African for the *status* of slavery." They "embitter by their presence the happiness of those who remain slaves. They entice them and furnish them with facilities to elope." They were potential allies of the slaves in the event of a rebellion. In 1830, David Walker, a free Negro who moved from North Carolina to Boston, wrote and attempted to circulate in the South a pamphlet which urged the slaves to fight for their freedom. He thus aroused southern legislatures to the menace of the free Negro.[9]

The trend of ante-bellum legislation was toward ever more stringent controls. Free Negroes could not move from one state to another, and those who left their own state for

---

8 Austin *Texas State Gazette*, July 22, 1854.
9 Jackson *Mississippian*, February 26, 1858; Tallahassee *Floridian and Journal*, April 11, 1857; *American Farmer*, XI (1829), p. 167; Johnson, *Ante-Bellum North Carolina*, pp. 515–16.

any purpose could not return. In South Carolina and the Gulf states Negro seamen were arrested and kept in custody while their vessels were in port. Though free Negroes could make contracts and own property, in most other respects their civil rights were as circumscribed as those of slaves. They were the victims of the white man's fears, of racial prejudice, and of the desire to convince slaves that winning freedom was scarcely worth the effort.

Many Southerners desired the complete expulsion of the free Negroes, or the re-enslavement of those who would not leave. Petitions poured in to the state legislatures demanding laws that would implement one or the other of these policies. In 1849, a petition from Augusta County, Virginia, asked the legislature to make an appropriation for a program of gradual removal; all free Negroes who refused to go to Liberia should be expelled from the state within five years.[1] In 1859, the Arkansas legislature required sheriffs to order the state's handful of free Negroes to leave. Those who remained were to be hired out as slaves for a year, after which those who still remained were to be sold into permanent bondage.

A Texas editor caught the spirit of the extreme proslavery element during the 1850's when he proclaimed that the time was "near at hand for determined action." Southern free Negroes were "destined to be remitted back into slavery," which was their "true condition." [2] In this last ante-bellum decade most states adopted laws authorizing the "voluntary enslavement" of these people and enabling them to select their own masters. Virginia went a step further and permitted the sale into "absolute slavery" of free Negroes convicted of offenses "punishable by confinement in the penitentiary"; Florida applied the same penalty to those who were "idle" or "dissolute." This problem,

---

[1] Virginia Legislative Petitions.
[2] Austin *Texas State Gazette*, September 12, 1857.

some apparently felt, would remain unsolved until all Negroes and "mulattoes" were not only *presumed* to be slaves
but were in *fact* slaves.

6

"A slave," said a Tennessee judge, "is not in the condition of a horse. . . . He has mental capacities, and an immortal principle in his nature." The laws did not "extin-
guish his high-born nature nor deprive him of many rights
which are inherent in man." [3] All the southern codes recognized the slave as a person for purposes other than holding
him accountable for crimes. Many state constitutions required the legislature "to pass such laws as may be necessary to oblige the owners of slaves to treat them with
humanity; to provide for them necessary clothing and provisions; [and] to abstain from all injuries to them, extending to life or limb."

The legislatures responded with laws extending some
protection to the persons of slaves. Masters who refused to
feed and clothe slaves properly might be fined; in several
states the court might order them to be sold, the proceeds
going to the dispossessed owners. Those who abandoned or
neglected insane, aged, or infirm slaves were also liable to
fines. In Virginia the overseers of the poor were required
to care for such slaves and to charge their masters.

Now and then a master was tried and convicted for the
violation of one of these laws. In 1849, the South Carolina
Supreme Court upheld the conviction of a slaveholder who
"did not give his negroes enough even of [corn] meal, the
only provision he did give." In such a case, said the court,
the law had to be enforced for the sake of "public sentiment, . . . and to protect property from the depredation

---

[3] Catterall (ed.), *Judicial Cases*, II, p. 530.

of famishing slaves." [4] But prosecutions were infrequent. Since a slave could neither file a complaint nor give evidence against his master, action depended upon the willingness of whites to testify in the slave's behalf. This happened only under unusual circumstances.

Some of the codes regulated the hours of labor. As early as 1740, South Carolina limited the working day to fifteen hours from March to September and fourteen hours from September to March. All the codes forbade field labor on Sunday. In Virginia, a master who worked his slaves on Sunday, "except in household or other work of necessity or charity," was to be fined two dollars for each offense. It was permissible, however, to let slaves labor on the Sabbath for wages; and the North Carolina Supreme Court ruled that it was not an indictable offense to give them Sunday tasks as a punishment. [5] With rare exceptions, masters who were so inclined violated these laws with impunity.

The early colonial codes had assessed only light penalties, or none at all, for killing a slave. South Carolina, "to restrain and prevent barbarity being exercised toward slaves," provided, in 1740, that a white who willfully murdered a slave was to be punished by a fine of seven hundred pounds or imprisonment at hard labor for seven years. Killing a slave in "sudden heat or passion" or by "undue correction" carried a fine of three hundred and fifty pounds. In Georgia prior to 1770, and in North Carolina prior to 1775, taking a slave's life was not a felony.

After the American Revolution there was a drastic change of policy. Virginia, in 1788, and North Carolina, in 1791, defined the malicious killing of a slave as murder subject to the same penalty imposed upon the murderer of a freeman. In 1817, North Carolina applied this principle to persons convicted of manslaughter. Georgia's Constitution

---

[4] Catterall (ed.), *Judicial Cases*, II, pp. 412–13.
[5] *Ibid.*, II, p. 107.

of 1798 contained a clause that was copied, in substance, into the constitutions of several states in the Southwest: "Any person who shall maliciously dismember or deprive a slave of life shall suffer such punishment as would be inflicted in case the like offence had been committed on a free white person."

Eventually all the southern states adopted laws of this kind. In 1821, South Carolina belatedly provided that a person who killed a slave "willfully, maliciously, and deliberately" was to suffer death, and a person who killed a slave in "sudden heat or passion" was to be fined up to five hundred dollars and imprisoned up to six months. In Alabama a person who, "with malice aforethought," caused the death of a slave "by cruel whipping or beating, or by any inhuman treatment, or by the use of any weapon in its nature calculated to produce death," was guilty of murder in the first degree. A master or overseer causing death by cruel whipping or by other cruel punishment, "though without any intention to kill," was guilty of murder in the second degree.

By the 1850's, most of the codes had made cruelty a public offense even when not resulting in death. Alabama masters and overseers who inflicted brutal punishments were subject to fines of from twenty-five to one thousand dollars. A person who committed an assault and battery upon a slave not his own, "without just cause or excuse," was guilty of a misdemeanor. Louisiana prohibited the owner from punishing a slave with "unusual rigor" or "so as to maim or mutilate him." Georgia more explicitly prohibited "cutting, or wounding, or . . . cruelly and unnecessarily biting or tearing with dogs." In Kentucky, a slave who was treated cruelly might be taken from his master and sold.

But these laws invariably had significant qualifications. For example, the accidental death of a slave while receiving "moderate correction" was not homicide. Killing a slave in the act of rebellion or when resisting legal arrest was always "justifiable homicide." South Carolina permitted a white person to "apprehend and moderately correct" a slave who was at large without a pass and refused to submit to examination; "and if any such slave shall assault and strike such white person, such slave may be lawfully killed." The South Carolina law against cruelty concluded with a nullifying clause: "nothing herein contained shall be so construed as to prevent the owner or person having charge of any slave from inflicting on such slave such punishment as may be necessary for the good government of the same." Southern courts, by their interpretations of the laws, in effect added further qualifications. Thus the North Carolina Supreme Court ruled that a homicide upon a slave did not require as much provocation as a homicide upon a white to make it justifiable.

Under most circumstances a slave was powerless to defend himself from an assault by a white man. According to the Tennessee Supreme Court, severe chastisement by the master did not justify resistance. If a master exercised his right to punish, "with or without cause, [and] the slave resist and slay him, it is murder . . . because the law cannot recognize the violence of the master as a legitimate cause of provocation." According to the Georgia Supreme Court, even if the owner should "exceed the bounds of reason . . . in his chastisement, the slave must submit . . . unless the attack . . . be calculated to produce death." [6]

On rare occasions a court refused to convict a bondsman for killing a brutal overseer (never a brutal master) while resisting an assault that might have caused his death. In 1834, the North Carolina Supreme Court reversed the decision of a lower court which had sentenced a slave to be hanged for the homicide of an overseer under these circum-

[6] Catterall (ed.), *Judicial Cases*, II, pp. 549–50; III, pp. 35–36.

stances. Though the slave's *"general* duty" was unconditional submission, he nevertheless had the right to defend himself against "an unlawful attempt . . . to deprive him of life." But Chief Justice Thomas Ruffin, in a similar case, expressed the apprehension many Southerners felt when a slave was exonerated for an assault on a white man. To hold that slaves could decide when they were entitled to resist white men was a dangerous doctrine, said Ruffin. It might encourage them to denounce "the injustice of slavery itself, and, upon that pretext, band together to throw off their common bondage entirely." [7]

In a few notable cases the courts enforced the laws against the killing of slaves. A North Carolinian was sentenced to death for the murder of his own female chattel. Over a period of months he had "beat her with clubs, iron chains, and other deadly weapons, time after time; burnt her; inflicted stripes . . . which literally excoriated her whole body." The court held him "justly answerable" for her death, though he did not "specially design it." The Virginia Court of Appeals, in approving a similar conviction, explained precisely how far a master could go before the law would intervene. For the sake of securing "proper subordination and obedience" the master would not be disturbed even though his punishment were "malicious, cruel and excessive." But he "acts at his peril; and if death ensues in consequence of such punishment, the relation of master and slave affords no ground of excuse or palliation." In Mississippi, too, a white man was hanged for killing another man's slave. "In vain," argued the state Supreme Court, "shall we look for any law passed by the . . . philanthropic legislature of this state, giving even to the master, much less to a stranger, power over the life of a slave." [8]

Decisions such as these were exceptional. Only a handful

---

[7] *Ibid.*, II, pp. 70–71, 132–34.
[8] *Ibid.*, I, pp. 223–25; II, pp. 85–86; III, pp. 283–84.

of whites suffered capital punishment for murdering slaves, and they were usually persons who had committed the offense upon slaves not their own. When a master was convicted, it was generally for a lesser crime, such as killing in "sudden heat or passion" or by "undue correction." And a convicted killer, whether or not the master, rarely received as heavy a penalty as he would have for a homicide upon a white.

Actually, the great majority of whites who, by a reasonable interpretation of the law, were guilty of feloniously killing slaves escaped without any punishment at all. Of those who were indicted, most were either acquitted or never brought to trial. For several reasons this was almost inevitable.

One major reason was that neither slaves nor free Negroes could testify against whites. There were, as one Southerner observed, "a thousand incidents of plantation life concealed from public view," witnessed only by slaves, which the law could not reach. One of slavery's "most vulnerable points," a defender of the institution agreed, was the "helpless position of the slave" when his master was "placed in opposition to him." His "mouth being closed as a witness," he had to depend upon whites to testify in his behalf.[9]

But here was the second major obstacle in the way of convictions: white witnesses were reluctant to testify against white offenders. Most white men were obsessed with the terrible urgency of racial solidarity, with the fear that the whole complex mechanism of control would break down if the master's discretion in governing slaves were questioned. It took a particularly shocking atrocity to break through this barrier—to enable a white man to win the approval of

---

[9] Henry, *Police Control*, p. 79; Thomas R. R. Cobb, *An Inquiry into the Law of Negro Slavery in the United States of America* (Philadelphia, 1858), pp. 97–98.

his neighbors for giving evidence against another white. A North Carolinian knew of "a number" of instances in which "nobody in the neighborhood had any doubt that the death of the slave was caused by the severity of his treatment," but no guilty party was indicted or brought to trial. Frederick Douglass cited the case of a Maryland woman who murdered a slave with a piece of firewood. A warrant was issued for her arrest, but it was never served.[1]

There was still a third obstacle. Even when whites agreed to testify, there remained the problem of getting a white jury to convict. A Louisiana planter made a terse notation in his diary: "Went to town[.] man tried for Whipping a negro to Death. trial will continue till tomorrow—deserves death—Cleared!" A South Carolinian reported that two whites who had murdered a slave "were cleared by a dirty ragged ———— Jury, the only reason I have heard for it was that a former jury had cleared men of . . . murder who were as guilty as these." The foreman of a South Carolina jury declared frankly that he "would not convict the defendant, or any other white person, of murdering a slave." [2] This was the feeling of most jurymen.

In Maryland, Frederick Douglass remembered hearing white men say that it was "worth but half a cent to kill a nigger, and half a cent to bury him." [3] This surely was not the attitude of the average Southerner, but it did indicate how lightly all too many of them regarded the laws against the killing of slaves. It would be too much to say that the codes gave slaves no protection at all. But it would also be too much to say that they extended equal justice and protection to slaves and freemen. If they had, there would

---

1 Bassett, *Slavery in North Carolina*, pp. 91–92; Douglass, *My Bondage*, pp. 125–26.
2 Davis (ed.), *Diary of Bennet H. Barrow*, p. 148; Gavin Diary, entries for November 4, 16, 1857; Catterall (ed.), *Judicial Cases*, II, p. 343.
3 Douglass, *My Bondage*, p. 127.

unquestionably have been fewer felonious assaults upon slaves.

"There are many persons," complained a Mississippi editor, "who think they have the same right to shoot a negro . . . that they have to shoot down a dog, but there are laws for the protection of slaves as well as the master, and the sooner the error alluded to is removed, the better it will be for both parties." [4] Slavery and the racial attitudes it encouraged caused this "error" to persist throughout the ante-bellum period.

7

The fate of a slave who was the principal, rather than the victim, of an alleged misdemeanor or felony was highly uncertain. The state codes established regular judicial procedures for the trial of slaves accused of public offenses, but probably most minor offenses, such as petit larceny, were disposed of without resort to the courts. For instance, when an Alabama slave was caught stealing from a neighboring plantation, the proprietor agreed not to prosecute if the overseer punished the slave himself. The state Supreme Court sanctioned the informal settlement of such cases. Even though an offense was "criminally punishable," said the court, so far as the public was concerned it was better to have the punishment "admeasured by a domestic tribunal." [5]

Nevertheless, many bondsmen who violated the law were given public trials. In colonial days they were always arraigned before special "Negro courts," which were usually less concerned about the formalities of traditional English justice than about speedy verdicts and certain punishments. A slave accused of a capital offense, according to the South

---

[4] Quoted in Sydnor, *Slavery in Mississippi*, pp. 250–51.
[5] Catterall (ed.), *Judicial Cases*, III, pp. 158–59.

Carolina code of 1740, was to be tried "in the most summary and expeditious maner"; on conviction he was to suffer death by such means as would be "most effectual to deter others from offending in the like maner." Justice in the "Negro courts" was at best capricious.

For misdemeanors, and in some states for crimes not punished capitally, the summary processes of "Negro courts" survived until the abolition of slavery. Louisiana tried slaves for noncapital felonies before one justice and four slaveholders, Mississippi before two justices and five slaveholders, and Georgia before three justices. Alabama tried slaves for minor offenses before a justice (who could assign a maximum penalty of thirty-nine lashes), and for noncapital felonies before the judge of the probate court and two justices of the peace. The states of the Upper South generally subjected slaves accused of misdemeanors to similar informal and summary trials.

In the nineteenth century, most states gave slaves jury trials in the regular courts when accused of capital crimes; some went further and gave them this privilege when accused of any felony. The Missouri Constitution of 1820 and the Texas Constitution of 1845 provided that in criminal cases slaves were to have an impartial trial by jury. On conviction, a Missouri slave was to suffer "the same degree of punishment, and no other, that would be inflicted on a free white person for a like offense." North Carolina slaves accused of capital offenses were tried in the superior courts, and the law required the trials to be conducted as the trials of freemen. In Alabama, they were tried before the circuit court of the county, "in the mode provided by law for the trial of white persons," except that two-thirds of the jurors had to be slaveholders. In Georgia, capital crimes continued to be tried before three justices until 1850, when the superior courts were given jurisdiction.

A few states never granted jury trial or abandoned the

informal courts and summary procedures even in capital cases. The Virginia code declared that the county and corporation courts, consisting of at least five justices, "shall be courts of *oyer* and *terminer* for the trial of negroes charged with felony. . . . Such trials shall be . . . without a jury." Louisiana tried slaves for capital offenses before two justices and ten slaveholders, and South Carolina tried them for all offenses before a justice and five freeholders without a jury.

Many Southerners trained in the law recognized the possibilities for miscarriages of justice in the "Negro courts." A South Carolina judge called these courts "the worst system that could be devised." In his message to the legislature, in 1833, Governor Robert Y. Hayne acknowledged that reform was "imperiously called for." "Capital offenses committed by slaves, involving the nicest questions of the law, are often tried by courts composed of persons ignorant of the law." An editor affirmed that the life of the slave and the property of the master were in jeopardy "from the ignorance and malice of unworthy magistrates." [6] However, criticism such as this produced few reforms.

In practice, the quality of justice slaves received from juries and regular courts was not consistently better than the justice they received from "Negro courts." When tension was great and the passions of white men were running high, a slave found it as difficult to get a fair trial before a jury in one of the superior courts of North Carolina or Alabama as he did before the justices in one of the informal courts of South Carolina or Virginia. Nowhere, regardless of constitutional or statutory requirements, was the trial of a bondsman apt to be like the trial of a freeman. Though counsel was guaranteed, though jurors might be challenged, though Negroes could testify in cases involving

---

[6] Henry, *Police Control*, pp. 58–61, 63–64; letter from Albert Rhett in Charleston *Courier*, January 27, 1842.

members of their own race, the trial of a slave was never the trial of a man by his peers. Rather, it was the trial of a man with inferior rights by his superiors—of a man who was property as well as a person. Inevitably, most justices, judges, and jurors permitted questions of discipline and control to obscure considerations of even justice.

A slave accused of committing violence upon another slave, rather than upon a white, had a better chance for a fair trial. Here the deeper issues of discipline and racial subordination were not involved, and the court could hear the case calmly and decide it on its merits. Moreover, the penalty on conviction was usually relatively light. Slaves were capitally punished for the murder of other slaves almost as rarely as whites were capitally punished for the murder of slaves. A bondsman in Rapides Parish, Louisiana, accused of beating another bondsman to death, was found guilty of "misbehavior" and sentenced to receive one hundred lashes on four successive days and to wear a ball and chain for three months. A slave in Clay County, Missouri, convicted of murdering another slave, received thirty-nine lashes and was sold out of the state.[7]

The southern codes did not prescribe lighter penalties for slaves who murdered other slaves than for slaves who murdered whites. The theory of the law was that one offense was as serious as the other. But the white men who applied the law usually thought otherwise.

8

When a Louisiana slave accused of murdering a white man (not his master) had the benefit of two mistrials, an overseer wrote in disgust: "there are some slave owners who think that a white man's life is worth nothing in com-

---

[7] Alexandria (La.) *Red River Republican*, January 8, 1848; Trexler, *Slavery in Missouri*, p. 79.

parison with that of a slave." [8] For some, such as this overseer, the wheels of justice even in the "Negro courts"
turned all too slowly; and critics often held the masters responsible for it.

Fortunately for the slave, his lack of civil rights and helplessness in the courts was mitigated somewhat by either the
master's self-interest or paternalism, or both. Sometimes
bondsmen had the help of their masters in escaping conviction for legal offenses or were sheltered from the harsh-
est features of the slave codes. On a Mississippi plantation
a field-hand once "rose upon" the overseer and "came near
killing him." His master kept him in irons for a few days,
but when the overseer recovered, the slave was sent back
to work. Though he had committed a capital crime, this
slave was never prosecuted for it.[9] On a Louisiana plantation a female domestic, while resisting punishment, threw
her mistress down and "beat her unmercifully on the head
and face." At her trial before a "Negro court," her mistress
"plead so hard for the girl's life to be spared" that she was
sentenced to life imprisonment.[1] Thus a slave escaped capital punishment because a "Negro court" indulged the
whim of her mistress.

Some good-natured masters winked at other regulations
in the codes. They permitted slaves to gather in illegal assemblies, to go at large without passes, to trade without per-
mits, to purchase liquor, and to hunt with guns. Despite the
laws, they allowed slaves to hire their own time and were
seldom prosecuted for it. Sometimes they encouraged slaves
to learn to read and write. A small Mississippi planter reported that one of his slaves had taught all the rest to read

[8] Moore Rawls to Lewis Thompson, n.d., Lewis Thompson Papers.
[9] Newstead Plantation Diary, entries for June 8–11, 1860.
[1] Rachel O'Connor to A. T. Conrad, May 26, 1836; *id.* to Mary C.
Weeks, June 5, 1836, Weeks Collection.

and that he had not objected. When told that there was a law prohibiting this, he claimed never to have heard of it.[2] The southern press complained incessantly about violations of the codes and demanded more rigorous enforcement.

Though slaves were not legally permitted to live independently, a few masters nevertheless gave them virtual freedom. The North Carolina Supreme Court noted a custom that had developed, "particularly among that class of citizens who were opposed to slavery, of permitting persons of color, who, by law, are their slaves, to go at large as free,—thereby introducing a species of *quasi* emancipation, contrary to the law, and against the policy of the State." Quakers frequently owned slaves "having nothing but the name, and working for their own benefit." Free Negroes with titles to slaves usually made their bondage nominal. Maryland doubtless contained more Negroes living in an "intermediate status between slavery and freedom" than any other southern state.[3]

Masters softened the state codes not only by evading them but also by going beyond the mere letter of the law in recognizing their slaves as human beings. No slaveholder needed to respect the marital ties of his slaves; yet a Tennesseean purchased several slaves at a public sale, not because he needed them, but because of "their intermarriage with my servants and their appeals to me to do so." A Kentucky mistress tried to buy the wife of her slave before moving to Missouri. Another Kentuckian, when obliged to sell his slaves, gave each an opportunity to find a satisfactory

---

[2] Olmsted, *Back Country*, pp. 143–44.

[3] Catterall (ed.), *Judicial Cases*, II, pp. 161–62; John Hope Franklin, "Slaves Virtually Free in Ante-Bellum North Carolina," *Journal of Negro History*, XVIII (1943), pp. 284–310; Richard B. Morris, "Labor Controls in Maryland in the Nineteenth Century," *Journal of Southern History*, XIV (1948), pp. 385–87.

purchaser and refused to sell any to persons residing outside the neighborhood.[4]

Finally, a few slaveholders tempered the codes by refusing to bequeath their human chattels as they did ordinary
property. True, wills showing solicitude for slaves were unusual; they often singled out just one or two from the rest
for special consideration; and the favored ones were nearly
always being rewarded for loyalty and obedience. Even so,
these expressions of gratitude were touching reminders
that some masters could never completely forget the human qualities in their "people."

When Mary Weems, of Prince Georges County, Maryland, wrote her will in 1840, she devoted a clause to one of
her female slaves. This woman, she instructed her heirs, was
not to be separated from her daughter, was to be given the
choice of working in the field or in the house, and was to
be "well and kindly treated, these wishes being expressed
in behalf of one who has been ever faithful and kind to me
and attentive to my wants when I have been sick." In 1846,
John Armstrong, of Fairfield District, South Carolina,
willed that a "favorite negro woman" was to be kept with
her children and not required to "perform the duties of a
slave." Instead, she was to "work for her own support alone,
and her time be allowed her as a free person, so far as by
the laws of this State it can be done."

Some testators made more general provisions for the welfare of all their slaves. In cases where slaves had to be sold
they prohibited the division of families, restricted sales to
purchasers within the county or state, or permitted slaves
to select their own masters. In 1837, Joseph Martin, of Talbot County, Maryland, realizing that his property would be
sold to pay his debts, ordered his executor to sell the slaves

---

[4] Bills Diary, entry for January 22, 1850; Sarah G. Yeates to her brother,
February 1, 1857, Buckner Family Papers; W. F. Bullock to Isaac P.
Shelby, December 21, 1850, Shelby Family Papers.

within the state and to "exercise the utmost humanity . . . by disposing of them in families as far as practicable." His son was "to take care of and tenderly treat" two old slaves "and furnish them with comfortable lodging and clothing and wholesome food, so long as they shall respectively live." In 1832, Elizabeth Carver, of Cumberland County, North Carolina, charged two of her children "with the maintenance and support of all my old and faithful Negro Slaves . . . during [their] natural lives."

John Clark, a small, obscure slaveholder who lived in Abbeville District, South Carolina, provided a striking example of inconspicuous paternalism. Clark, a childless widower, resided on his estate "without the society of white persons." To his slaves, twelve in number, he was "indulgent to a degree hurtful to his pecuniary interest and he regarded them as objects of care and regard." His will stipulated that his slaves were to be kept together on his land, the proceeds from their labor used for their comfort and support, and his household furniture divided among them. Clark's heirs contested the will on the ground that its purpose was to emancipate the slaves illegally, but the probate court denied that it violated state law.[5]

This decision was as unique as the will that precipitated it. Masters who ignored the demands of discipline by flagrantly violating the slave codes, who elevated their slaves to virtual freedom, who treated them with utter disregard for their status as property, and who strictly regulated their use when bequeathing them to heirs, are justly celebrated in the folklore of slavery. But they are celebrated because their conduct was so abnormal. Had other masters imitated them, the slave system would have disintegrated—and a nation might have been spared a civil war.

---

[5] Abbeville District, South Carolina, Judge of Probate Decree Book, 1839–1858.

9

"A free African population is a curse to any country," the Chancellor of the South Carolina Court of Appeals once flatly affirmed. "This race, . . . in a state of freedom, and in the midst of a civilized community, are a dead weight to the progress of improvement." Free Negroes became "pilferers and maurauders," "consumers, without being producers . . . governed mainly by the instincts of animal nature." [6] Racial attitudes such as these, the fear of free Negroes as a social menace, and respect for the rights of property caused the southern states to adopt constitutional prohibitions against the legislative emancipation of slaves without the consent of their owners.

But the state constitutions put few obstacles in the way of masters who wished to manumit their own slaves. In the border states of Delaware, Maryland (until 1860), Kentucky, and Missouri, the sole legislative restrictions were that creditors' claims must be respected and that a manumitted slave must not become a burden to the public because of age or infirmity. Virginia added the further condition that a manumitted slave was not to remain in the state for more than a year "without lawful permission." A county or corporation court might grant this permission if it had evidence that the freedman was "of good character, sober, peaceable, orderly and industrious." In North Carolina an emancipated slave had to leave the state within ninety days, unless a superior court made an exception because of "meritorious service." In Tennessee a slave freed after 1831 had to be sent beyond her borders immediately; after 1854 he had to be sent to the west coast of Africa.

In the Deep South the trend was toward increasingly severe legislative restrictions. In Louisiana (for many years the most liberal of these states) an act of 1807 limited the

---

[6] Catterall (ed.), *Judicial Cases*, II, p. 442.

privilege of manumission to slaves who were at least thirty years old and who had not been guilty of bad conduct during the previous four years. In 1830, Louisiana required emancipated slaves to leave the state within thirty days; after 1852, they had to leave the United States within twelve months. Five years later, Louisiana entirely prohibited private emancipations within the state.

The remaining states of the lower South had outlawed private emancipations early in the nineteenth century, except when granted by a special act of the legislature as a reward for "meritorious service." The Georgia legislature once approved a request a master inserted in his will: "Whereas, from the fidelity of my negro man Joy, and my negro woman Rose, who not only saved and protected a great part of my property during the time the British occupied St. Simons, but actually buried and saved a large sum of money, with which they might have absconded and obtained their freedom; it is therefore my will, and I direct my executors to petition the Legislature to pass an Act for the manumission of my said negroes." The South Carolina legislature purchased the freedom of two slaves and granted them annual pensions of fifty dollars for betraying insurrection plots. The Louisiana legislature emancipated a slave and gave him a reward of five hundred dollars for the same "meritorious service." [7]

The laws prohibiting private emancipations did not in themselves prevent a testator from directing in his will that his slaves be removed from the state and freed elsewhere. But the court might scrupulously examine the wording of such a bequest. The Georgia Supreme Court invalidated wills specifying that slaves be "manumitted and sent to a free state," because "the emancipation . . . was to take ef-

---

[7] Catterall (ed.), *Judicial Cases*, III, p. 21; Henry, *Police Control*, pp. 17–18; Taylor, "Negro Slavery in Louisiana," pp. 203–204. In 1860, Maryland also prohibited private emancipations within the state.

fect in Georgia." However, if the verbs were transposed, if the slaves were to be "sent to a free state and manumitted," the will was valid, because it was not unlawful to direct emancipation outside the state. Judge Joseph H. Lumpkin urged the Georgia legislature to remedy this "defect" in the law. "I have no partiality for foreign any more than domestic manumission," he confessed. "Especially do I object to the colonization of our negroes upon our northwestern frontier. They facilitate the escape of our fugitive slaves. In case of civil war, they would become an element of strength to the enemy." [8]

Several states in the Deep South took the step Judge Lumpkin suggested and prohibited emancipation by last will and testament. South Carolina acted as early as 1841, when it voided all deeds and wills designed to free slaves before or after removal from the state. Mississippi, Georgia, Arkansas, and Alabama adopted similar laws during the next two decades.

Occasionally a testator attempted to circumvent the statutes against emancipation, but almost invariably the court invalidated his will. "This is another of those cases," the South Carolina Court of Appeals once complained, "in which the superstitious weakness of dying men, proceeding from an astonishing ignorance of the solid moral and scriptural foundations upon which the institution of slavery rests, . . . induces them, in their last moments, to emancipate their slaves, in fraud of the . . . declared policy of the State." A Charleston editor thought it was sheer hypocrisy for an "old sinner" who had "enjoyed the profits of the labor of his slaves, during his life time" to emancipate them on his death bed. [9]

The truth was, of course, that *living* masters in all the southern states—even in those which prohibited manumis-

---

[8] Catterall (ed.), *Judicial Cases*, III, pp. 1–3, 61.
    Ibid., II, p. 392; Charleston *Courier*, September 7, 1857.

sion by last will and testament—always had the right to remove their slaves to a free state and there release them from bondage. Though no slave state could deprive them of this right, few made use of it.

Moreover, only a handful of slaveholders wrote wills providing for manumissions in states where this continued to be legal. An even smaller number would have done so in the Deep South had the privilege remained open to them. In no slave state, early or late in the ante-bellum period, were the total yearly emancipations more than a small fraction of the natural increase of the slave population. For example, in 1859, only three thousand slaves were emancipated throughout the entire South. At that time both Virginia and Kentucky permitted manumissions by deed or will. Yet Virginia, with a slave population of a half million, freed only two hundred and seventy-seven; Kentucky, with a slave population of nearly a quarter million, freed only one hundred and seventy-six.

Clearly, if the decline of slavery were to await the voluntary acts of individuals, the time of its demise was still in the distant future. The failure of voluntary emancipation was evident long before the 1830's when, according to Judge Lumpkin, "the blind zealots of the North" began their "unwarrantable interference." [1] James H. Hammond got at the crux of the matter when he asked whether any people in history had ever voluntarily surrendered two billion dollars worth of property.

One of the minority, a North Carolinian, who willed the unconditional emancipation of his slaves gave four reasons for his action: "Reason the first. Agreeably to the rights of man, every human being, be his or her colour what it may, is entitled to freedom. . . . Reason the second. My conscience, the great criterion, condemns me for keeping them

---

[1] Catterall (ed.), *Judicial Cases*, III, pp. 1-2.

in slavery. Reason the third. The golden rule directs us to do unto every human creature, as we would wish to be done unto; and sure I am, that there is not one of us would agree to be kept in slavery during a long life. Reason the fourth and last. I wish to die with a clear conscience, that I may not be ashamed to appear before my master in a future World. . . . I wish every human creature seriously to deliberate on my reasons." [2]

[2] Catterall (ed.), *Judicial Cases*, II, pp. 49–50.

CHAPTER SIX

Slavemongering

The power of conveyance, inseparable from any species of private property, was a fundamental attribute of chattel slavery. Since titles to slaves were transferable, since slaves were not bound to the land like medieval serfs, they formed a reasonably mobile labor supply.

Much of the traffic in slaves involved private transactions between neighbors, in which sellers negotiated directly with buyers. Local sales were also arranged through newspaper advertisements or through the services of commission merchants, auctioneers, or brokers. In these ways many bondsmen changed hands within a neighborhood as masters, for one reason or another, found it necessary to dispose of all or part of their labor force.

The right of conveyance was significant not only because it made local transfers of ownership possible but also because slaves could be moved to new areas as they were opened to settlement. Among the ante-bellum Southerners who left the impoverished lands of the Southeast for the fresh lands of the Southwest—among those who cut down the forests, grubbed the stumps, cleared the cane brakes, drained the swamps, and broke the virgin soil—were Negro slaves as well as white pioneers. Hundreds of thousands of bondsmen were in the stream of settlers who filled the hemp and tobacco districts west of the Appalachians and expanded the Cotton Kingdom from the Georgia piedmont to the Texas prairies. Whenever the prices of southern staples were good, wherever the yield per acre was high, there arose an urgent demand for labor, and the slave coffles were on the move.

The Atlantic and border states, with Virginia constantly ranking first among them, were the exporters of slaves. In the three decades between 1830 and 1860, Virginia exported nearly three hundred thousand—almost the whole of her natural increase. Maryland and Kentucky each exported about seventy-five thousand, North Carolina about one hundred thousand, South Carolina about one hundred and seventy thousand, and Missouri and Tennesee smaller numbers. Total annual slave exports from these states averaged approximately twenty-five thousand. By the 1850's, Georgia's exports slightly exceeded her imports. The exports of Arkansas and the Gulf states remained negligible and were always greatly exceeded by imports.[1]

How did slaves become a part of this westward movement of population? Some of them were sent to new cotton and sugar lands by planters who did not themselves leave their family estates in the Southeast. Edward Lloyd, of Talbot County, Maryland, moved part of his force of several hundred slaves to a cotton plantation in Mississippi. Lewis Thompson, of Bertie County, North Carolina, put a large gang to work on a profitable sugar plantation in Rapides Parish, Louisiana. The Wade Hamptons, of South Carolina, increased their wealth from huge cotton and sugar plantations in Louisiana and Mississippi. These and other absentee owners shipped thousands of slaves to the Southwest and placed them under the control of their sons or of hired overseers.

More commonly, however, the master sold his old lands and accompanied his bondsmen. In the Southwest lived

---

[1] Bancroft, *Slave-Trading*, pp. 382 ff.

colonies of Virginians and Carolinians who had been driven from their old homes by economic necessity, or lured away by the irresistible prospect of large profits. Early in the nineteenth century the bulk of this migration was toward Kentucky, Tennessee, and the Georgia piedmont; after the War of 1812 it was toward Missouri, Alabama, Mississippi, and Louisiana; and during the prosperous 1850's it was increasingly toward Arkansas and Texas. Travelers in the Old South frequently encountered both large and small slaveholders driving their slaves, livestock, and wagonloads of other movable property to some promised land.

But a large proportion of the slaves who were transferred to the Southwest—perhaps a majority of them—reached their new homes through the facilities of the interstate slave trade.[2] They were usually moved by professional traders who purchased them from masters in the exporting states and sold them to masters in the importing states. This merchandising of bondsmen gave them their great mobility—made possible the transportation of much of the relatively abundant labor in the less prosperous older regions to the flourishing new districts where labor was scarce. The trader was therefore a key figure in the slave system; and many masters at one time or another utilized his services, either as sellers or buyers. Without him the slave economy of, say, Virginia or Mississippi, could not have functioned efficiently. Indeed, without him many slaveholders could not have survived.

However essential it was, this traffic in slaves—the most overtly commercialized aspect of the peculiar institution—was offensive not only to abolitionists but also to many of slavery's stanchest defenders. The more conscientious slaveholders made great financial sacrifices to avoid dealing with "speculators." Some patriarchal masters in Virginia and

2 *Ibid.,* p. 398.

elsewhere lived on the edge of bankruptcy rather than seek solvency through the sale of all or part of their "people." Other masters, more concerned about social prestige than about economic prosperity, feared to lose rank by marketing bondsmen.

When necessity dictated sales, masters often gave convincing evidence of the distress this misfortune caused them. A North Carolinian, informing his brother that some of the family slaves must be disposed of, wrote: "Father will not sell them himself, you know his nature in that respect. But he has intimated that he would be willing to give them to some of us, and that he would be satisfied if we chose to sell them." Another North Carolinian, after parting with some of his slaves, lamented: "I did not know until the time came what pain it would give me." "I earnestly pray," wrote an unhappy South Carolina mistress before the marketing of her slaves, that "the people may be fortunate in being owned by a good master." [3]

The majority of slaveholders agreed that only the most calamitous circumstances could justify dealings with professional traders. In fact, it was hard to find a master who would admit that he sold slaves as a deliberate "speculation"—a business transaction whose object was a profit—rather than as an unhappy last resort. Perhaps only a few masters wished to regard slaves as marketable commodities, though some certainly did so, but most of them had in their lexicons an extremely broad definition of "necessity." Somehow their necessities kept the auctioneers busy and enabled the traders to conduct a brisk traffic in human flesh. [4]

While some masters would not sell "surplus" slaves, i.e.,

[3] Walter W. Lenoir to Thomas I. Lenoir, July 2, 1850, Lenoir Family Papers; Taylor, *Slaveholding in North Carolina*, p. 70; Easterby (ed.), *South Carolina Rice Plantation*, p. 29.
[4] Bancroft, *Slave-Trading*, pp. 202–204.

the excess above the number they could use economically, most of them felt that the possession of a surplus created one of those fortuitous situations that necessitated sales. Farmers and planters whose slave stock increased beyond their labor needs often elected to sell the surplus rather than expand their agricultural operations. Many urban slaveholders marketed the surplus from their staffs of domestics.

Selling slaves to facilitate the division of an estate among heirs was also regarded as an involuntary transaction. So was an administrator's sale or an execution sale to satisfy the claims of creditors. If a master used his slaves as security for a loan and was later obliged to sell them to repay the loan, that was an unanticipated misfortune. In such cases the line between a speculative sale and an involuntary sale was a thin one, but it was nevertheless important to those who drew it.

The owner's moral right to sell trouble makers within his slave force was almost universally recognized. If a master were to remain a master, he could hardly be expected to retain slaves he could not manage, or to consider their sale as a matter within his control. Slaveholders in the border states saw the necessity of seeking out the trader when bondsmen gave evidence of contemplating escape to the free states. Accordingly, a North Carolina mistress sold two slaves, one because of his "insubordination and the apprehension . . . that he designed an escape into Canada," the other "on account of [her] bad qualities." Another North Carolinian discovered in his slave force two families who were "an injury to the others and to the farm to retain; and now seems to be the judicious time to let them go." "It is a melancholy fact," wrote a South Carolinian, "that a large proportion of our ablest and most intelligent slaves are annually sent out of the State for misconduct." [5]

---

[5] Catterall (ed.), *Judicial Cases*, II, pp. 118–19; Walter W. Lenoir to

Sometimes a master in financial straits used the transgressions of a slave as an excuse for selling him, when under happier circumstances he would not have considered such a sale. His rationalization protected him from loss of public esteem, but it did not always satisfy his troubled conscience. Such was the plight of a Maryland slaveholder who sold Eliza, a refractory slave mother, to a trader who in turn sold her to a Louisiana planter. Eliza compounded her old master's distress when she begged him (through a letter written by her new mistress) to restore her daughter Jennie to her. The transparent cant of his reply concealed neither his feelings of guilt nor the genuine pathos of his predicament:

> . . . As to letting Jennie go to live with you I can hardly make up my mind what to say. I would be reluctant to part with her. She has a good disposition, . . . is very useful for her services in the house, . . . and I should miss her very much. . . .
>
> However I profess to be a christian and have the happy and comforting assurance that I am . . . what I profess to be. . . . I think you will acknowledge that I was to you a kind and forbearing master and that you were an ungrateful servant, and I think you feel assured that if you had conducted yourself faithfully, no offer would have tempted me to part with you. . . . But situated as I was after the death of [my] dear beloved and still lamented wife, the only alternative presented to me was to quit housekeeping or part with you—a painful one. . . .
>
> . . . Let me advise you as your former Master . . . to cease to do evil and learn to do well, to live up to the precepts of the gospel. . . . Serve your heavenly Master and your present owners faithfully, and be assured that I greatly regret the occasion that resulted in the separation of you from your child.

Thomas I. Lenoir, July 2, 1850, Lenoir Family Papers; *Southern Agriculturist*, II (1829) , p. 575.

Though refusing her request, he extended to Eliza his "unfeigned benevolence and charity." [6]

A numerous minority of masters contributed slaves to the interstate trade under circumstances which their neighbors could hardly have considered creditable. Doubtless the slave-selling masters either professed to have legitimate reasons or hoped to conceal their actions from others. One such transaction came unexpectedly into the open when a slave trader sued a North Carolinian for fraud in the sale of a slave child who was physically "unsound." Speculators were frequently implicated with masters in covert or open attempts to dispose of "sickly" slaves. In an article on "Negro consumption," a southern doctor advised slaveholders to learn the symptoms of this affliction, because slaves suffering from it were often put on the market. A few speculators made a practice of purchasing diseased slaves at low prices with the expectation of good profits from those who recovered. A "Dr. J. King," of New Orleans, advertised that he would give "immediate attention" to communications from owners who had "slaves rendered unfit for labor by . . . diseases, and who wish to dispose of them on reasonable terms." [7]

An indignant Georgia editor pointed to another source from which traders drew their supplies. "We allude to . . . the introduction into our State, of the negro felons and desperadoes of all the other states. It is a common practice, for instance, for our sister State South Carolina, when they get hold of some desperate villain of a negro, who is convicted of crime, after the infliction of some punishment, to make it imperative that he shall be carried out of the State." In 1849, a court of freeholders and magistrates in Charleston confirmed this when it convicted four slaves of

---

[6] T. D. Jones to Eliza, September 7, 1860, Butler Family Papers.
[7] Catterall (ed.), *Judicial Cases*, II, p. 26; *De Bow's Review*, XI (1851), pp. 212–13; Lexington *Kentucky Gazette*, July 4, 1839.

riot and insubordination and sentenced them to six months of solitary confinement, fifteen lashes on the first day of each month, "and then to be placed in solitary confinement for five years, unless sent without the limits of the State." Owners occasionally tried secretly to dispose of slaves accused of felonies. A North Carolinian "secreted" one under suspicion of homicide and sold him to a trader with the understanding that he was to be taken out of the state. Slaveholders in all the states of the Deep South frequently echoed the protest of a Georgian who asked, "Is Georgia the Botany Bay, for the black criminals of the South?" [8]

Although the interstate slave trade had few defenders and found no place in romanticized versions of the antebellum South, it was nevertheless a crucial part of her economic life. How vital this traffic was to the economies of the exporting states was apparent in the fall of 1860 when the secession crisis disrupted it. "Money matters are tighter in Kentucky than ever I saw them," wailed a Lexington merchant, "and no one seems to know when they will change for the better. If we could get our usual supply of exchange from the South, at this season of the year, we might get along better, but the planters are not buying negroes, mules, horses nor anything else. . . . Asa Collins has been in Natchez ten or twelve days with forty-one negroes and sold nothing. . . . There are some negroes offering here, . . . but . . . hardly any selling." [9] A condition such as this brought distress to the entire commercial community.

---

[8] Milledgeville *Southern Recorder*, February 18, 1851; Charleston *Courier*, July 31, 1849; Catterall (ed.), *Judicial Cases*, II, p. 229; Bancroft, *Slave-Trading*, p. 270.

[9] F. G. Murphy to George ———— [?], September 26, 1860, Buckner Family Papers.

2

The magnitude of the interstate slave trade caused some critics to charge that many of those who supplied the speculators with merchandise were engaged in "slave breeding"—in raising slaves for the specific purpose of marketing them. In Virginia, Olmsted remarked, most "gentlemen of character seem to have a special disinclination to converse on the subject. . . . It appears to me evident, however, from the manner in which I hear the traffic spoken of incidentally, that the cash value of a slave for sale, above the cost of raising it from infancy to the age at which it commands the highest price, is generally considered among the surest elements of a planter's wealth. . . . That a slave woman is commonly esteemed least for her laboring qualities, most for those qualities which give value to a broodmare is, also, constantly made apparent." [1]

Slaveholders intensely resented this accusation, and proslavery writers vigorously denied its truth. A Virginian published an essay, entitled "Estimates of the Expenses and Profits of Rearing Slaves," to prove that holding them exclusively for breeding purposes yielded meager returns and was therefore never done. Post-bellum Southerners affirmed that those who made this charge had "adduced no shred of supporting evidence." [2]

The evidence of systematic slave breeding is scarce indeed, not only because it is unlikely that many engaged in it but also because written records of such activities would seldom be kept. But if the term is not used with unreasonable literalness, if it means more than owner-coerced matings, numerous shreds of evidence exist which indicate that slaves were reared with an eye to their marketability—that

---

[1] Olmsted, *Seaboard*, pp. 55-56.
[2] *Farmers' Register*, II (1834), pp. 253-55; Trexler, *Slavery in Missouri*, p. 45; Phillips, *American Negro Slavery*, pp. 361-62.

the domestic slave trade was not "purely casual." [3] Many masters counted the fecundity of Negro women as an economic asset and encouraged them to bear children as rapidly as possible. In the exporting states these masters knew that the resulting surpluses would be placed on the market. Though few held slaves merely to harvest the increase or overtly interfered with their normal sexual activity, it nevertheless seems proper to say that they were engaged in slave breeding.

For instance, a Virginia planter boasted to Olmsted that his slave women were "uncommonly good breeders; he did not suppose that there was a lot of women anywhere that bred faster than his." Every infant, he exulted, was worth two hundred dollars at current prices the moment it was born. "I have been making enquiries," wrote another Virginian to a friend who was selling slaves in Mississippi, "in regard to the prices of Negroes in our section and have attended several sales lately. . . . From what I observed healthy young women sell almost as well as men. . . . It has occurred to me that negro men would sell better in 'Orleans perhaps than here, but that women would bring more in Virginia." He advised his friend to bring his slaves back to Virginia—"or perhaps the men could be disposed of and the women brought back." [4]

A Tennessee court once protected the heirs to an estate by prohibiting the sale of a slave woman who had given birth to several children. To sell this slave, "so peculiarly valuable for her physical capacity of child-bearing," the court believed would have been an "enormous sacrifice." In fact, the modest profit gained from the labor of a gang

---

[3] See Gray, *History of Agriculture*, II, pp. 662–63, for an excellent analysis of this problem. See also Bancroft, *Slave-Trading*, pp. 67–87.

[4] Olmsted, *Seaboard*, p. 57; A. S. Dillon to William C. Powell, William C. Powell Papers.

of slaves in Tennessee made "an increase of the stock an object" of their owners.[5]

Late in the eighteenth century a South Carolinian advertised that he wished to sell fifty "prime orderly Negroes." He had, "with great trouble and expence, selected them out of many for several years past. They were purchased for stock and breeding Negroes, and to any Planter who particularly wanted them for that purpose, they are a very choice and desirable gang." Many years later, in 1844, another South Carolinian tried to sell two female slaves because they were afflicted with a malady which he thought "rendered them unprofitable as breeding women." James H. Hammond bemoaned the heavy mortality on his plantation: "Other people consider the . . . increase [of slaves] one of the greatest sources of profit to them. If they can make out to pay their way they expect to accumulate at a fair rate by course of nature." [6]

Even in Mississippi there is a record of a small planter who was "an unsuccessful farmer, generally buying his corn and meat," but who "succeeded very well in raising young negroes." And one of the early propagandists for Florida proclaimed: "The climate is peculiarly adapted and fitted to the constitution of the Negro. It is an excellent and cheap climate to breed and raise them. The offal of the Sugar House fattens them like young pigs." [7]

Masters who prized prolific Negro women not only tolerated but sometimes came close to promoting sexual promiscuity among them. A few sanctioned the breakup of marriages when one or the other partner gave evidence of

---

[5] Catterall (ed.), *Judicial Cases*, II, pp. 504–505, 579.

[6] Phillips (ed.), *Plantation and Frontier*, II, pp. 57–58; Catterall (ed.), *Judicial Cases*, II, p. 392; Hammond Diary, entry for November 2, 1841.

[7] Catterall (ed.), *Judicial Cases*, III, p. 356; *Southern Cultivator*, XVIII (1860), p. 324.

sterility. Some owners in the Upper South maintained an amazing imbalance of the sexes in their holdings. The will of a master in Caroline County, Virginia, for example, showed that he owned one adult male and eight adult females; and the inventory of a Maryland estate revealed a holding of fifty-six slaves, "mostly women and children." An advertisement in a Fredericksburg, Virginia, newspaper was inserted by someone who wished "to purchase 10 or 12 negroes, chiefly young females." [8]

In both the exporting and importing states, slaveholders almost inevitably made slave rearing a part of their business. Every child born to a slave woman became the master's property, and usually the child's ultimate capital value far exceeded the cost of raising him. A sagacious master, therefore, was solicitous about the natural increase of his slaves, whether he marketed the increase or used it to expand his own economic operations. Here was a situation in which humanity and self-interest both enjoined masters to bless motherhood—to give reasonable care to pregnant slave women and to the "sucklers" and their offspring.

Seldom did female chattels disappoint their owner. After all, sexual promiscuity brought them rewards rather than penalties; large families meant no increased responsibilities and, if anything, less toil rather than more. Slave women, Fanny Kemble observed on her husband's Georgia plantation, understood distinctly what it was that gave them value as property. "This was perfectly evident to me from the meritorious air with which the women always made haste to inform me of the number of children they had borne, and the frequent occasions on which the older slaves would direct my attention to their children, exclaim-

---

[8] Catterall (ed.), *Judicial Cases*, IV, p. 104; Bancroft, *Slave-Trading*, p. 26.

ing, 'Look missis! little niggers for you and massa; plenty little niggers for you and little missis!' " [9]

Slaveholders were often remarkably candid about their desire to exploit the procreative talents of their slaves. "Your negroes will breed much faster when well clothed, fed and housed," advised a Virginia planter in an agricultural periodical, "which fact, offers an inducement to those slave owners, whose hearts do not overflow with feelings of humanity." In demonstrating the superiority of slave labor over free, a Georgian observed that capital invested in bondsmen yielded a substantial return from the offspring of the women alone. "It is certain that multitudes of men have accumulated largely, merely by the increase of their slaves." Fecund slave women, argued a Mississippian, "if properly taken care of, are the most profitable to their owners of any others. . . . It is remarkable the number of slaves which may be raised from one woman in the course of forty or fifty years with the proper kind of attention." [1]

An Alabama planter felt cheated when a female he purchased as a "breeding woman" proved to be "incapable of . . . bearing children," and he sued the vendor for fraud. The Alabama Supreme Court agreed that any jury "would place a higher value on a female slave promising issue, than on one of a contrary description." A Tennessee planter wished that his agricultural enterprises were more remunerative but thought that he "ought perhaps be satisfied" because of the numerous births among his slaves. "We have the prospect of a pretty fair increase now, and if the children are not any thing but consumers in our day they will be of some value to our children." [2]

Planters usually ordered their overseers to be attentive

---

[9] Kemble, *Journal*, pp. 59–61.

[1] *Farmers' Register*, V (1837), p. 302; *North Carolina Planter*, II (1859), p. 163; Sydnor, *Slavery in Mississippi*, pp. 136–37.

[2] Catterall (ed.), *Judicial Cases*, III, pp. 138, 195; Gustavus A. Henry to his wife, November 28, December 3, 1846, Henry Papers.

to expectant mothers, to women with nursing babies, and to small children. "The children must be particularly attended to," wrote a Mississippian in his plantation rules, "for rearing them is not only a duty, but also the most profitable part of plantation business." The printed instructions in Thomas Affleck's plantation record book warned overseers to "bear in mind that a *fine crop* consists, first, in an increase in the number, and a marked improvement in the condition and value of the negroes." Responding to a similar warning, a Georgia overseer assured his employer that he used "every means" to promote an increase of the slave force. "I consider every child raised as part of the crop. . . . my ambition is to do better and better not to retrograde so if I fail do not blame me. blame *Luck*." [3]

Some owners tempted their slave women to be fruitful by rewarding them for each baby they bore. In an essay on plantation management one master recommended his policy to others: "No inconsiderable part of a farmer's profits being in little negroes he succeeds in raising; the breeding women, when lusty, are allowed a great many privileges and required to work pretty much as they please. When they come out of the straw, a nice calico dress is presented each one as a reward and inducement to take care of their children." The mistress of a Louisiana plantation ordered some gay calico from her business agent. "I have all ways given a dress of such to every woman after having a young child," she explained. "I am now in debt to four, that has young babes, *and fine ones too*—they do much better, by being encouraged a little, and I have ever thought they deserved it." [4]

---

[3] Andrew Flinn Plantation Book; R. King, Jr., to Thomas Butler, February 13, 1831, Pierce Butler Papers, Historical Society of Pennsylvania, Philadelphia (copy in possession of Prof. Ralph W. Haskins).

[4] *American Cotton Planter and Soil of the South*, I (1857), p. 375; Rachel O'Conner to A. T. Conrad, April 12, 1835, Weeks Collection.

VI: *Slavemongering*

The slaveholder's intervention in the process of procreation was usually limited to providing slave women with favorable conditions and attractive incentives such as these. If this was not slave breeding, at least it was slave rearing, which was inseparable from slavery. Owners calculated the natural increase as part of the profit upon their invested capital. They might realize this profit by putting additional acres under cultivation, or they might realize it by doing business with the slave traders.

3

In so far as the domestic slave trade was interstate commerce it was subject to Federal control. Antislavery groups tried repeatedly to persuade Congress to exercise its constitutional power to abolish this traffic, but they never succeeded. Only a few minor Federal regulations in any way affected it. A clause in the act which outlawed further importations from Africa after January 1, 1808, barred ships of less than forty tons burden from transporting slaves in the coastwise trade. As soon as Congress established its jurisdiction over the District of Columbia, it closed the District as a slave market; and in 1850 it closed the District as a depot for the collection of slaves to be sold elsewhere. In all other respects Congress left control of the trade to the individual states.

State regulation was sporadic and, for the most part, ineffective. A curious blend of self-interest and humanitarianism motivated such restraining legislation as was adopted. Unquestionably the chief objectives were to protect the interests of purchasers and to maintain the security of the white community; but a few states gave some thought to the plight of the bondsmen who were the victims of the traffic.

In the Upper South, Delaware alone refused to become a source of supply for speculators. The preamble to an act of 1787 noted that slaves were being "exported and sold into other States, contrary to the principles of humanity and justice, and derogatory to the honor of this State." This act prohibited even the master from exporting a slave without a permit; and a subsequent act gave freedom to any slave illegally exported. No other state, however, interfered with either masters or traders who wished to ship chattels beyond its boundaries.

Nor did any other state forbid masters to separate husbands and wives when put on the market. In Louisiana, slave children under ten were not to be sold or imported apart from their mothers. Alabama and Georgia placed rather slight restrictions on the breakup of families when slaves were sold to satisfy creditors, but neither these states nor the others applied the restrictions to masters who sold slaves voluntarily. In the chief exporting states owners legally could separate children of any age from their mothers.

Certain regulations the importing states enforced were clearly of a protective character. For example, they required vendors to give a written warrant of clear title and physical soundness. Louisiana and Mississippi also required sellers to prove the slave's good character with affidavits from two freeholders and the clerk of the county in which the slave had lived. All these states tried to prevent the importation of bondsmen who had been convicted of felonies. Cities which became major slave marts adopted ordinances designed to protect the community from disease. New Orleans required traders to keep their merchandise in clean, well-ventilated buildings at least two stories high, to report the outbreak of any contagious disease, and to send sick slaves to Charity Hospital (at the traders' own expense). During a cholera epidemic, in

1833, the town of Washington, Mississippi, entirely stopped slave trading within its limits.[5]

In the nineteenth century, at one time or another, the majority of southern states tried to prevent the speculators from marketing their merchandise within their borders. Most of the state constitutions contained clauses authorizing the legislature to "prohibit the introduction of any slave for the purpose of speculation, or as an article of trade or merchandise." Missouri, Arkansas, Texas, and Florida were the only states never to pass such laws. Until 1849, Kentucky even prohibited residents—but not immigrants—from importing slaves for their own use, unless they were acquired by inheritance. Elsewhere both residents and immigrants were always free to bring in slaves for personal use, although they were sometimes required to take an oath that their purpose was not to sell them.

With few exceptions, the laws against the introduction of slaves by professional traders remained in force for only short periods of time. Virginia and North Carolina repealed their laws early in the nineteenth century, South Carolina in 1848, Maryland in 1850, and Tennessee in 1855. Georgia barred the speculators briefly on three different occasions before 1850; Alabama from 1827 to 1829 and for a few months in 1832; Louisiana from 1826 to 1828 and from 1831 to 1834; and Mississippi from 1833 to 1846. But during the last ante-bellum decade none of the importing states had any such restriction, and the gates were thus again wide open to the slave traders.

Though humanitarianism was not the crucial force behind the adoption of these laws, it was never altogether absent even in the Deep South. Mississippi, explained an attorney before the state Supreme Court, had been "pecul-

---

[5] Taylor, "Negro Slavery in Louisiana," p. 64; Washington *Mississippi Gazette*, May 18, 1833.

iarly the theatre . . . of the unfeeling cruelty" of slave traders, "until all good men no doubt had become disgusted and possessed of a strong wish to exclude . . . this class of speculators." Mississippians, the Court agreed, "had seen and deplored the evils connected with it. The barbarities, the frauds, the scenes so shocking in many instances to our feelings of humanity and the sensibilities of our nature, which generally grew out of it, they, therefore, determined to prohibit in the future." [6] Yet here, as elsewhere, the trade eventually was reopened and the shocking scenes re-enacted.

One of the basic reasons for the attempts to close the trade was the alarm many whites in the importing states felt because of the rapid increase of the slave population. This, they feared, threatened their security. It was not a coincidence that Alabama, Mississippi, and Louisiana, the major importing states, outlawed the trade immediately after the Nat Turner rebellion—a time of more than normal fear that irresponsible speculators would introduce dangerous rebels from the Upper South. The traders wanted maximum profits, explained a Mississippian; hence they were tempted to buy the most "wicked" slaves because they were the cheapest. Mississippi was being "inundated" by "the insurgents and malefactors, the sweepings of the jails of other states." A Natchez newspaper reported that after the Turner rebellion Virginia was "swarming with Negro traders." Many rebels who had been "directly or indirectly engaged in the work of murder" would be brought to Mississippi "to instil in our slaves the poison of discontent." [7]

Some whites in the Deep South suspected that masters

---

[6] Catterall (ed.), *Judicial Cases*, III, p. 289; Sydnor, *Slavery in Mississippi*, pp. 157–58.

[7] Catterall (ed.), *Judicial Cases*, III, pp. 289–90, 534–35; Natchez *Gazette*, October 5, 1831.

in the Upper South were disposing of their property in anticipation of the abolition of slavery. "We are actually offering them inducements to become free States by allowing them to bring their slaves amongst us and paying them large prices for them," warned a Georgian. By closing this trade, "we will force them to keep their slaves, as well as make it their interest to protect the institution." Mississippi adopted her restriction, in part, "to compel these border States to stand firm by the institution . . . by cutting off their market. . . . It was feared that if these border States were permitted to sell us their slaves, . . . *they too* would unite in the wild fanaticism of the day, and render the institution . . . thus reduced to a few Southern States, an easy prey to its wicked spirit." [8]

The manner in which Mississippi applied her proscription of the trade seriously compromised her slave interest. The state Constitution of 1832 prohibited this traffic after May 1, 1833. But during the following four years the state made no serious effort to enforce this provision, and speculators continued to sell slaves in violation of it. Not until after the Panic of 1837, when the slave market collapsed, did the legislature take action and impose penalties upon professional traders. Then Mississippi slaveholders refused to honor the notes they had given to local speculators for slaves purchased on credit between 1833 and 1837. The slaveholders argued that all such transactions had been illegal—and the state courts upheld them. Thus, protested the counsel for an indignant speculator, Mississippians were "protected in the enjoyment of thousands of slaves, imported from different portions of the republic without paying for them." [9]

---

[8] Savannah *Republican*, January 22, 1849; Vicksburg *Weekly Whig*, July 30, 1845; Catterall (ed.), *Judicial Cases*, III, p. 361.

[9] Sydnor, *Slavery in Mississippi*, pp. 161–71; Catterall (ed.), *Judicial Cases*, III, pp. 295–96.

Actually, none of the laws against the introduction of slaves as merchandise were ever effectively enforced, for the speculators found numerous ways to evade them. Sometimes speculators imported slaves, held them on a farm for a short time, and then sold them. After the Mississippi legislature stopped the traffic in 1837, purchasers crossed the river at Natchez or Vicksburg and dealt with the traders in Louisiana. In Georgia, complained an editor, "the law is constantly evaded by corrupt speculators, and hundreds of negroes are annually introduced and sold. It is a practice among these speculators, after having agreed with their several purchasers upon the price to be paid, to take the Rail-Road or stage to the nearest point in Alabama or South Carolina, and there make out and sign their bills of sale. . . . All this is a corrupt violation of the law; and . . . we hope it will not longer be permitted." [1]

But the Georgia law was repealed rather than strengthened, and the introduction of slaves as merchandise remained legal to the end of the slave regime. Ultimately the convenience of the traffic to residents of both exporting and importing states outweighed the evils about which so many complained.

4

If most slaveholders condoned slave trading under conditions they accepted as unavoidable, few had a good word to say for the slavemongers themselves. Daniel R. Hundley reflected the attitude of most articulate Southerners when he wrote a defense of his section's institutions. The "hard-hearted Negro Trader" was "preeminent in villainy and a greedy love of filthy lucre." This "Southern Shylock," Hundley claimed, was usually "a coarse ill-bred person, provincial in speech and manners, with a cross-looking

---

[1] Savannah *Republican*, January 30, 1849.

phiz, a whiskey-tinctured nose, cold hard-looking eyes, a dirty tobacco-stained mouth, and shabby dress."

After drawing this contemptuous caricature of the typical speculator, Hundley catalogued his sins. He habitually separated mothers from their children, husbands from their wives, and brothers from their sisters; he generally dealt in "vicious" slaves "sold for crimes or misdemeanors, or otherwise diseased ones sold because of their worthlessness as property." He "dresses them up in good clothes, makes them comb their kinky heads into some appearance of neatness, rubs oil on their dusky faces to give them a sleek healthy color, gives them a dram occasionally to make them sprightly, and teaches each one the part he or she has to play. . . . At every village of importance he sojourns a day or two, each day ranging his 'gang' in a line on the most busy street; and whenever a customer makes his appearance, the oily speculator button-holes him immediately, and begins to descant in the most highfalutin fashion upon the virtuous lot of darkies he has for sale." [2]

Many speculators engaged in these and other unseemly practices which gave their profession its ill repute. They often purchased slaves in family groups and promised not to divide them, or pretended to buy them for personal use or for some kindly planter who wanted whole families. They made these promises to win good will or to quiet the consciences of the sellers. But a Louisianian observed that it was a "daily occurrence" for these slaves to be sold individually upon reaching the Deep South. For example, the sheriff of Chicot County, Arkansas, advertised that he had in his jail two fugitives, husband and wife, who had been "purchased by . . . a negro trader . . . in the State of Virginia, and taken to New Orleans." There the husband had been sold separately "to a gentleman whose name he

---

[2] Hundley, *Social Relations*, pp. 139–42.

does not know, as he runaway immediately on learning that he was sold from his wife." Traders frequently gave public notice that they had children under ten for sale apart from their mothers. One trader in North Carolina advertised that he would pay "fair prices . . . for young negroes, from 8 to 12 years old." [3]

The speculators sometimes made purchases from masters on the condition that the slaves were not to be removed from the state—then ignored the condition. They bought slaves accused of felonies and sold them with false warrants of good character. They acquired slaves sentenced to be transported beyond the limits of the United States and secretly disposed of them in the Deep South. A New Orleans trader was indicted for having imported from Virginia twenty-four slaves convicted of murder, burglary, rape, arson, manslaughter, and attempted insurrection. [4]

The least scrupulous of the traders obtained part of their supply from thieves and kidnappers. Throughout the South gangs of slave stealers—the Murrell gang, which operated in the Southwest during the 1830's, being the most notorious—were a constant source of concern to owners of slave property. Some of the thieves persuaded bondsmen to run away, permit themselves to be sold, and then run away again. They promised to reward the bondsmen ultimately with freedom, but more often they ended the sordid business with murder. Others kidnapped free Negroes in the Upper South or in the free states and sold them in the Deep South.

Speculators fraudulently trafficked in habitual runaways and in insubordinate, diseased, and senile slaves. A former slave recalled how he helped a St. Louis trader prepare the

[3] Bancroft, *Slave-Trading*, pp. 32, 208; Catterall (ed.), *Judicial Cases*, III, pp. 599–600; Little Rock *Arkansas State Gazette*, January 6, 1845; Raleigh *North Carolina Standard*, August 4, 1836.
[4] Catterall (ed.), *Judicial Cases*, III, pp. 558–59.

stock for market en route to New Orleans. "I was ordered to have the old men's whiskers shaved off, and the gray hairs plucked out, where they were not too numerous, in which case we had a preparation of blacking to color it, and with a blacking brush we would put it on. . . . These slaves were also taught how old they were . . . and after going through the blacking process, they looked ten or fifteen years younger." When some of Isaac Franklin's slave merchandise contracted cholera while awaiting sale in Natchez, his agent secretly dumped those who died in the swamp, hoping thus not to discourage potential purchasers. But local planters discovered this deception and indignantly threatened legal action against Franklin for exposing their slaves to this terrible disease.[5]

A trader in Lexington, Kentucky, who paid $1600 and $1700 for two young slave women obviously had the market for "fancy girls" in mind, because these prices were considerably above current prices for female field-hands or domestics, even when they were promising "breeding women." Lewis C. Robards, Lexington's best-known trader in the 1850's, had special quarters on the second floor of his "Negro jail" for his "choice stock" of quadroon and octoroon girls. "In several rooms," reported a visitor, "I found very handsome mulatto women, of fine persons and easy genteel maners, sitting at their needlework awaiting a purchaser. The proprietor made them get up and turn around to show to advantage their finely developed and graceful forms—and slaves as they were, this I confess, rather shocked my gallantry." New Orleans was known to be a good market for "fancy girls," but traders found purchasers elsewhere too.[6]

---

5 Brown, *Narrative*, pp. 42–43; Washington *Mississippi Gazette*, May 4, 1833.
6 Coleman, *Slavery Times in Kentucky*, pp. 158–59; Bancroft, *Slave-Trading*, pp. 328–30.

The vulgarity of the inspections of Robard's "choice stock" was only one illustration of the dehumanization of the slave by the slave trade. Prospective purchasers usually examined the trader's merchandise minutely to make sure that there were no physical defects or whip marks to indicate bad character. Buyers could hardly have been expected to invest in an expensive piece of property without this precaution; and anyone who had a mind to purchase, or pretended to have, was free to satisfy his curiosity. Though the spectacle was seldom edifying, an inspection and the accompanying sale never failed to attract a crowd of spectators. A visitor in Louisville attended a public auction where a pregnant slave woman was offered to the highest bidder: "the auctioneer standing by her side, indulged himself in brutal jests upon her thriving condition, and sold her for four hundred dollars." [7]

Most of the traders operated on a small scale with limited capital. In the exporting states they attended estate and execution sales and sought out private owners who wished to dispose of a slave or two. After purchasing a few dozen slaves they organized them into a coffle and drove them southward to the cotton and sugar districts. But a few of the traders operated on a large scale with substantial capital and elaborate business organizations. They employed agents to comb the countryside of the Upper South for merchandise; they maintained their own private depots in such trading centers as Baltimore, Alexandria, Richmond, Louisville, Lexington, and St. Louis; and they established their own facilities for displaying and vending their merchandise in the chief distribution centers of the Deep South.

The traders gave evidence of the nature and size of their enterprises through their advertisements in the southern

---

[7] Coleman, *Slavery Times in Kentucky*, p. 118 n.; Bancroft, *Slave-Trading*, pp. 106–108.

press. Thus a small speculator notified slaveholders around Jefferson City, Missouri, that he would stop there for a short time "for the purpose of purchasing a few negro slaves. Persons having young slaves for sale, will find this a favorable opportunity to sell." In Baltimore, Austin Woolfolk, a large trader, announced his desire to obtain three hundred slaves "from the ages of 13 to 25 years. Persons having such to sell shall have cash, and the highest prices. . . . Liberal commissions will be paid to those who will aid in purchasing for the subscriber." In Lynchburg, Seth Woodroof offered to buy slaves between the ages of ten and thirty. "His office is a newly erected brick building . . . where he is prepared . . . [to] keep them as secure as if they were placed in the jail of the Corporation." Hart & Davis, also of Lynchburg, were "anxious to purchase about 50 Negroes of both sexes, to complete our last shipment, for this season, and will pay the full Richmond prices if application be made shortly." Richmond's business directory of 1852 listed twenty-eight persons who were engaged in slave trading, and there were doubtless more; probably no city in the Upper South had as many involved in this business.[8]

The firm of Franklin & Armfield, organized in 1828, was the South's largest slave-trading enterprise during the period of great expansion before the Panic of 1837. John Armfield directed affairs at their headquarters in Alexandria, Virginia, and collected and shipped slaves to Isaac Franklin who supervised their marketing agencies at New Orleans and Natchez. Representatives of the firm were located at Richmond and Warrenton, Virginia, and at Frederick, Baltimore, and Easton, Maryland. A visitor to their establishment in Alexandria found Armfield to be "a man of fine personal appearance, and of engaging and graceful

---

[8] Bancroft, *Slave-Trading*, pp. 95–96.

manners." Although this visitor was a severe critic of Armfield's profession, he reported that the quarters for the slaves were spacious and clean and the food "wholesome and abundant." In the yard he saw nearly a hundred slaves, most of them between the ages of eighteen and thirty, "neatly and comfortably dressed." Armfield treated the firm's property with care and tried to send it to his partner in good condition and ready for the market.[9]

Slaves were usually exported to the Deep South between October and May, the period when they could be most easily acclimatized and prepared for the next growing season. Many of them were transported on coastwise vessels from such shipping points as Baltimore, Alexandria, Richmond, Norfolk, and Charleston. Franklin & Armfield operated their own "slavers," and when their business was at its peak they shipped cargoes of as many as a hundred slaves every fortnight. Kentucky and Missouri slaves were often sent "down the river" on flatboats and steamers.[1]

But most of the slave merchandise was transported overland in coffles. A former Maryland slave remembered how a trader to whom he had been sold organized a coffle of more than fifty slaves for the long journey. The women were tied together with a rope that was fitted like a halter around their necks; the men were fettered by a long chain attached to iron collars which were fastened with padlocks. "In addition to this, we were handcuffed in pairs, with iron staples and bolts, with a short chain about a foot long uniting the handcuffs and their wearers."[2] Thus secured they marched along the roads leading south, bivouacking in the

---

9 Wendell H. Stephenson, *Isaac Franklin: Slave Trader and Planter of the Old South* (Baton Rouge, 1938), *passim;* Andrews, *Slavery and the Domestic Slave Trade,* pp. 135–43.

1 Charles H. Wesley, "Manifests of Slave Shipments along the Waterways, 1808–1864," *Journal of Negro History,* XXVII (1942), pp. 155–74; Stephenson, *Franklin,* pp. 42–44.

2 Phillips (ed.), *Plantation and Frontier,* II, p. 59.

woods and fields at night, until several weeks later they reached their destination. Here they rested a while and received new clothing before being offered for sale.

Traders who used the land routes often stopped briefly in the towns along their line of travel to display their stock. But they took most of it to large trading centers such as New Orleans and Natchez. Here the dealers issued public invitations to buyers to visit them and examine their merchandise. In New Orleans, John E. Smith gave notice that he had "Just arrived, with a choice lot of VIRGINIA and CAROLINA NEGROES, consisting of Plantation hands, Blacksmiths, Carpenters, Cooks, Washers, Ironers and Seamstresses, and will be receiving fresh supplies during the season." A. Wiesemann announced: "Having permanently established myself in this city, I shall keep constantly on hand a full supply of negroes, selected for this market. . . . My stock already purchased is large, and will be added to as required during the season." In Houston, Walter L. Campbell advertised that he had for sale "a large supply of all classes of negroes . . . imported from Virginia, Maryland and Georgia. Hereafter during the whole season, the supply shall be kept good by the receipt of large lots of the choicest negroes to be had from the above States." [3]

At a crossroads on the outskirts of Natchez a visitor and his planter companion found the mart where the slave traders conducted their business. Entering a narrow courtyard, they saw a line of about forty slaves, neatly dressed, standing along the side. "With their hats in their hands . . . they stood perfectly still, and in close order, while some gentlemen were passing from one to another examining for the purpose of buying. With the exception of displaying their teeth when addressed, and rolling their great

---

[3] New Orleans *Picayune*, January 4, 1860; Houston *Weekly Telegraph*, October 12, 1859.

white eyes about the court—they were so many statues of the most glossy ebony." The planter joined in the scrutiny of the merchandise, "giving that singular look, peculiar to the buyer of slaves as he glances from head to foot over each individual." Now and then a sale was closed and one of the slaves left the line to follow his new master. The countless tragedies of the slave market were not always evident to the casual visitor, for many of the slaves outwardly seemed to be quite indifferent to the whole business, and some wore a cheerful air as they passed the time in idle waiting. The traders usually took pains to keep them comfortable and in good spirits.[4]

But tragedy was never far beneath the surface—to be caught in this traffic was one of the fears that haunted southern slaves. An unfavorable turn in the master's economic fortunes, a death and the subsequent settlement of an estate could at any time wrench a slave away from his family and friends, away from familiar places, and send him to a new life made dreadful by its uncertainties. Ultimately, of course, most of the slaves who were traded as merchandise recovered from this unsettling experience, but not always with ease. The slave Josephine, sold to a Mississippian in the New Orleans market, indicated that she was "a good deal dissatisfied by the purchase" by "crying and taking on considerably"; she no longer moved about "with the life and sprightliness" she had shown in the past.[5]

Only a few of the professional traders amassed great wealth; some lost money and failed. This business, engaged in by hundreds of small entrepreneurs, was highly competitive and speculative. Besides bearing the costs of transporting the slaves and supporting them until they were sold, the vendors risked losses through sickness, death, escapes,

---

[4] [Ingraham], *South-West*, II, pp. 192–94, 202; Bancroft, *Slave-Trading*, pp. 113–14.
[5] Catterall (ed.), *Judicial Cases*, III, p. 373.

and fluctuating prices; more, they had to contend with the methods of the least ethical members of their profession, and meet the expenses of lawsuits instituted by dissatisfied purchasers. The records of one small trader, who gathered his merchandise in Virginia and North Carolina during the 1850's, show that the sales which netted him unusually large profits were offset by sales which netted him no profits at all. His most lucrative transaction involved a slave woman and her child whom he purchased for $1275 and sold for $1700; his least fortunate transaction involved another slave woman whom he purchased for $700 and sold some months later for the same price. He sold most of his merchandise for $200 to $300 more than he paid, a markup of around 30 per cent. This brought him an average net profit of well over $100 on each sale.[6]

Among the minority of large-scale traders were some of the wealthiest businessmen of the Old South. Nathan Bedford Forrest, who later won fame as a Confederate cavalry commander, was the largest slave trader in Memphis during the late 1850's; he was reputed to have made a profit of $96,000 in a single year. But probably no trader ever exceeded the returns enjoyed by the firm of Franklin & Armfield. Before retiring from the business each of the partners accumulated fortunes in excess of a half million dollars.[7] Few who exploited slave labor, rather than trading in it, profited that much.

5

"This trade is a sore subject with the defenders of slavery," observed a critical English traveler. "It is difficult to weave it handsomely in among the amenities of the patri-

---

[6] A. and A. T. Walker Ms. Account Book; Phillips, *American Negro Slavery*, p. 201.

[7] Bancroft, *Slave-Trading*, pp. 263–64; Stephenson, *Franklin*, p. 93.

archal institution. They fain would make a scape-goat of the 'Trader,' and load all the iniquities of the system on his unlucky back." This, the Englishman thought, was unjust. "If slavery and the slave trade which it necessitates be in themselves right and proper, it is a wrong to visit with ignominy the instruments of the system." [8] The injustice of making scapegoats of these men was compounded by the element of social snobbery in it—the attitude of contempt for petty traders with their customary lack of the social graces, which Hundley's description of the "Negro trader" made so evident.

Moreover, slaveholders who did business with the speculators often deserved to share responsibility for practices for which the latter received the entire blame. Slaveholders themselves put in the hands of speculators the dangerous or "sickly" slaves who were offered to buyers in the Deep South. A lawyer whose planter client commissioned him to sell a slave explained how it was done: "Finding that I should not probably succeed in making an advantageous sale of the boy myself, so unpromising was he[,] I procured the services of a Broker whose business it is to do such things. He had his hair carded and his person washed and a supply of clothes was procured to set him off. After which you would hardly have known your own boy. A few days training improved his air and manner much and a sale was effected." [9]

If the dissolution of families was one of the cardinal sins of the traffic, masters merited some of the opprobrium that was heaped upon the traders. They frequently sold their slaves knowing full well that families would be broken whenever the traders found it to their advantage to do so. Sometimes the masters themselves agreed to dissolve fami-

---

[8] Stirling, *Letters*, pp. 292–93.
[9] Henry Watson, Jr., to Dr. J. W. Carrigan, November 27, 1852, Watson Papers.

lies. A Kentuckian advertised a slave woman and her four children whom he would sell "together or separately"; a Virginian agreed to sell a slave woman "with one or more Children, to suit the purchaser"; and another Virginian offered a reward for his runaway Nat who was "no doubt attempting to follow his wife, who was lately sold to a speculator." A mistress in Nelson County, Virginia, sent a female slave to an agent in Lynchburg with instructions "to see her sold." After being sold to a trader, this slave twice escaped and returned to her husband at her former home.[1] These were not isolated cases.

Purchasers in the Deep South selected from the trader's supply whatever slaves best satisfied their needs, occasionally whole families but usually not. For instance, an Arkansas planter visited the slave market in Memphis and bought five women with their children but not a single husband. In fact, when a trader or purchaser spoke of a "family" of slaves he was ordinarily referring only to a mother and her children. Thus a planter who thought of buying some slaves from a trader noted that the lot included "a family" consisting of "a woman 27 years old, five children and another hourly expected." The mother was "stout and healthy"; the children were "very likely, sprightly and smart" and seemed to be "all one man's children"; but the father was not part of the trader's stock.[2]

The southern gentry's traditional contempt for traders was directed chiefly against the more unsavory elements in the business. Substantial and trustworthy dealers often maintained cordial relations with members of the planter class. Peter Stokes and William H. Hatchett, slave traders

---

1 Coleman, *Slavery Times in Kentucky*, p. 119; Bancroft, *Slave-Trading*, p. 27 n.; Richmond *Enquirer*, April 1, 1834; Thos. Massie to Wm. H. Hatchett, December 15, 1845, William H. Hatchett Papers.
2 Leak Diary, entry for October 8, 1859; I. T. Lenoir to Albert S Lenoir, November 4, 1847, Lenoir Family Papers.

in Lunenburg County, Virginia, were on friendly terms
with neighboring lawyers and planters and probably received financial support from local businessmen. Indeed,
it was not at all uncommon for merchants or bankers in
the towns of the Upper South to act as silent partners of
the speculators. Moreover, many respectable commission
merchants, factors, general agents, and lawyers engaged in
a little slave trading as a side line.[8]

A few traders—for example, Thomas Norman Gadsden
and Louis D. DeSaussure, of South Carolina—belonged to
distinguished southern families whose social positions were
firmly established. Others whose origins were humbler used
slave trading as an avenue to ultimate membership in the
planter class. Such men may never have been able entirely
to escape the stigma of their earlier profession; but in the
Southwest, with its great social fluidity, they had reason to
believe that their children would. By the 1840's, Isaac
Franklin had retired from trading and invested his fortune
in slaves and plantations in Tennessee and Louisiana.
James D. Ware, a Virginia trader who for many years marketed slaves in Natchez, used his profits to buy a Mississippi plantation. Finally, in 1848, Ware informed a planter
friend: "I leave in a few days for Va. on the same old errand
and for the last time. This trip result as it may closes my
trading operations. So far a kind providence has sustained
and prospered my undertakings. I have made a compe-
tency. I wish to stay at home [in Mississippi] and enjoy
it . . . in such a manner as becomes a rational and accountable being."[4]

Many slaveholders by-passed the professional speculators

---

[8] Hatchett Papers, *passim;* Thomas D. Clark, "The Slave Trade between
Kentucky and the Cotton Kingdom," *Mississippi Valley Historical Review,* XXI (1934), p. 342; Bancroft, *Slave-Trading,* pp. 368–69.

[4] Bancroft, *Slave-Trading,* pp. 167–69, 186–90; James D. Ware to William M. Waller, April 11, 1848, William M. Waller Papers.

VI: *Slavemongering*

and participated directly in the interstate trade. Planters in the Deep South themselves often visited Virginia to purchase slaves for personal use. Masters in the Upper South often arranged for the marketing of their own bondsmen. Thus, John H. Anthony, of Halifax County, North Carolina, sent thirteen slaves to a relative in Mississippi who promised to sell them for him.[5] Virginians were frequently seen in the Southwest seeking buyers for slaves they had transported from their private estates.

William M. Waller, a planter in Amherst County, Virginia, left a full record of one such slave selling expedition. In 1847, Waller and his neighbor James Taliaferro decided they must sell some of their slaves to escape from heavy debts. Though electing to handle the sales themselves, they consulted an experienced speculator who informed them that Natchez was the most promising market and that early October was the best time to begin the trip.

After selecting twenty of his choicest slaves, Waller joined Taliaferro for the long overland journey to Mississippi. That his mission was distasteful and disquieting, Waller left no doubt. Compassion for his slaves, concern about the morality of his action, and a touch of self-pity caused him to brood over the matter incessantly while he was away from home. Only a "sense of duty" to his family, he repeatedly told his wife, supported him "in a trip that under any other consideration would be intolerable. I have already seen and felt enough to make me loath the vocation of slave trading." A few weeks later, after reaching Mississippi, Waller wrote: "I still think it was my duty. . . . I care not for my exposure, nor for my absence from home or for the privation of my usual comforts if I can effect my purpose—if I can return to you all freed from my bondage

---

[5] James Gordon to John H. Anthony, February 8, 1837, Lewis Thompson Papers.

[of debt] which has been for some years more awfully gall-
ing to my feelings, vastly more so, than the world sup-
poses." Still later he referred apprehensively to a report
that a Virginia friend had been "threatened by the church
for his supposed participation in the negro trade—is there
any thing of it and what?"

Waller suffered many disappointments, for in the fall of
1847 slave prices in Mississippi declined and purchasers
could not be found. After a month in northern Mississippi,
he related sadly: "As yet neither Mr. Taliaferro or I have
sold one nor does there appear the least prospect of our
doing so in any short time." In December, the two Virginians separated, and Waller took his merchandise to the
Hinds County plantation of his friend, Thomas S. Dabney,
who promised to help him find purchasers. "I have taken
away the most valuable portion of my slave property," he
wrote in despair, "and if now parted with without effecting
my purpose what will become of our children[?]"

Early in January, 1848, Waller made his first sale—a
slave woman for $675—to one of Dabney's neighbors. By
February he had sold seven, one of them in New Orleans.
He then took the remaining thirteen to Natchez where the
Virginia trader, James D. Ware, offered to assist him. Together they looked for a buyer who would agree to take the
entire lot. At last, on March 2, he rejoiced: "I have sold
out all my negroes to one man for eight thousand dollars. . . . I have not obtained as much as I expected, but
I try and be satisfied—the whole amount of the sales for
the twenty is $12,675." In April he was home again in Am-
herst County, confident that the proceeds of his expedition
would emancipate him from his bondage of debt.

Waller offered to compensate Ware for his help, but the
latter indignantly refused to accept it. Ware expected no
commission for what he regarded as a "mere act of cour-

tesy." This trader, who was about to retire to his Mississippi plantation, knew how a gentleman was expected to
behave.[6]

6

In the eighteenth century the slave trade between Africa
and America yielded fabulous profits to many European
and American merchants. By 1803, however, only South
Carolina's ports were still open to this traffic, and after
January 1, 1808, Federal law closed them too. But during
the next half century planters who needed additional laborers, and merchants who remembered the rich returns,
sometimes questioned the wisdom of this act.

In practice the prohibitory laws were never sufficiently
effective to wipe out the illicit trade that continued—and
at times flourished. The Federal statute of 1807 provided
fines and imprisonment for persons convicted of transporting and selling Africans, and fines for those who knowingly
bought them. But in the absence of special enforcement
machinery the law was violated with impunity; various estimates of slave importations between 1810 and 1820 run
as high as sixty thousand. Not until 1819 did Congress authorize the use of armed cruisers to patrol the coasts of the
United States and West Africa. A year later, another statute
made participation in the African trade piracy and imposed a death penalty.

Thereafter the Federal government made fitful efforts at
enforcement, but its patrol system was always inadequate,
and the executive department often showed little real interest in more vigorous action. During the 1850's, the illicit
commerce reached such proportions as almost to constitute
"a reopening of the slave-trade." Many of the slavers were

---

[6] Correspondence from July, 1847, to April, 1848, relating to this expedition is in the Waller Papers.

fitted out in New York City, and some of their cargoes were unloaded with scarcely any attempt at secrecy. When, occasionally, African traders were brought to trial, southern juries refused to convict. Indeed, the first conviction and execution for piracy under the law of 1820 occurred after the outbreak of the Civil War.[7]

On the eve of the Civil War, some defenders of slavery in the Deep South argued that self-interest and moral consistency required Southerners to seek the repeal of these hostile laws. If slavery were a positive good, if it were a kindness to the Negro to rescue him from Africa for labor in the South, then the means by which this was accomplished were surely not immoral. Southerners, asserted a Texan, could not "eulogize slavery and denounce the slave trade in the same breath, without stultifying themselves with the grossest and most suicidal inconsistency."

The Federal law defining this trade as piracy, according to a Texas editor, had "subverted every principle of justice, . . . slandered the memories of our honored ancestors, and . . . trampled upon the common sentiment of the Southern States." More, it violated the southern doctrine of free trade. "The same reason which would induce us to oppose a high protective tariff . . . leads us to protest against the fanatical laws passed to prohibit the African slave trade. We can distinguish no great difference between the trade in African negroes, and the trade in any other article of property. Nothing but sectional malice and narrow bigotry prevents the trade in slaves from being left to the great laws of commerce, which can best adjust the relation between supply and demand." To the argument that the trade was cruel, the answer was that the illegal

---

[7] DuBois, *Suppression of the African Slave-Trade, passim;* Harvey Wish, "The Revival of the African Slave Trade in the United States, 1856–1860," *Mississippi Valley Historical Review,* XXVII (1941), pp. 569–88; Gray, *History of Agriculture,* II, p. 650.

trade was more cruel. If the trade were recognized and regulated by law, steps could be taken "to compel the humane treatment of slave emigrants." Legalization would thus be "a measure of humanity." [8]

In their reckless but devastating criticism of southern inconsistencies, advocates of the renewal of the African trade attacked slaveholders in the Upper South for opposing it. Though for the past half century Virginians had monopolized the domestic trade, they had no "vested right to perpetuate that monopoly." If the importing states could buy more cheaply in Africa than in Virginia, they had a "natural right" to do so. Why was it immoral to import from Africa if it was moral to import from Virginia? [9]

Moreover, if the peculiar institution were to be preserved, masters in the Upper South had to be forced to hold their slaves. The current high prices and great demand tempted them to send their human chattels to the Deep South at an unprecedented rate, and thus the "circle of slave labor and southern institutions" was gradually contracting. Unless this were stopped, one result would inevitably follow: "Free labor will necessarily take the place of slave labor, and when [it] preponderates . . . they will become anti-slavery States." To prevent this, labor had to be imported from Africa to drive the slaves of the Upper South out of the market. [1]

There was no denying that during the 1850's the Southwest suffered from an acute labor shortage. Arkansas planters complained that the resulting exorbitant slave prices prevented most of the good cotton lands from being culti-

---

8 Little Rock *Arkansas Gazette and Democrat*, December 4, 1858; Austin *Texas State Gazette*, December 18, 1858; Jackson *Mississippian*, September 17, 1858; *Southern Cultivator*, XVI (1858), pp. 233–36.

9 Austin *Texas State Gazette*, January 1, 1859; *Southern Cultivator*, XVI (1858), pp. 233–36.

1 Montgomery *Advertiser*, quoted in Jackson *Mississippian*, January 28, 1859.

vated. "To remedy this evil African slaves should be imported into the country," advised a Little Rock editor. "Otherwise our resources may never be developed." Texans made the same complaint; one advocate of the African trade estimated that Texas needed at least six million more Negroes. Even South Carolinians complained about the high price of labor, because few of them could outbid Southwesterners for male field-hands. "A young girl, who would breed like a cat would tell differently," explained a South Carolina planter, "but such hands cannot do the heavy labor of mine or any other plantation. Then where am I to get laborers? I say, emphatically, import them from Africa." [2]

Many Southerners believed that the inadequate labor supply was responsible for the wasteful, extensive system of agriculture which was rapidly wearing out their lands. In the South "the natural balance between land and laborers has been wantonly destroyed," and "one of the most obvious effects has been a continuous effort to make the most of a comparatively little labor by extending it over too much surface of soil." Unless the slave supply were increased, "our present practice of skinning and bleeding the soil will not be abandoned for many years. The public interest demands more laborers in the planting States." [3]

Proslavery leaders also feared that, unless there was an increase in the supply of slaves, ownership would be limited to a dangerously small proportion of the southern whites. If a small group monopolized this form of labor, the foundation of the institution would be weak; if slaveownership were diffused "more generally among the people,"

[2] *De Bow's Review*, XXV (1858), pp. 491–506; Little Rock *Arkansas Gazette and Democrat*, October 2, 1858; Austin *Texas State Gazette*, December 18, 1858; January 15, February 19, 1859; *American Cotton Planter and Soil of the South*, III (1859), pp. 75–76.
[3] *De Bow's Review*, XXIV (1858), pp. 202–203; *Southern Cultivator*, XVI (1858), pp. 233–36.

the foundation would be strong. Every white family should own at least a household servant—in fact, "we do not wish to see the white man of the South act as a boot-black, a cook, a waiter, or as one of a gang of laborers in the sugar and cotton fields." The small farmers were the ones most grievously wronged by the closing of the African trade. Unable to buy slaves, they were compelled to toil in their fields and to put their young sons to work "when they should either be at school or at play." [4]

The introduction of free white farm hands to solve the South's labor problem, it was said, would merely create a new evil. "To hire white men," explained a South Carolina planter, "will be to bring about an association between my negroes, and a set of drinking, vagabondish foreigners; for native born white laborers are never to be seen for hire in this country." Fill the South with immigrant laborers, "and you will have voters enough among these new comers to abolish slavery in every State where it exists." Too many had come already. "It would be a happy riddance if they were not among us—they are the only opposing element to slave labor in the South." [5]

Finally, the reopening of the African slave trade would help to restore the political balance between North and South. "Every five slaves," the argument ran, "gives us the equivalent in the basis of federal representation which the North claims for three whites." Why debate the right of slavery to expand into the territories when there were not enough slaves to satisfy the labor needs of the existing southern states? If the South were to match the North in territorial growth, "the labor system of the South must

---

[4] *De Bow's Review*, XXV (1858), pp. 491–506; Austin *Texas State Gazette*, July 17, December 18, 1858; January 15, 1859.
[5] *American Cotton Planter and Soil of the South*, III (1859), pp. 75–76; *Southern Cultivator*, XVI (1858), pp. 233–36; Little Rock *Arkansas Gazette and Democrat*, October 2, 1858.

have the same access to the labor markets of the world that the labor system of the North has." There was only one way to "expand the area of slavery, . . . to enlarge the circle of slaves States," and to establish southern equality within the Union: "In plain terms [the South] must have slave emigration—the slave trade." [6]

This was the cry that went up from some southern politicians in Congress and in the state legislatures. In 1857, a southern commercial convention, meeting at Knoxville, appointed a committee to investigate the subject. The next year the chairman of this committee, L. W. Spratt, of South Carolina, an ardent advocate of the African trade, submitted a report to another commercial convention at Montgomery. Spratt's report urged the adoption of a resolution declaring that since slavery was right "there can be no wrong in the natural means to its formation," and that "it is expedient and proper [that] the foreign slave trade should be re-opened." The Convention took no action.[7]

Almost everyone who favored the renewal of this trade realized that there was not the remotest chance of getting Congress to pass such a measure; hence they proposed that the states evade Federal law through some form of subterfuge. The Louisiana legislature several times considered an "African Apprentice Bill" which would have authorized the importation of Negro laborers under fifteen-year indentures. In 1858, this measure passed the lower house of the legislature but failed in the upper house. A year later, some of the most active supporters of the apprentice scheme organized the African Labor Supply Association and elected J. B. D. De Bow, of New Orleans, as its president. Meanwhile, a group of Mississippians considered forming an

---

[6] Austin *Texas State Gazette*, June 26, December 18, 1858; Wilmington (N.C.) *Journal*, June 25, 1858; Little Rock *Arkansas Gazette and Democrat*, October 2, 1858; *De Bow's Review*, XXV (1858), pp. 491–506.
[7] *De Bow's Review*, XXIV (1858), pp. 473–91, 576–606.

African Labor Immigration Company to bring in indentured Negro apprentices, but the project never materialized. An impatient Florida editor openly invited the African traders to land their cargoes in his state without waiting for friendly legislation. Commenting on the high slave prices, he reported that "advocates for the re-opening of the trade in 'wool' are increasing. An investment in a ship load to be landed on the coast of Florida would be profitable. Who'll take stock?" [8]

Not many would. In spite of all the talk, advocates of reopening the African slave trade were in the minority even in the states of the Southwest. "We are fully aware that our position is not a popular one," confessed one of the most clamorous members of this group in Arkansas. Two months later the Arkansas Senate overwhelmingly defeated a resolution favoring the repeal of the Federal law which made it piracy to import Africans. No such resolution ever passed a southern legislative body. [9]

There were several practical reasons for this. Slaveholders in the Upper South feared the competition of the African traders in the markets of the slave importing states. Masters with an adequate supply of labor opposed a measure that would inevitably depress the price of slaves and (in the long run by increasing production) the price of southern staples as well. Moderates throughout the South knew that agitation for reopening the African slave trade would merely intensify sectional bitterness, and they regarded its sponsors as disunionists.

There were moral reasons too. It may have been inconsistent, as some contended, to defend slavery and the do-

---

[8] Taylor, "Negro Slavery in Louisiana," pp. 73–76; *De Bow's Review*, XXIV (1858), pp. 421–24; XXVII (1859), pp. 231–35; Jackson *Mississippian*, January 12, 1858; Tallahassee *Floridian and Journal*, February 19, 1859.

[9] Little Rock *Arkansas Gazette and Democrat*, October 2, December 4, 1858; New Orleans *Picayune*, March 21, 1858.

mestic slave trade while condemning further importations from Africa. But most Southerners preferred to waive consistency, for on this point there was "a healthy moral feeling." Few of them, according to a Georgian, were willing "to roll back the tide of civilizaton and christianity of the nineteenth century, and restore the barbarism of the dark ages." [1]

---

[1] Milledgeville *Southern Recorder*, January 11, 1859.

CHAPTER SEVEN

Maintenance, Morbidity, Mortality

The proprieties of a slaveholding society, explained a Virginian, obligated the bondsman to labor diligently and to respond "submissively and honestly" to his master's commands. In return, he was "entitled to an abundance of good plain food; to coarse but comfortable apparel; to a warm but humble dwelling; to protection when well, and to succor when sick." Defenders of slavery believed that common sense and self-interest, as well as justice and humanity, caused the master to provide adequately for his slave's material needs. The master knew that "men, like animals, cannot work unless there is furnished them the necessary comforts which by nature they require." [1]

Seldom did a planter fail to refer to this subject when he prepared a body of instructions for his overseer. "See that their necessities be supplied, that their food and clothing be good and sufficient, their houses comfortable, and be kind and attentive to them in sickness and in old age," admonished Joseph Acklen, of Louisiana. In a written contract, John Ambler, of Virginia, imposed the following obligations upon his overseer: "To make the negroes keep their houses clean and tightly covered. . . . To attend to the clothing of the negroes—and to have them well nursed and taken care of when they are sick."[2] Masters who did not employ overseers looked to these matters themselves.

Expenditures for food, clothing, shelter, and medical care were, in a sense, the wages paid a slave for his labor; but the master usually thought of them as maintenance costs—expenditures necessary for the upkeep of slave property. How much he spent for these necessities, the quality and quantity he believed essential, depended upon a number of things. First, it depended upon how well informed the master was upon such subjects as diet, hygiene, and the causes and treatment of disease. Even a well-intentioned master could, from sheer ignorance, cause his bondsman much misery. Second, it depended upon where the master lived. In new regions, where semi-frontier conditions still prevailed, the master himself enjoyed few of the amenities; as late as 1848, a visitor described the "big house" of a wealthy Mississippi planter as "nothing better than a log one of four rooms," in which the white family ate from "common pine tables" and sat upon "split bottom chairs."[3] Under these circumstances the slave perforce endured the crudest, most meager comforts. Third, it depended upon the slave's status. A domestic, a skilled artisan, or a foreman was usually the recipient of more of the master's bounty than a common field-hand. Fourth, and most important, it depended upon the master's disposition—upon how close to the margin of subsistence he chose to keep his workers. Except for the few who hired their own time, slaves seldom had much control over their own well-being. The master determined what part of his annual revenues he would appropriate for their maintenance.

A young North Carolinian described conditions on his father's plantation illustrating the maximum living standard which the most fortunate slaves might enjoy. Here

[2] *De Bow's Review*, XXII (1857), pp. 376–79; Ambler Family Papers.
[3] William M. Waller to his wife, January 3, 1848, Waller Papers.

they ate what the white family ate, lived in well-built houses, had plenty of firewood, and received good shoes and ample clothing. When ill they were treated by the best doctors in the neighborhood; the "breeding women" were never overstrained. "When any of the slave children were very sick they were brought into the [master's] house . . . and there attended as one of the white children." Every adult slave had "a 'patch of ground' and the time to work it, in order that each might have some money of his own to spend as he chose." [4] If the relative advantages of slavery and freedom were measured exclusively in terms of the material comfort of the worker, the ante-bellum free laborer could not always have boasted that he was better off than the slaves of this North Carolina master.

Few freemen would have accepted this simple criterion, but surely the comparative standard of living of free and slave laborers was not altogether irrelevant. Proslavery writers frequently contended that northern workers suffered greater privation than southern slaves. They demonstrated this by contrasting the hardships of the lowest paid, most heartlessly exploited factory hands with the comforts of the best-treated bondsmen. They found abundant evidence of widespread poverty among new immigrants and among unskilled or semi-skilled workers in the industrial towns of the Northeast, especially during periods of economic depression.

But the typical ante-bellum northern "free laborer" was not a half-starved hireling of a large, impersonal, industrial corporation. Rather, he was a small farmer, a farm laborer, a journeyman or master artisan, or an employee of a small manufacturing enterprise managed by its owner. The great mass of northern workers enjoyed, by and large, an income that afforded them a reasonably comfortable standard of

---

[4] Quoted in John S. Bassett, *Slavery in the State of North Carolina* (Baltimore, 1899), pp. 87–88

living—a standard of living considerably higher than that of the mass of southern slaves. For the average slave lived in nothing like the material comfort which that philanthropic North Carolina master provided his "people."

Though one hears of slaves who were given opportunities to earn a little money and who were indulged in other ways, most of them were limited to the bare necessities and lived at the subsistence level. Unlike the free laborer, the average slave could not attain an appreciably higher living standard, no matter how hard he strived. The slave's labor was controlled labor: his bargaining power was, by design, severely circumscribed. His labor was cheap labor: his compensation was, also by design, kept at a minimum. The free worker was, inevitably, more independent, more often successful in his efforts to increase his material comforts; and as a rule his labor was therefore more expensive.[5] In short, one might dispute the proslavery argument on economic as well as moral grounds: freedom was clearly a practical advantage to the laborer himself.

2

A peck of corn meal and three or four pounds of salt pork or bacon comprised the basic weekly allowance of the great majority of adult slaves. These rations, to which were frequently added a few supplementary items, usually provided a diet of sufficient bulk but improper balance. The slaves who consequently suffered from dietary deficiencies were sometimes the victims of penurious masters, but probably they were more often the victims of ill-informed masters—of the primitive state of the science of dietetics. Even the master and his family rarely had a balanced diet, though they generally enjoyed a wider variety (and a

---

[5] See below, Chapter IX. See also Olmsted, *Seaboard*, pp. 686–711.

higher quality) of foods than did the slaves. In any case, the adequacy of the provisions furnished the slaves must be judged in the light of what ante-bellum Southerners knew about the principles of nutrition.

In 1859, Dr. John H. Wilson, of Columbus, Georgia, published an essay on the feeding of Negroes, which illustrated the confusing mélange of science and quackery that influenced the practices of even the best-informed slaveholders. Wilson divided all foods into two categories: "*nitrogenized* or muscle-producing and *non-nitrogenized* or heat-producing." It was a common notion, he observed, "that fat bacon and pork are highly nutritious; but almost everything, even the lightest and most watery vegetables contain more nutritive muscle-building elements. Yet these fatty articles of diet are peculiarly appropriate on account of their heat-producing properties; they generate sufficient heat to cause the wheels of life to move glibly and smoothly, . . . and hence negroes who are freely supplied with them grow plump, sleek and shiny. . . . Corn, abounding as it does in oily matter, is also a heat-producing agent, acting precisely like fat meat; and in addition to this its other elements render it a valuable muscle-producing food. How fortunate that pork and corn, the most valuable of all articles of diet for negroes, may be so readily produced throughout the whole region where slaves are worked!" Wilson warned masters, however, that Negroes and whites "are very different in their habits and constitutions, and that while fat meat is the life of the negro, . . . it is a prolific source of disease and death among the whites." In addition to corn and pork, "negroes should be liberally supplied with garden vegetables, and milk and molasses should be given out occasionally at least. These afford an agreeable variety and serve as preventives to scurvy and other diseases." Among the fruits, he particularly recommended figs because of their nutritiousness; among the vegetables,

peas "on account of the large quantity of oil they contain." [6]

Few slaveholders knew more than Dr. Wilson about food
chemistry; none had heard of vitamins or of the connection
between vitamin deficiencies and certain diseases that puzzled them; and none had any precise knowledge of the proportions of various foods in a balanced diet. Yet, those who
followed Wilson's advice to add milk, molasses, vegetables,
and fruits to the allowances of corn and pork were seldom
troubled with slaves who suffered seriously from malnutri-
tion. Some did provide a diet as varied as this; some went
further and added such items as Irish or sweet potatoes,
eggs and poultry, beef and mutton, perhaps even coffee and
sugar. In the coastal regions masters could easily furnish
fish, lobsters, crabs, clams, and oysters; almost everywhere
they could make it possible for their slaves to feast occasionally on wild game.

There seemed to be no appreciable difference in the
quality or variety of foods given slaves in the Upper South
and in the Deep South, or in the practices of large and
small slaveholders. The important difference was between
masters who assumed direct responsibility for supplying
their slaves with all the food they needed, and those who
merely supplied pork and corn and a plot of ground on
which slaves might produce some supplementary items if
they cared to. Too often the slaves lacked the time or energy to cultivate their own plots in addition to performing
their other tasks.[7] In either case, fresh vegetables were only
available "in season"; during the winter months few slaves
escaped the monotony of a "hog-and-hominy" diet.

Indeed, everywhere in the South a depressingly large
number of slaves lived on little else than this dismal fare
throughout the year. On countless farms and plantations

---

[6] *American Cotton Planter and Soil of the South*, III (1859), p. 197.
[7] Olmsted, *Seaboard*, p. 108.

the laborers never tasted fresh meat, milk, eggs, or fruits, and rarely tasted vegetables. "All that is allowed," recalled a former slave on a cotton plantation, "is corn and bacon, which is given out at the corncrib and smoke-house every Sunday morning. Each one receives, as his weekly allowance, three and a half pounds of bacon, and corn enough to make a peck of meal." No slave on this estate, he added bitterly, was "ever likely to suffer from the gout, superinduced by excessive high living." [8]

An experienced Louisiana physician claimed that the diet of slaves on the majority of plantations was "mostly salt pork, corn bread, and molasses—rarely . . . fresh meat and vegetables." An Alabamian reported that planters in his region had the "erroneous impression . . . that *Pork*—and the fatter the better—is the only proper substance of animal food for Negroes." A Virginian affirmed that "corn meal, with little or no meat, and no vegetable diet is extremely hard fare. I believe that there are extremely few masters who starve their slaves to actual suffering, . . . [but] I have no doubt that the slow motion, and thin expression of countenance, of many slaves, are owing to a want of a sufficiency of nourishing food." Olmsted agreed that not many slaves were denied an adequate quantity of food, but he claimed that the fare was generally "coarse, crude, and wanting in variety." [9] This condition was by no means peculiar to the large plantations.

The minority of masters who gave their slaves an insufficient supply even of corn and pork were usually so preoccupied with the staple crops that they neglected to produce enough food. Such masters were obliged to purchase sup-

---

[8] Northup, *Twelve Years a Slave*, pp. 168–70.
[9] V. Alton Moody, "Slavery on Louisiana Sugar Plantations," *Louisiana Historical Quarterly*, VII (1924), p. 263; *Southern Cultivator*, VIII (1850), p. 4; *Farmers' Register*, V (1837), p. 32; Olmsted, *Seaboard*, p. 700.

plies, and some of them tried to reduce operational costs by issuing meager rations. This short-sighted policy caused the mistress on a Louisiana plantation to hope certain masters would learn that it was to their own advantage to give slaves "more and better food," so that self-interest might effect "what humanity failed to secure." A North Carolinian complained, "There are many farmers who feed their negroes sparingly, believing that it is economy[,] that they save by it, but such is not the fact." [1] In times of economic stringency masters who relied upon food purchases sometimes lacked either the cash or credit to obtain what they needed, and their slaves suffered accordingly.

"I practice on the plan, that all of us would be better to be restrained, and that health is best subserved by not over-eating," explained a small planter. There was much truth in this, but some slaveholders seemed to underestimate the amount of food that a hard-working field-hand needed. Various slaves claimed that they sometimes consumed their weekly rations within four or five days and then had to make night raids on the hog pen or corn crib. Fanny Kemble noted that on her husband's Georgia plantation slaves approached her almost daily to beg for rice or meat. James H. Hammond was convinced that his slaves were "too well fed," yet he complained that in one year they had stolen and killed a hundred of his hogs.[2] Much of this pilfering was committed by slaves whose purpose was to trade plantation supplies for whisky or tobacco; but some of it was to enrich their diet. It indicated that the slaves themselves were not always satisfied with the quality or quan-

[1] William D. Postell, *The Health of Slaves on Southern Plantations* (Baton Rouge, 1951), p. 78; *Farmer's Journal*, II (1853), p. 53.
[2] *De Bow's Review*, XI (1851), pp. 369–71; Drew, *The Refugee*, p. 155–56; Kemble, *Journal, passim;* Hammond Diary, entry for October 22, 1843.

tity of their rations—that they, like their masters, preferred a fine ham to the cheaper cuts of pork. Most masters, therefore, kept their smokehouses carefully locked.

The problem of slave sustenance involved not only the need for an ample and balanced diet but also the need for a practical system of food preparation. Usually the master held each family of slaves responsible for cooking their own food and paid little attention to how well they did it. He required them to carry their noon meals to the fields in the morning and to wait for their evening meals until they returned to their cabins at night. In some cases he expected the slaves to grind their own corn and gather their own firewood, a great burden after a long day of toil. He did not always provide cooking utensils. Without these, cooking was a simple process, as a former slave recalled: "When the corn is ground, and fire is made, the bacon is . . . thrown upon the coals to broil. . . . The corn meal is mixed with a little water, placed in the fire, and baked. When it is 'done brown,' the ashes are scraped off, and being placed upon a chip, which answers for a table, the tenant of the slave hut is ready to sit down upon the ground to supper."[3] The majority of masters provided iron pots, for cooking vegetables and fat pork and "grits," and frying pans for preparing bacon and corn pone.

Many slaveholders vigorously condemned the practice of requiring slaves to cook their own meals. "It encroaches upon the rest they should have both at noon and at night," one planter explained. "The cooking being done in a hurry, is badly done; being usually burnt on the outside while it is still raw within; and consequently unhealthy. However abundant may be the supply of vegetables, the hands have no time to cook them, and consequently are

---

[3] Northup, *Twelve Years a Slave*, pp. 168–70.

badly fed, and have not the strength to do as much labor as they could otherwise perform with comfort." [4] Masters who shared this point of view used slave cooks to prepare at least breakfasts and dinners in a common kitchen or "cook house," though they might expect slave families to prepare their own suppers. If communal cooking increased the regimentation of slave life and destroyed almost the last vestige of the family's significance, it nevertheless resulted ordinarily in a better diet.

On the smaller holdings the same cook often prepared the food for both the white family and the slaves. The proprietor of a modest-sized Mississippi plantation told Olmsted that he called his field-hands up to the house for their dinners when they were within a reasonable distance. They came to the master's kitchen and ate the same food that he ate, "right out of the same frying-pan." The larger plantations had special cooks and kitchens, from which breakfasts and dinners were sent to the fields in buckets. In the morning the hands customarily worked from sunrise until about eight o'clock before having breakfast. At noon they ate again, then rested for an hour or two.[5]

Some slaves were provided with tables and utensils that enabled them to eat with reasonable decorum, but most of them were obliged to eat in a primitive fashion. On one Georgia plantation they had no chairs, tables, plates, knives, or forks; "they sat . . . on the earth or doorsteps, and ate out of their little cedar tubs or an iron pot, some few with broken iron spoons, more with pieces of wood, and all the children with their fingers." On a Maryland farm where Frederick Douglass was a child, "the corn-meal mush . . . was placed in a large wooden tray. . . . This tray was set down, either on the floor of the kitchen, or out

---

[4] *De Bow's Review*, X (1851), pp. 325–26; XIII (1852), pp. 193–94; *Farmers' Register*, IV (1836), p. 495.
[5] Olmsted, *Back Country*, p. 153; *id., Seaboard*, pp. 108–10, 431–32.

of doors on the ground; and the children were called, . . . and like so many pigs would come, and literally devour the mush—some with oyster shells, some with pieces of shingles, and none with spoons." [6] In Africa the Negro had rarely consumed his food with less dignity and grace than this.

3

Examples of deliberate stinting of rations were fortunately few; and the imbalance of the average slave's diet resulted from ignorance more often than penuriousness. But cases of poorly clad slaves were far more numerous, and the master's ignorance was less often the cause. Carelessness, indifference, and economy—a desire to reduce annual expenditures for clothing which, unlike food, usually involved cash outlays—these were the chief reasons why a large proportion of the slaves wore shabby and insufficient apparel made from some variety of cheap "Negro cloth." During the long summers, ragged and meager clothing merely added to the drabness of slave life; but during the winters it caused real discomfort and posed a serious threat to health.

The elegantly dressed slaves who promenaded the streets of southern towns and cities on Sundays, the men in fine linens and bright waistcoats, the women in full petticoats and silk gowns, were usually the domestic servants of wealthy planters or townspeople. Butlers, coachmen, maids, and valets had to uphold the prestige of their white families. "My own are supplied *without limit* to insure a genteel and comfortable appearance," wrote a South Carolina rice planter. Wealthy Southerners, an English visitor noted, "feel as natural a pride in having their personal attendants to look well in person and in dress, when slaves, as they do

---

[6] Kemble, *Journal*, pp. 64–65; Douglass, *My Bondage*, pp. 132–33.

when their servants are free." [7] Accordingly, they furnished domestics with good apparel, some of it from their own wardrobes.

Many ordinary slaves acquired a little holiday finery as gifts at Christmas, or with money earned from extra work or from the sale of their small crops. A woman might own some cheap jewelry, a printed calico dress, and a colorful handkerchief for her head; a man might own a felt hat, a fine cotton shirt, and a good pair of woolen trousers. Often the master hoped to improve the morale of his slaves by encouraging them to take pride in their appearance and by permitting them to possess a few frills. "They should be induced to think well of themselves," advised a Georgia planter, "so they should always be aided and encouraged in dressing, and their own peculiar fancies indulged to a reasonable extent." The clean, well-dressed slave who made "a decent appearance in the eyes of others" also felt "the touch of an honest pride in himself, and of friendship for his master, which lightens his tasks and sweetens all his toils." Above all, good clothing was conducive to good health; generous disbursements for an adequate supply was money well spent.[8]

The clothing regularly allotted to the slaves was made sometimes from homespun woven on the farm or plantation, sometimes from cloth manufactured in southern mills, but most of it came from northern or English factories. Southern merchants kept in stock numerous kinds of "Negro cloth," including calicoes, nankeens, osnaburgs, tows, linsey-woolseys, cassimeres, ducks, kerseys, and Kentucky jeans. On large, well-managed plantations several slave women might spend most of their time making cloth-

---

[7] Easterby (ed.), *South Carolina Rice Plantation*, p. 347; Buckingham, *Slave States*, I, p. 131.

[8] *De Bow's Review*, XVII (1854), p. 424; James Ewell, *The Planter's and Mariner's Medical Companion* (Philadelphia, 1807), pp. 13–14.

ing under the supervision of the plantation mistress or the overseer's wife. On smaller establishments the mistress often made the clothing herself, but frequently each slave family made its own. Although some slave forces included a shoemaker, "Negro brogans" were customarily purchased ready-made.

James H. Hammond's plantation manual described the clothing allowance that masters commonly provided: "Each man gets in the fall 2 shirts of cotton drilling, a pair of woolen pants and a woolen jacket. In the spring 2 shirts of cotton shirting and 2 pr. of cotton pants. . . . Each woman gets in the fall 6 yds. of woolen cloth, 6 yds. of cotton drilling and a needle, skein of thread and ½ dozen buttons. In the spring 6 yds. of cotton shirting and 6 yds. of cotton cloth similar to that for men's pants, needle thread and buttons. Each worker gets a stout pr. of shoes every fall, and a heavy blanket every third year." Some masters also gave socks and wool caps to the men, stockings and sunbonnets or kerchiefs to the women.

The children on Hammond's plantation received two shirts, "made very long," each fall and spring; but like most slave children they received no shoes. As a child in Maryland, Frederick Douglass "was kept almost in a state of nudity; no shoes, no stockings, no jacket, no trousers; nothing but coarse sack-cloth or tow-linen, made into a sort of shirt, reaching down to my knees. This I wore night and day, changing it once a week." Douglass wore the usual costume of slave children throughout the South. A visitor pictured the children on a South Carolina plantation as "ragged, dirty, shoeless urchins"—and this was an accurate picture of most of them everywhere.[9]

Field-hands, who did rough outdoor work, could not keep themselves comfortably clad throughout the year with

---

[9] Douglass, *My Bondage*, pp. 101, 132; Russell, *Diary*, p. 126.

the amount of clothing that was normally given to them. Most of them lacked the time or inclination to keep their meager apparel clean and mended, and so their garments were in tatters before the next allotment was distributed. Those who observed slaves working in the fields or lounging in the quarters often commented upon their shabby appearance—so often, in fact, that this condition must have been very common. Most of the slaves, both children and adults, lacked sufficient clothing to keep warm when the temperature dropped below freezing. Many of them went barefoot even in winter weather, or wore out their shoes before spring; hence they often limped about on frost-bitten feet.

A North Carolinian divided the masters in his state into "two well-known classes." One class owned slaves who were "ragged" and "filthy"; the other owned slaves whose needs were adequately filled.[1] So it was throughout the South.

4

In the towns and on the farms each slave family had its own cabin near the master's house, as a rule; on the plantations the slaves lived in little villages, called the quarters, within sight of the overseer's cottage. The quarters consisted of a single or double row of cabins or multiple-unit tenements for families and dormitories for unmarried men and women. Since slave mothers and fathers both customarily labored full-time for the master, while their children were supervised by the mistress or by an old slave woman, their cabins merely served as places to sleep and as shelters during inclement weather. Most of their dwellings were obviously designed for these simple purposes, not as centers of an active family life.

---

[1] Johnson, *Ante-Bellum North Carolina*, p. 526.

VII: *Maintenance, Morbidity, Mortality*

Southern agricultural periodicals bristled with warnings to masters about the importance of furnishing good houses for their laborers. They emphasized the need to elevate the cabins at least two feet above the ground, to make them weatherproof, and to provide plank flooring, glazed windows, a hinged door, and a large fireplace. The cabins should never be small and crowded: "One sixteen or eighteen feet square is not too large for a man and woman and three or four small children." They should be whitewashed inside and out at least twice a year, and the ground under and around them should be kept free of litter. Slave quarters should always be located on high ground where they would be free from the "impurities of stagnant waters." They should be protected by shade trees and near a supply of pure drinking water.[2]

A substantial minority of southern farmers and planters observed these standards and built snug dwellings of logs covered with weather-boarding, or frame houses of bricks, clapboards, or shingles. On many of the farms the slave cabins were not much inferior to the master's cabin; on some plantations they were nearly as comfortable as the overseer's cottage. A Louisiana sugar planter, Olmsted reported, provided slave houses "as neat and well-made externally as the cottages usually provided by large manufacturing companies in New-England, to be rented to their workmen." On Colonel Acklen's plantations the slaves lived in "neat frame houses, on brick pillars, . . . furnished with good bedding, mosquito bars, and all that is essential to health and comfort." A South Carolina rice planter built frame dwellings, boarded and whitewashed on the outside and lathed and plastered on the inside. They were forty-two feet long and twenty-one feet wide, divided into two family tenements, and each tenement parti-

---

2 *De Bow's Review*, III (1847), p. 419; X (1851), p. 623.

tioned into three rooms. The tenements had brick fire-places, cock-lofts, closets with locks, front and back doors, and windows closed by hinged wooden shutters.[3] Wealthy planters provided dwellings as elaborate as these more of-ten than the smaller slaveholders.

But on units of all sizes housing of such quality was the exception and not the rule. The common run of slave cab-ins were cramped, crudely built, scantily furnished, un-painted, and dirty. A resident of Liberty County, Georgia, presented a picture of slave housing which he thought would be "recognized by the well-informed as a fair aver-age" for the entire South. These "average" dwellings were covered with crudely cut, loose-fitting clapboards. They were not lined within, "so that only the thickness of a sin-gle board kept out the winter's air and cold." They were warmed by a clay chimney; the windows were unglazed.[4]

That an appalling amount of slave housing was of a quality far below this "average," well-informed Southern-ers frequently admitted. Poor housing was at least as com-mon as insufficient clothing, and southern doctors lectured incessantly to slaveholders about their shortsightedness. "One of the most prolific sources of disease among ne-groes," wrote an Alabama physician, "is the condition of their houses. . . . Small, low, tight and filthy; their houses can be but laboratories of disease." According to a Missis-sippian, "Planters do not always reflect that there is more sickness, and consequently greater loss of life, from the de-caying logs of negro houses, open floors, leaky roofs, and crowded rooms, than all other causes combined." Occasion-ally a slaveholder learned the truth of this complaint from his own experience. A Louisianian finally concluded that

3 Olmsted, *Seaboard*, pp. 422, 659–60; *Southern Cultivator*, X (1852), p. 227.
4 Robert Q. Mallard, *Plantation Life before Emancipation* (Richmond, 1892), pp. 29–30.

most of the sickness among his slaves was "owing to work-ing all day without rest and then sleeping in crowded dirty apartments." He resolved to cover the dirt floors with plank.[5]

On South Carolina and Georgia rice and cotton planta-tions visitors found houses "in the most decayed and de-plorable condition." Some of them were not more than twelve feet square, "built of logs, with no windows—no opening at all, except the doorway, with a chimney of sticks and mud." The three slave cabins on a small plantation in northern Mississippi were "small, diladpidated and dingy; the walls were not chinked, and there were no windows—which, indeed, would have been a superfluous luxury, for there were spaces of several inches between the logs, through which there was unobstructed vision. . . . Every-thing within the cabins was colored black by smoke." On a Maryland farm a former slave remembered houses that were "but log huts—the tops partly open—ground floor—rain would come through." [6]

Everywhere houses such as these were plentiful. The dwellings of the great mass of southern slaves were drab and cheerless, leaky in wet weather, drafty in cold. Like their food and clothing, their housing usually did not much exceed the minimum requirements for survival.

5

To slavery's defenders it was axiomatic that Negroes were peculiarly fitted for agricultural labor in the South. Of course, white yeoman farmers produced a large propor-tion of southern crops, but proslavery writers had particu-

---

[5] *Southern Cultivator*, VIII (1850), p. 66; *De Bow's Review*, X (1851), p. 623; Nutt Plantation Journal, entry for June 17, 1846.

[6] Bremer, *Homes of the New World*, I, pp. 288–89; Olmsted, *Seaboard*, pp. 140–41, 386; Drew, *The Refugee*, p. 155.

larly in mind the Deep South's alluvial river bottoms where the great cotton, sugar, and rice plantations were located and where the slaves heavily outnumbered the whites. In these lowlands under the hot southern sun, it was argued, white laborers would have perished "by the thousands," whereas the Negroes flourished.[7]

In spite of the relatively salubrious climate of some regions, such as the piedmont plateau, the South as a whole did have certain peculiarly difficult health problems. The survival of frontier conditions, the inadequate medical facilities typical of rural areas, the superabundance of undrained swamps and ponds, and the long summers and mild winters which enabled insects to thrive and increased the difficulty of preserving foods, all helped to make Southerners exceptionally vulnerable to epidemic and endemic diseases.[8] These, however, were the very conditions which Negroes presumably could endure without injurious effects; and one would therefore expect to find much lower morbidity and mortality rates among them than among the whites. The slave of tradition was a physically robust specimen who suffered from few of the ailments which beset the white man. A tradition with less substance to it has seldom existed. In the South, disease did not discriminate among men because of the color of their skins; wherever it was unhealthful for whites to live it was also unhealthful for Negroes.

Apart from the proslavery polemics, white Southerners themselves gave overwhelming testimony on this point. One doctor often heard planters say that *"sickness amongst negroes"* gave them their "greatest trouble." According to a South Carolinian, the lowlands were "deleterious to the

---

[7] *De Bow's Review*, XXI (1856), p. 467; XXIV (1858), p. 63.

[8] Richard H. Shryock, "Medical Practice in the Old South," *South Atlantic Quarterly*, XXIX (1930), pp. 160–63.

constitutions of both" races. When Negroes were moved from the Upper South to the Deep South they, like the whites, had to be acclimatized, and this process took its toll of human lives. "The hearse has been running regularly . . . bearing dead bodies from the negro Market to the publick Cemetery," wrote a resident of Natchez.[9]

In the rice districts of South Carolina and Georgia, Olmsted observed how difficult it was to keep slaves in good health and concluded that the "subtle poison of the miasma" was "not innocuous to them." Few rice planters saw their labor forces grow by natural increase; they did well if they could prevent a decline in numbers; and many of them were obliged to make periodic purchases to keep their forces at full strength. A South Carolina master refused to buy two hundred acres of tideland on the Savannah River because of the "great mortality" among the Negroes there. He learned "that it was never expected by the Planters on that river that the number of their people should increase. If they could keep up the force—which in very many cases they could not do—it was all they hoped." This, he thought, was the chief reason why these fertile lands were offered for sale at comparatively low prices.[1] Clearly, laboring in the rice swamps had a decidedly unfavorable effect upon the health of slaves.

The picture was essentially the same on the bottom lands in the cotton districts of the Deep South. The overseer on a Georgia cotton plantation reported to his employer that "from the great loss of time from Sickness and the deaths of so many fine Negroes . . . there can be but very little

---

9 *American Cotton Planter and Soil of the South,* II (1858), pp. 293–94; *Columbian Carolinian,* quoted in Charleston *Courier,* September 6, 1855; Joseph T. Hicks to Samuel S. Downey, May 14, 1836, Downey Papers.

1 Olmsted, *Seaboard,* pp. 418–19; Easterby (ed.), *South Carolina Rice Plantation,* p. 30; Grimball Diary, entry for June 6, 1832.

profit." James H. Hammond filled his diary with frightful accounts of sickness at Silver Bluff Plantation, on the Savannah River: "Great God what have I done. Never was a man so cursed! Never has death been so busy in any spot of earth." "All the plagues [of] Egypt still infest these Negroes. I don't believe there is a disease to which the human family is subject that is not to be seen here in the run of the year." Yet Hammond insisted that he had done everything he could and that his plantation was "as healthy as anywhere about here." In spite of this, "The fact is my negroes decrease . . . and I am hampered and alarmed beyond endurance by sickness." One evening, another South Carolina planter wrote a terse but significant entry in his journal: "Not a negro sick to day!!!!!!!!!!" [2]

To owners of river-bottom plantations in Alabama and Mississippi reports of "a great deal of sickness among negroes" were distressingly familiar. In the Alabama Black Belt a planter observed that "in a sickly year a man . . . has his hands full." On a plantation in the cane brakes of Marengo County, "*Every* person, *old* and *young, black* and *white*," had been "prostrated"; eventually the proprietor abandoned the place because he "had so much sickness and lost so many negroes." A slaveholder reported that in the Mississippi lowlands between the Yazoo River and the Big Black River "the negroes die off every few years"—it was a "sickly country." [3]

The Louisiana Sugar Country was apparently "healthy for neither whites nor blacks." In 1840, the mistress of a

[2] Stephen Newman to Mary Telfair, February 28, 1837, Telfair Plantation Records; Hammond Diary, *passim;* Gaillard Plantation Journal, entry for May 31, 1856.

[3] Henry Watson, Jr., to his mother, October 27, 1843, Watson Papers; C. S. Howe to William Lenoir, January 8, 1844; Julia Howe to Louisa S. Lenoir, January 4, 1845, Lenoir Family Papers; J. G. de R. Hamilton (ed.), *The Papers of Thomas Ruffin* (Raleigh, 1918–20), II, p. 77.

cotton plantation in West Feliciana Parish wrote sadly that slaves were "dying all round the neighborhood"; for many months she had been "constantly nursing sick negroes," while her neighbors were "in distress at the loss of so many." In the fall of 1833, the proprietor of a cotton plantation in eastern Texas noted that "we have done verry little since the middle of June as the Blacks were all sick as well as ourselves." [4]

The cotton plantations which lined the banks of the Arkansas River took an especially heavy toll. The "whole country" was "full of sickness," according to the overseer on a Jefferson County estate. The absentee owner of a plantation near Pine Bluff, where the death rate was staggering, was bedeviled by his brother who insisted that it was "morally wrong to settle one's negroes in any place where there are good grounds for the belief that their lives will be shortened thereby." But slaveholders were resourceful in solving moral problems. The owner's pious answer was that God must have created the river bottoms for a "wise purpose"—He designed them to be cultivated by the Negro. In reply the nagging brother suggested that the bottoms were "intended for aligators," and that "ten bales to the hand," rather than Providence, explained why slaves were sent to these unhealthy lands. As if this were not enough, the overseer also complained about the awful sickness and the numerous deaths. The harassed proprietor scolded him for constantly looking on the dark side of things, "an ugly habit which he ought to correct whilst he is young." Since the present overseer "harped upon the cripples and invalids," perhaps another should be employed

---

4 Sitterson, *Sugar Country*, pp. 92–93; Rachel O'Conner to Frances Weeks, October 2, 1840; *id.* to Mary C. Weeks, November 28, 1840, Weeks Collection; Abigail Curlee, "The History of a Texas Slave Plantation, 1831–63," *Southwestern Historical Quarterly*, XXVI (1922), p. 92.

who was more "accustomed to the chills, mud, and water of the Arkansas bottoms." [5]

Though the health problem was most acute in the lowlands of the Deep South, it was often serious even in areas such as Middle Tennessee, the Kentucky bluegrass, and the Virginia piedmont. In the Virginia tidewater, the slaves on Hill Carter's Shirley Plantation, on the James River, suffered severely during the "sickly season" in late summer. On the Pettigrew plantations in the swamplands of Tyrrell County, North Carolina, considerable sickness during August and September was taken as a matter of course; the proprietor frequently observed that his slaves were "as well as this season of the year will admit." On September 19, 1836, Ebenezer Pettigrew reported, "All the country as far as I hear is little else than a hospital, and I find the fevers among my negroes of the most obstinate character." [6]

Slaveholders gave many different names to the "fevers" to which Pettigrew alluded, among them, "ague," "shakes," "chills and fever," "bilious fever," "remittent fever," "intermittent fever," "miasmatic fever," and "autumnal fever." In most cases these "fevers" were clearly some form of malaria. The belief that Negroes were practically immune to malaria was altogether incorrect, as ante-bellum doctors and slaveholders knew all too well. "Fever," asserted a southern physician, "has always prevailed among the slave population . . . to a remarkable extent"; it was "the principal disease to which the race has been subject." Malaria may have been somewhat less severe and less often fatal among Negroes than among whites, but even this is uncertain. Some doctors claimed that there was "but little, if any difference, either in liability or fatality between the

---

[5] Willie Empie to James Sheppard, August 29, 1858, Sheppard Papers; Leak Diary, entries for January 27, 30, February 19, 26, June 7, 1859.
[6] Shirley Plantation Journal, *passim;* Pettigrew Family Papers, *passim.*

two races under similar circumstances of exposure, regimen, etc." In 1849, according to the seventh census, the proportion of deaths from "fever" in the total deaths was substantially higher for Negroes than for whites. This can be explained by the fact that so many slaves lived in the malarial river bottoms, but it is still convincing evidence that malaria found its victims among members of both races.[7]

When masters enumerated the diseases which afflicted their slaves, malaria often headed their lists. Year after year they waited in bewildered resignation for the "sickly season" to begin. In July and August, wrote a small planter in South Carolina's Colleton District, "the fever commenced and almost every family and plantation were more or less sick, and it was very fatal."[8] Until the heavy frosts of fall, the anopheles mosquitoes swarmed out of the swamps to infect blacks and whites with the parasites that caused malaria—while men lived in dread of atmospheric "miasmata" and night mists which they believed were the real sources of this disease.

Like malaria, yellow fever baffled ante-bellum Southerners; epidemics took a fearful toll of the whites in port towns such as Charleston, Savannah, and New Orleans. The Negroes seemed to have greater resistance to the toxin of the yellow fever virus, but they were not immune to the disease itself. Rather, they usually contracted it in a milder form and suffered fewer fatalities. In 1855, more than a score of slaves on an Adams County, Mississippi, planta-

---

7 *Memphis Medical Recorder*, quoted in *De Bow's Review*, XX (1856), pp. 612–14; Richard H. Shryock (ed.), *Letters of Richard D. Arnold, M.D., 1808–1876* (Durham, 1929), pp. 66–67; Felice Swados, "Negro Health on the Ante-Bellum Plantations," *Bulletin of the History of Medicine*, X (1941), pp. 463–64; Lewis, *Biology of the Negro*, pp. 192–96.

8 Hammond Diary, entry for May 22, 1832; Gavin Diary, entry for November 20, 1857.

tion were "taken down with yellow fever," but apparently none died. During this same year, several hundred cases occurred among the slaves in Rapides Parish, Louisiana; all the time of a local physician was "taken up with his Yellow fever Negroes." He reported only one death.[9]

The epidemics of Asiatic cholera, the first of which hit the United States in 1832, were if anything more deadly to the Negroes than to the whites. In the South, the cholera epidemics were most severe in the Mississippi delta where they spread from New Orleans to the plantations of Louisiana and Mississippi. Other regions suffered periodically from this "scourge of nations." In 1833, cholera caused more than three hundred deaths in Lexington, Kentucky; a year later, it produced "great consternation and alarm" in Middle Tennessee and killed many slaves in the vicinity of Savannah. Even a rumor that cholera was in a neighborhood was enough to cause masters to abandon their crops and flee with their slave property. In each of the great epidemics, cholera, which struck its victims with terrifying suddenness and ran its course with dramatic speed, was fatal to thousands of slaves and reduced some of their owners to financial ruin.[1]

In the long run, the "fevers" and other endemic diseases which attacked the slaves steadily, year after year, caused infinitely greater damage than the occasional ravages of cholera. During the summer months, "bowel complaints," or the "bloody flux" (usually some form of dysentery or diarrhea) , matched the debilitating effects and mortality of

---

[9] Lewis, *Biology of the Negro*, pp. 210–14; Jenkins Diary, entries for September 25 to October 6, 1855; Reuben Carnal to Lewis Thompson, October 18, 1855; Kenneth M. Clark to *id.*, November 2, 1855, Lewis Thompson Papers.

[1] Martha Carolyn Mitchell, "Health and the Medical Profession in the Lower South, 1845–1860," *Journal of Southern History*, X (1944) , pp. 430–31; Postell, *Health of Slaves*, pp. 5–6, 76; Washington *Mississippi Gazette*, May 18, 1833.

malaria. During the winter months, pleurisy, pneumonia, and pleuropneumonia cut down the poorly clothed and improperly housed field-hands who were too much exposed during cold or wet weather. A Louisiana physician reported that pneumonia was "one of the most formidable complaints," "more fatal than any other." Entries in the diary of a Mississippi slaveholder, during January, 1852, tell a grim story. January 21: "A very cold morning. . . . A great deal of Sickness through the Country from Colds and a great many *deaths* among the *negroes*." January 23: "A hard freeze and frost this morning. . . . great Complaint among people . . . great many negroes *dieing*." January 30: "There has been during the Cold weather a great deal of Typhoid Neumonia and very fatal among negroes." [2]

Because both doctors and masters often made crude diagnoses and gave vague names to the diseases they treated, one cannot always be sure what it was that caused a slave's death. According to their records, many suffered from "decline and debility," "effusion on chest," "inflammation of lungs," "congestion of brain," "marasmus," and "lingering disease," but each of these terms might have described several specific maladies. Even so, the records do identify clearly other diseases that commonly afflicted slaves. Sore throats, colds, thrush, measles, mumps, influenza, whooping cough, dengue, scrofula, scarlet fever, rheumatism, typhoid, typhus, smallpox, diphtheria, and dropsy, all were mentioned frequently. Tuberculosis, or "Negro consumption," was prevalent, though it probably never reached the proportions in the rural South that it did among postbellum Negroes in the cities of the North. Syphilis, originally contracted from the whites, was present in the towns and on scattered plantations, but it did not spread rapidly. Diseases of the heart and arteries and malignant tumors

---

[2] *De Bow's Review*, XI (1851), p. 209; Postell, *Health of Slaves*, pp. 81–82; Eli J. Capell Ms. Diary.

accounted for few slave deaths—other afflictions were usually fatal before these scourges of old age became a major menace.

The mortality from tetanus was incredibly high among slaves of all ages, but it was highest among newborn infants who received the infection through improperly dressed umbilical cords. Fanny Kemble observed that slave babies often fell victim to "lockjaw" a week or two after birth—and confessed that she was "utterly incapable" of explaining it. A North Carolina doctor wrote: "I am now . . . attending a Boy, with that terrible disease, *Tetanus*—he had his leg severely lacerated ten days ago and Lock jaw has supervened. I have little hope of his recovery." Tetanus, which occurred even after minor injuries, and whose cause remained a mystery, was nearly always fatal.[3]

Cachexia Africana (dirt-eating), another malady which puzzled masters and physicians, appeared with particular frequency on the plantations of the Southwest. According to a Louisiana physician, several slaves on almost every large plantation were addicted to eating such substances as clay, mud, sand, chalk, and ashes. Masters usually thought this to be merely a vile habit and tried to cure it by forcing the victims to wear wire masks or iron gags. But dirt-eating was a symptom of disease—in most cases it was probably a symptom of hookworm infection. A few southern doctors suggested that it might have resulted from severe treatment or from a "deficiency of suitable nutriment." Certainly many slaves did show other signs of such dietary-deficiency diseases as pellagra, beriberi, and scurvy.[4]

The image of the Negro whose broad grin revealed two

---

[3] Swados, "Negro Health," *loc. cit.*, pp. 464–65; Kemble, *Journal*, p. 39; W. C. Warren to Ebenezer Pettigrew, August 7, 1831, Pettigrew Papers.
[4] Moody, "Slavery on Louisiana Sugar Plantations," *loc. cit.*, p. 272 n.; Swados, "Negro Health," *loc. cit.*, pp. 467–68; Postell, *Health of Slaves*, p. 85.

even rows of glistening white teeth needs drastic modification, unless it can be demonstrated that slaves with dental caries had a special inclination to run away. For a very high proportion of the advertisements for fugitives described bondsmen with teeth "much rotten" or "somewhat decayed." Few slave children enjoyed the kind of diet that helped to produce good teeth; few received dental care; and, as a result, most adults suffered from tooth decay and kept the doctors busy making extractions.

Contrary to tradition, slaves also suffered from mental and nervous disorders. The census of 1840 seemed to indicate that the number of mentally defective and insane was proportionally higher among whites than among Negroes, and this presumably proved the psychic serenity of the unharried slaves. Actually, it only proved that psychotic bondsmen, unlike whites, were rarely institutionalized unless they were dangerous. Most of them could still be employed profitably, and in any case it was less expensive to support them at home than to pay their expenses in an asylum. Many masters owned slaves whom they described as "mentally unsound," "demented," suffering from "brain fever," "laboring under an aberration of mind," or afflicted with epilepsy.[5] Moreover, the occurrence of various mild and acute forms of neurosis almost certainly exceeded the rate in twentieth-century urban populations. "Surly," "sullen," "grum," "speaks quick," "stammers," "stutters," "easily frightened," "easily excited"—terms such as these hardly fitted the gay, carefree clowns of legend; yet masters often used such terms when they attempted to describe or identify their slaves.

Finally, slaves were the victims of numerous occupa-

---

[5] Albert Deutsch, "The First U. S. Census of the Insane (1840) and Its Use as Pro-Slavery Propaganda," *Bulletin of the History of Medicine*, XV (1944), pp. 469–82; Lewis, *Biology of the Negro*, p. 266; Postell, *Health of Slaves*, pp. 86–87.

tional disorders. "Female complaints" belong in this category, because slave women were troubled with them a great deal more than white women. "Reasoning *a priori*," wrote a Georgia physician, "one would suppose that the delicate white female should have a much oftener demand for the physician, than the coarse muscular negress,—but such is not the fact. . . . This tendency on the part of the slaves to womb diseases, originates, I doubt not, from two causes, —their great exposure and severe labor, and their vicious habits,—and not, as many planters suppose, from an unnatural tendency in the mother to destroy her offspring." Painful or irregular menses, suppurative infections of the generative tract, and prolapsus uteri were extremely common; sterility, spontaneous abortions, stillbirths, and death in childbirth occurred two or three times as frequently among slave women as among white. "Eliza had a child born dead last night," a South Carolina master noted. "This makes five miscarriages this Spring and but two live births." [6]

A Savannah physician believed that a Philadelphian who had developed an improved truss would find a good market in the South, because hernia was "a very common disease among Negroes." (Unfortunately, slaveholders generally preferred "the penny wisdom of buying the common and cheap trusses at the Apothecaries." [7]) Hernia was an occupational affliction of slaves who performed heavy labor. Similarly, round shoulders resulted from constant bending, and sore and infected fingers from picking cotton. In the dust-laden air of hemp factories slaves contracted diseases of the lungs. On the railroads and in the mines, mills, and factories they were crippled and maimed through indus-

---

[6] *Charleston Medical Journal*, VII (1852), p. 455; Postell, *Health of Slaves*, pp. 117–18; Swados, "Negro Health," *loc. cit.*, pp. 468–70; Hammond Diary, entry for March 31, 1834.

[7] Shryock (ed.), *Letters of Richard D. Arnold*, pp. 13, 19.

trial accidents. Few were without a scar or two somewhere on their bodies.

6

Not many masters left the treatment of disease to the untutored slave himself. When a bondsman was reputed to be a gifted healer, then sometimes they did give a trial to his "charms" or brews of root and bark. Thus a Virginian sent one of his hands to "the Old Man Docr. Lewis," a slave, "to be cured of being poisoned," and the treatment (a "decoction of herbs") was successful.[8] But masters generally agreed that ministering to the sick was their own responsibility.

Unfortunately, the state of ante-bellum medical science made it uncertain that even the most conscientious master would invariably prescribe better remedies than the superstitious slave healer. For example, Dr. James Ewell's *Planter's and Mariner's Medical Companion*, which went through several editions and guided many slaveholders, advised that cancer of the breast be treated by "wearing a hare or rabbit skin over the part affected." For "remittent fevers," Dr. Ewell prescribed "bleeding, cathartics, emetics and diluents, with such medicines as have a tendency to solicit the circulation of the fluids to the surface." For prolapsus uteri, a Mississippian administered cream of tartar, calomel pills, rhubarb, and aloes. For dropsy, a Virginian recommended a brew made from juniper berries, black mustard seed, and ashes of grape vine mixed in a gallon of hard cider—"to which add half a pound of rusty nails." Sore throats and "fall complaints," according to a Georgian, responded to doses of red pepper which created "a glow over the whole body" and produced "general arterial excitement." When a woman was about to miscarry, Hill

---

[8] John Walker Diary, entry for July 19, 1833.

Carter had her "copiously bled" and gave her a grain of opium and three grains of sugar of lead.[9]

Diseased slaves who received remedies such as these could have counted themselves fortunate if the remedies did not retard recovery or hasten death. Some were not this fortunate. A Louisiana slave took a dose of a "Tonic Mixture" prescribed by a respected physician; an hour later he told his master "that he felt very strange, as if his insides were coming up, as if the top of his head was coming off." He soon died.[1]

Prior to 1860, such heroic remedies as bloodletting and violent purging were still popular. Physicians, masters, and overseers frequently used the lancet and administered huge doses of castor oil, calomel, jalap, Glauber salts, and blue mass. They were also generous patrons of the patent medicine manufacturers whose tonics, elixirs, and panaceas promised miraculous cures for every malady from carbuncles to cancer. Many still believed that various diseases were caused by atmospheric "miasmata" resulting from decaying animal and vegetable matter; few fully understood the hygienic value of a piece of soap. Add to this surviving mass of ignorance the shortage of properly trained physicians and the profusion of quacks—hydropaths, eclectics, and botanics, among others—and the picture of medical practice in the Old South is a depressing one for both whites and blacks.[2]

Another sign of the state of southern medicine was the common (though not universal) belief that the physical

---

[9] Franklin L. Riley (ed.), "Diary of a Mississippi Planter," *Publications of the Mississippi Historical Society*, X (1909), p. 331; John Ambler to John Jacquelin Ambler, March 29, 1831, Ambler Family Papers; *De Bow's Review*, XVII (1854), p. 426; Shirley Plantation Journal, volume dated "1828–1839."

[1] William J. Minor Ms. Plantation Diary, entry for September 24, 1857.

[2] Postell, *Health of Slaves, passim;* Shryock, "Medical Practice," *loc. cit.*, pp. 171–72; Mitchell, "Health and the Medical Profession," *loc. cit.,* pp. 425, 437–39.

and emotional differences between Negroes and Caucasians were too great to permit the same medical treatment for both races. Dr. John S. Wilson, of Columbus, Georgia, affirmed that "the peculiarities in the diseases of negroes are so distinctive that they can be safely and successfully treated . . . only by Southern physicians." Dr. Samuel Cartwright, of Louisiana, the most distinguished advocate of this viewpoint, repudiated the "abolition theory that the negro is only a lamp-blacked white man." The Negro, said Cartwright, was sensual rather than intellectual; he normally suffered from a "deficiency of red blood in the pulmonary and arterial systems" and from a "defective atmospherization or arterialization of the blood in the lungs." The "seat" of "Negro consumption," he wrote, was not in the lungs but in the mind; it was caused by "bad government on the part of the master, and superstition or dissatisfaction on the part of the negro." "Facts" such as these caused Cartwright to urge medical schools to give special study to "Negro diseases," and to warn doctors that remedies which would cure a white man might injure or even kill a Negro.[3]

Most southern doctors did not actually put Cartwright's theories into practice, and a few of them ridiculed the theories. "Grant that the Negro is *black* to the bone," protested a South Carolina medic. "Admit that his shins are curved, his nose flat, his lips thick; still, we see no ground here on which to base the idea that he is governed by separate and distinct physiological laws." No good would result from Cartwright's "mixture of medicine and politics."[4]

This plea for professional integrity, for the scientific

---

3 *American Cotton Planter and Soil of the South*, II (1858), p. 293; III (1859), pp. 228–29; *De Bow's Review*, XI (1851), pp. 65–69, 209–13, 331–36, 504–508.
4 *Charleston Medical Journal*, VII (1852), pp. 89–98.

spirit in medicine, won the support of the South's best physicians. Like the leaders of their profession everywhere, they questioned more and more sharply many of the traditional ideas about the cause and treatment of disease—to the benefit of slaves and masters alike. Empirical observation caused a few to suggest that the use of pure water would prevent cholera and numerous other diseases, to doubt that all "fevers" were merely varieties of one, and to see dimly a connection between malaria and the mosquito, or at least between the prevalence of the disease and the presence of stagnant water. As early as 1842, a doctor wrote: "So far from musketoes being regarded as an evil, they should be viewed as kind messengers sent to warn the agriculturist against the danger of suffering stagnant pools of impure water to be about his premise." In the lowlands of the Deep South some planters gave their slaves mosquito bars, and many more learned the value of locating the quarters on high ground away from the swamps. From "long observation and suffering" a planter in eastern North Carolina concluded that stagnant water was "the great cause of most of our sickness in this country." "If I knew anything that would induce me to accept the dictatorship of a country it would be that of having the power to constrain the inhabitants in the bilious fever region to remove all stagnant waters from it." [5]

Late in the ante-bellum period trained physicians began to doubt the therapeutic value of bleeding and purging. In 1859, a Georgia doctor deplored the application of these remedies to "fever" patients before giving quinine. It was a mistake, he affirmed, to think that Negroes could "bear almost any amount of puking, purging and bleeding. The fact is, excessive physic[k]ing is a very common error in do-

---

[5] Shryock, "Medical Practice," *loc. cit.*, pp. 163–65; Mitchell, "Health and the Medical Profession," *loc. cit.*, p. 437; *American Agriculturist*, I (1842), p. 216; *Farmers' Register*, VIII (1840), p. 141.

mestic practice, both among whites and negroes, and thousands are thus hurried to the grave annually."[6]

One of the most hopeful signs was the gradual appreciation of the value of cleanliness as a disease preventive. Doctors warned slaveholders about the tragic results of overcrowding in the quarters, of permitting filth to accumulate in or around the cabins, and of the failure to require slaves to bathe and to keep their clothing and blankets clean. The best informed, most humane, and most efficient slaveholders responded to these admonitions. "The people," wrote a North Carolina master, "are at present too much crowded, and it is my intention . . . to afford them more room; thereby, they will be enabled to keep their houses more cleanly, which . . . will conduce much towards health." Some masters conducted weekly inspections to make sure that the slaves had bathed, washed their clothing, aired their blankets, swept their houses, and scoured their cooking utensils. Each spring and fall James H. Hammond appointed a day for a thorough cleaning of the quarters. The houses were completely emptied and everything was exposed to the sun; the floors and walls were washed, the mattresses filled with fresh hay, the yards cleaned, and the trash burned. Once a year the houses were whitewashed inside and out.[7] These sanitary measures were worth all the time and expense they entailed.

To treat their sick slaves, many masters employed trained physicians, often the same ones who treated the white families. A few large planters retained resident doctors on their estates; occasionally several small planters together contracted with a doctor for his full-time service. More commonly a slaveholder made a yearly contract with a physi-

---

6 *American Cotton Planter and Soil of the South*, III (1859), pp. 228–29.

7 William S. Pettigrew to James C. Johnston, September 1, 1849, Pettigrew Family Papers; Hammond Plantation Manual.

cian who agreed to charge a fixed amount for each visit. "Bargained today with Dr. Trotti to practice at the plantation," Hammond noted in his diary. "He agrees to charge only $2.50 a visit without reference to the number of sick prescribed for." Another planter cautioned his overseer, "Strong medicines should be left to the Doctor; and since the Proprietor never grudges a Doctor's bill, however large, he has a right to expect that the Overseer shall always send for a Doctor when a serious case occurs." Slaveholders, both large and small, sometimes spent generous sums for skilled medical treatment for their "people." To prove that there was "no class of working people in the world better cared for," one southern physician declared that he had often received large fees for attending even senile and worthless slaves.[8]

This statement was much too optimistic, but it did give recognition to a class of humane masters whose expenditures for medical service went far beyond the simple dictates of self-interest. In mourning the death of an old slave woman, a North Carolinian noted that his physician had given the case "asiduous attention" for six months, "devoting to it more reflection and research than he had (as he informs me) to any case within ten years."[9] This thought might lighten a little the moral burden which weighed so heavily upon a sensitive slaveholder.

A few masters patronized hospitals which were built and maintained especially for the care of sick slaves. During the 1850's, three Savannah physicians ran a slave hospital for "lying-in" women as well as for medical and surgical cases; similar institutions existed in Charleston, Montgomery, Natchez, and New Orleans. But plantation proprietors usu-

[8] Hammond Diary, entry for October 19, 1833; *De Bow's Review*, XXI (1857), pp. 38–44; XXIV (1858), pp. 321–24.
[9] William S. Pettigrew to Ann B. Pettigrew, November 2, 1850, Pettigrew Family Papers.

ally established their own hospitals where the sick could be attended by physicians or slave nurses. "All sick persons are to stay in the hospital night and day, from the time they first complain to the time they are able to go to work again," a South Carolinian instructed his overseer. "Hopeton," James Hamilton Couper's Georgia rice plantation, contained a model hospital where ailing slaves received the best medical attention the South could provide. The hospital was well ventilated and steam heated; it contained an examining room, medicine closet, kitchen, bathing room, and four wards, all of which were swept every day and scrubbed once a week.[1]

Wise and humane masters gave proper attention to slave women who were either expectant or nursing mothers. A Mississippian ordered his overseer to treat them with "great tenderness." A South Carolinian required "lying-in women" to remain at the quarters for four weeks after parturition, because their health might be "entirely ruined by want of care in this particular." Hammond gave the "sucklers" lighter tasks near the quarters and insisted that they be cool and rested before nursing.[2]

Some masters were equally solicitous about the care of slave children. On the smaller establishments they appointed an old woman to watch the children while the mothers worked in the fields. On the plantations they built nurseries where the plantation nurse cooked for the children, mended their clothing, and looked after them during illness. "My little negroes are consequently very healthy," boasted a South Carolina planter, "and . . . I am confident that I raise more of them, than where a different sys-

---

[1] *Charleston Medical Journal,* VII (1852), p. 724; XII (1857), p. 134; Postell, *Health of Slaves,* pp. 129, 138–40; *De Bow's Review,* XXI (1857), pp. 38–44; *Southern Agriculturist,* VI (1833), p. 574.
[2] Flinn Plantation Book; *De Bow's Review,* XXI (1857), pp. 38–44; Hammond Plantation Manual.

tem is followed." A rice planter maintained a summer house on high ground for his slave children "as a retreat from the bad summer climate of our rice fields." [3]

Conscientious masters and mistresses gave close personal attention to their diseased slaves, not only because they feared to lose valuable property but also because they felt that they owed this to their "people." In the North men and women of the leisure class devoted time and money to charities; in the South the gentry did their "settlement work" among their own slaves. "When people talk of my having so many slaves, I always tell them it is the slaves who own me," sighed a South Carolina mistress. "Morning, noon, and night, I'm obliged to look after them, to doctor them, and attend to them in every way." During a siege of "fever" a Louisiana plantation mistress complained that the slaves scarcely let her "set half an hour at a time." On another occasion she reported that "poor little Isaac has been sick, three or four days. . . . I keep him and his mother in my room, with me at night." [4] These touching scenes were enacted on farms and plantations scattered throughout the South.

7

But masters who maintained efficient medical regimes for the protection of health and the treatment of disease—who enforced sanitary regulations, established clean hospitals and nurseries, and employed trained physicians regularly— were the exception and not the rule. The average slaveholder was more or less unaware of the importance of these

---

[3] *Farmers' Register*, IV (1836), p. 495; Phillips (ed.), *Plantation and Frontier*, I, p. 148.

[4] Russell, *Diary*, p. 141; Rachel O'Connor to David Weeks, August 4, 1831; *id.* to Mary C. Weeks, September 1, 1833, Weeks Collection.

measures, or was not sufficiently concerned about his patriarchal obligations, or tried to economize by keeping down
his medical costs. Unquestionably, slaves were attended by
trained physicians and received good medical care less often
than whites.

Though some slaveholders spared neither time nor expense in ministering to their "people," others were guilty
of astonishing neglect. Often they possessed neither a sense
of duty nor a practical concern for the protection of their
property. They misused their lands, tools, and livestock as
well as their human chattels with a singular disregard for
the dictates of self-interest. Indeed, economic self-interest
did not always impel a calloused master to give medical aid
to an ailing slave, for it might tempt him to withhold this
aid either because the case seemed hopeless or because the
slave was worthless. For this reason one southern doctor opposed insuring the lives of slaves lest the "Almighty Dollar" silence the "soft, small voice of humanity" still more.[5]
Whatever the reason, neither humanity nor self-interest induced the generality of masters to protect the health of
their bondsmen as well as they might have done.

Except in the most "obscure" or "desperate" cases, the
master or overseer usually made his own diagnoses and prescribed remedies without the aid of a doctor. According to
a Georgian, " 'To send for the doctor' was, in plantation
belief, to give up the case." A standard set of instructions
to overseers declared, "A great majority of the cases you
should yourself be competent to manage, or you are unfit
for the place you hold." From personal experience one
overseer included among the "qualifications and duties"
of a man in his profession "a tolerable knowledge of physic,
that he may be able to administer medicine *properly*," and

---

[5] Shryock, "Medical Practice," *loc. cit.*, pp. 174–75; *De Bow's Review*,
IV (1847), pp. 286–87.

sufficient skill in surgery "that he may be able with *safety* to open a vein, extract a tooth, or bandage a broken limb." [6]

In their records or in their instructions to overseers, slaveholders often inserted prescriptions for all the common diseases—and thus clearly indicated that they employed doctors as infrequently as possible. A Georgian required his overseer to sign the following agreement: "There being no Physician engaged on the place I [the overseer] will provide myself with a good book of medical instruction and be careful to have at hand the few requisite Plantation Medicines and I will attend myself to mixing and instructing the nurses how to administer them." Another Georgian told his overseer that a certain slave woman was the "Doctress of the Plantation. In case of extraordinary illness, when she thinks she can do no more for the sick, you will employ a Physician." Subsequently his overseer boasted, "I have generally attended the Sick . . . with as good Success as I could Expect and have been so fortunate as to keep clear of the Doctors bills." [7]

Slave midwives commonly handled obstetrical cases. There was a prevalent notion that Negro women "were not subject to the difficulty, danger, and pain which attended women of the better classes in giving birth to their offspring." Moreover, most of them received improper prenatal and post-natal care. Too often, complained one observer, "nothing but actual confinement releases them from the field; to which the mother soon after returns, leaving an infant a few days old at the 'quarters.'" [8]

Some, thinking more of saving a crop than of guarding

---

[6] Shryock, "Medical Practice," *loc. cit.*, p. 174; Mallard, *Plantation Life,* pp. 33–34; Affleck, *Plantation Record and Account Book*; Charleston *Courier,* November 15, 1839.

[7] Phillips (ed.), *Plantation and Frontier,* I, pp. 124, 126–28; Elisha Cain to Alexander Telfair, October 10, 1829; January 16, 1830, Telfair Plantation Records.

[8] Olmsted, *Back Country,* p. 78; [Ingraham], *South-West,* II, p. 125.

health, kept their Negroes out of doors in the most inclement weather. One sugar planter forced his slaves to cut and haul cane on a "dreadful stormy day" when it was so cold they "could scarcely stay in the field," and another employed them for six weeks "constantly in the water" draining fields and repairing levees until they began to "fail very fast from sore feet and swelled legs." This was "bad economy," warned a critic. "The loss of time, and sometimes of life, from such causes, together with the doctor's bill, doubles the amount of gain that can ever accrue from such means." [9] But it was painful to lose a crop, and some gambled with the lives of Negroes to prevent it.

That most overseers neglected ailing slaves was one of the major complaints of employers. After visiting their Alabama plantation, the wife of an absentee owner wrote: "I begin very much to fear that the children are neglected. . . . I almost wish that we were living down there when I see how much they might be relieved by a little attention and care." But doctors scolded masters too for failing to provide hospitals and for "tampering with their sick negroes for one, two, or more days before applying for medical aid." Slaveholders would employ a skilled mechanic to put a spoke in a cart wheel, "but of the intricate mechanism of man . . . their knowledge is . . . sufficient, in their own estimation." [1]

Fanny Kemble's description of the hospitals on Pierce Butler's rice and cotton plantations was an accurate description of the hospitals on many other plantations as well. The floors were "merely the hard damp earth itself," most of the windows were unglazed, the rooms were dirty and malodorous, and the inmates "lay prostrate on the

---

[9] McCollam Diary, entry for November 30, 1845; Sitterson, *Sugar Country*, p. 22; *Southern Cultivator*, II (1844), p. 180.
[1] Sophia Watson to Henry Watson, Jr., June 26, 1848, Watson Papers; Swados, "Negro Health," *loc cit.*, pp. 466–67.

floor, without bed, mattress, or pillow, buried in tattered and filthy blankets." Sick and well alike were "literally encrusted with dirt" and infested with "swarms of fleas." Slave mothers were dismayed at the suggestion that they wash their babies. A condition of more complete indifference toward the invalids and disregard for the most elementary rules of sanitation could scarcely be imagined.[2]

Hired slaves doubtless suffered most from lack of medical care. Owners frequently sued hirers for damages when there was evidence that a slave had died from neglect. In Virginia, according to an agent who handled the hiring of slaves, it was "well known" that hired slaves were "much neglected" and that their owners had "sustained heavy losses in consequence." [3]

The combination of lower living standards, greater exposure, heavier labor, and poorer medical care gave slaves a shorter life expectancy and a higher mortality rate than whites. The census of 1850 reported average ages of 21.4 for Negroes and 25.5 for whites at the time of death. In 1860, 3.5 per cent of the slaves and 4.4 per cent of the whites were over sixty; the death rate was 1.8 per cent for the slaves and 1.2 per cent for the whites. Ante-bellum mortality statistics were not very reliable, but slave deaths went unreported more often than white. If anything, the disparity between slave and white death rates was greater and not less than recorded in the census returns.

These statistics discredit one of the traditions about slavery days: that a substantial number of aged "aunties" and "uncles" spent their declining years as pensioners living leisurely and comfortably on their masters' bounty. A few did, of course, but not enough reached retirement age to be more than a negligible expense to the average owner.

---

2 Kemble, *Journal*, pp. 23–24, 32–34, 63–64, 133, 214–15.
3 Catterall (ed.), *Judicial Cases*, II, pp. 541–42; Richmond *Enquirer*, December 6, 1836.

Doubtless most Negroes in their sixties were not very productive, but they usually did enough work at least to pay for their support. Even slaves over seventy were not always an absolute burden, though it may be assumed that most were. In 1860, however, only 1.2 per cent were over seventy; thus the owner of as many as a hundred seldom had more than one or two senile slaves to support.

The percentage of aged Negroes was somewhat higher in the older districts of the Southeast than in the newer districts of the Southwest. In 1842, Edward Lloyd, of Talbot County, Maryland, owned 211 slaves, of whom 11 were over seventy. This was far above average—in fact, it would be hard to find a master anywhere with a larger proportion of senile slaves. In the Southwest, plantations often contained none at all. In 1860, Francis T. Leak had a force of 93 slaves on his estate in Tippah County, Mississippi; the oldest was sixty-two, and only 5 were over fifty. In 1855, Thomas W. Butler listed 109 slaves on his sugar plantation in Terrebonne Parish, Louisiana, the oldest of whom was sixty-seven.

A study of life expectancy in ante-bellum Mississippi indicates that twenty-year-old Negroes "could, on the average, look forward to a somewhat shorter life" than whites of the same age. The life expectancy of slaves at this age was 17.5 years, of whites 19.2 years.[4] But in Mississippi, as in all the slave states, the difference between slave and white life expectancy widened considerably when infants were included in the statistics. Among white infants the mortality was distressingly high; among slave infants it was fantastic. In 1850, the white and Negro populations of Charleston were almost equal, but deaths among infants under five numbered 98 for the whites and 201 for the Negroes. In Mississippi, where the Negro population only

---

4 Charles S. Sydnor, "Life Span of Mississippi Slaves," *American Historical Review*, XXXV (1930) , pp. 566–74.

slightly exceeded the white, Negro infant deaths numbered 2,772 and white infant deaths numbered 1,315. In Virginia, the Negro population was only half the size of the white, but there were nearly 500 more deaths among Negro infants than among white infants. Everywhere the Negro infant mortality rate was more than double the white.

Slaveholders who kept their own vital statistics produced grim documentation of these conditions. William J. Minor had one of the least disheartening records on his Louisiana sugar plantation, "Waterloo," where out of 209 live births between 1834 and 1857, only 44 (21 per cent) died before the age of five. In Bertie County, North Carolina, Stephen A. Norfleet listed 24 births during the 1850's, of whom sixteen (67 per cent) died in infancy. In Charleston District, South Carolina, Keating S. Ball recorded 111 births during an eleven-year period, of whom 38 died before the age of one and 15 more between the ages of one and four. On St. Simon Island, Georgia, Fanny Kemble interviewed 9 slave women who together had had 12 miscarriages and 55 live births; 29 of their children were dead.[5] These infants were the victims of the ignorance that made tetanus such a killer, of neglect by slave mothers whose days were spent in the fields, and of "mismanagement" by their masters.[6]

In spite of the high mortality, the southern slave population, between 1830 and 1860, grew by natural increase at a rate of about 23 per cent each decade. The director of the seventh census gave the only possible explanation: "The marriages of slaves . . . take place, upon the average, much earlier than those of the white or free colored, and are probably more productive than either."[7] Though

---

[5] Kemble, *Journal*, pp. 190–91.
[6] *American Cotton Planter and Soil of the South*, III (1859), p. 228.
[7] *Compendium of the Seventh Census*, p. 92.

ante-bellum white families also were large, slave women had to bear many more children than white women to make this natural increase possible. For a slave mother gave birth to two or three babies in order that one might grow to be a "prime hand" for her master.

CHAPTER EIGHT

Between Two Cultures

The evil that confounds men in the present often causes them to look nostalgically to the good they think they see in some misty past. For example, the racial tension that followed emancipation fostered a legend of racial harmony under slavery. Among white Americans the popular tradition about slavery days emphasizes the love that united benevolent "massas" and pampered servants, not the hostility that divided harsh overseers and disgruntled field-hands. After a century, few remember that southern slavery was not so much a patriarchal institution as a practical labor system. Few recall that slaveholders were more often ambitious entrepreneurs than selfless philanthropists. And few ask what the slaves themselves thought of bondage.

The legend tells of a good time long ago when Negroes and whites abided happily together in mutual understanding. Slaveholders themselves created the legend, giving it both its kernel of fact (by their numerous kindnesses toward slaves) and its texture of fancy (in their proslavery polemics). The kernel of fact—the reality of ante-bellum paternalism—needs to be separated from its fanciful surroundings and critically analyzed. How much paternalism was there? Under what circumstances did it occur? What was its nature?

A South Carolinian once described the kinds of slaves

who aroused paternalistic impulses in their owners. There was the "faithful and kind old nurse" who watched over her master in his infancy; the body servant who cared for him during sickness and anticipated all his wants; and the "faithful and devoted" field-hand who earned his regard "by implicit obedience to all his command[s]." These cases were not imaginary but arose "out of real life." Harriet Martineau wasted little of her charity upon slaveholders, but she did acknowledge that some showed deep gratitude for such services from bondsmen. "Nowhere, perhaps, can more touching exercises of mercy be seen than here," she confessed. "The thoughtfulness of masters, mistresses, and their children about, not only the comforts, but the indulgences of their slaves, was a frequent subject of admiration with me." A former slave, in recalling his life on a Louisiana plantation, thought it was but "simple justice" to observe that his owner had been a "kind, noble, candid, Christian man, . . . a model master, walking uprightly, according to the light of his understanding." [1]

Visitors often registered surprise at the social intimacy that existed between masters and slaves in certain situations. A Northerner saw a group of Mississippi farmers encamped with their slaves near Natchez after hauling their cotton to market. Here they assumed "a 'cheek by jowl' familiarity . . . with perfect good will and a mutual contempt for the nicer distinctions of colour." Domestics moved freely among the whites at social functions and sat with them in public conveyances. On a train in Virginia Olmsted saw a white woman and her daughter seated with a Negro woman and her daughter. The four of them talked and laughed together, while the girls munched candy out of the same bag "with a familiarity and closeness" which

---

[1] Abbeville District, South Carolina, Judge of Probate Decree Book, 1839–58, May term, 1841; Martineau, *Society in America,* II, p. 107; Northup, *Twelve Years a Slave,* p. 90.

would have astonished and displeased most Northerners. As an infant a master might have been nourished at the breast of one of his female chattels. A young South Carolinian noted in his diary: "Meta has nursed sister's baby as well as her own for three days—but she cant support it—and they intend making Tibbi nurse it." Olmsted concluded, "When the negro is definitely a slave, it would seem that the alleged natural antipathy of the white race to associate with him is lost." [2]

From such close associations an owner might develop a deep affection for a slave. An Alabama mistress wrote with great tenderness about the death of a nurse who had been the playmate of all her children: "When I saw that Death had the mastery, I laid my hands over her eyes, and in tears and fervor prayed that God would cause us to meet in happiness in another world. I knew, at that solemn moment, that color made no difference, but that her life would have been as precious, if I could have saved it, as if she had been white as snow." A South Carolinian mourned the loss of his "old man Friday" who had known three generations of his family: "He seemed like a connecting link between me and grand-father and grand-mother . . . for he could . . . tell me of the actings and doings of them and others of the olden time." A Louisiana mistress confessed that her heart was "nearly broke" when she "lost poor *Leven*, one of the most faithful black men, ever lived." And a North Carolinian sent his brother the sad news of the death of "our faithful old servant William." This event deprived their family "of a friend over whom they should weep," and it cast over him "a feeling of solitude and desolation." [3]

---

[2] [Ingraham], *South-West*, II, p. 26; Olmsted, *Seaboard*, pp. 17–18; Grimball Diary, entry for May 23, 1832.

[3] Gayle Journal, entry for May 4, 1834; Gavin Diary, entry for September 13, 1856; Rachel O'Conner to Mary C. Weeks, September 4, 1840, Weeks Collection; William S. Pettigrew to Charles L. Pettigrew, September 28, 1844, Pettigrew Family Papers.

VIII: *Between Two Cultures*

These were the facts "out of real life" from which grew the legend of racial harmony in the Old South—the facts which proslavery writers enlarged into a generalized picture of bondage as a patriarchal institution. Many of the best illustrations of paternalism were drawn from small establishments where absentee ownership was rare, where overseers were seldom employed, and where contacts between masters and slaves were numerous. Here the discipline tended to be less severe and the system generally less rigid. Olmsted described the "great difference in the mode of life of the slaves when living on the large plantations, and when living on farms or in town establishments, or on such small plantations that they are intimately associated with white families." [4] Only a minority of the slaves, however, lived in holdings so small that the master was more or less constantly in close association with them. Moreover, while there were numerous exceptions, most small slaveholders tried to operate their agricultural enterprises in an efficient, businesslike way and not as easygoing patriarchs.

On the plantations the master's intimate personal contacts were confined almost exclusively to household servants; rarely did he have more than a casual acquaintanceship with the mass of common field-hands. For instance, when a personal attendant died, a South Carolina planter wrote a sentimental tribute to him and affirmed that his loss was "irreparable." But he recorded the deaths of more than a hundred other slaves with no comment at all. In 1844, James H. Hammond was saddened by the loss of his gardener and plantation "patriarch" who had been a "faithful friend" and "one of the best of men." But the deaths of two other slaves in the same year stirred no deep emotions: "Neither a serious loss. One valuable mule has also died." A Mississippi planter grieved at the death of a slave child,

---

[4] Olmsted, *Back Country*, pp. 156, 158.

whom his whole family had loved, as if he "had lost some dear relative." More commonly, however, his grief seemed to arise from the loss of property. "Dick died last night, curse such luck," he wrote. And again: "Mary's son, Richard, died tonight. Oh! my losses almost make me crazy." [5]

Even the most benevolent masters usually did not hold all their slaves in equal esteem; being human, they developed affections for some and animosities for others. A Virginian gave evidence of the mixed attitudes that planters often exhibited. He described the deaths of Sam and Delph as great tragedies, for Sam had been "the very best servant I ever knew" and Delph had been "faithful and affectionate, and a great favorite with all our white family"; but he regarded the death of Betsy, if anything, as a relief, for she had been a "worthless lazy thing . . . good for nothing from the time I bought her." [6]

Plantation paternalism, then, was in most cases merely a kind of leisure-class family indulgence of its domestics. In these households, an English visitor observed, "there are often more slaves than are necessary for the labor required of them, many being kept for state, or ostentation." Since the domestics were continually in the presence of the master and mistress and their guests, they were usually treated with great liberality. [7]

A planter sometimes whimsically selected a slave or two for special pets. He pampered them, consulted them with mock gravity about large matters, and permitted them to be impertinent about small. In Charleston a visitor went for a drive with a mistress who asked her coachman to take them down a certain street. But the coachman ignored all her pleas and took them a different way. The guest of a

---

[5] Keating S. Ball Ms. Record of Births and Deaths; Hammond Diary, entries for April 29, June 22, 1844; Riley (ed.) , "Diary of a Mississippi Planter," *loc. cit.,* pp. 334, 450, 469.

[6] William Massie Ms. Slave Book.

[7] Buckingham, *Slave States,* I, p. 200.

Georgia planter told of another coachman who suddenly stopped the carriage and reported that he had lost one of his white gloves and must go back to find it. "As time pressed, the master in despair took off his own gloves, and . . . gave them to him. When our charioteer had deliberately put them on, we started again." A neighbor told Fanny Kemble "with great glee" that his valet had asked him for his coat as a loan or gift. This, she thought, furnished a good example of the extent to which planters "capriciously permit their favorite slave occasionally to carry their familiarity. . . . I had several of these favorite slaves presented to me, and one or two little negro children, who their masters assured me were quite pets." [8]

This kind of paternalism (Fanny Kemble likened it to "that maudlin tenderness of a fine lady for her lapdog"), which often arose from the master's genuine love for his slave, gave its recipient privileges and comforts but made him into something less than a man. The most generous master, so long as he was determined to *be* a master, could be paternal only toward a fawning dependent; for slavery, by its nature, could never be a relationship between equals. Ideally it was the relationship of parent and child. The slave who had most completely lost his manhood, who had lost confidence in himself, who stood before his master with hat in hand, head slightly bent, was the one best suited to receive the favors and affection of a patriarch. The system was in its essence a process of infantilization—and the master used the most perfect products of the system to prove that Negroes were a childlike race, needing guidance and protection but inviting paternal love as well. "Oh, they are interesting creatures," a Virginian told Olmsted, "and, with all their faults, have many beautiful traits. I

---

[8] Sir Charles Lyell, *Travels in North America in the Years 1841–1842* (London, 1845), I, pp. 169–70; Bremer, *Homes of the New World*, I, pp. 391–92; Kemble, *Journal*, pp. 67–68.

can't help being attached to them, and I am sure they love us." This Virginian's manner toward his slaves was "familiar and kind; and they came to him like children who have been given some task, and constantly are wanting to be encouraged and guided." [9]

It was typical of an indulgent master not to take his slaves seriously but to look upon them as slightly comic figures. He made them the butt of his humor and fair game for a good-natured practical joke. He tolerated their faults, sighed at their irresponsibility, and laughed at their pompous pretensions and ridiculous attempts to imitate the whites. This amiable attitude was evident in a Southerner's jocose description of old "family Negroes." These "plantation oracles," he wrote, usually possessed a "very sage, sober look," shook their heads "with utmost gravity," and loved "a wee drop too much of the 'critter' on all holiday occasions." They thought they knew "much more than their masters, whom they always looked upon as *young*," and they advised him "with all oracular dignity" on how to run his estate. They were generally pious and "great on quotations from 'scripter,' " and many of them were preachers or exhorters—though sometimes their manner of expression was "a little ludicrous, thus giving rise to many amusing anecdotes." [1]

Even the most sensitive master called adult slave men "boys" and women "girls," until in their old age he made them honorary "aunties" and "uncles." In addressing them, he never used courtesy titles such as "Mr.," "Miss," and "Mrs."; except in Maryland he seldom identified them by family names. But in selecting given names the master often let his sense of humor have full play. If familiar with the classics, he found a yard full of Caesars, Ciceros, Pompeys, Catos, Jupiters, Venuses, and Junos deliciously ludi-

[9] Olmsted, *Seaboard*, pp. 45–46.
[1] Hundley, *Social Relations*, pp. 88–89.

crous; and he saw to it that every distinguished soldier and statesman had his slave namesake. When a clergyman visited a Mississippi plantation to baptize forty slave children, he could "scarcely keep his countenance" as he administered the sacrament to "Alexander de Great," "General Jackson," "Walter Scott," "Napoleon Bonaparte," and "Queen Victoria," among others. This "scandalous naming" originated in the "merry brain" of the planter's sister, and the white visitors found "the whole scene irresistible." [2]

The weddings, balls, and other social functions which a generous master arranged for his slaves were equally "irresistible." The white family found it a pure delight to watch a bride and groom move awkwardly through the wedding ceremony, to hear a solemn preacher mispronounce and misuse polysyllabic words, or to witness the incredible maneuvers and gyrations of a "shakedown." A Tennessee planter once noted in his diary that he gave his slaves a holiday and took a group of white children to the quarters to "enjoy the Negro *dance* and Barbecue." [3] In the sentimental recollections of the whites, these gay times in the quarters gave plantation life much of its charm. But these affairs were as much performances for the whites as celebrations for the slaves.

Clearly, to enjoy the bounty of a paternalistic master a slave had to give up all claims to respect as a responsible adult, all pretensions of independence. He had to understand the subtle etiquette that governed his relations with his master: the fine line between friskiness and insubordination, between cuteness and insolence. A nurse might scold the white child under her care; a cook might be a petty tyrant in her kitchen; an old servant might gravely advise on family affairs; a child pet might crawl on mas-

---

[2] Ingraham (ed.), *Sunny South*, pp. 68–70.
[3] Bills Diary, entry for July 4, 1860.

ter's lap and sleep in his bedroom; a field-hand and a small farmer might work together and eat from the same frying pan. But between master and slave there was still a formidable barrier, a barrier that prevented either from being entirely candid with the other. A slave was always reticent, never entirely at ease, except in the company of other slaves.

Plantation domestics, as a rule, enjoyed their privileges and basked in the affection of their masters. And yet some of them occasionally felt isolated and lonely in the "big house" and looked wistfully to the relative privacy of the quarters. Though the domestics were expected to remain aloof from the field-hands, they sometimes went to the quarters for company and relaxation. "You have no idea of the corruption to house servants to have a gang of negroes in the yard," a plantation mistress complained. Olmsted believed that the field-hands preferred the "comparatively unconstrained life of the negro-settlement" and disliked "the close control and careful movements required of house-servants." [4] Living intimately with even a paternal master was not in all respects as completely satisfying as the whites liked to think.

This raises a question about the benefits, from the slave's point of view, of being owned by a small slaveholder. It is by no means certain that the bondsman thought that the advantages of living on a farm in close association with his master outweighed the disadvantages of living on a plantation remote from his master. In the first place, there is reason to doubt that the slaves invariably desired and enjoyed these intimate contacts. In the second place, the modest slaveholdings were usually located in regions where Negroes were a small minority of the population—where the slave groups were like tiny islands in a sea of suspicious

---

[4] Ann Pettigrew to Ebenezer Pettigrew, January 23, 1830, Pettigrew Family Papers; Olmsted, *Seaboard*, p. 421.

and unfriendly whites. Here the bondsmen could have no social milieu of their own, no relief from the constant scrutiny of white men, no escape from the consciousness of inferior status. For instance, a former slave on a Tennessee farm recalled that he ate in the same room with the white family, but at a separate table. The arrangement made him extremely uncomfortable, and his ardent wish was to get away by himself.[5]

On the large plantations the field-hands were often worked harder and disciplined more severely; but there were compensations. Here they found conditions which made it easier for some to achieve, with advancing years, the kind of inward serenity that comes when one is reconciled to his earthly lot. For here they lived together in their own substantial communities in regions where the majority of people were of their own race and status. Thus they had fewer humiliating contacts with the whites; and in their free time they could be at ease, express their thoughts and feelings with less restraint, and find their diversions amid a wide circle of friends. Above all, they played less at the game which etiquette demanded even when master and slave were showing affection for each other.

2

The ante-bellum South had a class structure based to some extent upon polite breeding but chiefly upon the ownership of property. Superimposed upon this class structure was a caste system which divided those whose appearance enabled them to claim pure Caucasian ancestry from those whose appearance indicated that some or all of their forebears were Negroes. Members of the Caucasian caste, regardless of wealth or education, considered themselves

---

[5] Jermain W. Loguen, *The Rev. J. W. Loguen, as a Slave and as a Freeman: a Narrative of Real Life* (Syracuse, 1859), pp. 164–66.

innately superior to Negroes and "mulattoes" and therefore entitled to rights and privileges denied to the inferior
caste. They believed in "white supremacy," and they maintained a high degree of caste solidarity to secure it.

The slaves were "caste conscious" too and, despite the
presence of some "white man's Negroes," showed remarkable loyalty toward each other. It was the exception and
not the rule for a slave to betray a fellow slave who "took"
some of the master's goods, or shirked work, or ran away.
In Tennessee, for example, Jim killed Isaac for helping to
catch him when he was a fugitive; and he clearly had the
sympathy of the other slaves. At Jim's trial the judge observed that "Isaac seems to have lost *caste*. . . . He had
combined with the white folks . . . no slight offense in
their eyes: that one of their own color, subject to a like
servitude, should abandon the interests of his *caste*,
and . . . betray black folks to the white people, rendered
him an object of general aversion." Former slaves testified
that when a newly purchased chattel was sent to the quarters he was immediately initiated into the secrets of the
group. He was told what he "had better do to avoid the
lash." [6]

In the quarters the bondsman formed enduring friend-
ships. He became attached to the community—to the soil
on which he labored and to the people who shared his hardships and fears, his hopes and joys. Between the slaves on a
plantation there developed, one Southerner observed, "a
deep sympathy of feeling" which bound them "closely together." It was back to old friends and familiar places that
the runaway often fled. As a Kentucky slave began a dash
for freedom, he "took an affectionate look at the well-
known objects" on his way and confessed that sorrow was
mingled with his joy. The slave, explained Frederick

---

[6] Catterall (ed.), *Judicial Cases*, II, pp. 522–23; Douglass, *My Bondage*, p. 269; Drew, *The Refugee*, p. 199.

Douglass, had "no choice, no goal, no destination; but is pegged down to a single spot, and must take root there or nowhere." [7]

This was why estate and execution sales were such tragedies; for each of them involved, besides the breakup of families, the disintegration of a community, the dispersion of a group of people who might have lived together for a generation or more. After the death of a Tennessee planter, one of the heirs noted that the slaves were "much opposed to being broken up." While Fanny Kemble resided on her husband's Georgia plantation, slaves came to her to express their gratitude that she had had children. They regarded the children as security "against their own banishment from the only home they knew, and separation from all ties of kindred and habit, and dispersion to distant plantations." [8] These fears might have caused a group of slaves to grieve at the death of even a severe master.

Although slaves were generally loyal to their caste and fond of their communities, they, like the whites, had their own internal class structure. Their masters helped to create a social hierarchy by giving them specialized tasks for the sake of economic efficiency, and by isolating domestics and artisans from the field-hands as a control technique. But the stratification of slave society also resulted from an impelling force within the slaves themselves—a force which manifested itself in their pathetic quest for personal prestige. Slaves yearned for some recognition of their worth as individuals, if only from those in their own limited social orbit; for to them this wholly human aspiration was, if anything, more important than it was to the whites. Each

---

[7] Harrison, *Gospel Among the Slaves*, p. 102; Josiah Henson, *Father Henson's Story of His Own Life* (Boston, 1858), p. 107; Douglass, *My Bondage*, p. 176.

[8] Allen Brown to Hamilton Brown, December 7, 1834, Hamilton Brown Papers; Kemble, *Journal*, pp. 165–66.

slave cherished whatever shreds of self-respect he could preserve.

The bondsmen, of course, were cut off from the avenues which led to success and respectability in white society. The paragon of virtue in materialistic nineteenth-century America—at least in its white middle-class segment, both urban and rural—was the enterprising, individualistic, freedom-loving, self-made man. Ideally he was the head of a family which he provided with the comforts and luxuries that symbolized his material success. He sought through education to give his children culture and social poise; he emancipated his wife from household drudgery; and he subscribed to the moral code of the Victorian age. Southern masters more or less conformed to this pattern and thus gained dignity and prestige; but the white caste's whole way of life was normally far beyond the reach of slaves. In slave society, therefore, success, respectability, and morality were measured by other standards, and prestige was won in other ways. The resulting unique patterns of slave behavior amused, or dismayed, or appalled the whites and convinced most of them that Negroes were innately different.

Many domestics did adopt part of the white pattern of respectability, were proud of their honesty and loyalty to the white family, and frowned upon disobedient or rebellious behavior. Some bondsmen at times seemed to fear or disapprove of a trouble-maker lest he cause them all to suffer the master's wrath. But most of them admired and respected the bold rebel who challenged slave discipline. The strong-willed field-hand whom the overseer hesitated to punish, the habitual runaway who mastered the technique of escape and shrugged at the consequences, each won personal triumphs for himself and vicarious triumphs for the others. The generality of slaves believed that he who knew how to trick or deceive the master had an enviable talent, and they regarded the committing of petit larceny as both thrilling and praiseworthy. One former slave recalled with great satisfaction the times when he had caught a pig or chicken and shared it with some "black fair one." These adventures made him feel "good, moral, [and] heroic"; they were "all the chivalry of which my circumstances and condition of life admitted." [9]

The unlettered slaves rarely won distinction or found pleasure in intellectual or esthetic pursuits. Theirs was an elemental world in which sharp wits and strong muscles were the chief weapons of survival. Young men prided themselves upon their athletic skills and physical prowess and often matched strength in violent encounters. Having to submit to the superior power of their masters, many slaves were extremely aggressive toward each other. They were, insisted a Georgian, "by nature tyrannical in their dispositions; and if allowed, the stronger will abuse the weaker; husbands will often abuse their wives, and mothers their children." Slave foremen were notoriously severe taskmasters and, when given the power, might whip more cruelly than white masters. Fanny Kemble discerned the brutalizing effects of bondage in the "unbounded insolence and tyranny" which slaves exhibited toward each other. "Everybody, in the South, wants the privilege of whipping somebody else," wrote Frederick Douglass.[1]

Each community of slaves contained one or two members whom the others looked to for leadership because of their physical strength, practical wisdom, or mystical powers. It was a "notorious" fact, according to one master, "that on almost every large plantation of Negroes, there is one

9 Henson, *Story*, pp. 21–23.
1 *Southern Cultivator*, XII (1854), p. 206; Drew, *The Refugee*, p. 45; Kemble, *Journal*, p. 239; Douglass, *My Bondage*, pp. 69–72, 74–75, 129–32.

among them who holds a kind of magical sway over the minds and opinions of the rest; to him they look as their oracle. . . . The influence of such a Negro, often a preacher, on a quarter is incalculable." A former slave on a Louisiana plantation remembered "Old Abram" who was "a sort of patriarch among us" and was "deeply versed in such philosophy as is taught in the cabin of the slave." On a Mississippi plantation everyone stood in awe of "Old Juba" who wore about his neck a half dozen charms and who claimed to have seen the devil a hundred times. On Pierce Butler's Georgia plantation Sinda prophesied the end of the world, and for a while no threat or punishment could get the hands back to work. A Louisiana planter noted angrily that "Big Lucy" was the leader who "corrupts every young negro in her power." [2] These were the self-made men and women of slave society.

Slaves who lacked the qualities which produce rebels or leaders had to seek personal gratification and the esteem of their fellows in less spectacular ways. They might find these things simply by doing their work uncommonly well. Even some of the field-hands, though usually lacking the incentive of pecuniary gain, were intrigued by the business of making things grow and enjoyed reputations as good farmers. To be able to plow a straight furrow, to master the skills required in cultivating one of the southern staples, to know the secrets of harvesting and preparing it for market—these activities brought personal rewards which might not be completely lost because all was done for another man's profit. Patsy, for example, was "queen of the field" on a small Louisiana plantation, since the "lightning-like motion" of her fingers made her the fastest cotton picker. Whatever she thought of bondage, Patsy was absorbed in

---

[2] *Southern Cultivator*, IX (1851), p. 85; Northup, *Twelve Years a Slave*, pp. 186–87; Ingraham (ed.), *Sunny South*, pp. 86–87; Kemble, *Journal*, p. 84; Davis (ed.), *Diary of Bennet H. Barrow*, p. 191.

her work and found pleasure in her own special kind of creativeness.[3]

This was still more true of slave artisans whose work often won great admiration. An English visitor affirmed that their aptitude for the mechanical arts should "encourage every philanthropist who has had misgivings in regard to the progressive power of the race." Again it was pride in craftsmanship, not monetary rewards, which gave most carpenters, blacksmiths, coopers, cobblers, and wheelrights their chief incentive. The carpenters on a North Carolina plantation must have gained additional satisfaction from the knowledge that a white laborer had asked for permission to work with them "for the sake of Instruction." In Louisiana, a white engineer who was training a slave gave the master a favorable report: "I have seldom met with a Negro who shewed more anxiety to learn everything pertaining to a Steam Engine . . . and I have no hesitation in saying that with a little more practice, he will make a competent careful Engineer." [4]

The well-trained domestic also obtained a pleasant feeling of self-importance from the tactful performance of his services. A first-rate plantation cook wallowed in admiration; a personal servant who could humor his master and bandy innocuous pleasantries with him possessed the rare talent of a diplomat. Most domestics were proud of their positions of responsibility, of their fine manners and correct speech, and of their handsome clothing and other badges of distinction. They were important figures in their little world.

Indeed, the domestics, artisans, and foremen constituted the aristocracy of slave society. "I considered my station a

---

[3] Northup, *Twelve Years a Slave*, pp. 188–89.
[4] C. P. Phelps to Ebenezer Pettigrew, March 2, 1831, Pettigrew Papers; Lyell, *Second Visit*, I, p. 360; John B. Clarkson to Phanor Prudhomme, February 3, 1854, Phanor Prudhomme Papers.

very high one," confessed an ex-slave who had been his master's body servant. Many visitors to the South commented on how the domestics flaunted their superiority over "the less favored helots of the plough"—"their assumption of hauteur when they had occasion to hold intercourse with any of the 'field hands.'" And former slaves described the envy and hatred of the "helots" for the "fuglemen" who "put on airs" in imitation of the whites.[5]

Thus, ironically, a slave might reach the upper stratum of his society through intimate contact with the master, by learning to ape his manners, and by rendering him personal service, as well as by being a rebel or a leader of his people. And a bondsman, in his own circle, was as highly sensitive to social distinctions as ever was his master. In a society of unequals—of privileged and inferior castes, of wealth and poverty—the need to find some group to feel superior to is given a desperate urgency. In some parts of Virginia even the field-hands who felt the contempt of the domestics could lavish their own contempt upon the "coal pit niggers" who were hired to work in the mines.[6]

Everywhere, slaves of all ranks ridiculed the nonslaveholders, especially the poor whites—the dregs of a stratified white society—whom they scornfully called "po' buckra" and "white trash." Those who belonged to a master with great wealth and social prestige frequently identified themselves with him and looked disdainfully upon those who belonged to humbler masters. "They seemed to think that the greatness of their masters was transferable to them," wrote Frederick Douglass. "To be a slave, was thought to be bad enough; but to be a *poor man's* slave, was deemed a disgrace, indeed." Another former slave criticized the "foolish pride" which made them love "to boast of their master's

---

[5] Thompson, *Life of John Thompson*, pp. 24–25; Ingraham (ed.), *Sunny South*, p. 35; Steward, *Twenty-Two Years a Slave*, pp. 30–32.
[6] Bancroft, *Slave-Trading*, pp. 153–55.

wealth and influence. . . . I have heard of slaves object to being sent in very small companies to labor in the field, lest that some passer-by should think that they belonged to a poor man, who was unable to keep a large gang." A northern visitor described the house servant of a wealthy planter as "full of his master's wealth and importance, which he feels to be reflected upon himself." A domestic on a Louisiana sugar plantation was once asked to attend a sick overseer. "What do you think he says," reported the irritated mistress, "he aint used to waiting on low rank people." [7]

Many whites also heard slaves boast of the prices their masters had paid for them, or of the handsome offers their masters had rejected from would-be purchasers. A thousand-dollar slave felt superior to an eight-hundred-dollar slave. "When we recollect that the dollars are not their own," wrote an amused traveler, "we can hardly refrain from smiling at the childlike simplicity with which they express their satisfaction at the high price set on them." [8] But this attitude was not as simple as it seemed. Seeing the master exhibit his wealth as evidence of his social rank, the slave developed his own crass measure of a man's worth and exhibited his price tag.

But the most piteous device for seeking status in the slave community was that of boasting about white ancestors or taking pride in a light complexion. In the eyes of the whites the "mulatto" was tainted as much as the "pure" Negro and as hopelessly tied to the inferior caste; but this did not prevent some slaves of mixed ancestry (not all) from trying to make their Caucasian blood serve as a mark of superiority within their own caste. Fanny Kemble told of a slave woman who came to her and begged to be re-

---

[7] Douglass, *My Bondage*, p. 118; Steward, *Twenty-Two Years a Slave*, p. 101; [Ingraham], *South-West*, II, p. 248; Sitterson, *Sugar Country*, p. 91.

[8] Lyell, *Travels*, I, pp. 182–83.

lieved from field labor "on *'account of her color.'*" This slave made it evident that, "being a mulatto, she considered field labor a degradation."[9] Such an attitude may have been sheer opportunism, or it may have indicated that some slaves had been effectively indoctrinated with the idea of their racial inferiority. But in many cases it was merely another example of the bondsman's search for dignity and self-respect.

3

In Africa the Negroes had been accustomed to a strictly regulated family life and a rigidly enforced moral code. But in America the disintegration of their social organization removed the traditional sanctions which had encouraged them to respect their old customs. Here they found the whites organized into families having great social and economic importance but regulated by different laws. In the quarters they were usually more or less encouraged to live as families and to accept white standards of morality.

But it was only outwardly that the family life of the mass of southern slaves resembled that of their masters. Inwardly, in many crucial ways, the domestic regimes of the slave cabin and of the "big house" were quite different. Because the slaves failed to conform to the white pattern, the master class found the explanation, as usual, in the Negro's innate racial traits. Actually, the differences resulted from the fact that slavery inevitably made much of the white caste's family pattern meaningless and unintelligible—and in some ways impossible—for the average bondsman. Here, as at so many other points, the slaves had lost their native culture without being able to find a workable substitute and therefore lived in a kind of cultural chaos.

The most obvious difference between the slave family and the white family was in the legal foundation upon

[9] Kemble, *Journal*, pp. 193–94.

which each rested. In every state white marriages were recognized as civil contracts which imposed obligations on both parties and provided penalties for their violation. Slave marriages had no such recognition in the state codes; instead, they were regulated by whatever laws the owners saw fit to enforce.

A few masters arbitrarily assigned husbands to women who had reached the "breeding age"; but ordinarily they permitted slaves to pick their own mates and only required them to ask permission to marry. On the plantations most owners refused to allow slaves to marry away from home and preferred to make additional purchases when the sexes were out of balance. Thus an Alabama overseer informed his employer that one slave was without a wife and that he had promised to "indever to git you to Bey a nother woman sow he might have a wife at home." [1] Still, it did frequently happen on both large and small estates that husbands and wives were owned by different masters. Sometimes, when a slave wished to marry the slave of another owner, a sale was made in order to unite them.

Having obtained their master's consent, the couple might begin living together without further formality; or their master might hastily pronounce them man and wife in a perfunctory ceremony. But more solemn ceremonies, con-ducted by slave preachers or white clergymen, were not un-common even for the field-hands, and they were customary for the domestics. The importance of the occasion was sometimes emphasized by a wedding feast and gifts to the bride.

After a marriage many masters ignored the behavior of the couple so long as neither husband nor wife caused any loud or violent disturbances. Others insisted that they not only live together but respect their obligations to each

---

[1] J. B. Grace to Charles Tait, April 25, 1835, Charles Tait and Family Papers.

other. A Louisianian made it a rule that adultery was to be "invariably punished." On a Mississippi plantation, the husband was required to provide firewood for his family and "wait on his wife"; the wife was to do the family's cooking, washing, and mending. Failure to perform these duties was "corrected by words first but if not reformed . . . by the whip." According to a Georgian, "I never permit a husband to abuse, strike or whip his wife. . . . If the wife teases and provokes him . . . she is punished, but it sometimes happens that the husband petitions for her pardon, which I make it a rule not to refuse, as it imposes a strong obligation on the wife to . . . be more conciliating in her behavior." [2] Some masters apparently ran domestic relations courts and served as family counselors.

Divorce, like marriage, was within the master's jurisdiction. He might permit his slaves to change spouses as often and whenever they wished, or he might establish more or less severe rules. A Louisiana master granted a divorce only after a month's notice and prohibited remarriage unless a divorcee agreed to receive twenty-five lashes. James H. Hammond inflicted one hundred lashes upon partners who dissolved their marriage and forced them to live singly for three years. One day in 1840, Hammond noted in his diary: "Had a trial of Divorce and Adultery cases. Flogged Joe Goodwyn and ordered him to go back to his wife. Dito Gabriel and Molly and ordered them to come together again. Separated Moses and Anny finally. And flogged Tom Kollock . . . [for] interfering with Maggy Campbell, Sullivan's wife." [3] While one master might enforce divorce laws as rigid as these, his neighbor might tolerate a veri-

---

[2] *De Bow's Review*, XXII (1857), pp. 376–79; Plantation Rules in William Erwin Ms. Diary and Account Book; *Southern Agriculturist*, IV (1831), p. 351.

[3] Sitterson, *Sugar Country*, p. 58; Hammond Plantation Manual; Hammond Diary, entry for December 26, 1840.

table regime of free love—of casual alliances and easy separations. Inevitably the rules on a given estate affected the family life of its slaves.

Not only did the slave family lack the protection and the external pressure of state law, it also lacked most of the centripetal forces that gave the white family its cohesiveness. In the life of the slave, the family had nothing like the social significance that it had in the life of the white man. The slave woman was first a full-time worker for her owner, and only incidentally a wife, mother, and home-maker. She spent a small fraction of her time in the house; she often did no cooking or clothes making; and she was not usually nurse to her husband or children during illness. Parents frequently had little to do with the raising of their children; and children soon learned that their parents were neither the fount of wisdom nor the seat of authority. Thus a child on a Louisiana farm saw his mother receive twenty-five lashes for countermanding an order his mistress had given him.[4] Lacking autonomy, the slave family could not offer the child shelter or security from the frightening creatures in the outside world.

The family had no greater importance as an economic unit. Parents and children might spend some spare hours together in their garden plots, but, unlike rural whites, slaves labored most of the time for their masters in groups that had no relationship to the family. The husband was not the director of an agricultural enterprise; he was not the head of the family, the holder of property, the provider, or the protector. If his wife or child was disrobed and whipped by master or overseer, he stood by in helpless humiliation. In an age of patriarchal families, the male slave's only crucial function within the family was that of siring offspring.

---

4 Marston Diary, entry for June 12, 1829.

Indeed, the typical slave family was matriarchal in form, for the mother's role was far more important than the father's. In so far as the family did have significance it involved responsibilities which traditionally belonged to women, such as cleaning house, preparing food, making clothes, and raising children. The husband was at most his wife's assistant, her companion, and her sex partner. He was often thought of as her possession ("Mary's Tom"), as was the cabin in which they lived.[5] It was common for a mother and her children to be considered a family without reference to the father.

Given these conditions—the absence of legal marriages, the family's minor social and economic significance, and the father's limited role—it is hardly surprising to find that slave families were highly unstable. Lacking both outer pressures and inner pulls, they were also exposed to the threat of forced separations through sales. How dispersed a slave family could be as a result of one or more of these factors was indicated by an advertisement for a North Carolina fugitive who was presumed to be "lurking in the neighborhood of E. D. Walker's, at Moore's Creek, who owns most of his relations, or Nathan Bonham's who owns his mother; or, perhaps, near Fletcher Bell's, at Long Creek, who owns his father." A slave preacher in Kentucky united couples in wedlock "until death or *distance* do you part." When Joshua and Bush asked for permission to marry, their Virginia master read them a statement warning that he might be forced to separate them, "so Joshua must not then say I have taken his wife from him."[6] Thus every slave family had about it an air of impermanence, for

---

[5] Johnson, *Sea Islands*, pp. 135, 137–38; *id., Ante-Bellum North Carolina*, p. 535.

[6] Wilmington (N.C.) *Journal*, May 2, 1851; Coleman, *Slavery Times in Kentucky*, pp. 58–59; Massie Slave Book, entry for September 24, 1847.

no master could promise that his debts would not force sales, or guarantee that his death would not cause divisions.

If the state did not recognize slave marriages, the churches of the Protestant South might have supplied a salutary influence, since they emphasized the sanctity of the home and family. The churches did try to persuade their own slave members to respect the marriage sacrament and sometimes even disciplined those who did not. But they were quite tolerant of masters who were forced by "necessity" to separate husbands, wives, and children. For example, in 1856, a committee of the Charleston Baptist Association agreed that slave marriages had "certain limitations" and had to be "the subject of special rules." Hence, though calling these marriages "sacred and binding" and urging that they be solemnized by a religious ceremony, the committee raised no objection to the separation of couples against their wills. Apparently the only sinful separation was one initiated by the slaves themselves.[7]

The general instability of slave families had certain logical consequences. One was the casual attitude of many bondsmen toward marriage; another was the failure of any deep and enduring affection to develop between some husbands and wives. The South abounded in stories of slaves who elected to migrate with kind masters even when it meant separation from their spouses. "Ef you got a good marster, foller him," was the saying in Virginia, according to an ex-slave. An equally common story, which was often true, was that chattels were not severely disturbed by forced separation and soon found new husbands or wives in their new homes. All who were familiar with the Negro, wrote a South Carolinian, understood how difficult it was "to educate even the best and most intelligently moral of

---

[7] Charleston *Courier*, August 5, 1857.

the race to a true view and estimation of marriage." [8] Here, presumably, was proof that separations through the slave trade caused no real hardship.

Still another consequence was the indifference with which most fathers and even some mothers regarded their children. An angry Virginian attributed the death of a slave infant to "the unnatural neglect of his infamous mother"; he charged that another infant was "murdered right out by his mother's neglect and barbarous cruelty." Fanny Kemble observed the stolid reaction of slave parents to the death of their children. "I've lost a many; they all goes so," was the only comment of one mother when another child died; and the father, "without word or comment, went out to his enforced labor." [9] Many slaveholders complained that mothers could not be trusted to nurse their sick children, that some showed no affection for them and treated them cruelly. This, of course, was not a manifestation of Negro "character" as masters seemed to think. How these calloused mothers could have produced the affectionate slave "mammies" of tradition was never explained. But one master spoke volumes when he advocated separating children from their parents, because it was "far more humane not to cherish domestic ties among slaves." [1]

The final consequence of family instability was widespread sexual promiscuity among both men and women. The case of a Kentucky slave woman who had each of her seven children by a different father was by no means unique. This was a condition which some masters tried to control but which most of them accepted with resignation, or indifference, or amusement. As to the slave's moral habits, wrote one discouraged owner, "I know of no means

[8] Smedes, *Memorials*, p. 48; Olmsted, *Seaboard*, pp. 556–57; Charleston *Courier*, September 15, 1857.
[9] Massie Slave Book; Kemble, *Journal*, p. 95.
[1] Lyell, *Travels*, I, p. 184.

whereby to regulate them, or to restrain them; I attempted it for many years by preaching virtue and decency, . . . but it was all in vain." Olmsted cited numerous instances of masters who regarded the whole matter with complete unconcern; and masters themselves rarely gave any sign of displeasure when an unmarried slave woman became pregnant. A Virginia planter kept a record of the fathers of his slave children when he knew who the fathers were, but often he could only guess—and sometimes he suggested that the child was sired "by the Commonwealth," or "by the Universe," or "God knows who by." Overseers were generally even less concerned; as one overseer explained, the morals of the slaves were "no business of his, and he did not care what they did." Nor was the law concerned. In Mississippi, when a male slave was indicted for the rape of a female slave, the state Supreme Court dismissed the case on the ground that this was not an offense known to common or statute law.[2]

If most slaves regarded the white man's moral code as unduly severe, many whites did too. Indeed, the number of bastardy cases in southern court records seems to confirm the conclusion that women of the poor-white class "carried about the same reputation for easy virtue as their sable sisters." Marriage, insisted Frederick Douglass, had no existence among slaves, "except in such hearts as are purer and higher than the standard morality around them." His consolation was that at least some slaves "maintained their honor, where all around was corrupt."[3]

That numerous slaves did manage somehow to surmount the corrupting influences everywhere about them, their

---

[2] Brown, *Narrative*, p. 13; *De Bow's Review*, X (1851), p. 623; Olmsted, *Back Country*, pp. 89, 113, 154; Massie Slave Book; Catterall (ed.), *Judicial Cases*, II, pp. 544–45; III, p. 363.

[3] Avery O. Craven, "Poor Whites and Negroes in the Ante-Bellum South," *Journal of Negro History*, XV (1930), pp. 17–18; Douglass, *My Bondage*, p. 86.

masters themselves freely admitted. A South Carolinian
admired the slave mother's "natural and often ardent and
endearing affection for her offspring"; and another declared that "sound policy" as well as humanity required
that everything be done "to reconcile these unhappy beings
to their lot, by keeping mothers and children together."
The majority of slave women were devoted to their children, regardless of whether they had been sired by one or
by several fathers. Nor was sexual promiscuity a universal
trait of southern Negroes even in bondage. Many slave
couples, affirmed a Georgian, displayed toward each other
a high degree of "faithfulness, fidelity, and affection." [4]

Seldom, when slave families were broken to satisfy creditors or settle estates, was a distinction made between those
who were indifferent to the matter and those who suffered
deeply as a consequence. The "agony at parting," an ex-
slave reminded skeptics, "must be seen and felt to be fully
understood." A slave woman who had been taken from her
children in Virginia and sent to the Southwest "cried many
a night about it; and went 'bout mazin' sorry-like all day, a
wishing I was dead and buried!" Sometimes the "derange-
ment" or sudden rebelliousness of a slave mother was attributed to "grief at being separated from her children."
Often mothers fought desperately to prevent traders from
carrying off their children, and often husbands and wives
struggled against separation when they were torn apart. [5]

But the most eloquent evidence of the affection and devotion that bound many slave families together appeared in
the advertisements for fugitives. A Virginian sought a run-

[4] *De Bow's Review*, XVII (1854), pp. 425–26; Abbeville District, South
Carolina, Judge of Probate Decree Book, 1839–1858, May term, 1841;
Catterall (ed.), *Judicial Cases*, II, p. 314.
[5] Henson, *Story*, pp. 10–11; Ingraham (ed.), *Sunny South*, p. 439; Cat-
terall (ed.), *Judicial Cases*, I, p. 298; III, p. 632; V, p. 229–30; Loguen,
Narrative, pp. 112–20; Andrews, *Slavery and the Domestic Slave
Trade*, pp. 128–33.

348

away whose wife had been transported to Mississippi, "and I understand from some of my servants, that he had been speaking of following her." A Maryland master was convinced that a female fugitive would attempt to get back to Georgia "where she came from, and left her husband and two children." Even when fugitives hoped to reach the free states, husbands often took their wives and parents their children, though this obviously lessened their chance of a successful escape. Clearly, to many bondsmen the fellowship of the family, in spite of its instability, was exceedingly important.

Some of the problems that troubled slave families, of course, had nothing to do with slavery—they were the tragically human problems which have ever disturbed marital tranquillity. One such domestic dilemma involved a slave whose wife did not return his devotion. "He says he loves his wife and does not want to leave her," noted the master. "She says she does not love him and wont live with him. Yet he says he thinks he can over come her scruples and live happily with her." [6] For this slavery was not the cause nor freedom the cure.

But other kinds of family tragedies were uniquely a part of life in bondage. A poignant example was the scene that transpired when an overseer tied and whipped a slave mother in the presence of her children. The frightened children pelted the overseer with stones, and one of them ran up and bit him in the leg. During the ruction the cries of the mother were mingled with the screams of the children, *"Let my mammy go—let my mammy go."* [7]

---

[6] Gustavus A. Henry to his wife, December 11, 1839, Henry Papers.
[7] Douglass, *My Bondage*, pp. 92–95.

4

Everywhere in the ante-bellum South marriages between whites and Negroes or "mulattos," whether free or unfree, were prohibited. The prohibition against marriages, however, did not prevent other forms of interracial sexual contacts. Sometimes these extra-legal alliances were remarkably open and durable, but usually they were clandestine, casual, and brief—a simple matter of a white using a Negro to satisfy an immediate sexual urge. All adult slaves must have been aware of the reality of miscegenation; and they doubtless detected the element of hypocrisy in white criticism of their moral laxity.

The failure of the color barrier to prevent miscegenation in the Old South is hardly surprising, for this has always been the case when two races have intermingled. The English, Dutch, Spanish, and Portuguese had mixed their blood with the Africans long before black laborers were brought to the North American colonies. Only in the mythology of race can one find biological "proof" of the evils of miscegenation—for example, "proof" that children of mixed ancestry are likely to be mentally or physically inferior to children of racially "pure" ancestry. The real evils of miscegenation were purely social; they were evident in the opprobrium heaped upon both parents and offspring, in the emotional disturbances resulting from prejudice, and, above all, in the fact that the slaves did not ordinarily have an altogether free choice in the matter.

To measure the extent of miscegenation with precision is impossible, because statistical indexes are crude and public and private records fragmentary. But the evidence nevertheless suggests that human behavior in the Old South was very human indeed, that sexual contacts between the races were not the rare aberrations of a small group of depraved whites but a frequent occurrence involving whites of all social and cultural levels. It was a practice, a Kentucky judge avowed, "but too common, as we all know"; a practice, Olmsted was told, that pervaded the "entire society." "How many have fallen before this temptation!" wrote a Virginian. "So many that it has almost ceased to be a temptation to fall!" Many parents traced the moral ruin of their sons "to temptations found in female slaves in their own or neighbour's households." With this in mind, one slaveholder advised white families to use "elderly servants only" and to put all young slaves to work in the fields. Permitting them to grow up in the house, he warned, was "fraught with evil." [8]

The result of miscegenation, of course, was the emergence of a racially mixed group which constantly increased in size and which contained every shade of color. According to the census of 1860, more than a half million (about twelve per cent) of the colored people in the slave states were "mulattoes." This was certainly an underestimate, because the census takers classified each individual entirely on the basis of his appearance. Persons whose complexions were very dark were listed as Negroes, though they might have had some white ancestors.[9] Others whose complexions were very light were listed as whites, though they might have had some Negro ancestors. (The practice of "passing over" had already begun in the ante-bellum South.) The judicial records of South Carolina describe a family with remote Negro ancestors whose members were nevertheless recognized as whites, "received into society, . . . and married into respectable families." [1] Clearly, the "taint of the inferior race" was more widely diffused and

---

[8] Catterall (ed.), *Judicial Cases*, I, p. 318; Olmsted, *Seaboard*, pp. 601–602; James H. Johnston, *Miscegenation in the Ante-bellum South* (Chicago, 1939), pp. 1–2; *Southern Agriculturist*, VIII (1835), p. 8.

[9] For example, in the manuscript census returns of 1860, a slave mother was often listed as a "mulatto" and her children as "black."

[1] Catterall (ed.), *Judicial Cases*, II, pp. 358–59.

miscegenation more common than slavery's defenders cared to concede. Nor is it necessary to take seriously James H. Hammond's assertion that the "chief offenders" were "natives of the North or foreigners," for Hammond knew very well the frailties of native southern whites.[2]

Though white women were less involved in interracial sexual contacts than men, their role, especially in the colonial period when slaves and indentured servants worked on the same estates, was never entirely negligible. A Maryland statute of 1663 noted that "divers freeborn *English* women, forgetful of their free condition, and to the disgrace of our nation, do intermarry with negro slaves"; but the penalties provided in this and other southern statutes did not put an end to the practice. "There must always be women of the lower class of whites, so poor that their favors can be purchased by the slaves," a Southerner told Olmsted.[3]

But these women were not all paupers or prostitutes. In New Orleans a "seemingly respectable" white female was arrested on a charge of having been in an "indecent companionship" with a slave. Numerous white men attempted to divorce their wives for allegedly having had sexual relations with slaves. In one such case the wife not only admitted her intimacy with a slave but confessed that he had made her love him "better than any body in the world, and she thought he must have given her something." In some cases, after having intercourse with a slave the white woman claimed that she had been raped, but the evidence was not always very convincing. Occasionally a white female who loved her colored paramour lived with him as a common-law wife.[4]

<hr>

[2] *De Bow's Review*, VII (1849), p. 494.
[3] Olmsted, *Seaboard*, pp. 508–509.
[4] New Orleans *Picayune*, September 9, 1851; Catterall (ed.), *Judicial Cases*, I, p. 357; II, pp. 63–64, 117, 119, 167; Johnson, *Ante-Bellum North Carolina*, pp. 588–91.

Most miscegenation, however, involved white males and slave females. To be sure, many white men abstained altogether and few of them wallowed in lechery; but it would contradict neither the evidence nor the realities of southern life to say that a large proportion of them, particularly in the cities and plantation districts, had one or more sexual contacts with slave women. If it cannot be said that this practice ever won social approval, neither can it be said that detection carried severe penalties. The white female who was known to have cohabited with a Negro irretrievably lost the respect of society, but the white male paid no such price. There might be some clucking of tongues, a few crude jokes, but more than likely it would soon be forgotten. Besides, with a little caution the chance of detection was not great.

Men of the nonslaveholding class were responsible for much of the miscegenation. Masters often complained that whites in the neighborhood interfered with their slave women. "Cato born of Dinah, by some white chap on the commons," a Virginian noted in his records. Another Virginian affirmed that one of his slave women had all of her children "by whoredom most of them gotten by white men" at a neighbor's house. For years, he wrote, these men had been sending for his women "to whore it with" whenever he was away. Female slaves were quite accessible to both rural and urban nonslaveholders who desired casual sexual partners. Sometimes, however, the intentions of these men were what under other circumstances might have been called "honorable," for they sought more permanent union in defiance of law and property rights. For example, a Florida master advertised that a white man had stolen one of his slave women with the intention of having her "answer the place of a wife." [5]

---

[5] Massie Slave Book, entry for May 25, 1858; Walker Diary, entries for July 5, 8, 1834; Pensacola *Gazette*, August 11, 1838.

Overseers often succumbed to the temptations surrounding them. Though many of the planters seemed to be quite indifferent about it, some complained that the tendency of overseers to "equalize" with slave women resulted in "evils too numerous to be . . . mentioned." One master pointed to a specific evil when he noted that his overseer was causing his "negro *men* [to] run away by interfering with their wives." In his instructions to overseers a Louisiana planter warned that "intercourse with negro women" would not be tolerated, because it bred "more trouble . . . on a plantation than all else put together." For this reason, the author of an essay on overseers advised, "let him be a married man." [6]

On a Louisiana plantation, an overseer, named Patrick, caused his employer no end of trouble because of his habit of "sneaking about after . . . negro girls"; and when he was discharged he left behind a brood of mulatto children. The new overseer, named Mulkey, was married but proved to be "nearly as bad as Patrick in the same way." Mulkey's dismissal came after a "great fuss" which occurred when a slave told Mrs. Mulkey about her husband's escapades in the quarters. During her search for still another overseer the plantation mistress refused to hire an unmarried applicant, because "he would soon be like the others," and have a harem of "six or seven ladies." Instead she employed a man who was "too fond of his wife" to behave "as overseers commonly did amongst the negroes." This time she was not disappointed, and two years later she rejoiced that her overseer had "no favorite misses to fight and abuse the boys about." He was the first one she had ever employed who was innocent of such "meanness." [7]

[6] Memorandum Book for 1836 in Tait Papers; Nutt Journal of Araby Plantation; *American Cotton Planter and Soil of the South*, II (1858), p. 197.
[7] Rachel O'Conner to David Weeks, July 8, 1832; October 23, November 16, 20, 1833; *id.* to A. T. Conrad, April 12, 1835, Weeks Collection.

The lower-class whites, however, were by no means the only Southerners who had sexual relations with slave women and fathered the mulatto population. Unmarried slaveholders and the young males who grew up in slaveholding families, some bearing the South's most distinguished names, played a major role. Indeed, given their easy access to female slaves, it seems probable that miscegenation was more common among them than among the members of any other group.

Again, most of the relationships between slave women and males of the slaveholding class were the casual adventures of adolescents engaged in sexual experimentation, of college students on concupiscent larks, and of older bachelors or widowers periodically demanding the favors of one of their female chattels.[8] But some of the relationships developed into forms of concubinage which lasted until marriage and occasionally through life. Though the cases of concubinage involving young Louisiana Creoles and quadroon women are familiar, these alliances were confined neither to persons of French or Spanish descent nor to the state of Louisiana. Men with Anglo-Saxon names such as Turner and Crocker acknowledged having slave mistresses. A South Carolinian "lived for many years in a state of illicit intercourse" with a slave woman "who assumed the position of a wife"; another permitted a female slave "to act as the mistress of his house" and control his domestic affairs. A Kentuckian owned a woman who was his concubine and "possessed considerable influence over him." And a Virginian, his colored mistress, and their mulatto children lived "as a family upon terms of equality, and not as a master with his slaves."[9]

---

[8] Gavin Diary, entries for September 29, December 24, 1855; July 9, 1856.
[9] Catterall (ed.), *Judicial Cases*, I, pp. 227–28, 302; II, pp. 375, 451; III, pp. 655–56.

These sexual relationships with slaves did not always end when the master married; and others actually began after, rather than before, his marriage. When the husband's infidelity was casual and infrequent he doubtless managed often to conceal it from his wife. But when it was repeated frequently and indicated either that he had tired of his wife or desired a polygamous arrangement, the facts did not long remain a secret. Such cases sometimes found their way into the courts in the form of divorce actions or disputes over property settlements. Thus a Louisiana woman separated from her husband because he "had more regard for" a female domestic than for her. In Texas a wife divorced her husband for his "improper intimacy with the negress Jane" and for "obstinately persisting continuously to live in a negro house with his negro woman." A North Carolina divorce case involved a husband who had not only "bedded with . . . negro Lucy" but placed her in full control of his household.[1] When the aggrieved wife did not leave her husband, his relationship with the slave woman was sooner or later broken off or gradually lost its ardor.

Southern white women apparently believed that they suffered most from the effects of miscegenation. "Under slavery we live surrounded by prostitutes," one of them wrote bitterly. "Like the patriarchs of old, our men live all in one house with their wives and their concubines; and the mulattoes one sees in every family partly resemble the white children. Any lady is ready to tell you who is the father of all the mulatto children in everybody's household but her own. These, she seems to think, drop from the clouds. My disgust sometimes is boiling over." A Virginia woman grieved for the "white mothers and daughters of the South" who had "seen their dearest affections trampled upon—their hopes of domestic happiness destroyed"

---

[1] Catterall (ed.), *Judicial Cases*, II, p. 139; III, p. 491; V, p. 297.

by husbands, sons, and brothers who gratified their passions with female slaves.[2]

Southern males who venerated white womanhood were hit in a sensitive spot by charges such as these. Some of them denied the charges; others argued disingenuously that miscegenation was a boon to white women because it protected their chastity. In the South, various male Southerners explained, young men found carnal pleasure with Negro females rather than white; thus slavery gave southern women their high reputation for virtue.[3] But white women were not comforted by special pleading such as this. They watched their men suspiciously, because they knew much and doubtless suspected more.

White women, however, were not the only Southerners who were in some way distressed by miscegenation, for white men were not always able to indulge in it without personal complications. There were, of course, insensitive males who had sexual relations with slave women without concern about the effects upon others, without emotional involvement, and without feelings of guilt. Some felt no responsibility for the offspring of these unions and could forget the mothers when it seemed convenient. Some could brazenly sell their former mistresses to get them out of the way, as well as their own children to remove a further source of embarrassment.[4] But for many white men the problem was not so simple. Often the matter weighed heavily upon their consciences long after the affair had ended. Others suffered because they felt a deep attachment for

---

[2] Ben Ames Williams (ed.), *A Diary from Dixie* (Boston, 1949), pp. 21–22; Olmsted, *Seaboard*, pp. 601–602.

[3] *De Bow's Review*, IX (1850), pp. 498–502; XX (1856), p. 656; Charleston *Courier*, October 17, 1849.

[4] Catterall (ed.), *Judicial Cases*, III, p. 199; Brown, *Narrative*, pp. 46–48; Buckingham, *Slave States*, II, pp. 213–14. By some strange logic, to many it seemed morally more reprehensible to sell one's own children than to sell someone else's.

357

some slave women and knew that marriage was impossible. For them the alternatives were a painful separation, a secret alliance, or a life beyond the pale of respectable white society.

A man who was not necessarily troubled by an enduring love might still feel obligated to care for his slave mistress and her children. This explains many of the emancipating clauses in wills, though they did not always openly acknowledge the relationship. For instance, a master in Southampton County, Virginia, freed Hannah for "meritorious service" and gave her fifty acres of land, a house, and an annual pension of fifty dollars. Others frankly admitted their transgressions, as did a Baltimore slaveholder who devised most of his estate to his "natural daughter Louisa Gooding . . . born of a certain colored woman known by the name of Clara." Many times masters who waited until death had their wishes frustrated by unsympathetic heirs who contested their wills, or by state laws prohibiting the bequeathing of freedom or property to slaves. Thus the offspring of the deceased father remained in bondage.

Fearing such an outcome, some masters took care of these matters before they died. A Virginian who petitioned for the freedom of a mulatto boy, acknowledged "with blushes and confusion" that he was the boy's father and felt "great solicitude for his future welfare and liberty." After an unsuccessful attempt to educate his mulatto son in a local school, a South Carolinian sent him to Indiana "where he had him settled, and provided him, from time to time with considerable sums of money." [5] A distinguished southern planter and statesman who had children by two slave women concluded that it would be cruel to free them and send them to the North. Instead, he gave the children and

---

[5] Johnston, *Miscegenation*, p. 3; Catterall (ed.), *Judicial Cases*, II, p. 375.

their mothers to a legitimate son (who also seemed to have been involved with one of the women) with instructions that they be treated well and never be sold to strangers. Keeping them as slaves within the family, the father believed, was the best that could be done for them.[6] This tangled situation doubtless caused the father as much anguish as it did the white women of his family.

It requires a special variety of obtuseness to be able to overlook the fact that miscegenation also had a sharp psychological impact upon the Negroes. A devoted slave husband who was unable to protect his wife from the master or overseer, or whose wife willingly submitted to the advances of a white man, faced a personal crisis of major proportions. Occasionally the husband ignored the consequences and retaliated violently against a white man for taking liberties with his wife. On the other hand, a male bondsman might incur the master's hostility if he won the affection of a female in whom the master also had an interest. Thus an Alabama slave found himself in trouble when the master "became jealous" of him for "running after one of his women." [7]

Slave women did not always regard a sexual contact with a white male as a privilege which was in no case to be rejected. Many whose sexual behavior was altogether promiscuous doubtless gave their favors without restraint to whites and Negroes alike. Others who were less promiscuous and would have rejected most whites, out of sheer opportunism willingly submitted to the master or overseer with the hope that special privileges—perhaps even freedom—would be their reward.[8] But some slave women, be-

----

6 The author was unable to obtain permission to cite the document containing this information.

7 Henson, *Story*, pp. 2–7; Catterall (ed.), *Judicial Cases*, III, pp. 228, 362–63; Douglass, *My Bondage*, pp. 85–88.

8 Cf. Northup, *Twelve Years a Slave*, p. 65; Phillips and Glunt (eds.), *Florida Plantation Records*, pp. 156–57.

cause of devotion to their husbands, or because of a belief that it was morally wrong, or for some other inhibiting reason, did not voluntarily have sexual relations even with their masters. If they submitted, it was only under coercion. Indeed, some miscegenation was little more than rape, though no such offense against a slave woman was recognized in law. The Louisiana Supreme Court regretfully confessed that the female slave was "peculiarly exposed . . . to the seductions of an unprincipled master." [9]

When the effects of miscegenation upon all groups in southern society have been measured, one can hardly escape the conclusion that the principal victims were the colored females who were directly involved in it. There is no way to gauge precisely the psychological consequences of sexual promiscuity for slave women, but it is certain that few escaped without serious damage to their psyche. The concubine suffered profoundly if she became emotionally involved with her white paramour, for sooner or later the relationship would probably be broken off. The shock to an inhibited slave female whose submission was more or less coerced is obvious enough. Moreover, the woman who entered a prolonged alliance, willingly or unwillingly, was bound to feel the resentment of other slaves—to find herself isolated from her own people and yet unable to gain access to white society. If she did not share her master's passion, or affection, she was exposed to his wrath. Finally, miscegenation exposed her to the jealous anger of the white wife. For this reason, a Texas judge was sympathetic when a master conveyed his slave mistress and two mulatto children to a relative, in order to separate them from his "infuriated wife, who would possibly, yea, probably, inflict severity, cruelty and hardship on them." [1]

Miscegenation under slavery, then, was above all an in-

---

[9] Catterall (ed.) , *Judicial Cases*, III, p. 613.
[1] *Ibid.*, V, p. 294.

dignity to Negro women. It was an indignity to them, first, because they were rarely in a position freely to accept or reject the advances of white men; second, because those who enslaved them took advantage of the sexual promiscuity that slavery itself encouraged; and last, because the veneration of white womanhood combined with the disrespect for Negro womanhood was a peculiarly cynical application of a double standard.

5

What else was there in the lives of slaves besides work, sleep, and procreation? What filled their idle hours? What occupied their minds? What distinguished them from domestic animals? Much will never be known, for surviving records provide only brief glimpses into the private life of the slave quarters. But much can be learned from Negro songs and folklore, from the recollections of former slaves, and from the observations of the more perceptive and sensitive whites.

The average bondsman, it would appear, lived more or less aimlessly in a bleak and narrow world. He lived in a world without schools, without books, without learned men; he knew less of the fine arts and of aesthetic values than he had known in Africa; and he found few ways to break the montonous sameness of all his days. His world was the few square miles of earth surrounding his cabin—a familiar island beyond which were strange places (up North where people like him were not slaves), frightening places ("down the river" where overseers were devils), and dead places (across the ocean where his ancestors had lived and where he had no desire to go). His world was full of mysteries which he could not solve, full of forces which he could not control. And so he tended to be a fatalist and futilitarian, for nothing else could reconcile him to his life.

When they left Africa the Negroes carried with them a knowledge of their own complex cultures. Some elements of their cultures—or at least some adaptations or variations of them—they planted somewhat insecurely in America. These surviving "Africanisms" were evident in their speech, in their dances, in their music, in their folklore, and in their religion. The amount of their African heritage that remained varied with time and place. More of it was evident in the eighteenth century when a large proportion of the slaves were native Africans, than in the mid-nineteenth century when the great majority were second- and third-generation Americans. Field-hands living on large plantations in isolated areas, such as the South Carolina and Georgia sea islands, doubtless preserved more "Africanisms" than slaves who were widely dispersed in relatively small holdings or who lived in their master's houses as domestics. How substantial and how durable the African heritage was is a question over which students of the American Negro have long disagreed.[2]

But the disagreement has been over the size of what was admittedly a fragment; few would deny that by the antebellum period slaves everywhere in the South had lost most of their African culture. In bondage, the Negroes lacked cultural autonomy—the authority to apply rigorous sanctions against those who violated or repudiated their own traditions. Instead, they were exposed to considerable pressure to learn and accept whichever of the white man's customs would help them to exist with a minimum of friction in a biracial society. Before the Civil War, American Negroes developed no cultural nationalism, no conscious pride in African ways. At most they unconsciously pre-

---

[2] The literature on this subject is vast, but for the two points of view see Robert E. Park, "The Conflict and Fusion of Cultures with Special Reference to the Negro," *Journal of Negro History*, IV (1919), pp. 111–33; Melville J. Herskovits, "On the Provenience of New World Negroes," *Social Forces*, XII (1933), pp. 247–62.

served some of their old culture when it had a direct relevance to their new lives, or they fused it with things taken from the whites.

If anything, most ante-bellum slaves showed a desire to forget their African past and to embrace as much of white civilization as they could. They often looked with contemptuous amusement upon newly imported Africans. When a Tennesseean attempted to teach a group of slaves a dance he had witnessed on the Guinea coast, he was astonished by their lack of aptitude and lack of interest. In fact, the feelings of these slaves were "hurt by the insinuation which his effort conveyed." [3] Thus the "Africanisms" of the slaves —even of the Gullah Negroes of the South Carolina sea islands—were mere vestiges of their old cultures. For example, a few African words remained in their speech; the rest was the crude and ungrammatical English of an illiterate folk.

There was an element of tragedy in this. The slaves, having lost the bulk of their African heritage, were prevented from sharing in much of the best of southern white culture. There were exceptions, of course. Occasionally a gifted slave overcame all obstacles and without formal education became a brilliant mathematician or a remarkable linguist. A few showed artistic talents of a high order. Others learned to read and write, or, in the case of house servants, manifested polite breeding which matched—and sometimes surpassed—that of their masters. But the life of the generality of slaves, as a visitor to South Carolina observed, was "far removed from [white] civilization"; it was "mere animal existence, passed in physical exertion or enjoyment." Fanny Kemble saw grown slaves "rolling, tumbling, kicking, and wallowing in the dust, regardless alike of decency, and incapable of any more rational amuse-

---

[3] Ingraham (ed.), *Sunny South*, pp. 146–47.

ment; or lolling, with half-closed eyes, like so many cats and dogs, against a wall, or upon a bank in the sun, dozing away their short leisure hour." [4]

This was essentially the way it had to be as long as the Negro was held in bondage. So far from slavery acting as a civilizing force, it merely took away from the African his native culture and gave him, in exchange, little more than vocational training. So far from the plantation serving as a school to educate a "backward" people, its prime function in this respect was to train each new generation of slaves. In slavery the Negro existed in a kind of cultural void. He lived in a twilight zone between two ways of life and was unable to obtain from either many of the attributes which distinguish man from beast. Olmsted noted that slaves acquired, by example or compulsion, some of the external forms of white civilization; but this was poor compensation for "the systematic withdrawal from them of all the usual influences which tend to nourish the moral nature and develop the intellectual faculties, in savages as well as in civilized free men." [5]

What, then, filled the leisure hours of the slaves? The answer, in part, is that these culturally rootless people devoted much of this time to the sheer pleasure of being idle. Such activities as they did engage in were the simple diversions of a poor, untutored folk—activities that gave them physical pleasure or emotional release. Slaves probably found it more difficult to find satisfying amusements on the small farms where they had few comrades, than in the cities and on the plantations where they could mix freely with their own people.

"I have no desire to represent the life of slavery as an ex-

---

[4] Harrison, *Gospel Among the Slaves*, p. 245; [Ingraham], *South-West*, II, p. 194; Kemble, *Journal*, p. 66.
[5] Olmsted, *Back Country*, pp. 70–71.

perience of nothing but misery," wrote a former bondsman. In addition to the unpleasant things, he also remembered "jolly Christmas times, dances before old massa's door for the first drink of egg-nog, extra meat at holiday times, midnight visits to apple orchards, broiling stray chickens, and first-rate tricks to dodge work." Feasting, as this account suggested, was one of the slave's chief pleasures, one of his "principle sources of comfort." The feast was what he looked forward to not only at Christmas but when crops were laid by, when there was a wedding, or when the master gave a reward for good behavior. "Only the slave who has lived all the year on his scanty allowance of meal and bacon, can appreciate such suppers," recalled another ex-bondsman. Then his problems were forgotten as he gave himself up "to the intoxication of pleasurable amusements." Indeed he might when, for example, a Tennessee master provided a feast such as this: "They Barbecue *half* a small Beef and two fat shoats and some Chickens —have peach pies—Chicken pies, beets[,] Roasting Ears and potatoes in profusion." [6]

Occasions such as Christmas or a corn-shucking were times not only for feasting but also for visiting with slaves on nearby establishments. In Virginia a visitor observed that many bondsmen spent Sundays "strolling about the fields and streets" finding joy in their relative freedom of movement. They dressed in bright-colored holiday clothes, which contrasted pleasantly with their drab everyday apparel. The slaves seemed to welcome each holiday with great fervor, for they found in it an enormous relief from the boredom of their daily lives. "All are brushing up, putting on their best rigging, and with boisterous joy hailing

---

[6] Henson, *Story*, pp. 19–20, 56; Northup, *Twelve Years a Slave*, pp. 213–16; Steward, *Twenty-Two Years a Slave*, pp. 28–31; Bills Diary, entry for July 24, 1858.

the approach of the Holy days," noted an Arkansas master at the start of the Christmas season.[7]

Dancing was one of the favorite pastimes of the slaves, not only on special holidays but on Saturday nights as well. A few pious masters prohibited this diversion, as did a Virginian who was shocked when neighborhood slaves attended a dancing party: "God forbid that one of my Family either white or colored should ever be caught at such an abominable wicked and adulterous place." But most masters, too wise to enforce a regime so austere, permitted a shuffle at least occasionally. "This is Saturday night," wrote a Louisianian, "and I hear the fiddle going in the Quarter. We have two parties here among the Negroes. One is a dancing party and the other a Praying party. The dancers have it tonight, and the other party will hold forth tomorrow." [8]

The kinds of jigs and double shuffles that slaves indulged in were once described as "dancing all over"; they revealed an apparent capacity to "agitate every part of the body at the same time." Such dances were physical and emotional orgies. Fanny Kemble found it impossible to describe "all the contortions, and springs, and flings, and kicks, and capers" the slaves accomplished as they danced "Jim Crow." A visitor at a "shake-down" in a Louisiana sugar house found the dancers in a "thumping ecstasy, with loose elbows, pendulous paws, angulated knees, heads thrown back, and backs arched inwards—a glazed eye, intense solemnity of mien." [9] Slaves danced to the music of the fiddle or banjo, or they beat out their rhythm with sticks on tin pans or by clapping their hands or tapping their feet.

---

[7] Emerson Journal, entry for September 19, 1841; John W. Brown Diary, entry for December 25, 1853.

[8] Walker Diary, entry for February 13, 1841; H. W. Poynor to William G. Harding, March 22, 1850, Harding-Jackson Papers.

[9] *De Bow's Review*, XI (1851), p. 66; Kemble, *Journal*, pp. 96–97; Russell, *Diary*, pp. 258–59.

These ancestors of twentieth-century "jitterbugs" developed their own peculiar jargon too. In Virginia a skilled dancer could "put his foot good"; he was a "ring-clipper," a "snow-belcher," and a "drag-out"; he was no "bug-eater," for he could "carry a broad row," "hoe de corn," and "dig de taters." [1]

Other holiday amusements included hunting, trapping, and fishing. In spite of legal interdictions, slaves gambled with each other and with "dissolute" whites. But some found both pleasure and profit in using their leisure to pursue a handicraft; they made brooms, mats, horse collars, baskets, boats, and canoes. These "sober, thinking and industrious" bondsmen scorned those who wasted time in frivolities or picked up the white man's vices. [2]

A few things in the lives of slaves belonged to them in a more intimate and personal way; these were things which illustrated peculiarly well the blending of African traditions with new experiences in America. For instance, folklore was important to them as it has always been to illiterate people. Some of it preserved legends of their own past; some explained natural phenomena or described a world of the spirits; and some told with charming symbolism the story of the endless warfare between black and white men. The tales of Br'er Rabbit, in all their variations, made virtues of such qualities as wit, strategy, and deceit—the weapons of the weak in their battles with the strong. Br'er Bear had great physical power but was a hapless bumbler; Br'er Fox was shrewd and crafty as well as strong but, nonetheless, was never quite a match for Br'er Rabbit. This was a scheme of things which the slave found delightful to contemplate. [3]

---

[1] *Farmers' Register*, VI (1838), pp. 59–61.

[2] Johnson, *Ante-Bellum North Carolina*, pp. 555–57; Douglass, *My Bondage*, pp. 251–52.

[3] Crum, *Gullah*, p. 120; Benjamin A. Botkin (ed.), *Lay My Burden Down*, p. 2.

The bondsmen had ceremonial occasions of their own, and they devised special ways of commemorating the white man's holidays. At Christmas in eastern North Carolina, they begged pennies from the whites as they went "John Canoeing" (or "John Cunering") along the roads, wearing masks and outlandish costumes, blowing horns, tinkling tambourines, dancing, and chanting

> Hah! Low! Here we go!
> Hah! Low! Here we go!
> Hah! Low! Here we go!
> Kuners come from Denby!

Virginia slaves had persimmon parties where they interspersed dancing with draughts of persimmon beer and slices of persimmon bread. At one of these parties the banjo player sat in a chair on the beer barrel: "A long white cowtail, queued with red ribbon ornamented his head, and hung gracefully down his back; over this he wore a three-cocked hat, decorated with peacock feathers, a rose cockade, a bunch of ripe persimmons, and . . . three pods of red pepper as a top-knot." On some Louisiana sugar plantations, when the cutters reached the last row of cane they left the tallest cane standing and tied a blue ribbon to it. In a ceremony which marked the end of the harvest, one of the laborers waved his cane knife in the air, "sang to the cane as if it were a person, and danced around it several times before cutting it." Then the workers mounted their carts and triumphantly carried the last cane to the master's house where they were given a drink.[4]

Rarely did a contemporary write about slaves without mentioning their music, for this was their most splendid vehicle of self-expression. Slave music was a unique blend of "Africanisms," of Protestant hymns and revival songs,

---

4 Johnson, *Ante-Bellum North Carolina*, p. 553; *Farmers' Register*, VI (1838), pp. 59–61; Moody, "Slavery on Louisiana Sugar Plantations," *loc. cit.*, p. 277 n.

and of the feelings and emotions that were a part of life in servitude.[5] The Negroes had a repertory of songs for almost every occasion, and they not only sang them with innumerable variations but constantly improvised new ones besides. They sang spirituals which revealed their conceptions of Christianity and professed their religious faith. They sang work songs (usually slow in tempo) to break the monotony of toil in the tobacco factories, in the sugar houses, on the river boats, and in the fields. They sang whimsical songs which told little stories or ridiculed human frailties. They sang nonsense songs, such as "Who-zen-John, Who-za" sung by a group of Virginia slaves as they "clapped juber" to a dance:

> Old black bull come down de hollow,
> He shake hi' tail, you hear him bellow;
> When he bellow he jar de river,
> He paw de yearth, he make it quiver.
> Who-zen-John, who-za.[6]

Above all, they sang plaintive songs about the sorrows and the yearnings which they dared not, or could not, more than half express. Music of this kind could hardly have come from an altogether carefree and contented people. "The singing of a man cast away on a desolate island," wrote Frederick Douglass, "might be as appropriately considered an evidence of his contentment and happiness, as the singing of a slave. Sorrow and desolation have their songs, as well as joy and peace." [7] In their somber and mournful moods the bondsmen voiced sentiments such as these: "O Lord, O my Lord! O my good Lord keep me from sinking down"; "Got nowhere to lay my weary head"; "My trouble is hard"; "Nobody knows the trouble I've

---

5 The most recent collection of slave songs is Miles Mark Fisher, *Negro Slave Songs in the United States* (Ithaca, 1953).

6 *Farmers' Register*, VI (1838), pp. 59–61.

7 Douglass, *My Bondage*, pp. 99–100.

seen"; and "Lawd, I can't help from cryin' sometime." The Gullah Negroes of South Carolina sang:

> I know moon-rise, I know star-rise,
>   Lay dis body down.
> I walk in de moonlight, I walk in de starlight,
>   To lay dis body down.
> I'll walk in de graveyard, I'll walk through de graveyard,
>   To lay dis body down.
> I'll lie in de grave and stretch out my arms;
>   Lay dis body down;
> I go to de judgment in de evenin' of de day,
>   When I lay dis body down;
> And my soul and your soul will meet in de day
>   When I lay dis body down.[8]

One final ingredient helped to make pleasant the leisure hours of numerous slave men and women: alcohol in its crudest but cheapest and most concentrated forms. To be sure, these bibulous bondsmen merely indulged in a common vice of an age of hard liquor and heavy drinkers; but they, more than their masters, made the periodic solace of the bottle a necessity of life. In preparing for Christmas, slaves somehow managed to smuggle "fresh bottles of rum or whisky into their cabins," for many thought of each holiday as a time for a bacchanalian spree. Indeed, recalled a former bondsman, to be sober during the holidays was "disgraceful; and he was esteemed a lazy and improvident man, who could not afford to drink whisky during Christmas." [9] No law, no threat of the master, ever kept liquor out of the hands of slaves or stopped the illicit trade between them and "unscrupulous" whites. Some masters themselves furnished a supply of whisky for holiday oc-

---

[8] Thomas Wentworth Higginson, *Army Life in a Black Regiment* (Boston, 1870) , p. 209.

[9] Hundley, *Social Relations*, pp. 359–60; Olmsted, *Seaboard*, pp. 75, 101–102; Adams Diary, entry for December 29, 1857; Douglass, *My Bondage*, pp. 251–52.

casions, or winked at violations of state laws and of their own rules.

There was little truth in the abolitionist charge that masters gave liquor to their slaves in order to befuddle their minds and keep them in bondage. On the other hand, many bondsmen used intoxicants for a good deal more than an occasional pleasant stimulant, a mere conviviality of festive occasions. They found that liquor provided their only satisfactory escape from the indignities, the frustrations, the emptiness, the oppressive boredom of slavery. Hence, when they had the chance, they resorted to places that catered to the Negro trade or found sanctuaries where they could tipple undisturbed. What filled their alcoholic dreams one can only guess, for the dreams at least were theirs alone.

6

Most slaves took their religion seriously, though by the standards of white Christians they sinned mightily. In Africa the Negro's world was inhabited by petulant spirits whose demands had to be gratified; his relationship to these spirits was regulated by the rituals and dogmas of his pagan faith. Some of this was in the corpus of "Africanisms" brought to America. But most of it was lost within a generation, not only because of the general decay of Negro culture but also because new problems and experiences created an urgent need for a new kind of religious expression and a new set of beliefs. What the slave needed now was a spiritual life in which he could participate vigorously, which transported him from the dull routine of bondage and which promised him that a better time was within his reach. Hence, he embraced evangelical Protestantism eagerly, because it so admirably satisfied all these needs.

"The doctrine of the Savior comes to the negro slaves

as their most inward need, and as the accomplishment of the wishes of their souls," explained a visitor to the South. "They themselves enunciate it with the purest joy. . . . Their prayers burst forth into flame as they ascend to heaven." On many plantations religious exercises were almost "the only habitual recreation not purely sensual," Olmsted noted; hence slaves poured all their emotions into them "with an intensity and vehemence almost terrible to witness." A former slave recalled the ecstasy he felt when he learned that there was a salvation *"for every man"* and that God loved black men as well as white. "I seemed to see a glorious being, in a cloud of splendor, smiling down from on high," ready to "welcome me to the skies." [1]

Like the whites, many slaves alternated outbursts of intense religious excitement with intervals of religious calm or indifference, for both races participated in the revivals that periodically swept rural America. At the emotional height of a revival, most of the slaves in a neighborhood might renounce worldly pleasures and live austere lives without the fiddle, without dancing, and without whisky. But this could not last forever, and gradually they drifted back to their sinful ways. [2] And their masters often drifted with them; for although many used religion as a means of control, many others neglected it between revivals.

Of the Protestant sects, the Baptists and Methodists proselytized among the slaves most vigorously and counted among their members the great majority of those who joined churches. The decorous Episcopalians were ineffectual in their missionary work; even masters who adhered to this sect seldom managed to convert their own slaves. The Presbyterians had greater success than the Episco-

---

[1] Bremer, *Homes of the New World*, II, p. 155; Olmsted, *Back Country*, p. 106; Henson, *Story*, pp. 28–29.

[2] Smedes, *Memorials*, pp. 161–62; Henry Watson, Jr., to his mother, July 7, 1846, Watson Papers.

palians but far less than the Baptists or Methodists. Indeed, Presbyterian clergymen who preached to the slaves were advised to write out their sermons in advance and to discourage "exclamations," "outcries," and "boisterous singing." As a result, explained a Methodist, while the Presbyterian parson was composing his sermon the Methodist itinerant traveled forty miles and gave "hell and damnation to his unrepentant hearers." According to an ex-slave, the Methodists "preached in a manner so plain that the way-faring man, though a fool, could not err therein." [8] So did the Baptists—and, in addition, their practice of baptism by immersion gave them a special appeal.

In the North, Negroes organized their own independent churches; in the South, except in a few border cities, the laws against slave assemblies prevented them from doing this before the Civil War. Many slaves attended the white-controlled churches or were preached to by white ministers at special services. This inhibited them and limited both the spiritual and emotional value of their religious experience, because there was an enormous gap between a congregation of slaves and even the most sympathetic white clergyman. As one missionary confessed, "The pastor will meet with some rough and barren spots, and encounter tardiness, indifference, heaviness of eyes and inattention—yea, many things to depress and discourage." [4]

Yet it was from white preachers that the slaves first received their Christian indoctrination. To many bondsmen affiliation with a white church was a matter of considerable importance, and they did not take lightly the penalty of being "excluded from the fellowship" for immorality or "heathenism." Some white clergymen preached to them

---

[8] Jones, *Suggestions on the Religious Instruction of the Negroes*, pp. 14–15; Carter G. Woodson, *The History of the Negro Church* (Washington, D.C., 1921), pp. 97–98; Thompson, *Life*, p. 18.

[4] Jones, *Suggestions on the Religious Instruction of the Negroes*, p. 17.

with great success. Nor was it uncommon to see whites and slaves "around the same altar . . . mingling their cries for mercy" and together finding "the pearl of great price." [5]

Even so, most bondsmen received infinitely greater satisfaction from their own unsupervised religious meetings which they held secretly or which their masters tolerated in disregard of the law. In these gatherings slaves could express themselves freely and interpret the Christian faith to their own satisfaction, even though some educated whites believed that their interpretation contained more heathen superstition than Christianity. The slaves, observed Olmsted, were "subject to intense excitements; often really maniacal," which they considered to be religious; but "I cannot see that they indicate anything but a miserable system of superstition, the more painful that it employs some forms and words ordinarily connected with true Christianity." [6]

Not only the practice of voodooism which survived among a few slaves in southern Louisiana, but the widespread belief in charms and spirits stemmed in part from the African past. Frederick Douglass learned from an old African (who had "magic powers") that if a slave wore the root of a certain herb on his right side, no white man could ever whip him. Slave conjurers accomplished wondrous feats with "root work" and put frightful curses upon their enemies. A Louisiana master once had to punish a slave because of "a phial which was found in his possession containing two ground puppies as they are called. The negroes were under some apprehension that he intended to do mischief." [7]

---

[5] Flat River Church Records (Person County, North Carolina) ; Harrison, *Gospel Among the Slaves*, pp. 199–201.

[6] Olmsted, *Seaboard*, p. 114.

[7] Sitterson, *Sugar Country*, p. 102; Douglass, *My Bondage*, p. 238; Hammond Diary, entry for October 16, 1835; Marston Diary, entry for November 25, 1825.

VIII: *Between Two Cultures*

But slave superstitions did not all originate in Africa, and it would even be difficult to prove that most did. For the slaves picked up plenty of them from "the good Puritans, Baptists, Methodists, and other religious sects who first obtained possession of their ancestors." (Indeed, more than likely Negroes and whites made a generous exchange of superstitions.) There is no need to trace back to Africa the slave's fear of beginning to plant a crop on Friday, his dread of witches, ghosts, and hobgoblins, his confidence in good-luck charms, his alarm at evil omens, his belief in dreams, and his reluctance to visit burying grounds after dark. These superstitions were all firmly rooted in Anglo-Saxon folklore. From the whites some slaves learned that it was possible to communicate with the world of spirits: "It is not at all uncommon to hear them refer to conversations which they allege, and apparently believe themselves to have had with Christ, the apostles, or the prophets of old, or to account for some of their actions by attributing them to the direct influence of the Holy Spirit, or of the devil." During the 1840's, many slaves heard about Millerism and waited in terror for the end of the world.[8] The identification of superstition is, of course, a highly subjective process; and southern whites tended to condemn as superstition whatever elements of slave belief they did not happen to share—as they condemned each other's sectarian beliefs.

The influence of Africa could sometimes be detected in the manner in which slaves conducted themselves at their private religious services. In the sea islands, for example, a prayer meeting at the "praise house" was followed by a "shout," which was an invigorating group ceremony. The participants "begin first walking and by-and-by shuffling around, one after the other, in a ring. The foot is hardly taken from the floor, and the progression is mainly due to

---

[8] Olmsted, *Back Country*, p. 105; Davis (ed.), *Diary of Bennet H. Barrow*, pp. 283–85.

a jerking, hitching motion, which agitates the entire shouter, and soon brings out streams of perspiration. Sometimes they dance silently, sometimes as they shuffle they sing the chorus of the spiritual, and sometimes the song itself is sung by the dancers." This, a white witness believed, was "certainly the remains of some old idol worship." Olmsted reported that in social worship the slaves "work themselves up to a great pitch of excitement, in which they yell and cry aloud, and, finally, shriek and leap up, clapping their hands and dancing, as it is done at heathen festivals." [9]

But again it is not easy to tell how much of their "heathenism" the slaves learned in the white churches and at white revival meetings. One Sunday morning, in Accomac County, Virginia, a visitor attended a Methodist church where the slaves were permitted to hold their own services before the whites occupied the building. "Such a medley of sounds, I never heard before. They exhorted, prayed, sung, shouted, cryed, grunted and growled. Poor Souls! they knew no better, for I found that when the other services began the sounds were similar, which the white folks made; and the negroes only imitated them and shouted a little louder." [1]

A camp meeting in South Carolina provided an equally striking illustration of this point. When the services began, a great crowd assembled around a wooden platform, the Negroes on one side and the whites on the other. On the platform stood four preachers, and between the singing of hymns two of them exhorted the Negroes and two the whites, "calling on the sinners . . . to come to the Savior, to escape eternal damnation!" Soon some of the white people came forward and threw themselves, "as if overcome," before the platform where the ministers re-

[9] Johnson, *Sea Islands*, pp. 149–51; Olmsted, *Seaboard*, pp. 449–50.
[1] Emerson Journal, entry for September 26, 1841.

ceived their confessions and consoled them. Around a white girl, who had fallen into a trance, stood a dozen women singing hymns of the resurrection. "In the camp of the blacks is heard a great tumult and a loud cry. Men roar and bawl out; women screech like pigs about to be killed; many, having fallen into convulsions, leap and strike about them, so that they are obliged to be held down." The Negroes made more noise and were more animated than the whites, but the behavior of the two races did not differ in any fundamental way. Except for condemning a "holy dance" which some Negro women engaged in for a new convert, the whites did not appear to think that the Negroes acted in an outrageous or unchristian fashion.[2]

In short, the religion of the slaves was, in essence, strikingly similar to that of the poor, illiterate white men of the ante-bellum South.

7

Since the masters kept diaries and wrote letters, books, and essays, it is relatively easy to discover their various attitudes toward slaves. What the slaves thought of their masters (and of white people generally) is just as important to know but infinitely more difficult to find. Not only did slaves and ex-slaves write a good deal less but most of them seemed determined that no white man should ever know their thoughts. As Olmsted observed, the average slave possessed considerable "cunning, shrewdness, [and] reticence."[3]

Several points, however, are clear: (1) slaves did not have one uniform attitude toward whites, but a whole range of attitudes; (2) they gave much attention to the

---

[2] Bremer, *Homes of the New World*, I, pp. 306–315.
[3] Olmsted, *Back Country*, p. 384.

problem of their relationship with whites; and (3) they found the "management of whites" as complex a matter as their masters found the "management of Negroes." Every slave became conscious of the "white problem" sometime in early childhood; for in a society dominated by whites, Negro children have always had to learn, more or less painfully, the meaning of caste and somehow come to terms with it.[4] In bondage, they also had to learn what it meant to be property.

During the first half dozen years of their lives neither caste nor bondage had meaning to the children of either race, and blacks and whites often played together without consciousness of color. But it was not long before the black child, in some way, began to discover his peculiar position. Perhaps his mother or father explained his status to him and told him how to behave around the master and other whites. ("My father always advised me to be tractable, and get along with the white people in the best manner I could," recalled a former slave.[5]) Perhaps the slave child saw the white child begin to assume an attitude of superiority prior to their separation. Perhaps he first encountered reality when the master or overseer began to supercede parental authority—or, in a more shocking way, when he saw the master or overseer administer a reprimand or corporal punishment to one of his parents. Thus the young slave became conscious of the "white problem," conscious that the white man was a formidable figure with pretensions of omniscience and omnipotence. As he became involved with white men, the slave gradually developed an emotional attitude toward them.

His attitude, while perhaps seldom one of complete confidence, was frequently one of amiable regard, sometimes of

---

[4] Cf. E. Franklin Frazier, *Negro Youth at the Crossways* (Washington, D.C., 1940) , *passim*.
[5] Drew, *The Refugee*, p. 358.

deep affection. A slave who lived close to a warm, generous, and affectionate master often could not help but reciprocate these feelings, for the barriers of bondage and caste could not prevent decent human beings from showing sympathy and compassion for one another—slave for master as well as master for slave. The domestic's proverbial love for the white family was by no means altogether a myth. But it should be remembered that a slave's love for the good white people he knew was not necessarily a love of servitude, that a slave could wish to be free without hating the man who kept him in chains. A Negro woman who escaped from bondage in Missouri remembered fondly her master and many other whites she had known.[6]

Some slaves, in dealing with whites, seemed to be coldly opportunistic; they evidently had concluded that it was most practical to use the arts of diplomacy, to "keep on the right side" of their masters, in order to enjoy the maximum privileges and comforts available to them in bondage. So they flattered the whites, affected complete subservience, and behaved like buffoons. When Olmsted was introduced to a slave preacher he shook the Negro's hand and greeted him respectfully; but the latter "seemed to take this for a joke and laughed heartily." The master explained in a "slightly humorous" tone that the preacher was also the driver, that he drove the field-hands at the cotton all week and at the Gospel on Sunday. At this remark the preacher "began to laugh again, and reeled off like a drunken man —entirely overcome with merriment." Thus, remarked Olmsted, having concluded that the purpose of the interview was to make fun of him, the preacher "generously" assumed "a merry humor."[7] This slave, like many others, seemed willing enough to barter his self-respect for the privileges and prestige of his high offices.

---

6 *Ibid.,* pp. 299–300.
7 Olmsted, *Seaboard,* p. 451.

Other slaves exhibited toward whites no strong emotion either of affection or hatred, but rather an attitude of deep suspicion. Many contemporaries commented upon their "habitual distrust of the white race" and noted that they were "always suspicious." When this was the Negro's basic attitude, the resulting relationship was an amoral one which resembled an unending civil war; the slave then seemed to think that he was entitled to use every tactic of deception and chicanery he could devise. Many ex-slaves who spoke of their former masters without bitterness still recalled with particular pleasure the times when they had outwitted or beguiled them (" 'cause us had to lie") .[8]

To a few slaves this civil war was an intense and serious business, because they felt for their masters (sometimes for all whites) an abiding animosity. In speaking of the whites, such bondsmen used "the language of hatred and revenge"; on one plantation the slaves in their private conversations contemptuously called their master "Old Hogjaw." Externally these slaves wore an air of sullenness. "You need only look in their faces to see they are not happy," exclaimed a traveler; instead, they were "depressed" or "gloomy." Field-hands often gave no visible sign of pleasure when their master approached; some made clumsy bows, but others ignored him entirely.[9]

The poor whites were the one group in the superior caste for whom the slaves dared openly express their contempt, and the slaves did so in picturesque terms. Masters often tolerated this and were even amused by it. However, it is likely that some slaves were thereby expressing their opinion of the whole white race. A transparent example of the

[8] Olmsted, *Back Country*, p. 114; Bremer, *Homes of the New World*, I, p. 292; Botkin, *Lay My Burden Down, passim*.
[9] Northup, *Twelve Years a Slave*, pp. 62–63, 197; Russell, *Diary*, pp. 133, 146–47, 258, 262; Stirling, *Letters*, p. 49; Buckingham, *Slave States*, I, pp. 62–63.

malice that a portion of the slaves bore the whites occurred in St. Louis when a mob tarred and feathered a white man. "One feature of the scene I could not help remarking," wrote a witness: "the negroes all appeared in high glee, and many of them actually danced with joy." [1]

But the predominant and overpowering emotion that whites aroused in the majority of slaves was neither love nor hate but fear. "We were always uneasy," an ex-slave recalled; when "a white man spoke to me, I would feel frightened," another confessed. In Alabama, a visitor who lost his pocketbook noted that the slave who found it "was afraid of being whipped for theft and had given it to the first white man he saw, and at first was afraid to pick it up." A fugitive who was taken into the home of an Ohio Quaker found it impossible to overcome his timidity and apprehension. "I had never had a white man to treat me as an equal, and the idea of a white lady waiting on me at the table was still worse! . . . I thought if I could only be allowed the privilege of eating in the kitchen, I should be more than satisfied." [2]

The masters themselves provided the most vivid evidence of the frightening image that white men assumed in the minds of many slaves. When they advertised for runaways, the owners frequently revealed a distressing relationship between the two races, a relationship that must have been for these slaves an emotional nightmare. In their advertisements no descriptive phrases were more common than these: "stutters very much when spoken to"; "speaks softly and has a downcast look"; "has an uneasy appearance when spoken to"; "speaks quickly, and with an anxious expression of countenance"; "a very down look, and easily

---

[1] Drew, *The Refugee*, pp. 156–57; Benwell, *Travels*, p. 99.
[2] Drew, *The Refugee*, pp. 30, 86; Watson Diary, entry for January 1, 1831; Brown, *Narrative*, pp. 102–103.

confused when spoken to"; "stammers very much so as to be scarcely understood."

"I feel lighter,—the dread is gone," affirmed a Negro woman who had escaped to Canada. "It is a great heaviness on a person's mind to be a slave." [8]

---

[8] Drew, *The Refugee*, p. 179.

CHAPTER NINE

Profit and Loss

In searching for evidence to justify their cause, southern proslavery writers showed remarkable resourcefulness. In persuasive prose their polemical essays spun out religious, historical, scientific, and sociological arguments to demonstrate that slavery was a positive good for both Negroes and whites—that it was the very cornerstone of southern civilization. But they rarely resorted to the most obvious and most practical argument of all: the argument that the peculiar institution was economically profitable to those who invested in it. Rather, most of the polemicists insisted that slaves were a financial burden and that the institution continued to exist for noneconomic reasons. They apparently thought that to admit that men could make money from slave labor would seriously damage their cause. "In an economical point of view," wrote James H. Hammond, "slavery presents some difficulties. As a general rule, I agree that . . . free labor is cheaper than slave labor. . . . We must, therefore, content ourselves with . . . the consoling reflection, that what is lost to us is gained to humanity." [1]

Outside the South, doctrinaire liberals, with whom the major tenets of Adam Smith were articles of faith, sup-

---

ported the defenders of slavery on this point at least. The liberals, to be sure, criticized slavery because they believed in the moral goodness of a competitive society of free men, a society in which labor is rewarded with the fruits of its toil. But they also criticized slavery because they were convinced that free labor was, for a number of reasons, cheaper to employ. John E. Cairnes, the English economist, could reason from his liberal assumptions that slavery was unprofitable. Olmsted, though his position was somewhat ambiguous and his evidence conflicting, also reached the general conclusion that slave labor was more costly than free. Solon Robinson, a northern agricultural expert, reported after a tour of the South that planters were earning meager returns on their investments.[2]

Numerous historical treatises on slavery accept the verdict of these contemporaries; they agree that, except on the fresh lands of the Southwest, slavery had nearly ceased to be profitable by the close of the ante-bellum period—that some masters made money "in spite of slavery rather than because of it." Indeed, a doubt has been raised about whether slaves were a sound investment "year in and year out" even in Mississippi.[3]

If the employment of slaves was unprofitable (or nearly so), it must somehow be explained why slaves brought high prices in the market and why masters continued to use them. To say that no other form of labor was available hardly answers the question, for slave labor could have been converted into free labor by emancipation. And would not an employer use no labor at all in preference to a kind that gave him no return on his investment? Perhaps it was the mere expectation of profit, though seldom or

---

[2] Cairnes, *Slave Power, passim;* Olmsted, *Seaboard, passim;* Kellar (ed.), *Solon Robinson,* II, pp. 240–45.

[3] Phillips, *American Negro Slavery,* pp. 391–92; James D. Hill, "Some Economic Aspects of Slavery, 1850–1860," *South Atlantic Quarterly,* XXVI (1927), pp. 161–77; Sydnor, *Slavery in Mississippi,* pp. 199–201.

never realized, that kept him going from year to year. Perhaps the slaveholder did not keep careful and accurate business records and therefore did not realize that he was on an economic treadmill. Or perhaps slavery, having been profitable in the past, survived now only because of custom and habit—because of a kind of economic lethargy. These are possible explanations, or partial explanations, why an unprofitable labor system might survive for a considerable length of time.

Moreover, slavery in the ante-bellum South was not purely or exclusively an economic institution: it was also part of a social pattern made venerable by long tradition and much philosophizing. One cannot assume that a Southerner would have promptly liquidated his investment in land and slaves whenever he found some other form of investment that promised him larger returns. For many slaveholders were emotionally and ideologically committed to the agrarian way of life—to the Jeffersonian idea that those who lived on the land were more virtuous than those who engaged in commerce or industry. "To day Mr T L Pleasants came over to consult about breaking up and going into a mercantile business," wrote a small Virginia planter. "To me it seems to be a wild idea, hope he will give it up and be satisfied to Farm." An Alabamian refused to abandon farming to engage in mining operations, for "I believe Farming is the safest and most honorable *calling* after all."[4]

No other profession gave a Southerner such dignity and importance as the cultivation of the soil with slave labor. The ownership of slaves, affirmed Cairnes, had become "a fashionable taste, a social passion"; it had become a symbol of success like "the possession of a horse among the Arabs: it brings the owner into connexion with the privileged

---

[4] Adams Diary, entry for June 6, 1859; William A. Dickinson to Ebenezer Pettigrew, January 21, 1843, Pettigrew Papers.

class; it forms the presumption that he has attained a certain social position." Slaves, therefore, were "coveted with an eagerness far beyond what the intrinsic utility of their services would explain." Cairnes concluded that it would be futile to propose compensated emancipation, for this would be asking slaveholders to renounce their power and prestige "for a sum of money which, if well invested, might perhaps enable them and their descendants to vegetate in peaceful obscurity!" [5]

Southern merchants often put at least part of their savings in slaves and plantations, as did lawyers, doctors, and clergymen, without always considering whether this was the most profitable investment. In 1834, Henry Watson, Jr., of East Windsor, Connecticut, moved to Greensboro, Alabama, and after the Panic of 1837 made a modest fortune as a lawyer. Then, like numerous other Yankees in the South, Watson sought admission to the gentry through the purchase of land and Negroes. [6] Since he bought wisely at depression prices, his investment proved to be rewarding economically as well as socially; but it would be hard to say which reward he found more gratifying.

The desire for profits was no more the exclusive factor in the use and management of slaves than it was in their accumulation. Because masters enjoyed status from the ownership of a large force, they sometimes supported more field-hands and domestics than they could employ with maximum efficiency. Nor did planters think only in economic terms when they debated leaving their exhausted lands in the East for fresh lands in the West. One North Carolinian refused to move because of his "local attachments"; another decided not to settle in Louisiana because the country was "sickly" and lacked "good society." "This is a miserably poor place," wrote James H. Hammond of

---

[5] Cairnes, *Slave Power*, pp. 137–46.
[6] Watson Papers, *passim*.

his South Carolina plantation. Yet, "I have hung on here . . . partly because I did not wish to remove from my native state and carry a family into the savage semi-barbarous west."[7] Far from being strictly economic men, southern masters permitted numerous other considerations to help shape their decisions about the acquisition and utilization of slave labor.

The proslavery writer's favorite explanation for the survival of an allegedly unprofitable labor system was that Negroes were unfit for freedom. Slavery existed because of the "race problem"—because the presence of a horde of free Negroes would pose an immense social danger and threaten southern civilization. Slavery was, above all, a method of regulating race relations, an instrument of social control. The master kept possession of his slaves from a sense of duty to society and to his "people." To destroy the system, according to the proslavery argument, would be a tragedy for both races.

But surely there are limits beyond which it is unreasonable to credit noneconomic factors for the survival of slavery. One can concede that the desire for status stimulated the acquisition of slave property, that fear of the free Negro created a demand for a system of social control, and that some masters had a paternalistic quality in their make-up. Forces even as strong as these, however, could not long prevent an archaic labor system from collapsing of its own weight. There is no evidence that a substantial number of masters held their human property *chiefly* to gain status, or to help the South solve its "race problem," or from a patriarchal sense of duty to the Negroes. Had the possession of slaves been a severe economic burden, it is certain that the great mass of slaveholders would have

---

[7] William S. Pettigrew to J. Johnston Pettigrew, March 8, 1859, Pettigrew Family Papers; Henry Alexander to Ebenezer Pettigrew, November 5, 1838, Pettigrew Papers; Hammond Diary, entry for March 31, 1841.

thrown them on the market—or, if necessary, abandoned them. Even Cairnes conceded that the survival of bondage warranted the inference that the institution was at least self-supporting.[8]

As long as slavery showed no sign of decline or decay, the system was probably accomplishing a good deal more than merely supporting itself. If slavery appeared to be flourishing, it must have been justifying itself economically and not simply surviving on the strength of a sentimental tradition. And during the 1850's slavery did in fact give much evidence of continued vigorous growth. Slave prices were higher than ever before, and everywhere in the South the demand for Negro labor exceeded the supply. The railroads were just beginning to open new cotton lands which had not previously been exploited for lack of transportation. Even Virginians were complaining about a labor shortage, and slavery was, if anything, more securely entrenched in the Old Dominion than it had been a generation earlier. Hence, the claim that slavery had "about reached its zenith by 1860" and was on the verge of collapse is far from convincing.[9] It appears that the noneconomic factors involved in the survival of slavery have been overemphasized; for the realities of 1860 create a presumption that the institution was still functioning profitably.

2

If one is to investigate the profitability or unprofitability of slavery, it is essential to define the problem precisely. Profitable for whom? Bondage was obviously not very prof-

---

[8] Cairnes, *Slave Power*, p. 64.
[9] Gray, *History of Agriculture*, II, pp. 641–42. For a different point of view see Charles W. Ramsdell, "The Natural Limits of Slavery Expansion," *Mississippi Valley Historical Review*, XVI (1929), pp. 151–71.

itable for the bondsmen whose standard of living was kept at the subsistence level; but bondage was not designed to enrich its victims. Nor was it introduced or preserved to promote the general welfare of the majority of white Southerners, who were nonslaveholders. The question is not whether the great mass of southern people of both races profited materially from slavery.

Moreover, the question is not whether a Southerner would have gained by selling his slaves, leaving his section, settling somewhere in the North, and investing in commerce or industry. He might have, but this involves the question of whether agriculture, in the long run, ever yields profits equal to those gained from manufacturing and trade. With or without slavery, planters and farmers were the victims of uncontrolled and wildly fluctuating prices, of insect pests, and of the weather. The year 1846, mourned one Mississippi planter, "will ever be memorable in the history of cotton planting from the ravages of the army worm which has no doubt curtailed the crop . . . at least Six Hundred Thousand Bales, worth Twenty Millions of Dollars." A rice planter surveyed the ruin following a "violent gale accompanied by immense rain. . . . The little that remained of the Crop after the two last gales, may now be abandoned. Not even the fragments of the wreck are left. Such is planting." Time after time the growers of southern staples saw their crops wither in severe droughts during the growing season—or rot in heavy rains at harvest time. Everything, concluded a discouraged planter, "seems to be against Cotton, not only the Abolitionists: but frost, snow, worms, and water." [1] These were the hazards of husbandry in an age without crop insurance, price supports, or acreage restrictions. But they have no

---

[1] Jenkins Diary, entry for November 2, 1846; Grimball Diary, entry for September 1, 1837; H. W. Poyner to William G. Harding, April 14, 1850, Harding-Jackson Papers.

bearing upon the question of whether those who chose to risk them found it profitable to employ slave labor.

Here, then, is the problem: allowing for the risks of a laissez-faire economy, did the average ante-bellum slaveholder, over the years, earn a reasonably satisfactory return from his investment? One must necessarily be a little vague about what constitutes a satisfactory return—whether it is five per cent, or eight, or more—because any figure is the arbitrary choice of the person who picks it. The slaveholders themselves drew no clear and consistent line between satisfactory and unsatisfactory returns. In an absolute sense, of course, anything earned above operating expenses and depreciation is a profit. The question is whether it was substantial enough to be satisfactory.

It may be conceded at the outset that possession of a supply of cheap slave labor carried with it no automatic guarantee of economic solvency, much less affluence. An incompetent manager moved with steady pace toward insolvency and the inevitable execution sale. Even an efficient manager found that his margin of profit depended upon the fertility of his land, proximity to cheap transportation, and the ability to benefit from the economies of large-scale production. Moreover, nearly every slaveholder saw his profits shrink painfully during periods of agricultural depression such as the one following the Panic of 1837; and many who had borrowed capital to speculate in lands and slaves were ruined. In short, there were enormous variations in the returns upon investments in slave labor from master to master and from year to year. For the "average slaveholder" is, of course, an economic abstraction, albeit a useful one.

3

The adversities that at some time or other overtook most slaveholders, the anxieties to which their business operations subjected them, and the bankruptcy that was the ultimate reward of more than a few, have produced an uncommon lot of myths about the economic consequences of slavery for both the slaveholder and the South as a whole. One of the most durable of these myths is that the system unavoidably reduced masters to the desperate expedients of carrying a heavy burden of mortgage indebtedness and of living upon credit secured by the next crop. Actually, the property of most slaveholders was not mortgaged; and when they were troubled with debt, slavery was not necessarily the cause. Many of the debt-burdened planters gave evidence not of the unprofitability of slavery but of managerial inefficiency or of a tendency to disregard the middle-class virtue of thrift and live beyond their means. "There is a species of pride," complained one Southerner, "which prompts us to . . . imitate, if not exceed, the style of our neighbors . . . and it very often occurs that the deeper we are involved, the more anxious do we become to conceal it from the world, and the more strenuous to maintain the same showy appearance. . . . We cannot bear the thought that the world should know that we are not as wealthy, as it was willing to believe us to be, and thus lose the importance attached to our riches." Even during the depression years of the early nineteenth century, thriftless Virginia planters still hired tutors for their children, surrounded themselves with an army of servants, and entertained on a grand scale.[2] It was not slavery itself but the southern culture that required these extravagances.

Other slaveholders went into debt to begin or to enlarge their agricultural operations. So long as their investments were sound, there was nothing reckless about launching an

---

[2] *Southern Agriculturist*, VII (1834), pp. 288; Larry Gara (ed.), "A New Englander's View of Plantation Life: Letters of Edwin Hall to Cyrus Woodman, 1837," *Journal of Southern History*, XVIII (1952), pp. 343–54.

enterprise or expanding it on borrowed capital. Indeed, many of them deliberately remained in debt because their returns from borrowed capital far exceeded the interest charges. But the planter often was unable to resist the temptation to overextend himself, especially in the thriving regions of the Southwest. "This credit system is so fascinating," confessed a Mississippian, that it entices "a man [to] go farther than prudence would dictate." A critic of the Louisiana planters claimed that one of their "leading characteristics" was "an apparent determination to be always in debt; notwithstanding the sufficiency of their ordinary incomes to support them in ease and affluence." It seemed to this conservative critic that a planter ought not to become obsessed with "rearing up a mammoth estate, to add to his cares and anxieties in this world"; rather, he "should be satisfied with an income of 15 or $20,000"! [3] When a sudden decline of staple prices caused the speculative bubble to burst, the ambitious Louisianian, like the extravagant Virginian, was the victim of forces that were entirely unrelated to slavery. The frontier boomer and the reckless speculator were in no sense evils spawned by the South's labor system.

The slaveholder who expanded his enterprise with his own profits was obviously more fortunate and more secure than those who borrowed for this purpose. A fall in prices merely reduced his income but seldom threatened him with bankruptcy. Yet the condition of even this thoroughly solvent entrepreneur has been misunderstood. Such a planter, it has often been said, was caught in a vicious circle, because he "bought lands and slaves wherewith to grow cotton, and with the proceeds ever bought more slaves to make more cotton." [4] Surely this was not the essence of eco-

---

[3] Baker Diary, entry for September 28, 1855; E. G. W. Butler to Thomas Butler, May 5, 1830, Butler Family Papers.

[4] Phillips, *American Negro Slavery*, pp. 395-98.

nomic futility, for an entrepreneur could hardly be considered trapped by a system which enabled him to enlarge his capital holdings out of surplus profits. As long as the slaveholder earned returns sufficient to supply his personal needs, meet all operating expenses, and leave a balance for investment, he might count himself fortunate indeed!

The economic critics also blamed slavery for one of the South's chronic problems: the declining fertility of the land. This form of labor, they argued, was only adaptable to a one-crop system which used crude, unscientific methods and led relentlessly to soil exhaustion. Slaves, wrote Cairnes, were incapable of working with modern agricultural implements; lacking versatility, they could be taught little more than the routine operations required in the growth of a single staple. "Slave cultivation, therefore, precluded the conditions of rotation of crops or skillful management, tends inevitably to exhaust the land of a country, and consequently requires for its permanent success not merely a fertile soil but a practically unlimited extent of it."[5]

The proof seemed to be everywhere at hand, not only in the older tobacco and cotton districts on the Atlantic coast but also, by the last two ante-bellum decades, in areas that had not been settled until the nineteenth century. A Georgian described the "barren waste" into which parts of Hancock County had been transformed by careless husbandry: "Fields that once teemed with luxuriant crops . . . are disfigured with gaping hill-sides, chequered with gullies, coated with broom straw and pine, the sure indices of barrenness and exhaustion—all exhibiting a dreary desolation." In 1859, a Southerner noted that the process of soil exhaustion was far advanced in Mississippi and Alabama, and that the slaveholders were now ready "to wear out the

---

[5] Cairnes, *Slave Power*, pp. 47–58.

Mississippi bottom, . . . Arkansas, Texas and all other slave soil in creation." Even in Texas Olmsted often observed "that spectacle so familiar and so melancholy . . . in all the older Slave States": the abandoned plantation with its worn-out fields. By way of explanation a northern agricultural expert affirmed that "in many of the cotton plantations, the most destructive system of farming is pursued that I ever saw." [6]

If slavery had been the cause of soil exhaustion, this would provide convincing evidence that it was a general economic blight upon the South; but even this would not necessarily be relevant to the question of whether slavery was profitable to individual masters. For many of them found it highly rewarding to exhaust their lands within a few years and then move on to fresh lands. However, there was in reality little connection between slavery and the extensive, soil-mining type of agriculture that characterized the ante-bellum South. How else account for the fact that many nonslaveholders, North and South, used the same wasteful methods in the cultivation of their farms? The explanation in both cases was that land was relatively cheap and abundant and labor relatively expensive and scarce; and in an agricultural milieu such as this landowners were reluctant to employ labor in the manuring of exhausted fields to restore their fertility. The one-crop system prevailed throughout much of the South, because one or another of the great staples seemed to promise the largest returns on capital investments. The expectation of profits from staple production, not the limitations of slavery, led to specialization rather than diversification, and caused some planters to fail to produce enough food for their own needs. Nor can slavery be blamed for the managerial inefficiency of unsupervised overseers who introduced slovenly

---

[6] *Southern Cultivator*, II (1844), p. 9; XVII (1859), p. 69; Olmsted, *Texas*, p. xiv; Kellar (ed.), *Solon Robinson*, II, p. 27.

agricultural methods on many estates. "Depend upon it that it is not our negroes, but our white managers, who stand in the way of improvement," asserted a South Carolinian.[7] Finally, soil erosion was not the product of slavery but of the hilly, rolling terrain, of heavy rains, and of the failure to introduce contour plowing and proper drainage. This trouble, too, afflicted slaveholders and nonslaveholders alike.

As conditions changed in the older parts of the South, tillage methods also changed. Out of economic depression, which resulted from declining staple prices and rising production costs on depleted lands, there appeared an increasingly obvious need for agricultural reform. "Formerly, when lands were fresh and cotton high," observed a Southerner, "planters had very little difficulty in getting along, and with the least industry and economy, accumulated property rapidly. . . . Twenty cents a pound for cotton cured all defects in management, and kept the sheriff at bay; but six cents a pound for cotton is quite another thing." Then, for the first time, some of those who had been mining the southern soil began to show an interest in conserving it.[8]

And wherever in the South improved methods were adopted, the slaveholders usually took the lead. They promoted the organization of local agricultural societies, sponsored essay contests on agricultural topics, and provided most of the support for the numerous periodicals which preached reform. They did most of the experimenting with new crops, with systems of crop rotation, with new implements and techniques, and with fertilizers. In Virginia,

---

[7] *American Agriculturist*, IV (1845), p. 319.

[8] *Southern Cultivator*, IV (1846), p. 106. See also Gray, *History of Agriculture*, I, pp. 447–48, 458–59, 470; Craven, *Soil Exhaustion*, pp. 11–24; Robert R. Russel, "The General Effects of Slavery upon Southern Economic Progress," *Journal of Southern History*, IV (1938), pp. 35–36.

slaveholders such as Edmund Ruffin, Hill Carter, and John Seldon abandoned tobacco culture, or at least rotated tobacco with wheat and clover; they were the first to enrich their lands with marl and with animal and vegetable manures. In short, they were responsible for the agricultural renaissance that Virginia enjoyed during the generation before 1860. "It is true," admitted Ruffin, "that *good farming* is rare here; and so it is elsewhere." But, he added, "our best farming in lower and middle Virginia is always to be found in connection with . . . [the] use of slave labor."[9]

In the Deep South, slaveholding planters such as James H. Hammond, of South Carolina, and Dr. Martin W. Phillips, of Mississippi, led similar movements to save the soil. Throughout the South, most of the improved farming was being done on lands worked by bondsmen; the "model" farms and plantations were almost invariably operated with their labor. Thus a substantial minority of the landowners demonstrated that slaves could be used efficiently in a system of intensive, scientific, and diversified agriculture. It is a mistake, therefore, to attribute soil exhaustion to slavery, or to assume that the institution was working such general economic havoc as to be rushing headlong toward destruction.[1]

But slavery was alleged to be economically injurious to the South not only because it fostered one-crop agriculture but also because it produced a generally unbalanced economy. Southerners, according to this argument, had never been able to accumulate capital for manufacturing, because so much of their wealth was invested in their labor force. Critics such as Cairnes insisted that slaves were, "from the nature of the case, unskilled" and hence could

---

9 *Farmers' Register,* VII (1839), pp. 235–38; Craven, *Soil Exhaustion,* pp. 122–61.

1 Gray, *History of Agriculture,* I, pp. 449–50; Flanders, *Plantation Slavery in Georgia,* pp. 90–93; Kellar (ed.), *Solon Robinson,* I, pp. 456–57.

not "take part with efficiency in the difficult and delicate operations which most manufacturing and mechanical processes involve." Slaves, concluded Cairnes, have "never been, and can never be, employed with success in manufacturing industry." [2]

It is doubtful, however, that slavery in any decisive way retarded the industrialization of the South. After the African slave trade was legally closed, the southern labor system absorbed little new capital that might have gone into commerce or industry. Then only the illegal trade carried on by northern and foreign merchants drained off additional amounts of the South's liquid assets. The domestic slave trade involved no further investment; it merely involved the transfer of a portion of the existing one between individuals and regions. Obviously, when one Southerner purchased slaves another liquidated part of his investment in slaves and presumably could have put his capital in industry if he cared to.[3] To define the cost of raising a young slave to maturity as a new capital investment is quite misleading. It would be more logical to call this a part of the "wage" a slave received for his lifetime of labor; or to call it—as most slaveholders did—a part of the annual operating expense. Southerners *did* have capital for investment in industry, and the existence of slavery was not the reason why so few of them chose to become industrialists.

After innumerable experiments had demonstrated that slaves could be employed profitably in factories, Southerners were still divided over the wisdom of such enterprises. Some of the opponents were devoted to the agrarian tradition and contended that industrialization was an evil under all circumstances. Others insisted that nonagricultural occupations should be reserved for free white labor and

---

[2] Cairnes, *Slave Power*, pp. 65–66.
[3] Gray, *History of Agriculture*, I, pp. 459–60; Russel, "General Effects of Slavery," *loc. cit.*, pp. 52–53.

that white men should not be degraded by slave competition. In addition, many feared that removing slaves from the farms and plantations and increasing their numbers in the cities would undermine the peculiar institution. "Whenever a slave is made a mechanic, he is more than half freed," argued one master. "Wherever slavery has decayed, the first step . . . has been the elevation of the slaves to the rank of artisans and soldiers."[4]

Those who favored employing slaves in industry believed that this was the most practical way for the South to diversify its economy and to become more nearly self-sufficient. They protested that the attempt to confine slaves to agriculture was an attack upon slavery itself. It was the work of abolitionists. To prohibit masters from training slaves for any occupation "in which they may be profitably employed . . . would be fatal to the institution of Slavery, and an infringement on the rights of those on whom has devolved the responsibility of taking care of dependents." Finally, promoters of industry pointed to the record of successes where slaves were being used in mines, cotton mills, iron foundries, and tobacco factories.[5]

The appeal of such promoters had little effect, however, for Southerners put only a small amount of capital into industry before the Civil War. Many of those who sold slaves to the traders used the money to support an extravagant standard of living rather than for new investments. But in the nineteenth century most of the South's surplus capital went into land and agricultural improvements; and the reason for this was simply that in the competition for funds agriculture was able to outbid industry. Men invested in land not only because of the agrarian tradition and the

---

[4] Wesley, *Negro Labor in the United States*, pp. 71–73; *De Bow's Review*, VIII (1850), p. 518.

[5] *De Bow's Review*, VIII (1850), p. 76; Flanders, *Plantation Slavery in Georgia*, pp. 205–207.

prestige derived from the ownership of real estate, but also
because the production of one of the staples seemed to be
the surest avenue to financial success. Besides, southern industry faced the handicap of competition from northern industry which enjoyed the advantages of greater experience,
more efficient management, more concentrated markets,
more numerous power sites, and better transportation.[6] All
of these factors destined the South, with or without slavery,
to be a predominantly agricultural region—and so it continued to be for many years after emancipation.

Another supposed disadvantage of the southern labor
system was that slaves were less productive than free workers and therefore more expensive to their employers.
Cairnes explained that since slaves could be offered no incentives, "fear is substituted for hope, as the stimulus to
exertion. But fear is ill calculated to draw from a labourer
all the industry of which he is capable." A second critic declared, "Half the population of the South is employed in
seeing that the other half do their work, and they who do
work, accomplish half what they might do under a better
system." After visiting a number of plantations in Virginia, Olmsted concluded that slaves "can not be driven by
fear of punishment to do that which the laborers in free
communities do cheerfully from their sense of duty, self-
respect, or regard for their reputation and standing with
their employer." [7]

To be sure, the slave's customary attitude of indifference
toward his work, together with the numerous methods he
devised to resist his enslavement, sharply reduced the master's potential profits. It does not follow, however, that a
slaveholder who was a reasonably efficient manager would

[6] Gray, *History of Agriculture*, II, pp. 933–34; Russel, "General Effects
of Slavery," *loc. cit.*, pp. 47–49.
[7] Cairnes, *Slave Power*, pp. 43–47; Lyell, *Second Visit*, II, pp. 84–85;
Olmsted, *Seaboard*, pp. 44–47, 195–98, 203–205.

have found free labor cheaper to employ. Slavery's economic critics overlooked the fact that physical coercion, or the threat of it, proved to be a rather effective incentive, and that the system did not prevent masters from offering tempting rewards for the satisfactory performance of assigned tasks.

Besides, slave labor had several competitive advantages over free white labor. In the first place, it was paid less: the average wage of a free laborer exceeded considerably the investment and maintenance costs of a slave. In the second place masters exploited women and children more fully than did the employers of free labor. Finally, the average bondsman worked longer hours and was subjected to a more rigid discipline. Slaveholders were less troubled with labor "agitators" and less obligated to bargain with their workers. The crucial significance of this fact was dramatically demonstrated by a Louisiana sugar planter who once experimented with free labor, only to have his gang strike for double pay during the grinding season.[8] "Slave labor is the most constant form of labor," argued a Southerner. "The details of cotton and rice culture could not be carried on with one less constant." No conviction was more firmly embedded in the mind of the planter than this. Many employers "hire slaves in preference to other laborers," explained a southern judge, "because they believe the contract confers an absolute right to their services during its continuation."[9] These advantages more than compensated for whatever superiority free labor had in efficiency.

Indeed, some southern landowners who employed Irish immigrants or native whites even doubted that they were more diligent than slaves. One employer complained that

---

[8] Gray, *History of Agriculture*, I, pp. 464, 471, 474–75; Phillips, *American Negro Slavery*, p. 337.

[9] *North Carolina Planter*, II (1859), p. 163; Catterall (ed.), *Judicial Cases*, V, pp. 188–89.

no matter how well white workers were treated, "except when your eyes are on them they cheat you out of the labor due you, by lounging under the shade of the trees in your field." A Maryland planter assured Olmsted that "at hoeing and any steady field-work" his slaves accomplished twice as much, and with less personal supervision, than the Irish laborers he had used. North Carolina farmers told him that poor whites were "even more inefficient and unmanageable than . . . slaves."[1] Clearly, the productivity and efficiency of free labor was not so overwhelmingly superior as to make the doom of slavery inevitable.

Still another argument of the economic critics was that owners of slaves had to bear certain costs that employers of free labor did not bear. In a free labor system workers were hired and fired as they were needed; in a slave labor system workers had to be supported whether or not they were needed. In a free labor system the employer had no obligation to support the worker's dependents, or the worker himself during illness and in old age; in a slave labor system the employer was legally and morally obligated to meet these costs. Thus, presumably, slavery was at once more humane and more expensive.

This, too, is a myth. Employers of free labor, through wage payments, did in fact bear most of the expense of supporting the children of their workers, as well as the aged and infirm. Government and private charities assumed only a small part of this burden. Moreover, the amount that slaveholders spent to maintain these unproductive groups was not a substantial addition to their annual operating costs. The maintenance of disabled and senile slaves was a trivial charge upon the average master; and the market value of a young slave far exceeded the small expense of raising him.

---

[1] *American Farmer*, VI (1850), p. 171; Olmsted, *Seaboard*, pp. 10, 349-50.

Nor was the typical slaveholder faced with the problem of feeding and clothing surplus laborers; rather, his persistent problem was that of a labor shortage, which became acute during the harvest. Only a few masters had difficulty finding work for all available hands throughout the year. As for the need to support workers in time of economic depression, it must be remembered that the nineteenth-century agriculturist (unlike the manufacturer) did not ordinarily stop, or even curtail, production when demand and prices declined. Instead, he continued his operations—and sometimes even expanded them in an effort to augment his reduced income. During the depression of the 1840's, for example, both slaveholders and nonslaveholders strove for maximum production, and as a result there were few unemployed agricultural workers. Slave prices declined because nearly all prices declined, not because masters deliberately flooded the market with Negroes for whom there was no work. Rarely, then, did slaveholders pay for the support of idle hands.

But were there not other costs burdening the employer of slave labor which the employer of free labor escaped? The slaveholder, said the critics, bore the initial expense of a substantial investment in his laborers, the annual expense of interest and depreciation upon his investment, and the constant risk of loss through death by accident or disease. The employer of free labor, on the other hand, bore neither of these expenses and lost nothing when a worker died or was disabled. Here, many thought, was the most convincing evidence that slave labor was more costly than free.[2]

It is true that the purchase of slaves (which involves the capitalization of future income from their labor) increased the size of the capital investment in a business enterprise—

---

[2] Sydnor, *Slavery in Mississippi*, pp. 195–97; Flanders, *Plantation Slavery in Georgia*, p. 221.

and that most southern whites lacked the cash or credit to gain title to this form of labor. It is also true that an investment in slaves entailed the risk of serious losses, especially for the small slaveholder. Though most masters continued to assume this risk, late in the ante-bellum period a few began to protect themselves from such disasters by insuring the lives of slaves. More important, however, is the fact that in the general pricing of slaves these risks were discounted. Such dangers as death, long illness, permanent disability, rebelliousness, and escape were all weighed when a purchaser calculated the price he was willing to pay. Only an unfortunate minority, therefore, suffered severe losses from an investment in slaves.

But Depreciation on slave capital was not an operational expense for the average master. Not only were slave prices increasing, but with reasonable luck an investment in slaves was self-perpetuating. As one Southerner observed, "slaves . . . are not wasted by use, and if they are, that waste is supplied by their issue." Another added, "Their perpetuation by natural increase bears a strong resemblance to the permanency of Lands." Most slaveholders, in fact, were more fortunate than this, for their slave forces actually grew in size. With proper use, a master found his investment in slaves (sometimes in land too), unlike his investment in tools and buildings, appreciating rather than depreciating. This natural increase was a significant part of his profit.

The southern master's capitalization of his labor force has caused more confusion than anything else about the comparative cost of free and slave labor. This capital investment was not an added expense; it was merely the payment in a lump sum of a portion of what the employer of

---

3 Catterall (ed.), *Judicial Cases*, II, p. 69; Abbeville District, South Carolina, Judge of Probate Decree Book, 1839–1858, May term, 1841.

free labor pays over a period of years. The price of a slave, together with maintenance, was the cost of a lifetime claim to his labor; it was part of the wage an employer could have paid a free laborer. The price was what a master was willing to give for the right to maintain his workers at a subsistence level, and to gain full control over their time and movements. The interest he expected to accrue from his investment was not an operational expense to be deducted from profits, as it has often been called, unless the slaves were purchased on credit and interest therefore had to be paid to someone else. To deduct from the master's profit an amount equal to interest on his own capital invested in slaves is to create a fictitious expense and to underestimate his total earnings. There would be less confusion if this amount were called "profit on investment" rather than "interest on investment"; for as long as he earned it, this was a portion of his reward for risking his capital and managing his enterprise.[4] With scarcely an exception, southern slaveholders, like entrepreneurs generally, not only considered interest earned on investment as part of their total profit but lumped all sources of profit together without artificial and arbitrary divisions.

Calculated on this basis, discounting the myths, there is ample evidence that the average slaveholder earned a reasonably satisfactory return upon his investment in slaves.

4

Testimony concerning the profits derived from slave labor appears in the business records which many masters

---

[4] *De Bow's Review*, VII (1849), pp. 435–37; Gray, *History of Agriculture*, I, pp. 473–74; II, pp. 941 *et passim*; Thomas P. Govan, "Was Plantation Slavery Profitable?" *Journal of Southern History*, VIII (1942), pp. 514–18.

kept and in the reports which some prepared for southern periodicals. These records and reports must be used with care, however, because usually the slaveholder's bookkeeping and accounting methods left much to be desired. Often he overlooked certain legitimate costs such as depreciation on mules, machinery, tools, and farm buildings. Almost always he listed among operating expenses items which did not properly belong there. Most commonly he included personal expenditures and new capital investments among the year's production costs. For example, in the generally well-kept accounts of John C. Jenkins's two Mississippi plantations, household bills, $350 for an artist, and $50 for a church pew were counted with business expenses. James H. Hammond, of South Carolina, and Charles and Louis Manigault, of Georgia, maintained as full and systematic records as can be found; yet both added large sums spent for expansion or permanent improvements, as well as for household supplies, to their annual plantation costs. Slaveholders frequently thought of the cash expended for even such things as pianos, furniture, vacation trips, college tuition for their children, and additional land and slaves as charges against their business enterprises rather than as part of the profit.

Yet these records of expenses are important, because they indicate how modest the true costs of production were for the average slaveholder. Only the sugar planters and a few of the rice planters had heavy investments in machinery; for the rest the cost of capital depreciation was a relatively small item in proportion to the total capital investment. Direct taxes were so low as to be almost negligible. Masters generally paid no state tax on slave children or on the aged and infirm; the annual tax on able-bodied slaves was usually between fifty and seventy-five cents. In 1833, a Georgia planter paid a tax of $29.21 on 330 acres of land and 70

slaves; in 1839, a South Carolina planter paid a tax of
$136.55 on 10,000 acres of land and 153 slaves.[5] Freight was
the largest marketing cost, and this item varied with the lo-
cation of the shipper. In 1852, an Alabamian paid a comparatively high rate of two dollars a bale for shipping cotton by river from Florence to New Orleans. Other costs
included river and fire insurance, drayage, storage, weighing, and the factor's commission, and altogether amounted
to an additional two dollars a bale.[6] The cotton grower
commonly spent about ten per cent of the gross proceeds
from his crop for bale rope, cotton bagging, and marketing
charges.

By far, the master's greatest expense was the support of
his labor force. On the plantations this might include the
wages of an overseer, a cost which was proportionately
heavier for the small planters than for the large. Records of
yearly expenditures for the maintenance of individual
slaves demonstrate convincingly the cheapness of this form
of labor. "Negro shoes" could be purchased for a dollar or
less, hats and kerchiefs for a dollar, blankets for two dollars, and enough cloth for summer and winter clothing for
two or three dollars. "My medical bill for 1845," wrote a
Tennesseean, "is $50.00 for about 50 persons—it has been a
very sickly year." [7] Numerous estimates of the cost of feeding a slave ranged from $7.50 to $15.00 a year, the amount
depending upon how much pork and corn was produced
on the estate. Figured on an annual basis, five dollars
would easily cover the expense of housing a bondsman.
This means that the yearly charge for the support of an
adult slave seldom exceeded $35.00, and was often consid-
erably less than this.

To give some specific examples: Edmund Ruffin's yearly

[5] Manigault Plantation Records; Account Book in Hammond Papers.
[6] Sales account, dated February 3, 1852, in John Coffee Collection.
[7] Bills Diary, entry for January 16, 1846.

maintenance costs for the slaves on his Virginia plantation, Marlbourne, averaged less than $25.00 per slave during the five years from 1844 to 1848. James Hamilton supported each of the slaves on his Georgia sea-island cotton plantation for $18.33 a year over a forty-year period. In 1851, James A. Tait, of Alabama, estimated his maintenance costs at $34.70 per slave, including food, clothing, medical care, and taxes. In 1849, Thomas Pugh, of Louisiana, spent $23.60 per slave for all of these items, except taxes.[8] Maintenance was naturally more expensive in the towns and on plantations which produced no food, but slaves were then able to devote all of their time to other labor.

There was a second flaw in the typical slaveholder's business records, which caused him to underestimate the profitability of his enterprise. Rarely did he include all sources of income other than the net proceeds from the sale of his chief crop. Sometimes he neglected to list income from incidental crops and wood products, and from the occasional hiring out of slaves. He almost never thought of the personal services rendered by his domestics or of the food produced for his own family as part of his profit. Nor did he record his capital gains from the clearing and improvement of land and from the natural increase of his slave property. Yet a Virginian noted that in his state the chief profit of many planters was from "raising slaves and the increase in the value of their lands in consequence of improvements from marling and increase of population." A Georgian agreed that slave children paid "a good interest upon the amount of care and expense bestowed upon them." In Louisiana, an absentee cotton planter learned that his slaves were increasing rapidly, "and when you come to calculat-

---

[8] *American Farmer*, V (1849), p. 5; Johnson, *Sea Islands*, p. 102; Davis, *Cotton Kingdom in Alabama*, p. 186; Kellar (ed.), *Solon Robinson*, II, p. 198.

ing you will find your young negroes a figure in your favor." [9] This natural increase was often turned into cash
through sales.

After the necessary adjustments are made in costs and
total income, surviving business records reveal that during
the last ante-bellum decade slavery was still justifying itself
economically. Few masters, of course, enjoyed the bonanzas
which had made fortunes for Virginians in the seventeenth
century, South Carolinians in the eighteenth century, and
Alabamians and Mississippians in the early nineteenth cen-
ury. With the depression of the 1840's, those lush days had
permanently ended for all but a minority of slaveholders
in the Southwest. Only in the Mississippi delta, the Louisiana bayous, the Red River and Arkansas River valleys, and
the Texas prairies were men still earning fabulous profits
during the 1850's. In these flourishing districts, wrote Olmsted, "I have been on plantations . . . whereon I was assured that ten bales of cotton to each average prime field-
hand had been raised." At this level of production he calculated the profit per hand at a minimum of $250 a year.
"Even at seven bales to the hand the profits of cotton planting are enormous. Men who have plantations producing at
this rate, can well afford to buy fresh hands at fourteen
hundred dollars a head." In 1859, a Texan grew 254 bales
of cotton with 25 hands, and a planter on the Arkansas
River grew 366 heavy bales with 50 hands. Cotton growers,
observed a Louisianian, were "making oceans of money."
Among them were a few who produced gigantic crops of
more than two thousand bales, and who, together with several of the great sugar planters, ranked with the wealthiest
men in the United States before the Civil War.[1] Some of

[9] Hammond Diary, entry for February 12, 1841; *De Bow's Review*,
XVII (1854), pp. 423-24; Kenneth M. Clark to Lewis Thompson, December 17, 1854, Lewis Thompson Papers.
[1] Frederick L. Olmsted, *The Cotton Kingdom* (New York, 1861), I,
pp. 13-14; Leak Diary, entries for February 1, December 16, 1859;

them amassed their fortunes entirely from investments in virgin land and slave labor.

In the older cotton, sugar, and rice areas of the Deep South slaveholders seldom reaped profits as dazzling as these, but staple prices were high enough during the fifties to make returns of seven to ten per cent on capital investments common. In spite of inflated slave and land values, sugar growing in Louisiana was still a "healthy economic enterprise." In 1855, a Mississippian attempted to give a fair statement of the profits from cotton growing; he concluded that the planter earned about eight per cent on his capital—but this was an estimate of the net proceeds from the sale of cotton alone. Even the low prices of 1847 enabled one Alabama planter to make a net profit of ten per cent on his cotton crop. Six years later, another Alabamian concluded, "I can think of no investment so sure as a plantation and negroes." The prosperity of the decade before 1860 forced Olmsted to agree that the profit from slave labor in Alabama and Mississippi was "moderately good, at least, compared with the profit of other investments of capital and enterprise at the North." [2]

The rewards from agriculture in South Carolina and Georgia were less, on the average, than in the Southwest, but this does not mean that slavery had ceased to be profitable. Hammond, like many others, complained incessantly about meager earnings; yet by improving his methods he was able to share in the prosperity of the fifties. A proper balancing of expenses and income indicates that Louis Manigault was making ten per cent on his rice plantation

---

Pugh Diary, entry for April 6, 1860; Natchez *Free Trader*, quoted in *De Bow's Review*, XXVI (1859), p. 581.

[2] Sitterson, *Sugar Country*, pp. 181–82; *Southern Cultivator*, XIII (1855), p. 366; Gilmore & Co. to F. H. Elmore, March 18, 1847, Elmore Papers; Catterall (ed.), *Judicial Cases*, III, p. 188; Olmsted, *Back Country*, p. 294.

in Georgia. In 1850, John B. Grimball, a South Carolina rice planter, noted in his diary: "My pecuniary affairs although not flourishing are yet sufficiently easy to permit us to enjoy all the comforts and many of the luxuries of life." This might express the sentiment of numerous other rice growers, many of whom probably did not often net much above five per cent on the current cash value of their investments from the sale of their crops. A decade later, however, Grimball was benefiting from the general prosperity and earning well over ten per cent. Nearly all of the rice planters, in common with Nathaniel Heyward who was the greatest of them before his death in 1851, made their money from the soil without mules or machinery, "with only the Negro, the hoe, and the rice hook." [3]

Even in the Upper South slavery was amply rewarding those who took pains to preserve or restore the fertility of their soil and who directed their enterprises with reasonable efficiency. There is little foundation for the belief that the peculiar institution had ceased to be profitable for the average master in this region. The growing of tobacco and hemp with slave labor on medium-sized estates was still paying satisfactory returns in certain districts—and, indeed, the development of "Bright" tobacco in the Virginia-North Carolina piedmont just before the Civil War promised a new prosperity to those who possessed the thin, sandy soil on which it grew. Improved methods and crop rotation were once again making farming lucrative for many other slaveholders who lived north of the cotton belt. In Virginia, not only the competition of the Southwest but also the increasing employment of slaves in mining, industry, and internal improvements was forcing up slave

[3] Grimball Diary, entries for March 10, 1850; May 23, September 30, 1860; February 16, 1861; Heyward, *Seed from Madagascar*, p. 74.

410

prices and creating the labor shortage about which so many complained.[4]

The resulting rise in the capital value of slaves during the fifties created a deceptive picture of the Virginia slaveholder's plight, for inflated slave prices made him appear to be earning a small return on the market value of his investment. Actually these rising prices meant a substantial capital gain, a portion of which those who dealt with slave traders converted into money profits. No doubt the Virginian would have been wise to sell his slaves when prices reached their peak—but who could tell when the peak had been reached? And meanwhile it hardly seemed to be to his economic advantage to liquidate an investment whose value was steadily rising.

Moreover, it must be remembered that the typical master of the Upper South had inherited his slaves and had not purchased them at the high prices of the late ante-bellum period. When his profit is figured on the basis of the original cash investment, rather than at current slave prices, it was substantially higher and usually quite adequate. To some extent the inflated value of slaves on the market was offset by the low cost of land. As one Virginian observed, "So far as the prices for slaves have already exceeded the profits of their labor in Virginia, so far that excess has already checked the demand for investments in agriculture, and must operate to reduce the price of land. And the more that the price of slaves shall rise, still more, and in full proportion, will it operate further to reduce the price of land." At existing prices, he admitted, most Virginians were unable to make new investments in slaves. But for the man who already owned a slave force and did not enter the market as a buyer or seller, the commercial value of slaves

---

[4] Nannie May Tilley, *The Bright-Tobacco Industry, 1860–1929* (Chapel Hill, 1948), pp. 3–36; Bruce, *Virginia Iron Manufacture*, pp. 244–45.

had little meaning. The worth of his bondsmen depended upon "the actual value of the net products of their labor . . . and there is no difference to his income or interests whether his best slaves would sell for fifteen hundred dollars, or for but five hundred dollars." [5]

In 1852, another Virginian sketched a justifiably optimistic picture of the agricultural prospects in the eastern part of his state. Conceding the survival of "a great and lamentable amount of indolence, apathy, heedlessness, improvidence and wastefulness," he nevertheless affirmed that opportunities for substantial returns from agriculture existed once more. Hundreds of farmers "have derived and continue to derive profits which surpass any purely agricultural profits that can be made in the northern states, from free labor." [6] Numerous Virginians demonstrated this by earning more than ten per cent on their investments, after fertilizing their lands and turning to diversified farming. Their income from the production of corn, wheat, fruits, and vegetables enabled some of them even to purchase additional slaves.[7] This was the picture in other states of the Upper South too, including border states such as Maryland, Kentucky, and Missouri. A Fayette County, Kentucky, slaveholder understood the economic realities of slavery better than its critics when he wrote in his will: "I would prefer the Surplus of my estate (after the payment of my debts) Should continue in real estate and in Slaves rather than in money Stocks etc for the use and benefit of my descendants prefering the certainty of Revenue derivable therefrom to the chances of an increase by a resort to other means or pursuits."

Other things being equal, the owner of a large slave

---

[5] *Southern Planter*, XIX (1859), pp. 472–77.

[6] *Ibid.*, XII (1852), pp. 71–73.

[7] *American Farmer*, V (1849–50), pp. 2–11, 255–56; Massie Farm Journal, *passim;* Edmund Ruffin, Jr., Plantation Diary, *passim.*

gang earned a proportionately higher return on his investment than the owner of a small gang. The large operator
saved by purchasing supplies in big lots; he was often able
to withhold his crop from the market and sell at the most
opportune time; and he could afford to experiment with
improved tools and new methods of cultivation. He
achieved a maximum of labor specialization and found the
cost of management relatively low. As Olmsted noted, "A
man can compel the uninterrupted labor of a gang of fifty
cotton-hoers almost as absolutely as he can that of a gang
of five." [8] The ability of the large-scale staple producer to
cut costs and to survive at lower market prices encouraged
the ceaseless trend, in those parts of the South best suited
for commercial agriculture, toward the consolidation of
small units into big plantations.

But it must not be concluded therefore that the day of
the small slaveholder was passing. Far from it. Except in
the alluvial river bottoms, he was still an important figure
during the fifties; he produced a significant proportion of
the southern staples along with a great variety of other
farm products. Though the cotton farmer had to pay a toll
for the use of some planter's cotton gin, though he was unable to make a dozen economies that the planter made,
good management and a fair price still brought him a handsome profit from his investment in slaves. Most tobacco
was produced on small plantations and farms which employed only a few hands. In diversified farming the proprietor found that the ownership of a slave or two was an
enormous advantage; often it spelled the difference between mere subsistence and a cash income. This fact is evident in the inventories of estates preserved in southern
county records. These inventories show that the typical
master of one or two slaves lived in far greater comfort and

---

[8] Olmsted, *Back Country*, p. 226; Gray, *History of Agriculture*, I, p. 479.

died the possessor of far more worldly goods than the typical nonslaveholding farmer. In short, on both large and small estates, none but the most hopelessly inefficient masters failed to profit from the ownership of slaves.

5

In the final analysis, the high valuation of Negro labor during the 1850's was the best and most direct evidence of the continued profitability of slavery. Hiring rates varied with economic conditions, with the danger of the occupation, and with the slave's skill; but the rate per year usually ranged somewhere between ten and twenty per cent of the slave's market value, plus maintenance.[9] In 1859, Missouri field-hands hired for $225 for men and $150 for women. In 1860, a Virginian hired out 52 hands through an agent in Mobile, 35 at the rate of $225 and 17 at the rate of $200, the employer agreeing to pay for clothing, taxes, doctor bills, and all other expenses. Between 1844 and 1852 a group of Mississippi slaves were hired out at an annual rate averaging almost twenty per cent of their appraised value. Late in the 1850's, Louisiana sugar planters paid as much as $1.50 a day for hired slaves during the grinding season. The skilled artisans, owned by urban and plantation masters, often hired for twenty-five per cent of their cash value and were almost always uncommonly profitable investments.[1] There was considerable danger in hiring out slaves for labor in factories, mines, river boats, and internal improvements, but the rates were correspondingly high. In

---

[9] Bancroft, *Slave-Trading*, pp. 156–57.
[1] St. Louis *Missouri Republican*, January 10, 1859; Memorandum dated December 15, 1860, in Morton-Halsey Papers; Sydnor, *Slavery in Mississippi*, pp. 175–78; Sitterson, *Sugar Country*, pp. 61–62; Bassett, *Plantation Overseer*, pp. 162–63.

1858, slave deck hands on the steamers running between Galveston and Houston were hired for $480 a year; in 1859, a North Carolina internal improvements company offered to pay $312 a year for common laborers.[2]

These hiring rates brought masters excellent returns. Yet the employers paid such rates only after carefully calculating the immediate profits they could make with hired bondsmen. Thus a Kentucky hemp manufacturer estimated that his labor costs were one-third less when he hired slaves than when he employed free whites. In 1848, the Federal Commissioner of Patents reported that in agriculture the rates for hired slaves ranged from twenty to fifty per cent less than the wages of free labor.[3] Here was striking evidence of the competitive advantage of the slave system.

Slave prices were always influenced by staple prices and by other economic conditions, but from the colonial period to the Civil War the general trend was upward. In the nineteenth century, the sharpest and longest reverse of this trend came after the Panic of 1837 and lasted until the middle of the forties. Then prices began to climb again and during the prosperous fifties reached record highs. Between 1846 and 1859 the average value of slaves in Tennessee rose from $413.72 to $854.65. In 1856, a Tennessean attended a sale in Hardeman County where "A.1" men sold for $1350 and women for $1200, "the highest point for negroes during my time." The next year he purchased a fourteen-year-old girl for $1000.[4] In 1857, a Richmond price list quoted number one men, "extra," at $1450–$1550; number one men "good," at $1200–$1250; and number one men, "com-

---

2 Houston *Weekly Telegraph*, December 29, 1858; Raleigh *North Carolina Standard*, August 13, 1859.

3 Hopkins, *Hemp Industry*, pp. 135–37; *Compendium of the Seventh Census*, p. 164.

4 Mooney, "Some Institutional and Statistical Aspects of Slavery in Tennessee," *loc. cit.*, p. 199; Bills Diary, entries for February 29, 1856; March 2, 1857.

mon," at $1100–$1150. Women of corresponding grades sold for $200 less.[5]

Louisiana sugar planters who had been able to purchase prime field-hands in New Orleans for $600 during the 1820's, paid from $1200 to $1500 for them and from $2000 to $3000 for skilled artisans during the middle fifties. By 1859, prices were even higher. During a visit to New Orleans in February, a sugar planter "bought 14 head, 8 women and six men—the women from $1,325 to $1,400 men from $1,600 to $1,700—1 Blacksmith for $2,500." This was "very high," he complained, but "it seems we must have them at any price for fear they will go still higher." A month later his fear was realized when he purchased sixteen additional slaves: "four women for $1,500 each six for $1,600 each two for $1,650 each and one woman and her boy 11 years old at $2,400 and one man for $1,700 cash and a Blacksmith for $2,500." [6]

These inflated slave prices were in part the result of a speculative fever that swept through the Deep South during the fifties. "There is a perfect mania for Negroes here," wrote a Louisianian. Many feared that all would end in an economic panic similar to that of 1837 which had terminated an earlier boom. A Mississippian predicted, in 1859, that "a crash must soon come upon the country—just as soon as cotton dropped below ten cents, as no price below ten cents would be remunerative at the present price of negroes, land, mules etc." A Georgian warned that "in a short time we shall see many negroes and much land offered under the sheriffs hammer . . . and then this kind of property will descend to its real value. The old rule of pricing a negro by the price of cotton by the pound—that is to say, if cotton is worth twelve cents, a negro man is

---

[5] Newspaper clipping in Pré Aux Cleres Plantation Record Book.
[6] Sitterson, *Sugar Country*, p. 61; Pugh Plantation Diary, entries for February 4, 5, March 15, 1859.

worth $1200.00 if at fifteen cents, then $1500.00—does not seem to be regarded. . . . Men are demented upon the subject. A reverse will surely come." [7]

In so far as this Negro "mania" produced an overcapitalization of slave labor in relation to net earnings, it is reasonable to assume that the inflation would have been temporary and that a contraction of slave prices would have eventually occurred. But these rising prices were not entirely the result of speculation. They reflected, in addition, the prosperity of the fifties, the generally satisfactory prices of the southern staples, the agricultural renaissance in Virginia, and the chronic labor shortage. They also reflected increasing managerial efficiency and the increasing productivity of slave labor. Finally, they reflected the ability of the flourishing operators in the new bonanza regions of the Southwest to bid high for Negroes.[8] Eventually the flush times in Texas would have ended, as they had earlier in Alabama and Mississippi, and the gap between profit margins there and in the older regions would have narrowed. Then a more rational relationship between profits and slave prices would have been restored throughout the South.

Still, the crucial fact of the fifties was that, in the main, current hiring rates and sales prices were based on a solid foundation: the slave was earning for his owner a substantial, though varying, surplus above the cost of maintenance. For this reason, the critics of slavery who argued that the institution was an economic burden to the master were using the weakest weapon in their arsenal. There was no evidence in 1860 that bondage was a "decrepit institution tottering toward a decline"—and, indeed, if the slave-

---

[7] Kenneth M. Clark to Lewis Thompson, January 14, 1853, Lewis Thompson Papers; Leak Diary, entry for February 2, 1859; Phillips (ed.), *Plantation and Frontier*, II, pp. 73–74.

[8] Gray, *History of Agriculture*, I, pp. 476–77; II, p. 667; Sitterson, *Sugar Country*, pp. 127–28.

holder's economic self-interest alone were to be consulted, the institution should have been preserved.[9]

Nor is there any reason to assume that masters would have found it economically desirable to emancipate their slaves in the foreseeable future. "When the demand for agricultural labor shall be fully supplied," predicted a South Carolinian, "then of course the labor of slaves will be directed to other employments and enterprises. . . . As it becomes cheaper and cheaper, it will be applied to more various purposes and combined in larger masses. It may be commanded and combined with more facility than any other sort of labor; and the laborer, kept in stricter subordination, will be less dangerous to the security of society than in any other country, which is crowded and over-stocked with a class of what are called free laborers." [1]

In other words, even when there was an abundant supply of labor, the employer still enjoyed certain practical economic advantages from keeping his workers in bondage. The idea that free labor under any circumstances can be employed more cheaply than slave is patent nonsense. Fortunately, the critics of slavery had at their command numerous arguments with more substance than this.

---

[9] *Cf.* Gray, *History of Agriculture,* I, pp. 462–80; Govan, "Was Plantation Slavery Profitable?" *loc. cit.,* pp. 513–35; Robert Worthington Smith, "Was Slavery Unprofitable in the Ante-Bellum South?" *Agricultural History,* XX (1946), pp. 62–64; Russel, "General Effects of Slavery . . . ," *loc. cit.,* pp. 34–54.

[1] *De Bow's Review,* X (1851), p. 57.

CHAPTER TEN

He Who Has Endured

To-day is the annaversary of American independence,"
wrote an embittered South Carolina planter, in 1856.
"I have no doubt in many parts there will be pretensions
of great rejoicings, but I cannot really rejoice for a fredom
which allows every bankrupt, swindler, thief and scoundrel, traitor and seller of his vote to be placed on an equality with myself. . . . The Northern abolitionists are
threatening and planning to take away or destroy the value
of our Slave property, and the demon democracy by its
leveling principles, universal suffrage and numerous popular elections, homestead laws, and bribery are sapping the
foundations of the rights of property in every thing." [1]

Southern slaveholders were not the only nineteenth-
century Americans who took a pessimistic view of the
"demon democracy" and questioned the value of their
birthright of liberal ideals. In the North, too, many conservative men of property still nursed a Hamiltonian doubt
of the people's capacity to govern themselves. But no other
group was so solidly dedicated, by interest and necessity, to
the proposition that men were created unequal as were the
slaveholders of the Old South. No other group was so
firmly rooted in a dying past, so fearful of change, so alien-

---

[1] Gavin Diary, entry for July 4, 1856.

ated from the spirit of the age. In contrast to the "almost *diseased* activity" of the free North, boasted a defender of bondage, "it is the manifest interest of a slaveholding community to oppose social innovations, which, if not resisted, might undermine and finally destroy their system of servitude. . . . Communities of this kind are slow to receive new ideas in morals or politics, believing that stability better subserves their true interests than what is called progress." [2]

Proslavery partisans viewed with displeasure "nonsensical prating" about "abstract notions of human rights." "It is one of the distinguishing characteristics of the times," one complained, "that there is abroad a sickly sentimentalism, which is constantly showing itself in impractical schemes for the amelioration of the condition of the world. . . . Sometimes their universal benevolence expends itself upon negro abolitionism, sometimes in sympathy for the poor Indians, and sometimes these ambassadors of the whole human race, condescend to level their influence against abuses in the army and navy." At present they were demanding that the practice of punishing seamen by whipping be abolished. "Nothing can be more chimerical," this slaveholder assured the "sentimentalists" whose heads were so "filled with visions of equal rights." [3]

The equal-rights doctrine is nonsense, proclaimed John C. Calhoun, the most distinguished of the South's proslavery statesmen. The truth is, affirmed George Fitzhugh, of Virginia, that some men are "born with saddles on their backs and others booted and spurred to ride them, and the riding does them good." Both Calhoun and Fitzhugh, along with various other southern conservatives, concluded that the best way to protect property and prevent proletarian revolution was to reduce the laboring popula-

---

[2] *De Bow's Review*, XX (1856) , p. 657.
[3] *Ibid.*, XVIII (1855) , p. 713; Pensacola *Gazette*, March 21, 1840.

tion to servitude. "In all countries," one slaveholder explained, "where 'peculiar' institutions like our own do not exist, there is a conflict—a constant unremitting struggle for the mastery between *capital* and *labor* . . . which not unfrequently . . . [leads to] 'strikes,' mobs, bloodshed and revolution. . . . But is there no remedy for this state of things? . . . We answer *yes*, . . . [in] a system of labor such as the South is blessed with—a system which proclaims peace, perpetual peace, between the warring elements. Harmonizing the interest betwixt capital and labor, Southern slavery has solved the problem over which statesmen have toiled and philanthropists mourned from the first existence of organized society." [4]

If all this ever were to change, it was not within human power to tell when or how. "The institution of slavery," argued a Virginian, "is a fixed fact; and as wise and practical men, it is our duty to so regard it. Emancipation is an idle dream, beyond the reach of human power. . . . Let us be content with our condition." How, then, might the condition of the slaves be mitigated? "We answer that such mitigation is to be looked for only in the improvement of their masters. Children, in this section of the Union, . . . should be taught that it is their duty, to regard them with benevolence, to administer to their wants, and to protect them from injury." One should not waste time "in silly attacks upon institutions, that will die of themselves when their prolonged mission is fulfilled, and which can not be overthrown a day earlier." [5] In short, one must acquiesce in the *status quo* and leave the future to Providence.

Slavery, by its nature and influence, rendered the master class unfit to live easily in a society of free men. "I will

---

[4] *American Cotton Planter and Soil of the South*, III (1859), pp. 105–106.

[5] *American Farmer*, VII (1852), pp. 416–17; *Southern Agriculturist*, VIII (1835), p. 8; *Southern Cultivator*, XII (1854), p. 105.

only say," confessed a young planter to his father, "that I can never be too thankful to you for having situated me as I am,—on a plantation with negroes that understand their duty, and with but little necessity for dealing with whites, who are, I believe, less disposed to conduct themselves as they should than blacks who are properly raised and controlled." The slaveholder, Olmsted noted, was able to gratify, with little restraint, man's "natural lust for authority"; he could not endure an employee who made demands upon him, who could legally refuse to obey him, and who cherished his self-respect and personal dignity.[6]

Such was the impact of bondage upon the white masters. An abolitionist's feelings toward slaveholders were "greatly modified" during a residence among them, because he discovered so much that was fundamentally "noble, generous and admirable in their characters." "I saw so many demoralizing pro-slavery influences . . . brought to bear on their intellects from their cradle to their tomb, that from hating I began to pity them." [7] Slaveholders asked for pity from no one, least of all from abolitionists. Yet, who could withhold it? Who could help but feel compassion for men who found nothing more inspiring than the sterile rhetoric and special pleading of the proslavery argument to justify the institution upon which they lived? The pathos in the life of every master lay in the fact that slavery had no philosophical defense worthy of the name—that it had nothing to commend it to posterity, except that it paid.

Some liked to pretend that this was enough; and for a few, perhaps, it was. Impatient with theory, slaveholders "never inquire into the propriety of the matter, but just do as others do. Their ancestors owned slaves and they own them; they see their neighbors buying slaves, and they buy

---

6 William S. Pettigrew to Ebenezer Pettigrew, March 26, 1847, Pettigrew Papers; Olmsted, *Texas*, pp. xvi–xvii.

7 Redpath, *Roving Editor*, p. 82.

them. They invest their money in this sort of property, just as they invest it in cattle or real estate, leaving to others to discuss the right and justice of the thing." Only maudlin weaklings had "morbid sensibilities" about owning slaves or thought of freeing them in their wills. "Let our women and old men, and persons of weak and infirm minds, be disabused of the false . . . notion that slavery is sinful, and that they will peril their souls if they do not disinherit their offspring by emancipating their slaves!" It was high time masters "put aside all care or thought what *Northern people* say about them. Let us be independent in this at least!" [8]

But in this they could be independent least of all; for it was true, as one Southerner confessed, "that the world was against" them. They were disturbed to have the world against them—and what disturbed them even more (their denials notwithstanding) was the suspicion that the world might be right. A European traveler met few slaveholders who could "openly and honestly look the thing in the face. They wind and turn about in all sorts of ways, and make use of every argument . . . to convince me that the slaves are the happiest people in the world, and do not wish to be placed in any other condition." [9]

They were trying to convince themselves, too. The proslavery argument was more than a reply to their critics; it was also a reply to their own consciences. Masters recited it to themselves and to each other, over and over, as if to still their inward doubts. "My views respecting the responsibility under which the master of Negroes rests correspond precisely with yours," wrote a slaveholder to a fellow slaveholder. "That description of property is in our hands, and,

---

[8] Charleston *Courier*, August 29, 1857; Catterall (ed.), *Judicial Cases*, III, pp. 58–59, 292 n.; *Southern Agriculturist*, II (1829), pp. 575–76.
[9] Charleston *Courier*, May 14, 1847; Bremer, *Homes of the New World*, I, p. 275.

I believe, by the will of providence; and the fact of possess-ing them, is justified by the example and language of Patri-archs, Prophets and Apostles, from the day of Abraham to the period of St. John's revelation." The slaves were "in a happier—far happier condition—than if they were liberated." And so, he added bravely, "my conscience is clear." [1]

Of course, his conscience was *not* clear, or there would have been no need to dwell on the matter so much. There would have been no need for another troubled master to vow that he would practice the most rigid economy in or-der not to squander what the slave produced "by the hard-est labor and . . . greatest deprivation." Nor would there have been need for still another to confess pathetically to his wife that "I sometimes think my feelings unfit me for a slaveholder." [2]

But the feelings of most masters drove them to rational-ize the system rather than escape it, and this is why they were such tragic figures. They simply could not persuade themselves to forego slavery's rewards: its profits and con-veniences. During a residence on a Virginia plantation, a Northerner discovered for himself what self-denial aboli-tionists were demanding of slaveholders—how easy it was to be morally paralyzed in their situation. "Every night the servant comes in and gets my boots and cleans them. Every morning he comes in before I am up, brings me water to wash, brushes my clothes, and builds a fire when one is nec-essary. At night when I am down to prayers the chamber-maid comes in and turns down the bed clothes and puts things in order for me to go to bed. In fine everything is done for me, I have nothing to do and I find it really con-

---

[1] William S. Pettigrew to James C. Johnston, July 19, 1849; March 7, 1850, Pettigrew Family Papers.
[2] Baker Diary, entry for February 13, 1849; Gustavus A. Henry to his wife, December 2, 1837, Henry Papers.

venient to be waited upon." [3] It was a sign of their demor-
alization that slaveholders should have used a weapon as
feeble as the proslavery argument to escape this dilemma.
For, of course, they never did escape it until they ceased to
be slaveholders. When, at last, they lost the profits and con-
veniences of slavery, they won the chance to live in peace
with themselves and with their age. It was not a bad exchange.

2

The great mass of southern whites, who were nonslaveholders, gained not even the profits and conveniences of
slavery to offset its baleful impact upon their lives. Some
proslavery leaders, uneasy because so few Southerners had
a direct interest in bondage, searched for a way to check the
concentration of this form of property and to encourage its
diffusion. One proposal was to exempt all or a part of a
master's slaves from seizure for debt. This would "offer to
every man among us the strong inducement to become a
slave-owner," and thus everyone "would have an interest,
direct and abiding, in the existence and perpetuity of domestic slavery." [4] Failing in this, the institution's defenders
tried to convince nonslaveholders that Negroes, rather than
masters, were their mortal enemies. They painted frightening pictures showing how the poor man would fare if
abolitionists had their way—how slavery protected his wife
and children "from a state of horrors that he has never
dreamed of." What would the white working man gain if
a horde of free Negroes were turned loose to compete with
his labor and reduce him to their social level? "It is African slavery that makes every white man in some sense a
lord—it draws a broad line of distinction between the two

---

[3] Gara (ed.), "A New Englander's View of Plantation Life," *loc. cit.*,
p. 347.
[4] *De Bow's Review*, XXIII (1857), p. 212.

races, and color gives caste. . . . Here the division is between white free men and black slaves, and every white is, and feels that he is a MAN." [5]

That few nonslaveholders opposed slavery demonstrated the success of appeals such as these. Most of them felt a deep and abiding hatred of Negroes; they suffered from an intense fear that free Negroes would claim equality with them. As things stood, even in poverty they enjoyed the prestige of membership in the superior caste and proudly shared with slaveholders the burden of keeping black men in their place. Nonslaveholders could demand respect from other men's slaves, they could arrest slaves who ran away, and they could punish slaves when they rode on patrol. In short, "The humblest white man feels, and the feeling gives him a certain dignity of character, that where there are slaves he is not at the foot of the social ladder, and his own *status* is not the lowest in the community." [6]

For these prestige baubles the nonslaveholders paid a heavy price. As slaves the Negroes were, in fact, more ruinous economic competitors of white labor than they were as freemen. Everywhere, in nearly every occupation, white workers found their bargaining power severely restricted as long as employers were able to hire slaves and keep them at subsistence levels. In 1860, the average annual wage of textile workers in New England was $205; in the South it was $145. Even in industries that employed no slaves, the threat to employ them was always there nonetheless. The replacement of white labor with slaves after a strike in Richmond's Tredegar Iron Company was a dramatic illustration of the free worker's weak position in the South. A low standard of living for Negro labor meant a low standard of living for white labor too.

---

[5] Columbus (Ga.) *Times*, quoted in Memphis *Tri-Weekly Appeal*, August 24, 1850.
[6] *De Bow's Review*, XX (1856), p. 662.

White mechanics repeatedly demanded the passage of laws excluding slaves from their trades. "Negro mechanics," complained a petition to the Atlanta city council, "can afford to underbid the regular resident city mechanics of your city, to their great injury." [7] But the white mechanics seldom succeeded in the face of almost solid opposition from the slaveholders. Such laws, masters protested, were a "monstrous invasion of the right of private property." A supply of slave mechanics "is our bulwark against extortion and our safeguard against the turbulence of white mechanics, as seen in the great strikes, both in England and in the North, and is the only protection we have in any possible struggle between capital and white labor." "God forbid we should have any more white labor imported here among us," cried a master.[8] Unable to get legal protection, compelled to compete with slave artisans, the whites directed their resentment against the slaves more often than against their owners—and sometimes tried futilely to drive the black workers away with force.

Unquestionably the competition of slaves injured the dignity and lowered the self-respect of the white manual laborer. Both the skilled artisan and the unskilled wage earner felt humiliated when they had to bid for work against another man's slaves. How much slavery encouraged idleness and shiftlessness among the poor whites, how much it put a stigma on all forms of physical toil, it is hard to tell. Certainly the great majority of nonslaveholders labored diligently in order to survive, however degraded they may have felt as a consequence. But there were limits beyond which their pride would not let them go. They would seldom work with slaves, unless there was a clear di-

---

[7] Wesley, *Negro Labor in the United States*, pp. 71–73; Savannah *Republican*, May 26, 1851.

[8] Charleston *Courier*, December 12, 1840; *Southern Cultivator*, XVIII (1860), pp. 204–205, 288–89.

vision of labor. Nor would they perform menial tasks—
"nigger work"—as domestics. To render personal service
to a white employer—to cut his wood, cook his food, wait
his table, wash his clothes, or black his boots—was a form
of degradation that few white men would endure.

The yeoman farmer felt the economic effects of slavery
no less than the mechanic, for he too labored in competition with slaves. The price a farmer could get for what he
had to sell depended less upon his own production costs
than upon those of the planter with his superior efficiency
and cheap labor. How the white yeoman was rewarded for
his toil, therefore, was directly affected by the meager
rewards the slaves received. Poverty was contagious. Moreover, the slaveholder could usually outbid the nonslaveholder for the most fertile lands. By the end of the ante-
bellum period relatively few of the nonslaveholders were
cultivating the lands best suited for staple crops and commercial agriculture. Most of those who possessed such lands
had either prospered and risen into the slaveholding class
or sold out to their more successful neighbors. Usually one
either went up or out. Slavery did not destroy the South's
independent yeomanry; but to say that slavery did not ad-
versely affect this class is to ignore one of the prime facts of
the South's agricultural history.

And yet the majority of white farmers, like the white mechanics, were indoctrinated by the proslavery argument
and defended the peculiar institution. They too vented
their frustrations and resentments chiefly against the Negroes and not the slaveholders. Like Southerners generally,
they resented outsiders who "tampered" with slaves, and
they lived in dread of a slave insurrection. They joined the
mobs which sporadically dealt summary justice to lawless
slaves, punished strangers suspected of being abolitionist
agents, smashed antislavery presses, dispersed antislavery
meetings, and drove into exile native-born Southerners

guilty of heresy. As a group the nonslaveholders, urban and rural, were passionate conformists and demanded orthodoxy from their churches, their schools, and their public men.

In this chilling atmosphere the southern intellectual with an interest in social theory or moral philosophy played a stultifying role. If he remained in the South, the barriers raised by slavery circumscribed the areas of speculative thought open to him. Behind the barriers he performed the rituals which signified his loyalty to the South. He might debate with his fellows the grounds upon which slavery was to be justified: the scientist might speculate about whether or not Negroes and whites belonged to separate species of the genus, man; the clergyman might search the Scriptures for pronouncements on the obligations of master and slave; and the political economist might catalogue the weaknesses of a free society. On such matters the intellectual might speculate freely; but beyond them were the barriers, and beyond the barriers the dangerous morass of heterodoxy from which, once entered, there was no return.

3

Critics of slavery, certain white men think, err when they assume that Negroes suffered as much in bondage as white men would have suffered. One must remember, argue the critics of the critics, that to the Negroes slavery seemed natural; knowing no other life, they accepted it without giving the matter much thought. Not that slavery was a good thing, mind you—but, still, it probably hurt the Negroes less than it did the whites. Indeed, the whites were really more enslaved by Negro slavery than were the Negro slaves. This post-slavery argument, like the ante-bellum proslavery argument, is based upon some obscure and baffling logic. It is not unlike James H. Hammond's confident assertion that "our slaves are the happiest . . . human be-ings on whom the sun shines"; or his complaint that "into their Eden is coming Satan in the guise of an abolition-ist." [9]

A former slave once pronounced a simple and chasten-ing truth for those who would try to understand the mean-ing of bondage: "Tisn't he who has stood and looked on, that can tell you what slavery is,—'tis he who has endured." "I was black," he added, "but I had the feelings of a man as well as any man." [1] One can feel compassion for the ante-bellum southern white man; one can understand the moral dilemma in which he was trapped. But one must remember that the Negro, not the white man, was the slave, and the Negro gained the most from emancipation. When freedom came—even the quasi-freedom of "second-class citizen-ship"—the Negro, in literal truth, lost nothing but his chains.

[9] *De Bow's Review*, VIII (1850), p. 123.
[1] Drew, *The Refugee*, pp. 201–202.

Manuscripts Consulted, and Their Locations

Alabama State Department of Archives and History, Montgomery

John Coffee Collection.
William P. Gould, Rules and Regulations for the Management of the Hill of Howth Plantation. (Photostats.)
Israel Pickens, and Family, Papers. (Typescripts and some originals.)
Charles Tait, and Family, Papers.
James M. Torbert Plantation Diaries. (Typescripts.)
United States Census Bureau, Manuscript Census Returns for 1860, Schedule III for Alabama.

University of California Library, Berkeley

Peter Randolph Leigh Diary and Account Books. (Microfilms.)

Library of Congress

Charles Bruce Plantation Accounts.
Stephen D. Doar Plantation Accounts.
Franklin H. Elmore Papers.
James H. Hammond Papers.
William B. Randolph Plantation Accounts and Letters.
Turner Reavis Account Book.
Edmund Ruffin Diaries.
Shirley Plantation Farm Journals.
Slave Narrative Collection. (W.P.A. Federal Writers' Project.)

Duke University Library

William C. Adams Diary.
Alexander Robinson Boteler Diary.

Clement C. Clay Papers.
E. A. Crudup Plantation Diary.
Samuel Smith Downey Papers.
J. Milton Emerson Journal.
William H. Hatchett Papers.
Duncan G. McCall Plantation Journal and Diary.
Peter C. and Hugh Minor Notebooks.
Haller Nutt Journal of Araby Plantation.
William C. Powell Papers.
William W. Renwick Papers.
James Sheppard Papers.
United States Census Bureau, Manuscript Census Returns for 1860, Schedule III for Georgia, Kentucky, Louisiana, and Tennessee.
Henry Watson, Jr., Papers.
F. L. Whitehead and N. Lofftus Accounts of Slave Trading.
Samuel O. Wood Papers.

Fayette County Court House, Lexington, Kentucky

Fayette County Will Books, 1830–1860.

University of Kentucky Library

Buckner Family Papers.
J. Winston Coleman Papers on Slavery in Kentucky.
Shelby Family Papers.

Department of Archives, Louisiana State University

Butler Family Papers.
Thomas W. Butler Papers.
Eli J. Capell, and Family, Collection.
James A. Gillespie, and Family, Papers.
John C. Jenkins, and Family, Collection. (Typescripts and some originals.)
St. John R. Liddell, and Family, Collection.
Henry Marston, and Family, Papers.
William J. Minor Collection.

Pré Aux Cleres Plantation Record Books.
Alexander Franklin Pugh Diaries. (Typescripts.)
David Weeks, and Family, Collection.

Maryland Hall of Records, Annapolis

Baltimore, Prince Georges, and Talbot County Will Books, Inventories, and Administrator's Accounts, 1830–1860. (Microfilms.)

Maryland Historical Society, Baltimore

Lloyd Family Papers.
Jacob Michael Papers.
Ridgely Family Papers.
James W. Williams Farm Books.
Otho Holland Williams Papers.

National Archives

United States Census Bureau, Manuscript Census Returns for 1860, Schedules I and II.

North Carolina Department of Archives and History, Raleigh

Cumberland, Edgecombe, and Mecklenburg County Will Books, Inventories, and Minute Books, 1830–1860.
Pettigrew Papers.
United States Census Bureau, Manuscript Census Returns for 1860, Schedule III for North Carolina.

Southern Historical Collection, University of North Carolina

John D. Ashmore Plantation Journals.
James B. Bailey Papers.
Everard Green Baker Diaries and Plantation Notes.
Bayside Plantation Records.
John Houston Bills Diaries.
Hamilton Brown Papers.
John W. Brown Diary.

Henry King Burgwyn Papers.
Burton-Young Papers.
Cameron Family Papers.
Church of Bethany Session Book, 1775–1872, Iredell
   County, North Carolina. (Typescripts.)
Cole-Taylor Papers.
James Hamilton Couper Plantation Records.
Louis M. De Saussure Plantation Book.
William Erwin Diary and Account Book.
Flat River Primitive Baptist Church Records, Person
   County, North Carolina.
John Edwin Fripp Journals and Slave Lists.
David Gavin Diary.
Sarah A. Gayle Journal. (Typescripts.)
Globe Baptist Church Records, Caldwell County, North
   Carolina.
John Berkeley Grimball Diaries.
Peter W. Hairston Papers.
Harding-Jackson Papers.
William Hargrove Account Book and Slave Record.
Gustavus A. Henry Papers.
John Hill Plantation Diary.
Hubard Papers.
Franklin A. Hudson Diaries.
George J. Kollock Plantation Records.
Alexander K. Lawton Plantation Diary.
Francis Terry Leak Diaries.
Lenoir Family Papers.
Mrs. Andrew McCollam Diary.
Magnolia Plantation Journal.
Manigault Plantation Records.
Nicholas B. Massenburg Farm Journal.
Columbus Morrison Diary.
John Nevitt Plantation Journal.
Newstead Plantation Diary. (Microfilm.)
Stephen Andrews Norfleet Diaries.
Pettigrew Family Papers.
P. H. Pitts Diary and Account Book.

Phanor Prudhomme Papers.
Edmund Ruffin, Jr., Farm Journal and Plantation Diary.
Peter Evans Smith Papers.
Sparkman Family Papers.
William E. Sparkman Plantation Record.
John Thompson Plantation Book. (Microfilm.)
Lewis Thompson Papers.
A. and A. T. Walker Account Book.
John Walker Diaries. (Originals of first two volumes; remainder on microfilm.)

South Carolina Historical Commission, Columbia

Fairfield and Williamsburg District Will Books, 1830–1860. (Typescripts.)
South Carolina Slavery Manuscripts Collection.
United States Census Bureau, Manuscript Census Returns for 1860, Schedule III for South Carolina.

South Carolina Historical Society, Charleston

John Ball Plantation Books.
Thomas Aston Coffin Papers.
John B. Milliken Plantation Journals.

South Caroliniana Library, University of South Carolina

Abbeville and Union District Inventories and Appraisements, Guardian's Accounts, Commissioner's Minute Books, and Judge of Probate Decree Books, 1830–1860. (Typescripts.)
Keating S. Ball Record of Births and Deaths.
Caleb Coker Plantation Book.
Andrew Flinn Plantation Book.
S. Porcher Gaillard Plantation Journals.
Michael Gramling Record Book.
James H. Hammond Diary and Account Books.
William Gilmore Simms Plantation Book. (Photostats.)

Telfair Academy of Arts and Sciences, Savannah

Telfair Plantation Records.

Virginia Historical Society, Richmond

> William M. Waller Papers.
> Bickerton Lyle Winston Slave Account Book.

Virginia State Library, Richmond

> N. F. Cabell Collection of Agricultural Papers.
> Caroline, Henrico, Nelson, and Southampton County Minute Books, Order Books, and Will Books, 1830–1860. (Microfilms.)
> Jerdone Family Slave Book and Journal. (Photostats.)
> William Massie Slave Book and Farm Journals. (Photostats.)
> Virginia Legislative Petitions from Accomac, Albemarle, Alexandria, Allegheny, Amelia, Amherst, Appomattox, Augusta, Barbour, Bath, and Bedford Counties.

University of Virginia Library

> Ambler Family Papers.
> Bruce Family of Berry Hill Papers.
> Coleman Family Papers.
> John B. Garrett Farm Journal. (Microfilm.)
> Robert M. T. Hunter Papers.
> Richard Irby Papers. (Microfilms.)
> McDowell Family Papers.
> Morton-Halsey Papers.
> Pocket Plantation Papers.
> Virginia Slavery Collection of Receipts, Bills of Sale, and Lists and Evaluations of Slaves.

INDEX

Abbeville District, S.C., 231

Abolitionists, 20, 146, 207, 239, 371, 398, 419, 422, 425; on cruelty of slaveholders, 82, 180, 181, 187; and aid to runaways, 121, 153; alleged encouragement of rebellions by, 137–8

Absentee ownership: among planters, 43–4

Accomac County, Va., 376

Acklen, Col. J.A.S., 279, 293; plantation operations of, 42–3

Adams County, Miss., 301–2

Administrators: hiring out of slaves by, 69; sales of slaves by, 199–200, 201

Adultery: among slaves, 198

Affleck, Thomas, 173, 178, 250

Africa: peoples of, 9; cultures of, 12–13; slavery in, 17, 21

African Labor Supply Association, 276

African slave trade: beginning of, 17–18, 24; cruelty of, 24–5; abolition of, 25, 81, 271, 397; illegal, 271–2, 397; movement for reopening of, 272–8

"Africanisms": survival of, 362–3

Africans, see Negroes

Agriculture: southern advantages in, 4; inducements to use slaves in, 5, 400; southern white labor in, 7; movement for diversification of, 51–2; risks of, 389–90; alleged effects of slavery upon, 393–5; revival of, in South, 27, 395–6

Alabama, 7, 26, 185, 210, 239, 393; slaveholdings in, 30, 31; slave population of, 32 n; legal position of slaves in, 192–3; definition of mulatto in, 195; slave speculation in, 202; penalty for aiding slave rebellion in, 211; patrol system in, 214; penalty for killing slave in, 219; penalty for cruelty toward slaves in, 219; trial of slaves in,

Alabama (continued)
225, 226; restrictions on emancipation in, 234; regulation of slave trade in, 252, 253, 254; sickness among slaves in, 298; profits from slavery in, 408, 409

"Alabama fever," 27

Alabama, Florida, and Georgia Railroad Company: employment of slaves by, 62, 71

Alexandria, Va.: slave trade in, 260, 261–2

Ambler, John, 279–80

American Colonization Society, 94

Amherst County, Va., 269

Anderson, Joseph R., 65

Anglo-Saxons: alleged superiority of, 8

Anthony, John H., 269

Arcadia Cotton Factory, 66

Arkansas, 26, 29, 85, 194, 198, 239, 253, 394; slaveholdings in, 30; slave population of, 32 n; runaway slaves in, 120; insurrection panic in, 138; expulsion of free Negroes from, 216; restrictions on emancipation in, 234; sentiment for reopening African slave trade in, 273–4, 277; sickness among slaves in, 299–300; profits from slavery in, 408

Arkansas River, 185, 299

Armfield, John: slave trader, 261–2, 265

Armstrong, John, 230

Arson: by slaves, 127–8; penalty for, 210

Artisans, slave, 280; on small plantations, 37–8; on large plantations, 41–2; services of, 58–9; urban employment of, 63, 147; efficiency of, 63, 337; hiring of, 69, 167, 414; "hiring own time" by, 72–3; as runaways, 110; role of, in controlling slaves, 151, 333

Artisans, white, 29; employment of

Index

Constitution, Federal: and legality of slavery, 26

Cotton, 27; and alleged dependence upon Negro labor, 7; production of, with white labor, 7; labor routine in production of, 45–6, 55; growth of, by small farmers, 53; acres of, per field-hand, 56; overworking of slaves in production of, 82, 84–5; profits from production of, 408–9

Cotton presses: employment of slaves in, 63, 71

"Cotton snobs," 84, 185

Couper, James Hamilton, 313

Courts, southern: on powers of masters, 141; on valuation of slaves, 142–3; role of, in control of slaves, 192; and enforcement of slave codes, 193; litigation over slaves in, 203–4; protection of slaves by, 220–4; trials of slaves in, 224–7

Craftsmen, see Artisans

Creole: slave mutiny on, 138

Creoles, 70; and miscegenation, 355

Crime: among slaves, 124–32, 190–1; death penalty for, 210–11; trials for, 224–7

Cruelty: toward slaves, 111, 177–91, 204; legal penalties for, 219

Cuba, 21

Cumberland County, N.C., 205, 231

Cumberland Iron Works: employment of slaves in, 64–5

Cumberland River, 64

Curaçao, 17

Dabney, Thomas S., 74, 167, 270

Dahomey, 12

Dancing: among slaves, 168, 172, 366–7

Davis, Jefferson, 132, 151–2, 171–2

De Bow, J. B. D., 276

Deep South, 77, 78, 206, 210, 232, 244; white labor in, 7; slaveholdings in, 31–2; slave population of, 32; large plantations in, 43; sugar production in, 46–7; neglect of food crops by planters in, 50; runaway slaves in, 119; runaway slaves sold to, 154; slave fear of, 154; and movement to reopen African slave trade, 272–8; health problem in, 296, 297–300, 310

Delaware, 194; and prohibition of slave importations, 25; slaveholdings in, 30; slave population of,

Delaware (*continued*)
32; emancipation laws of, 232; and prohibition of slave exports, 251–2

Dengue: among slaves, 303

DeSaussure, Louis D.: slave trader, 268

Diarrhea: among slaves, 302

Diphtheria: among slaves, 303

"Dirt eating": among slaves, 304

Diseases: among slaves, 296–307; treatment of, 307–18

Dismal Swamp, 61

District of Columbia: runaway slaves in, 121; closing of slave trade in, 251

Divorce: among slaves, 342

Docks: employment of slaves on, 63

Dogs: use of, in tracking runaways, 189–90

Domestics, slave, 77, 161, 172, 280, 334, 363; on small plantations, 37–8; on large plantations, 41–2, 59; services of, 59; urban employment of, 62–3; hiring of, 69, 71; as runaways, 110; and aid to runaways, 116; theft among, 125, 126; murder of whites by, 130–1; role of, in controlling slaves, 151–3, 333; mulattoes as, 196; clothing of, 289–90; paternalism toward, 323–4, 325–6, 330; as slave aristocracy, 337–8, 339; devotion of, to whites, 379

Douglass, Frederick: on hiring own time, 72–3; on slave's desire for freedom, 89, 90; on slave resistance, 101; on slave theft, 127; on slave impudence, 145; on slave's fear of whites, 146; on fears of runaways, 154; on "breaking in" of slaves, 188; on murder of slaves, 223; on feeding of slaves, 288–9; on slave clothing, 291; on life in quarters, 332–3; on brutalizing effects of slavery, 335; on slave's search for prestige, 338; on slave marriages, 347; on slave music, 369; on slave superstition, 374

Drapetomania: alleged Negro disease, 109

Dred Scott case, 26

Drivers, slave, see Foremen

Dropsy: among slaves, 303

DuBose, Martha, 205

Dutch: and slave trade, 17–18; and miscegenation, 350

iii

Index

Georgia, 27, 206, 239, 243, 244; beginning of slavery in, 18; closing of African slave trade by, 25; slaveholdings in, 30, 31; slave population of, 32 n; sugar production in, 46; rice production in, 47–8; employment of slaves on railroads in, 62; penalties for killing slaves in, 218–19; law of, against cruelty, 219; trial of slaves in, 225; restrictions on emancipation in, 233–4; slave exports of, 238; regulation of slave trade by, 252, 253, 256; sickness among slaves in, 297–8; profits from slavery in, 409–10
Germans: as indentured servants, 16
Gold Coast, 12
Gramling, Michael, 47 n
Great Valley of Virginia, 37; slave iron workers in, 65
Greensboro, Ala., 386
Grimball, John B., 410
Gristmills: employment of slaves in, 61, 72
Guadeloupe, 17
Gullah Negroes, 363

Haiti: slave rebellion in, 20
Halifax County, N.C., 269
Hamilton, James, 407
Hammond, James H., 42, 79, 202, 235, 325, 386–7, 405; on working day of slaves, 44–5; on carelessness of slave labor, 102; on slave resistance, 105; and problem of runaways, 116; and techniques of slave control, 146, 151, 157, 169, 174, 175; on slave "breeding," 247; on feeding of slaves, 286; on clothing of slaves, 291; on slave sickness, 298; and protection of slave health, 311, 312, 313; and control of slave families, 342; on miscegenation, 352; on economics of slavery, 383, 409; as agricultural reformer, 396; and defense of slavery, 429–30
Hampton, Wade, 238
Hancock County, Ga., 393
Handicrafts: among slaves, 367
Hanover County, Va., 70, 78
Hardeman County, Tenn., 415
Harford County, Md., 36
Hart & Davis: slave traders, 261
Harvey, Thomas, 205–6

Hatchett, William H.: slave trader, 267–8
Hausas, 12
Hayne, Robert Y.: on "Negro courts," 226
Heathens: enslavement of, 16–17
Hemp: labor routine in production of, 49, 55; cultivation of, on small farms, 53
Hemp factories: employment of slaves in, 64, 72, 415; profits from, 410
Henrico County, Va., 135
Hernia: among slaves, 306
Heyward, Nathaniel, 410
Hillsboro, N.C., 36
Hinds County, Miss., 74, 270
Hired slaves, see Slaves
"Hiring own time": by slaves, 72–3, 90, 96, 147, 208, 228, 280
Hoe-hands, slave, 41, 55. See also Field-hands
Holidays: for slaves, 79, 365–6; as labor incentives, 168–70, 172
Hookworm: among slaves, 304
Hotels: employment of slaves in, 63, 71
Hottentots, 9
Housing, slave, 292–5
Houston, George, 205
Houston, Texas, 263
Hundley, Daniel R.: on cruelty toward slaves, 180; on slave traders, 256–7, 266

Indentured servants: in English colonies, 16, 18, 21–2, 24, 193
Indians, 71; as slaves, 17, 23; and intermarriage with Negroes, 23; enslavement of, prohibited, 23–4
Indigo: abandonment of, 47
Infant mortality: among slaves, 319–
Infidels: enslavement of, 16
Influenza: among slaves, 303
Insurrections, slave, 132–40, 190, 210; penalty for white aid to, 211
Internal improvements: employment of slaves in, 61–2
Iredell County, N.C., 161
Irish: as indentured servants, 16
Iron industry: employment of slaves in, 64–5, 72, 147
Irons: use of, to punish slaves, 174, 186

Issaquena County, Miss., 32

v

Index

About the Author

Kenneth M. Stampp, Morrison Professor of History Emeritus at the University of California, Berkeley, is a native of Wisconsin and received his higher education at the University of Wisconsin, from which he earned his doctorate in 1942. He was twice awarded John Simon Guggenheim Fellowships, has held two Fellowships at the Huntington Library, and has been a Visiting Fellow at All Souls College, Oxford. In addition to lecturing at various American colleges and universities, Mr. Stampp has been a Fulbright Lecturer at the Amerika Institute, University of Munich; a Commonwealth Fund Lecturer at the University of London; and Harmsworth Professor at Oxford University.

A specialist in nineteenth-century American history, Mr. Stampp is the author of *Indiana Politics during the Civil War, And the War Came, The Era of Reconstruction,* and *The Imperiled Union.*

Mr. Stampp is married and has four children.